The
Prentice Hall
Reader

THIRD EDITION

The Prentice Hall Reader

GEORGE MILLER

University of Delaware

PRENTICE HALL
Englewood Cliffs, New Jersey 07632

Library of Congress Cataloging-in-Publication Data

The Prentice Hall reader / [compiled by] George Miller.—3rd ed.
    p.   cm.
    ISBN   0–13–722059–6
    1. College readers.   2. English language—Rhetoric.   I. Miller,
  George.   II. Prentice-Hall, inc.
PE1417.P74   1992   91–29213
808'.0427—dc20   CIP

Acquisitions Editors: Tracy Augustine and Phil Miller
Production Editor/Designer: F. Hubert
Development Editors: Susan Alkana and Kate Morgan
Cover Designer: Ben Santora
Cover Photo: Don Spiro, The Stock Shop
Prepress Buyer: Herb Klein
Manufacturing Buyer: Patrice Fraccio
Editorial Assistant: Deborah Roff

Credits begin of page 584, which constitutes
a continuation of the copyright page.

© 1992, 1989, 1986 by Prentice-Hall, Inc.
A Simon & Schuster Company
Englewood Cliffs, New Jersey 07632

Printed in the United States of America

10   9   8   7   6   5   4   3   2

ISBN   0-13-722059-6   (student text)

ISBN   0-13-722067-7   (annotated instructor's edition)

Prentice-Hall International (UK) Limited, *London*
Prentice-Hall of Australia Pty. Limited, *Sydney*
Prentice-Hall Canada Inc., *Toronto*
Prentice-Hall Hispanoamericana, S.A., *Mexico*
Prentice-Hall of India Private Limited, *New Delhi*
Prentice-Hall of Japan, Inc., *Tokyo*
Simon & Schuster Asia Pte. Ltd., *Singapore*
Editora Prentice-Hall do Brasil, Ltda., *Rio de Janeiro*

For Lisa, her book

Contents

TWO

Narration   *83*

THREE

Description   *135*

FOUR

Division and Classification *191*

FIVE

Comparison and Contrast *253*

xi

SIX

Process *320*

SEVEN

Cause and Effect *382*

EIGHT

Definition *442*

xiv

NINE

Argumentation and Persuasion *501*

Alternate
Thematic Contents

Autobiography and Biography

Children and Family

Contemporary Phenomena and Issues

Discrimination

Feminists and Femininity

Growing Older

Humor and Satire

Men and Women

Minority Experience

Nature and the Environment

Psychology and Behavior

Reading, Writing, and Language

School and College

Self-Discovery

Preface

The Prentice Hall Reader is predicated on two premises: that reading plays a vital role in learning how to write and that writing and reading can best be organized around the traditional division of discourse into a number of structural patterns. Such a division is not the only way that the forms of writing can be classified, but it does have several advantages.

First, practice in these structural patterns encourages students to organize knowledge and to see the ways in which information can be conveyed. How else does the mind know except by classifying, comparing, defining, or seeking cause and effect relationships? Second, the most common use of these patterns occurs in writing done in academic courses. There students are asked to narrate a chain of events, to describe an artistic style, to classify plant forms, to compare two political systems, to tell how a laboratory experiment was performed, to analyze why famine occurs in Africa, to define a philosophical concept, or to argue for or against a nuclear freeze. Learning how to structure papers using these patterns is an exercise that has immediate application in students' other academic work. Finally, because the readings use these patterns as structural devices, they offer an excellent way in which to integrate reading into a writing course. Students can see the patterns at work and learn how to use them to become more effective writers and better, more efficient readers.

To these ends, the third edition of *The Prentice Hall Reader* includes 63 selections, ranging from classic to contemporary essays. Some of the selections and nearly all of the writers are old friends, but some fresh selections by young writers are included as well. Each reading was chosen to demonstrate the pattern under discussion and to be accessible to the college freshman.

What Is Different About This Book?

Even though rhetorically organized readers have similar tables of contents, they are not all alike. The third edition of *The Prentice Hall Reader* contains a number of unique or substantially different features that make it easier for students to use in learning how to write.

Prose in Revision

As every writing instructor knows, getting students to revise is never an easy matter. Having written a paper, most students do not even want to see it again, let alone revise it. Furthermore, for many students revising means making word substitutions and correcting grammatical and mechanical errors—changes that instructors rightfully regard as proofreading, not revising. To help make the need for revision more vivid and to show how writers revise, the third edition of *The Prentice Hall Reader* includes four features.

1. Each chapter now contains a selection by a professional writer showing a final version and an earlier draft. These selections were *not* commissioned for this reader; they are actual drafts of previously published works. Each example is accompanied by discussion questions that focus attention on *how* the writer revised. The writers represented in these examples of revision include Andrew Ward, Susan Allen Toth, Scott Momaday, James Villas, William Ouchi, Nora Ephron, Brent Staples, Susan Orlean, and Patricia McLaughlin.

2. The introduction to each chapter of readings includes a first draft of a student essay, a comment on the draft's strengths and weaknesses, and a final, revised version. These essays, realistic examples of student writing, model the student revision process.

3. An introductory essay on "How to Write an Essay" includes advice to students on how to revise a paper. This section, intended to supplement classroom activities, is written to the student and provides some simple tips on what to do when revising.

4. The second writing suggestion after each selection, which asks students to write an essay, is accompanied by prewriting and rewriting activities. In all, the text provides about 180 specific rewriting activities. These activities are designed to help students to organize ideas and to revise what they have written.

Selections

The third edition of *The Prentice Hall Reader* includes a large number of selections to offer the instructor maximum flexibility in choosing readings. No chapter has fewer than five selections and most have six or more. The readings are scaled in terms of length and sophistication. The selections in each chapter begin with a student essay. The student essay is then followed by several professional essays that gradually increase in length and difficulty. Each chapter concludes with a professional essay in both early and revised drafts.

Writing Suggestions

Each selection is followed by three writing suggestions: the first calls for a paragraph-length response; the second, an essay; and the third, an essay involving research. Each of the three suggestions is related to the content of the reading to which it is attached, and each calls for a response in the particular pattern being studied. The emphasis on the writing process is increased through the addition of prewriting and rewriting activities after the second writing suggestion for each selection.

Introductions

The introduction to each chapter offers clear and succinct advice to the student on how to write that particular type of paragraph or essay. The introductions anticipate students' questions, provide answers, and end with a checklist, titled "Some Things to

Remember," to remind students of the major concerns they should have when writing in a particular pattern.

How to Write an Essay

A new introductory section, "How to Write an Essay," offers an overview of every stage of the writing process, starting with advice on how to define a subject, purpose, and audience and an explanation of a variety of prewriting techniques. This section also suggests how to write a thesis statement, how to decide where to place that statement in an essay, and how to approach the problems of revising an essay. Finally, it contains a student essay as well as two drafts of the student's two opening paragraphs.

How to Read an Essay

A second introductory section offers advice on how to read an essay, following prereading, reading, and rereading models. A sample analysis of a professional essay shows how to use this reading model to prepare an essay for class.

Annotated Instructor's Edition

An annotated edition of *The Prentice Hall Reader* is available to instructors. Each of the selections in the text is annotated with teaching suggestions, additional classroom activities, important background information, and sample responses to the discussion questions. Emphasis is placed on how to teach each selection, how to develop class discussions and keep attention focused on how the selection works as a piece of writing. Tips on "related readings" suggest how to pair essays in the reader. At least one additional writing suggestion is provided with every essay. Many new class and collaborative activities have been added to the annotated instructor's edition. The third edition also introduces a new feature—"Links to Writing." This feature offers at least one and, often many, suggestions on how to use the reading to teach specific grammatical, mechanical, and rhetorical issues involved in writing. These "links" provide a bridge between your handbook and *The Prentice Hall Reader*.

The Structure of This Book

After an introductory chapter on writing and reading and the writing process, the next nine chapters follow a similar approach. Each chapter begins with an introduction to the pattern, which includes two drafts of a student essay and ends with a checklist.

The writing selections begin with example because example is essential in any type of effective writing. Narration and description are treated next, with a special emphasis on how each is used in expository writing. The key patterns of expository development—division, comparison and contrast, process, and cause and effect—follow. Definition, because it can include all of the other patterns, is placed at the end of the expository section. Argumentation and persuasion is the last and largest chapter.

Each selection has three groups of questions: a set on subject and purpose, directing the student to what was written about and why; a set on strategy and audience, asking the student to analyze how the essay is structured and how it is influenced by its intended audience; and a set on vocabulary and style, focusing attention on how style and language contribute to purpose. The apparatus after each reading also includes three writing suggestions. For the second of these three, specific prewriting and rewriting activities are given.

A glossary of terms can be found at the back of the text. For those instructors who wish to use the readings in a way other than by the rhetorical organization, an additional thematic table of contents is included. Sample syllabi keyed to the text and suggestions for how to handle collaborative and class activities can be found in the supplement *Teaching Composition with The Prentice Hall Reader*, available on request from your Prentice Hall representative.

What Is New in the Third Edition

The third edition of *The Prentice Hall Reader* features 63 selections, 18 of which are new. As in the previous editions, the readings are chosen on the basis of several criteria: how well they demonstrate a particular pattern of organization, appeal to a freshman audience, and promote interesting and appropriate discussion and writing activities. Some of the discussion questions have been changed; others have been reworded in more precise ways. Several new student essays have been added, including one that is followed through the writing process. Each chapter now contains an example of "prose in revision," two versions of a published selection by a professional writer. Also new are two introductory sections, "How to Write an Essay" and "How to Read an Essay," that offer advice on writing and reading and how the two processes are linked. The Annotated Instructor's Edition contains additional class and collaborative activities, as well as a new feature—"Links to Writing." These links show how the essays can be used to teach writing, providing a link or bridge between a handbook and the reader. For the instructor, additional teaching materials are provided in a new supplement, *Teaching Composition with The Prentice Hall Reader*, available from your Prentice Hall representative.

Acknowledgments

Although writing is a solitary activity, no one can write without the assistance of others. This text owes much to many people: To the staff at Prentice Hall who have continued to play a large role in helping to develop this reader, especially Phil Miller, Editor in Chief, Humanities; Tracy Augustine and Kate Morgan, Senior Editors, English, who have been supportive, sympathetic, and enthusiastic; Deborah Roff and Heidi Moore, Editorial Assistants; Susan Alkana, the Development Editor on this edition who watched my every word; Frank Hubert, the Production Editor; and Gina Sluss, Senior English Marketing Manager.

To my reviewers, who wrote extensive critiques of the manuscript and made many helpful suggestions: Ralph F. Voss, University of Alabama; Tahita Fulkerson, Tarrant County Junior College South; Bill M. Stiffler, Harford Community College; Cheryl L. Ware, McNeese State University.

To Laurie LoSasso, my editorial assistant on this edition, whose energy and thoroughness made everything so much easier. To the writing program staff at the University of Delaware and the students in my own writing classes who tested materials, offered suggestions, and contributed essays to the introductions. To my secretary, Deborah Lyall, who for sixteen years has made the chore of writing and rewriting easier. And finally to my children, Lisa, Jon, Craig, Valerie, and Eric, who have learned over the years to live with a father who writes.

George Miller
University of Delaware

THE NEW YORK TIMES and PRENTICE HALL are sponsoring A CONTEMPORARY VIEW: a program designed to enhance student access to current information of relevance in the classroom.

Through this program, the core subject matter provided in the text is supplemented by a collection of time-sensitive articles from one of the world's most distinguished newspapers, THE NEW YORK TIMES. These articles demonstrate the vital, ongoing connection between what is learned in the classroom and what is happening in the world around us.

To enjoy the wealth of information of THE NEW YORK TIMES daily, a reduced subscription rate is available. For information, call toll-free: 1-800-631-1222.

PRENTICE HALL and THE NEW YORK TIMES are proud to co-sponsor A CONTEMPORARY VIEW. We hope it will make the reading of both textbooks and newspapers a more dynamic, involving process.

The
Prentice Hall
Reader

How to Write an Essay

Watching a performance, whether it is athletic or artistic, our attention is focused on the achievement displayed in that moment. In concentrating on the performance, however, we might forget about the extensive practice that lies behind that achievement. Writing is no different. Although we imagine poets and novelists waiting for some brilliant flash of inspiration, more typically, writers rely on perspiration. An effective final product depends upon careful preliminary work.

A Writer's Subject

The first step in writing is to determine a subject. A subject is what a piece of writing is about. Once you have a subject, you will need to narrow or restrict it first into a more specific topic and then into a precise thesis. For now, however, think just about your general subject.

The majority of writing tasks that you face either in school or on the job require you to write in response to a specific assignment. Your instructor, for example, might ask you to use the specific writing suggestions that follow each reading in this book. Before you begin work on any writing assignment, take time to study what is being asked. What limits have already been placed on the assignment? What are the key words (for example, ''compare,'' ''analyze,'' ''define'') used in the assignment?

1

Once you have a subject, the next step is to restrict, focus, or narrow that subject into a workable topic. Although the words "subject" and "topic" are sometimes used interchangeably, think of "subject" as the broader, more general word. You move from a subject to a "topic" by limiting or restricting what you will include or cover. The shift from subject to topic is a gradual one that is not marked by a clearly definable line. Just remember that a topic is a more restricted version of a larger subject.

A Writer's Purpose

A writer writes to fulfill three fundamental purposes: to entertain, to inform, and to persuade. Obviously, those purposes are not necessarily separate. All three can be found together: an interesting, maybe even humorous, essay that documents the health hazards caused by smoking can, at the same time, attempt to persuade the reader to give up smoking. In this case the main purpose is still persuasion; entertainment and information play subordinate roles in catching the reader's interest and in documenting with appropriate evidence the argument being advanced.

These three purposes are generally associated with the traditional division of writing into four forms—narration, description, exposition (including classification, comparison and contrast, process, cause and effect, and definition), and argumentation. A narrative or descriptive essay typically tells a story or describes a person, object, or place in order to entertain a reader and recreate the experience. Expository essays primarily provide information for a reader. Argumentative or persuasive essays, on the other hand, seek to move a reader, to gain support, to advocate a particular type of action.

A Writer's Audience

Audience is a key factor in every writing situation. Writing is, after all, a form of communication and as such implies an audience. In many writing situations, your audience is a controlling factor that affects both the content of your paper and the style in which it is written. An effective writer learns to adjust to an audience and to write for that audience; for a writer, like a performer, needs and wants an audience.

Writers adjust their style and tone on a spectrum ranging from informal to formal. Articles that appear in popular, wide-circulation magazines often are written in the first person, use contractions, favor popular and colloquial words, and contain relatively short sentences and paragraphs. Articles in more scholarly journals exhibit a formal style that involves an objective and serious tone, a more learned vocabulary, and longer and more complicated sentence and paragraph constructions. In the informal style the writer injects his or her personality into the prose; in the formal style the writer remains detached and impersonal. A writer adopts whatever style seems appropriate for a particular audience or context. An effective writer does not have just one style or voice, but many.

Some Things to Remember

Before you begin even to prewrite, you need to think about your subject, purpose, and audience. Remind yourself of their importance in your writing process by jotting down responses to the following categories:

1. My general subject is ————————— .
2. My more specific topic is ————————— .
3. My purpose is to ————————— .
4. My intended audience is ————————— .

A Writer's Information

What makes writing entertaining, informative, or persuasive is information—specific, relevant detail. If you try to write without gathering information, you end up skimming the surface of your subject, even if you "know" something about it. To persuade a reader—even to interest a reader—you need specific information.

How you go about gathering information on your topic depends upon your subject and your purpose for writing. Some topics, such as those involving a personal experience, require a memory search; other assignments, such as describing a particular place, require careful observation. Essays that convey information or argue particular positions often demand information that must be gathered through research. Some possible strategies for gathering information and ideas about your topic are listed below. Before you start this step in your prewriting, remember three things.

First, **remember that different tactics work for different topics and for different writers.** No single strategy works every time for every writer. You might find that freewriting is great for some assignments, but not for others. As a writer, explore your options. Don't rule out any strategy until you have tried it. Second, **remember that prewriting activities sometimes produce information and sometimes just produce questions that you will then need to answer.** In other words, prewriting often involves learning what you don't know, what you need to find out. Learning to ask the right questions is just as important as knowing the right answers. Third, **remember that these prewriting activities are an excellent way in which to find a focus, to narrow a subject, or to suggest a working plan for your essay.** As you begin to explore a subject or topic, the possibilities spread out before you. Try not to be wedded to a particular topic or thesis until you have explored a subject through prewriting activities.

Writing from Personal Experience or Observation

Even you most unforgettable experience has probably been forgotten in part. If you are going to re-create it for a reader, you will have to do some active searching among your memories. By focusing your attention you can slowly recall more details. Ask yourself a series of questions about the chronology of the experience. For example, start with a particular detail and then try to stimulate your memory by answering questions: What happened just before? Just after? Who was there? Where did the experience take place? Why did it happen? When did it happen? How did it happen?

Sense impressions, like factual details, decay from memory. In the height of the summer, it is not easy to recall a crisp fall day. Furthermore, sensory details are not always noticed, let alone recorded. How many times have you passed by a particular location without really seeing it?

Descriptions, like every other form of writing, demand specific information, and the easiest way to gather that detail is to observe. Before you try to describe a person, place, or object, take some time to list specific details on a piece of paper. At first record everything you notice. Do not worry about having too much, for you can always edit later. At this stage it is better to have too much than to have too little.

The next step is to decide what to include in your description and what to exclude. As a general principle, an effective written description does not try to record everything. The selection of detail should be governed by your purpose in the description. Ask yourself what you are trying to show or reveal. For what reason? What is particularly important about this person, place, or object? A description is not the verbal equivalent of a photograph or a tape recording.

Writing to Inform or Persuade

If you are conveying information or trying to persuade a reader to do or believe something, you need specific information. A number of different prewriting activities can help you explore your topic and plan your piece of writing.

Freewriting

Putting words down on a page or a computer screen can be very intimidating. Your editing instincts immediately want to take over—are the words spelled correctly? Are the sentences complete? Do they contain any mechanical or grammatical errors? Not only must you express your ideas in words, but suddenly those words must be the correct words.

When you translate thoughts into written words and then edit those words at the same time, writing can seem impossible. Instead of allowing ideas to take shape in words or allowing the writing to stimulate your thinking, you become fearful of committing anything to paper.

Writing, however, can stimulate thought. Every writer has experienced times when an idea became clear because it was written down. If those editing instincts can be turned off, you can use writing as a way of generating ideas about a paper.

Freewriting is an effective way to deal with this dilemma. Write without stopping for a fixed period of time—a period as short as ten minutes or as long as an hour. Do not stop; do not edit; do not worry about mistakes. You are looking for a focus point—an idea or a subject for a paper. You are trying to externalize your thinking into writing. What emerges is a free association of ideas. Some are relevant; some are worthless. After you have ideas on paper, you can then decide what is worth saving, developing, or simply throwing away.

Journals

A daily journal can be an effective seedbed of ideas for writing projects. Such a journal should not be a daily log of your activities (got up, went to class, had lunch), but instead a place where you record ideas, observations, memories, feelings. Set aside a specific notebook or a pad of paper in which to keep your journal. Try to write for at least ten minutes every day. Over a period of time—such as a semester—you will be surprised how many ideas for papers or projects you will accumulate. When you are working on a paper, you might want to confine part of your daily journal entries to that particular subject.

Brainstorming and Mapping

A brainstorm is an oral freewriting in which a group of people jointly try to solve a problem by spontaneously contributing ideas. Whatever comes to mind, no matter how obvious or unusual, gets said. Hopefully out of the jumble of ideas that surface, some possible solutions to the problem will be found.

Although brainstorming is by definition a group activity, it can also be done by the individual writer. In the center of a blank sheet of paper, write down a key word or phrase referring to your subject. Then in the space around your subject, quickly jot down any ideas that come to mind. Do not write in sentences—just key words and phrases. Because you are not filling consecutive lines with words and because you have space in which the ideas can be arranged, this form of brainstorming often suggests structural relationships. You can increase the usefulness of such an idea generator by adding graphic devices such as circles, arrows, or connecting lines to indicate the possible relationships among ideas. These devices can be added to your brainstorming sheet later, and they become a map to the points you might want to cover in your essay.

Formal Questioning

One particularly effective way to gather information on any topic is to ask yourself questions about it. This allows you to explore the subject from a variety of different angles. After all, the secret to finding answers always lies in knowing the right questions to ask. A good place to start is with the list of questions below. Remember, though, that not every question is appropriate for every topic.

Illustration

1. What examples of _____ can be found?
2. In what ways are these things examples of _____?
3. What details about _____ seem the most important?

Comparison and Contrast

1. To what is _____ similar? List the points of similarity.
2. From what is _____ different? List the points of difference.
3. Which points of similarity or difference seem most important?
4. What does the comparison or contrast tell the reader about _____?

7

Division and Classification

1. Into how many parts can _____ be divided?
2. How many parts is _____ composed of?
3. What other category of things is _____ most like?
4. How does _____ work?
5. What are _____'s component parts?

Process

1. How many steps or stages are involved in _____?
2. In what order do those steps or stages occur?

Cause and Effect

1. What precedes _____?
2. Is that a cause of _____?
3. What follows _____?
4. Is that an effect of _____?
5. How many causes of _____ can you find?
6. How many effects of _____ can you find?
7. Why does _____ happen?

Definition

1. How is _____ defined in a dictionary?
2. Does everyone agree about the meaning of _____?
3. Does _____ have any connotations? What are they?
4. Has the meaning of _____ changed over time?
5. What words are synonymous with _____?

Argument and Persuasion

1. How do your readers feel about _____?
2. How do you feel about _____?
3. What are the arguments in favor of _____?
   List those arguments in order of strength.
4. What are the arguments against _____?
   List those arguments in order of strength.

Interviewing

Typically you gather information for college papers by locating printed sources—books, articles, reports. Depending upon your topic, however, printed sources are not always available. In that case, people often represent a great source of information for a writer. Obviously you should choose someone who has special credentials or knowledge about the subject.

Interviewing requires some special skills and tact. When you first contact someone to request an interview, always explain who you are, what you want to know, and how you will use the information. Remember that specific questions will produce more useful information than general ones. Take notes that you can expand later, or use a tape recorder. Keep attention focused on the information that you need, and do not be afraid to ask questions to keep your informant on the subject. If you plan to use direct quotations, make sure that the wording is accurate. If possible, check the quotations with your source one final time.

A Writer's Thesis

The information-gathering stage of the writing process is the time in which to sharpen your topic and to define first a tentative or working thesis for your paper and then a final thesis.

Thesis is derived from a Greek word that means "placing" or "position" or "proposition." When you formulate a thesis for your paper, you are defining your position on the subject. A thesis lets your reader know exactly where you stand in your paper. Because it represents your "final" position, a thesis is typically something that you develop and refine as you move through the prewriting stage of your paper, testing out ideas and gathering information. Don't try to start with a final thesis; begin with a tentative thesis (also called a *hypothesis*, from the Greek for "supposition"). Allow your final position to emerge based on what you have discovered in the prewriting stage.

Like any position statement, a thesis defines exactly what you are doing in this particular piece of writing. Before you write a thesis statement, though, you need to consider the factors that might initially control or influence the form that your thesis will take. For example, a thesis is a reflection of your purpose in writing. If your purpose is to persuade your audience to do or to believe something, your thesis will urge the reader to accept that position. If your purpose is to convey information to your reader, your thesis will indicate what you plan to say and how your paper will be organized.

Your thesis will also be shaped by the scope and length of your paper. Your topic and your thesis must be manageable within the space you have available; otherwise, you end up skimming the surface. A short paper requires a more precise focus than a longer one. As a result, when you move from subject to topic to thesis, make sure that each step is more specific and has an increasingly sharper focus. To check that focusing process, ask yourself the following questions:

What is my general subject?

What is my specific topic within that general subject area?

What is my position on that specific topic?

Writing a Thesis Statement

When you have answered the questions about your purpose, when you have sharpened your general subject into a topic, when you have defined your position toward that topic, you are ready to write a thesis statement. The process is simple. You write a thesis statement by linking together your topic and your position on that topic.

SUBJECT: Violence on television
TOPIC: The impact that viewing televised violence has on young children
THESIS: Televised violence makes young children numb to violence in the real world, distorts their perceptions of how people behave, and teaches them how to be violent.

An effective thesis, like any position statement, has a number of characteristics.

1. A thesis should clearly signal the purpose of the paper.
2. A thesis should state or take a definite position. It tells the reader what will be covered in the paper.

10

3. A thesis should express that definite position in precise, familiar terms. Avoid vague, abstract, or complicated technical terms.

4. A thesis should offer a position that can be explored or expanded within the scope of the paper. Remember that in moving from a general subject to a thesis, you have narrowed and sharpened your focus.

Placing a Thesis in Your Paper

Once you have written a thesis for your paper or essay, you must make two final decisions. First, you have to decide whether to include that explicit statement in your paper or just allow your paper's structure and content to imply that thesis. Second, if you decide to include a thesis statement, you must then determine where to place it in your paper. For example, should it appear in the first paragraph or at some point later in the paper?

If you look carefully at examples of professional writing, you will discover that neither question has a single answer. Writers make these decisions based upon the type of paper they are writing. As a student, however, you can follow several guidelines. Most pieces of writing done in college—either papers or essay examinations—should have explicit thesis statements and, typically, those statements should be placed early in the paper. The thesis will not always be in the first paragraph since your introduction might be designed to attract a reader's attention. Nevertheless, placing a thesis statement early in your paper will guarantee that the reader knows exactly what to expect.

Every argumentative or persuasive paper should have an explicitly stated thesis. Where you place that thesis depends upon whether the paper is structured deductively or inductively. Since a deductive argument begins with a general truth and then moves to a specific application of that truth, such an arrangement requires that the thesis be stated early. On the other hand, since an inductive argument moves in the opposite direction, starting with specific evidence and then moving to a conclusion, such an arrangement requires that the thesis be withheld until near the end of the paper.

Similarly, whenever your strategy in a paper is to build to a conclusion, a realization, or a discovery, you can withhold an explicit statement of your thesis until late in the paper. An early statement would spoil the suspense.

Revising an Essay

The idea of revising a paper may not sound appealing in the least. By the time you have finished the paper, the last thing you want to do is to revise it. Nevertheless, revising is a crucial step in the writing process, one you cannot afford to skip.

The word *revision* literally means "to see again." You do not revise a paper just by proofreading it for mechanical and grammatical errors, which is an expected final step in the writing process. Instead, a revision takes place after a draft of a whole paper or part of it has been completed, after a period of time has elapsed and you have had a chance to get some advice or criticism on what you wrote, after you can see what you wrote, not what you *think* you wrote. Revision should also involve an active, careful scrutiny on your part of every aspect of your paper—your subject, thesis, purpose, audience, paragraph structures, sentence constructions, and word choice.

Beginning a Revision

Revision should start not with the smallest unit—the choice of a particular word—but with the largest—the choice of subject, thesis, purpose, audience, and organization. A revision in its broadest sense involves a complete rethinking of a paper from idea through execution. Once you have finished a paper, think first about these five groups of questions—if possible, write out answers to each:

1. What is my *subject*? Is it too large? Too small? Is it interesting? Is it fresh or informative?
2. What is my *thesis*? Do I have a precise position on my subject?

12

Have I stated that thesis in a single sentence? Do I see the difference between having a subject and having a thesis?

3. What is my *purpose*? Why did I write *this* paper? Have I expressed my purpose in my thesis statement? Is everything in the paper related to that purpose?

4. Whom do I imagine as my *audience*? Who will read this? What do they already know about the subject? Have I written the paper with that audience in mind?

5. How is my paper *structured*? Have I followed the advice on structure given in the chapter introductions to this text? Is the organization of my paper clear and inevitable? Can it be outlined easily? Have I provided enough examples and details?

Using the Advice of Others

Another great help in revising is to find an editor/critic. If your writing instructor has the time to look at your draft or if your college or university has a writing center or a writing tutor program, you can get the advice of an experienced, trained reader. If your paper or part of it is discussed in class, listen to your classmates' comments as a way of gauging how successful your writing has been. If your writing class uses peer editing, you can study the responses of your editors for possible areas for revision.

Peer evaluation works best when readers start with a series of specific directions—questions to answer or things for which to look. If you are interested in trying peer evaluation, you and a classmate could start with an editing checksheet adapted from the "Some Things to Remember" section at the end of each introductory chapter in this book. Whenever you are responding to someone else's writing, remember that your comments are always more valuable if they are specific and suggest ways in which changes could be made.

It is often difficult to accept criticism, but if you want to improve your writing skills, you need someone to say, "why not do this?" After all, you expect that an athletic coach or a music or dance teacher will offer criticism. Your writing instructor plays the same role, and the advice and criticism he or she offers is meant to make your writing more effective; it is not intended as a personal criticism of you or your abilities.

Judging Length

After you have finished a draft of a paper, look carefully at how your response measures up to your instructor's guidelines about the length of the paper. Such guidelines are important for they give you some idea of the amount of space that you will need to develop and illustrate your thesis sufficiently. If your papers are consistently short, you probably have not included enough examples or illustrating details. Writing the suggested number of words does not, of course, guarantee a good essay, but writing only half of the suggested number because you fail to develop and illustrate your thesis can result in a lower grade.

Similarly, if your papers consistently exceed your instructor's guidelines, you have probably not sufficiently narrowed your subjects or you may have included too many details and examples. Of the material available to support, develop, and illustrate a thesis, some is more significant and relevant than the rest. Never try to include everything—select the best, the most appropriate, the most convincing.

Checking Paragraphs

The qualities of a good paragraph—things like unity, coherence, organization, completeness—have been stressed in every writing course you have taken. When you revise your paper, look carefully at each paragraph to see if it exhibits those qualities. How often have you paragraphed? If you have only one or two paragraphs in a several-page essay, you have not clearly indicated the structure of your essay to your reader or your essay does not have a clear, logical organization. On the other hand, if you have many short paragraphs, you are overparagraphing, probably shifting ideas too quickly and failing to develop each one adequately. A good paragraph is meaty; it is not a string of undeveloped ideas or bare generalizations.

Is an Error-Free Paper an "A" Paper?

Although good, effective writing is mechanically and grammatically correct, you cannot reverse the equation. It is perfectly possible to write a paper that has no "errors" but that is still a poor paper. An effective paper fulfills the requirements of the assignment, has something interesting or meaningful to say, includes specific evidence and examples rather than vague generalizations. Effective writing is a combination of many factors: appropriate content, a focused purpose, a clear organization, and effective expression.

Although perfect grammar and mechanics do not make a perfect paper, such things are important. Minor errors are like static in your writing. Too many of them distract your reader and focus the reader's attention not on your message, but on your faulty expression. Minor errors can undermine your reader's confidence in you as a qualified authority. If you make careless errors in spelling or punctuation, for example, your reader might assume that you made similar errors in reporting information. So while a revision is not just a proofreading, proofreading should be a part of the revision process.

A Student Writer's
Revision Process

The writing and rewriting process as outlined in this section can be seen in the evolution of Tina Burton's "The Watermelon Wooer." Tina's essay was written in response to a totally open assignment: she was just to write an essay, due in three weeks. The openness of the assignment proved initially frustrating to Tina. When she first began work on an essay, she started with a completely different topic. That weekend, however, she went home to visit her parents. Her grandfather had died just a few months before and the family was sorting through some photographs and reminiscing about him. Suddenly, Tina had the idea she wanted: she would write about her grandfather and her ambivalent feelings toward him.

Tina's first written work on the assignment came when she made a list of about 30 things that she remembered about him. "The list had to be cut," Tina said, "so I marked off those things which were too bawdy or too unbelievable." "I wanted to portray him as sympathetic," she added, "but I was really afraid that the whole piece would come off as too sentimental or drippy."

At the next class meeting, the instructor set aside some time for prewriting activities. The teacher recommended that the students try either a freewriting or a brainstorming exercise. Tina did the brainstorming that appears on the following page.

EARLIER DRAFT

From here, Tina wrote a draft—actually she wrote a complete draft in one sitting. She had the most difficulty with the beginning of the essay. "I kept trying to describe him, but I found that I was including too much," she commented. The breakthrough came through the advice of two other students in the class. Below is the first page of the first draft of Tina's essay. The handwritten comments were provided by Kathrine Varnes.

16

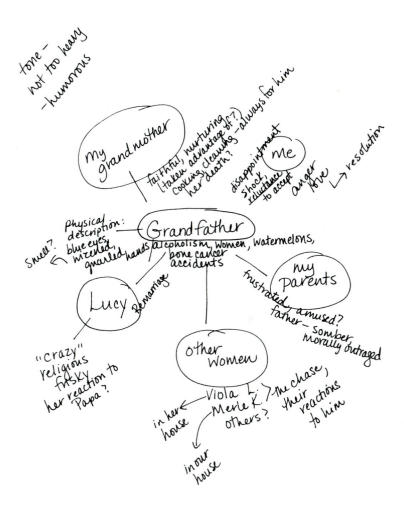

tone –
not too heavy
– humorous

my grandmother

faithful, nurturing
(taken advantage of?)
cooking, cleaning –always for him
her death?

me

disappointment
shock
reluctance
to accept
anger
love
↳ resolution

physical description:
Smell? blue eyes, wrinkled,
gnarled hands

Grandfather

alcoholism, women, watermelons,
bone cancer
accidents

my parents

frustrated, amused?
father – somber
morally outraged

Lucy

Remarriage

"crazy"
religious
frisky
her reaction to
Papa?

other women

Viola L.
Merle K.
others?

The chase,
their reactions
to him

in her house

in our house

The Watermelon Wooer

When someone you love dearly behaves in

a manner that offends you, do you stop

loving that person? Do you lose all respect

for that person because you cannot forget

repulsive [?]

the‸act (that you judged as repulsive) (On the *Eventually,* ?

contrary), ＊ you might (eventually) fondly recall   ＊*I have a*

personal

the once offensive behavior. (Perhaps,) in   *dislike for*

this 3-word

time, you might even understand why you   *transition*

so ?

found the behavior ‸ loathesome. Maybe, you

will reach a point in time when you will be   *Some way*

to

unable to think of your loved one without   *condense* ?

thinking of the once questionable behavior.

Such is the case with my grandfather.

Before I tell the story of how my

grandfather behaved in ways that I could

neither understand nor tolerate, I must

introduce ?

first (give some background information on)

him. A wizened little man with dancing blue

eyes and hands gnarled from years of

carpentry work, ''Papa'' was a notorious

womanizer and an alcoholic. Born and raised

18

in Halifax County, Virginia, he spent most

of his life building houses, distilling and

selling corn liquor, and chasing women.

After he and my grandmother had been married

for thirty years or so, he decided to

curtail some of his wild behavior and treat

her with more respect. Actually, he remained

both of these things? or respect by curtailing?

faithful to her only after he discovered

that she was ill and probably wouldn't be

around to feed and nurture him for much

longer. ~~So, as you can see,~~ my grandfather

didn't
(does not) have a spotless, or even a remotely

reputation
commendable record of personal achievements.

Use alternative diction to soften tone?

REVISED DRAFT

"Kathrine wanted me to condense and to find a way in which to jump right into the essay," Tina noted. "She also said, 'you're trying to tell too much. Let the story tell itself. Try to think of one thing that might capture something essential or important about him.'" In a second peer editing, Tina sought the advice of Stephen Palley, another classmate. Stephen offered these comments on this first page of the second draft.

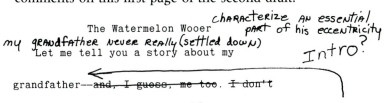

The Watermelon Wooer *chARActeRize AN essentiAl pART of his eccentricity*
my gRANdfAtheR NeveR ReAlly (settled dowN)
Let me tell you a story about my *Intro?*

grandfather--~~and, I guess, me too. I don't~~

19

~~pretend to know whether my story will shock~~,

~~offend, amuse, or bore~~. I only know that I

feel the need to tell ~~the story~~. *it*

For a time he
~~Before I tell the story of how~~ my

~~grandfather~~ behaved in ways that I could *but eventually*

neither understand nor tolerate, I must

(I see him now)   *Let me introduce*
first introduce him. A wizened little man

with ~~dancing blue eyes~~ and hands ~~gnarled~~

~~from years of carpentry work~~, ''Papa'' was a *smell?*

It's funny,
notorious womanizer and an alcoholic. Born

and raised in Halifax County, Virginia, he *but when*

I think of my
spent most of his life building houses, *grandfather*

I think 1ST
distilling and selling corn liquor, and

of the way
chasing women. After he and my grandmother *he smelled*

had been married for thirty years or so, he

decided to show her some respect by *Miller*

ponies,
curtailing his wild behavior. Actually, he *fertilizer*

remained faithful to her only after he

discovered that she was ill and probably

wouldn't be around to feed and nurture him

for much longer. Papa didn't have a spotless

reputation.

20

"Stephen offered me quite a few helpful suggestions," Tina recalled, "but he also suggested something that I just didn't quite feel comfortable with." As you can see in the revised draft, Tina had queried Stephen about possibly including her memories of odor. In a conversation Stephen urged Tina to substitute memories of smells for memories of sight. In the end, though, Tina observed, "I just couldn't do what Stephen suggested."

FINAL DRAFT

Before the three weeks were over, Tina actually wrote five separate drafts of her essay. "Everything here is true," she said, "but I worried so much about what I included, because I didn't want to embarrass anyone in my family." "Throughout the process," she added, "I was also worried about my tone. I wanted it to be funny; I wanted my readers to like my grandfather and his watermelon adventures."

Reproduced below is Tina's final draft of her essay.

```
            The Watermelon Wooer
               Tina M. Burton

      I see him now, sprawled on our couch, clutching a
 frayed afghan, one brown toenail escaping his sock. His
 darting eyes are betraying his withered body.
      Born and raised in backwoods Virginia, my
 grandfather spent most of his life building houses,
 distilling and selling corn liquor, and chasing women.
 After he and my grandmother had been married for thirty
 years or so, he decided to show her some respect by
 curtailing his wild behavior. Actually, he remained
 faithful to her only after he discovered that she was
 ill and probably wouldn't be around to feed and nurture
 him much longer. Papa didn't have a spotless
 reputation.
      Because he'd been on the wagon for several years
 and hadn't had any affairs for the last ten years, my
 family thought that Papa would continue to behave in a
 ''respectable'' manner even after my grandmother died.
 I guess we were hoping for some sort of miracle. After
```

my grandmother died in 1983, Papa became a rogue again: he insisted on reveling in wild abandon. When my father found out that Papa was drinking heavily again and crashing his car into mailboxes, houses, and other large obstacles, he asked Papa to move into our house. The fact that three of Papa's female neighbors had complained to the police about Papa's exposing himself probably had something to do with my father's decision.

The year that Papa lived with us rivaled the agony of Hell.

I was always Papa's favorite grandchild, his ''gal,'' and I worshipped him from the time that I was old enough to spend summers with him on his farm. Until I saw him every day, witnessed for myself his sometimes lewd behavior and his odd personality quirks, I never really believed the stories about him that I had heard from my mother and father. Every morning, he baited my mother with comments like ''the gravy's too thick,'' ''my room's too cold,'' ''your kids are too loud,'' and ''the phone rings too often.'' Against my mother's wishes, he smoked in the house. In mixed company, he gleefully explained how to have sex in an inner tube in the ocean without getting caught and gave detailed physical descriptions of the women he'd had sex with. It surprised me how much my opinion of Papa changed in one year.

During this one year, Papa did many things that I thought were embarrassing and inexcusable. I came face-to-face with the ''dark'' side of his personality. One week after moving into my parents' home, Papa began to sneak the orange juice from the refrigerator and doctor it with Smirnoff's vodka. I knew he'd been pickling his brain with alcohol for years and that this was part of the disease, but he'd said that he'd gone dry. Besides, he was violating my father's most important rule: no alcohol in the house. I didn't know that his drinking was only the first of a long line of incredible acts.

The behaviors that ultimately endeared Papa to me, that made me forgive him his shortcomings, are also those which I recall with a great deal of sadness. These are the memories of him that I treasure, the stories that I will tell to my grandchildren when they

22

are old enough to deal with graphic material. A year
ago, I never would have believed that I could fondly
remember, much less write about, these episodes.
    For about a year, Papa engaged in what I refer to
as the ''watermelon affairs.'' Perhaps because he had
lived on a vegetable farm for the majority of his life,
Papa had a special affinity for a wide variety of
fruits and vegetables. Especially dear to him were
watermelons. So, he assumed that other elderly people,
particularly women, shared his proclivity for produce.
One week after he moved into my parent's house, he
embarked upon his mission—to woo with watermelons as
many women as he could.
    A shrewd man, possessed of a generous supply of
common sense and watermelons, Papa decided to seduce a
woman who lived very close to him. This woman happened
to be my maternal grandmother who also lived in our
house. Unaware of his lascivious intentions and bent on
helping him assuage his grief over the loss of his
wife, Grandmother Merle prepared special meals for Papa
and spent long hours conversing with him about farming,
grandchildren, and life in the ''Old South.'' Merle
assumed that the watermelons Papa brought to her were
nothing more than a token of his appreciation for her
kindness. When Papa grabbed a part of Merle that she
preferred to remain untouched, these conversations came
to an abrupt halt. Of course, we were mortified by his
inappropriate behavior, but I suspect that my parents
secretly were amused. While Papa's indiscretion with
Merle was upsetting, at least no one other than members
of my immediate family knew about the incident. His
next romantic adventure earned him immediate notoriety
in the neighborhood. One afternoon, huge watermelon in
hand, he trotted over to visit Viola Lampson, a
decrepit and cranky elderly woman with whom my family
had been friendly for twenty years. Twenty minutes
after Papa entered her house, the police came. Poor
Viola was in a state of disrepair because my
grandfather had been chasing her around her kitchen
table demanding kisses. Fortunately, the policeman who
arrived at the scene of the crime was quite
understanding and polite; he advised my father to keep

a careful watch on Papa at all times. My somber father was very embarrassed. Finally, we were all beginning to see the relationship between watermelons and women. He'd disappear with a watermelon and return with the police.

I was mortified by Papa's lecherous desire for other women. After all, wasn't he supposed to be grieving over the death of my grandmother, his wife of fifty years? I resigned myself to the fact that I never would love him or respect him in the manner that I once had. For a while, I avoided his company and refused to answer his frequent questions about why I was avoiding him. I didn't think about why he was behaving the way he was; I simply cast judgement on his behavior and shut myself off from him. Not until Papa remarried did I even try to understand his needs or his behavior.

Approximately one year after his wife died, Papa remarried. Finally, he found a woman who not only loved watermelon but also loved him and his frisky behavior. Lucy, often referred to as ''crazy Lucy'' by her neighbors who had heard her speak of miracle healings and visions of Christ, wed Papa and took him into her already jam-packed home. Amazingly, she convinced him to stop drinking and to refrain from molesting other women. She could not, however, convince Papa to ''get the religion'' as she called it. My family was nonplussed both by Papa's decision to remarry at age 77 and to stop drinking after all these years. We all were annoyed by the fact that Lucy convinced him to do in several months what we had been trying to get him to do for many years.

Not until I learned that Papa was dying of bone cancer did I try to understand why he needed to remarry and why I found that fact unbearable. Until this time, I harbored the feeling that Papa somehow was degrading the memory of my grandmother by remarrying. His attempted seductions of women disturbed me, but his decision to marry Lucy saddened me. Only after I spent many afternoons with Papa and Lucy did I realize that they truly loved each other. More importantly, I realized that Papa, devastated by his wife's death, was

afraid to be alone in his old age. Perhaps sensing his
illness, even though he knew nothing of its development
at this time, he wanted to recapture some of his
stamina, some of his youth. He really wasn't searching
for someone to replace my grandmother: he simply wanted
to have a companion to comfort him, to distract him
from his grief.

Fortunately, I accepted Papa's actions and resolved
my conflict with him before he died. Once again, I was
his ''gal'' in spirit, and I even came to love and
respect Lucy. Now, I find that I cannot conjure images
of Papa without thinking of watermelons and his
romantic escapades. The acts that once troubled me
eventually allowed me to glimpse the frail side of my
grandfather, to see him as a human being possessed of
fears and flaws rather than a cardboard ideal.

Some Things to Remember When Revising

1. Put your paper aside for a period of time before you attempt to revise it.

2. Seek the advice of your instructor or a writing center tutor, or the help of classmates.

3. Reconsider your choice of subject. Were you able to treat it adequately in the space you had available?

4. State your thesis in a sentence as a way of checking your content. Is everything in the paper relevant to that thesis?

5. Check to make sure that you have given enough examples to support your argument or to make your thesis clear. Relevant specifics convince and interest a reader.

6. Look through the advice given in each of the introductions to this text. Have you organized your paper carefully? Is its structure clear?

7. Define your audience. To whom are you writing? What assumptions have you made about your audience? What changes are necessary to make your paper clear and interesting to that audience?

25

8. Check the guidelines your instructor provided. Have you done what was asked? Is your paper too short or too long?

9. Examine each sentence to make sure that it is complete and grammatically correct. Try for a variety of sentence structures and lengths.

10. Look carefully at each paragraph. Does it obey the rules for effective paragraph construction? Do your paragraphs clearly indicate the structure of your essay?

11. Check your word choice. Have you avoided slang, jargon, and clichés? Have you used specific words? Have you used appropriate words for your intended audience?

12. Proofread one final time.

How to Read
an Essay

When your grade in most writing courses is determined by the papers that you write, rather than by examinations based on the essays that you read in the course, you might wonder why any instructor would assign "readings" in a writing course. How do these two seemingly very different activities fit together?

How Does Reading Help You Write?

You read in a writing course for three purposes: First, the essays are a source of information: you learn by reading and what you learn can then, in turn, be used in your writing. Any paper that involves research requires selective, critical reading on your part as you search for and evaluate sources. Second, readings offer a perspective on a particular subject, one with which you might agree or disagree. In this sense readings can serve as catalysts or stimuli to provoke writing. Many of the writing suggestions in this text are outgrowths of the readings. You are asked to explore some aspect of the subject more fully, to employ the same type of strategy with a different subject, to reply to a writer's position, or to expand on or refine that position. And finally, readings offer models to a writer; they show you how another writer dealt with a particular subject or a particular writing problem.

The first two purposes—readings as a source of information or as a stimulus to writing—are fairly obvious, but the third purpose might seem confusing. Exactly how are you, as a student writer, to use an example, or a model, an essay written by a professional writer? Are you to suppose to sound like E. B. White or Joan Didion or Maya Angelou? Are you to imitate their styles or the structures that they use in their essays? To model in the sense that the word is being used here does not mean to produce an imitation. You are not expected to use the same organizational structure; you are not expected to imitate someone else's style, tone, or approach. Rather, what you can learn from these writers is how to handle information; how to adapt writing to a particular audience; how to structure the body of an essay; how to begin, make transitions, and end; how to construct effective paragraphs and achieve sentence variety. In short, the readings represent an album of performances, examples that you can use to study writing techniques.

Models or examples are important to a writer because you learn to write effectively in the same way that you learn to do any other activity. You study the rules or advice on how it is done; you practice, especially under the watchful eye of an instructor or a coach; and you study how others have mastered similar problems and techniques. A young musician learns how to read music and play an instrument, practices daily, studies with a teacher, and listens to and watches how other musicians play. A baseball player learns the proper offensive and defensive techniques, practices daily, is supervised by a coach, and listens to the advice and watches the performance of other players. As a writer in a writing class, you do the same thing: follow the advice offered by your instructor and textbooks, practice by writing and revising, listen to the advice and suggestions of your fellow students, and study the work of other writers.

How Does Writing Help You Read?

The interaction between reading and writing works in both ways: being a good reader will help you become a more effective writer and being a good writer will help you become a more effective reader. As a writer, you learn how to put an essay together, how to use examples to support a thesis, how to structure an argument, how to make an effective transition from one point to another. You learn how to write beginnings, middles, and ends, and most especially you learn how essays can be organized. For example, you know that a comparison and contrast paper can be organized either by the subject-by-subject or the point-by-point pattern. You know that narratives are structured in time and that cause and effect analyses are linear and sequential. As a result, when you read an essay you look for structure and pattern, realizing that such devices are not only creative tools you use in writing, but also analytical ones that can be used in reading. These devices help you understand what the essay says, by revealing to you an underlying organizational pattern. In order to become an efficient reader, however, you need to exercise the same care and attention that you do when you write. You do that by becoming an active rather than a passive reader.

Active Rather Than Passive Reading

Every reader first reads a piece of writing for plot or subject matter. On that level, the reader wants to know what happens, what is the subject, whether it is new or interesting. Generally that first reading is done quickly, even, in a sense, superficially. The reader is a spectator waiting passively to be entertained or informed. Only after the reader's curiosity about plot or subject has been satisfied does the next stage of active reading begin. On this level, the reader asks questions, seeks answers, looks for organizational structures, and concentrates on the thesis and the quality of evidence presented. Careful reading requires this active participation of the reader. Writing and reading are, after all, social acts and as such they involve an implied contract between a writer and an audience. A writer's job is to communicate clearly and effectively, but a reader's job is to read attentively and critically.

Because as a reader you need to become an active participant in this process of communication, you should never read any piece of writing just once. Reading an essay, like those found in this book, involves the same types of critical activities that you use when reading a poem, a novel, or a play. While an essay might be easier to read than a poem, it still demands your attention and your active involvement as a reader.

In addition to reading an essay you must study it. You must examine how the author embodies meaning or purpose in prose. You must seek answers to a variety of questions: How does the author structure the essay? How does the author select, organize, and present information? To whom is the author writing? How does that audience influence the essay?

You can increase your effectiveness as an active and critical reader by following the same three-stage model that you use as a writer: divide your time into prereading, reading, and rereading activities.

Prereading

Before you begin reading the essay, look first at the apparatus that accompanies it. Each essay is preceded by a biographical headnote describing the author and her or his work. The headnote and the accompanying credits also identify where and when the essay was originally published, including any special conditions or circumstances that surrounded or influenced its publication. A careful reading of this material can help prepare you to read the essay.

Look next at the text of the essay itself. What does the title tell you about the subject or the tone? A serious, dignified title such as "The Value of Children: A Taxonomical Essay" (p. 237) sets up a very different set of expectations than a playful title such as "Going to the Cats" (p. 391). Page through the essay— are there any obvious subdivisions in the text (extra spaces, sequence markers, subheadings) that signal an organizational pattern? Does the paragraphing suggest a particular structure?

Finally, look at the series of questions that follow each selection. Those questions always ask about subject and purpose, structure and audience, and vocabulary and style. Read through them so that you know what to look for when you read the essay. Before you begin to read, make sure that you have a pen or pencil, some paper on which to take notes, and a dictionary in which to check the meanings of unfamiliar words.

Reading

When you begin to read a selection in this book, you already have an important piece of information about its structure. Each selection was chosen to demonstrate a particular type of writing (narration, description, exposition, and argumentation) and a particular pattern of organization (chronological, spatial, division and classification, comparison and contrast, process, cause and effect, definition, induction or deduction). As you read, think about how the author organized the essay. On a separate sheet of paper, construct a brief outline. That will help you focus your attention on how the whole essay is put together.

Remember that an essay, like any work of literature, will typically express a particular idea or assertion **(thesis)** about a **subject** to an **audience** for a particular reason **(purpose).** Probably one reading of an essay will be enough for you to answer questions about **subject,** but you may have to reread the essay several times in order to identify the author's **thesis** and **purpose.** Keep these three elements separate and clear in your own mind. It will help to answer each of the following questions as you read:

1. **Subject:** What is this essay about?
2. **Thesis:** What particular point is the author trying to make about this subject?
3. **Audience:** To whom is the author writing? Where did the essay first appear? How does its intended audience help shape the essay and influence its language and style?
4. **Purpose:** Why is the author writing this? Is the intention to entertain? To inform? To persuade?

Effective writing contains specific, relevant details and examples. Look carefully at the writer's choice of examples. Remember that the author made a conscious decision to include

31

each of these details. Ideally, each is appropriate to the subject and each contributes to the thesis and purpose.

Rereading

Rereading, like rewriting, is not always a discrete stage in a linear process. Just as you might pause after writing several sentences and then go back and make some immediate changes, so as a reader, you might stop at the end of a paragraph and then go back and reread what you have just read. Depending upon the difficulty of the essay, it might take several rereadings for you to be able to answer the questions posed above about the writer's thesis and purpose. Even if you feel certain about your understanding of the essay, a final rereading is important.

In that rereading, focus on the essay as an example of a writer's craft. Look carefully at the paragraphing. How effective is the introduction to the essay? The conclusion? Have you ever used a similar strategy to begin or end an essay? How do both reflect the writer's purpose? Audience? Pay attention to the writer's sentence structures. How do these sentences differ from the ones that you typically write? Does the author employ a variety of sentence types and lengths? Is there anything unusual about the author's word choices? Do you use a similar range of vocabulary when you write? Remember that the writer of essays is just as conscious of craft as the poet, the novelist, or the playwright.

A Sample Reading

Before you begin reading in the third edition of *The Prentice Hall Reader*, you can see how to use these techniques of prereading, reading, and rereading in the following analyzed essay.

To Noble Companions

GAIL GODWIN

Born in 1937 in Birmingham, Alabama, Gail Godwin graduated with a B.A. from the University of North Carolina and then earned an M.A. and a Ph.D. from the University of Iowa. She has held a number of teaching positions in colleges and universities but now devotes her full time to writing. Her books include seven novels— The Perfectionists *(1970),* Glass People *(1972),* The Odd Woman *(1974),* Violet Clay *(1978),* A Mother and Two Daughters *(1982),* The Finishing School *(1985),* A Southern Family *(1987), and* Father Melancholy's Daughter *(1991)—and several collections of short stories. She has contributed essays, stories, and reviews to a wide range of periodicals. "To Noble Companions" was originally published in* Harper's *in a special section devoted to friendship. In this five-paragraph essay, Godwin explores the meaning of the word* friend.

Essay begins with a conventional definition of friendship.

Rejection of that definition

Godwin develops her own definition, using the extended metaphor of flying.

THE DUTIFUL FIRST ANSWER seems programmed into us by our meager expectations: "A friend is one who will be there in times of trouble." But I believe this is a skin-deep answer to describe skin-deep friends. There is something irresistible about misfortune to human nature, and standbys for setbacks and sicknesses (as long as they are not too lengthy, or contagious) can usually be found. They can be *hired*. What I value is not the "friend" who, looming sympathetically above me when I have been dashed to the ground, appears gigantically generous in the hour of my reversal; more and more I desire friends who will endure my ecstasies with me, who possess wings of their own and who will fly with me. I don't mean this as arrogance (I am too superstitious to indulge

1

33

Thesis: friends are
"persons whose
qualities groom me
and train me up
for love."

Origins of the word
friend

Body of paper   2
begins here. Author
includes three
examples of
friendship.

First example: a
childhood
experience

Second example: an   3
adult relationship

Third example: an   4
ideal or model
friendship

long in that trait), and I don't fly all that often. What I mean is that I seek (and occasionally find) friends with whom it is possible to drag out all those beautiful, old, outrageously *aspiring* costumes and rehearse together for the Great Roles; persons whose qualities groom me and train me up for love. It is for those people that I reserve the glowing hours, too good not to share. It is the existence of these people that reminds me that the words "friend" and "free" grew out of each other. (OE *freo*, not in bondage, noble, glad; OE *freon*, to love; OE *freond*, friend.)

When I was in the eighth grade, I had a friend. We were shy and "too serious" about our studies when it was becoming fashionable with our classmates to acquire the social graces. We said little at school, but she would come to my house and we would sit down with pencils and paper, and one of us would say: "Let's start with a train whistle today." We would sit quietly together and write separate poems or stories that grew out of a train whistle. Then we would read them aloud. At the end of that school year, we, too, were transformed into social creatures and the stories and poems stopped.

When I lived for a time in London, I had a friend. He was in despair and I was in despair, but our friendship was based on the small flicker of foresight in each of us that told us we would be sorry later if we did not explore this great city because we had felt bad at the time. We met every Sunday for five weeks and found many marvelous things. We walked until our despairs resolved themselves and then we parted. We gave London to each other.

For almost four years I have had a remarkable friend whose imagination illumines mine. We write long letters in which we often discover our strangest selves. Each of us appears, sometimes prophetically, sometimes comically, in the other's dreams. She and I agree that, at certain times, we seem to be parts of the same mind. In my most sacred and interesting moments, I often think: "Yes, I must tell ———." We have never met.

Restatement of thesis: A friend is more than a "Job's comforter."

It is such exceptional (in a sense divine) companions I wish to salute. I have seen the glories of the world reflected briefly through our encounters. One bright hour with their kind is worth more to me than a lifetime guarantee of the services of a Job's comforter whose "helpful" lamentations will only clutter the healing silence necessary to those darkest moments in which I would rather be my own best friend. 5

Prereading Godwin's Essay

The headnote to Godwin's essay gives you several important pieces of information. The essay originally appeared in a special section of *Harper's* focusing on friendship. Presumably Godwin was asked to contribute, in the form of a short essay, her thoughts on the subject. The context in which the essay originally appeared probably helped shape or influence its form—for example, its brevity and the quickness with which it jumps into the subject. Godwin's educational background might account for some of the details in the essay. That is, while many writers might make a reference to "Job's comforter," only someone with a more specialized knowledge might choose to include the references to the Old English (OE) origins for the words *friend* and *free*. The title of the essay indicates the subject, but it also suggests that what follows is not so much a definition as a "toast" to friendship. "To Noble Companions" occasions in the reader different expectations than "A Definition of a Friend."

Reading Godwin's Essay

If Godwin's essay were in the main portion of this book, it would be found in Chapter 8: Definition. Although a definition essay does not have a specific, predetermined structure, you would expect that it will extend a conventional dictionary definition through a series of examples. With a word such as "friend," you know that a simple definition such as "a person whom one knows well and is fond of" is hardly adequate. You expect that Godwin will include examples to illustrate her understanding of the word *friend*.

Godwin begins by rejecting one definition of the term—"a friend is one who will be there in times of trouble." A friend, she suggests, is someone with whom to endure "ecstasies," not "misfortunes." In paragraphs 2, 3, and 4, Godwin offers examples of friendships that she has experienced. Each example is developed in a single paragraph. The first two examples took place in an earlier time, and she links the two together by repeating the same structure for the first sentence of the paragraph:

When I was in the eighth grade, I had a friend.

When I lived for a time in London, I had a friend.

The third example—set in the present—is introduced in a slightly different, but clearly related, way: "For almost four years I have had a remarkable friend. . . ." The final paragraph returns to the distinction that Godwin had established in the first paragraph—a friend is someone who helps you grow, develop, and love.

The subject of Godwin's essay is, obviously, friendship. Her thesis is that a friend is someone with whom and through whom human potential and aspirations are realized. Presumably, her purpose is to illuminate for her readers other, less conventional, meanings to be found in the word *friend*.

As you read, always watch for words, phrases, or allusions that you do not recognize and always try to find a definition or explanation for each. A good college dictionary is an essential piece of equipment for any active reader, and it can often answer a range of different questions. In this case, for example, even the allusion to "Job's comforter" in paragraph 5 can be identified by using a dictionary ("a person who aggravates one's misery while attempting or pretending to comfort; see Job 16:1–5").

Rereading Godwin's Essay

Godwin's essay is both conventional and unconventional at the same time. At first, this five-paragraph essay on the topic "define a friend" probably recalls some of the writing that you did in high school. The similarity, though, ends with this superficial observation. From the opening sentence, Godwin's response is uniquely her own and cleverly crafted. You or I might open with a sentence such as "A friend is typically defined as 'one who will be there in times of trouble.' However, this definition does not do justice to a word that can mean many things." Godwin's sentence says much more in a distinctive way: "The dutiful first answer seems programmed into us by our meager expectations. . . ." The sentence is a response to the implied question, "What is a friend?"

Godwin's paragraphs and sentences depend heavily on parallelism. As you reread the essay, you probably noticed the repetitions that hold together paragraphs 2 and 3:

When I was . . .
We were shy . . .
We said little . . .
We would sit . . .
Then we would read . . .

When I lived . . .
He was in despair and I was in despair . . .
We met . . .
We walked . . . and then we parted . . .
We gave London . . .

Defining a complex term is never a simple matter, for words have not only denotations (explicit definitions) but also connotations (associations or suggestions). In this sense, defining can be a reductive act; it cannot always do justice to the complexities and subtleties that are inherent in a word. Godwin's strategy as a writer is to avoid a simple answer. She illustrates her definition with three experiences—arranged chronologically, with each contained within its own paragraph. In the end, though, she resists providing a one-sentence definition of the term, choosing instead to suggest through example and analogy what a friend really means to her.

Each of the essays in the third edition of *The Prentice Hall Reader* will repay you for the time and effort you put into reading it carefully and critically. Each essay shows an artful craftsperson at work, solving the problems inherent in communicating experiences, feelings, ideas, and opinions to an audience. Each writer is someone from whom you, as a reader and as a thinker, can learn. So when your instructor assigns a selection from the text, remember that as a reader you must assume an active role. Don't assume that reading an essay once—to see what it is "about"—will mean that you are prepared to write about it or that you have learned all that you can learn from the essay. Ask questions, seek answers to those questions, analyze, and reread.

Some Things to Remember When Reading

1. Read through the selection first to see what happens and to satisfy your curiosity.
2. Go back and read the headnote to the selection. How does this information help you to understand the writer and the context in which the selection was written?
3. Reread the selection several times, taking notes or underlining as you go.
4. Look at the questions that follow each reading. They will help focus your attention on the important aspects of the selection. Write out answers to each question.
5. Write or locate in the essay a thesis statement. Remember that the thesis is the particular point that the writer is trying to make about the subject.

6. Define a purpose for the essay. Why is the writer writing? Does the author make that purpose explicit?

7. Imagine the audience for such an essay. Who is the likely reader? What does that reader already know about the subject? Is the reader likely to have any preconceptions or prejudices about the subject?

8. Isolate a structure in the selection. How is it put together? Into how many parts can it be divided? How do those parts work together? Outline the essay.

9. Be sure that you understand every sentence. How does the writer vary the sentence structures?

10. Look up every word that you cannot define with some degree of certainty. Remember that you might misinterpret what the author is saying if you simply skip over the unfamiliar words.

11. Reread the essay one final time, reassembling its parts into the artful whole that it was intended to be.

ONE

Example

Effective writing in any form depends upon examples. Without them you are forced to rely on generalizations. Examples make writing vivid; they represent particular instances that illustrate the points you are trying to make. That general statement needs an example.

Life magazine asked writer Malcolm Cowley for an essay on what it was like to turn 80. The result was "The View from 80." Since nearly all of his readers would be less than 80, Cowley needed to show his readers what it was like to be "old." He does so through a series of examples, including at one point a simple list that begins like this:

The body and its surroundings have their messages for him, or only one message: "You are old." Here are some of the occasions on which he receives the message:

—when it becomes an achievement to do thoughtfully, step by step, what he once did instinctively

—when his bones ache

—when there are more and more little bottles in the medicine cabinet, with instructions for taking four times a day

—when he fumbles and drops his toothbrush (butterfingers)

—when his face has bumps and wrinkles, so that he cuts himself while shaving (blood on the towel)

—when year by year his feet seem farther from his hands

—when he can't stand on one leg and has trouble pulling on his pants

41

—when he hesitates on the landing before walking down a flight of stairs

—when he spends more time looking for things misplaced than he spends using them after he (or more often his wife) has found them

—when he falls asleep in the afternoon

—when it becomes harder to bear in mind two things at once

—when a pretty girl passes him in the street and he doesn't turn his head*

Cowley's list of examples is atypical. Most writing tasks do not involve quite so many illustrations, and most demand that the examples be worked into the paragraphs rather than set apart in a list.

How Important Are Examples?

Examples are very important, for they add life and interest to your writing and they support or illustrate the points you are trying to make. Russell Baker, in "Computer Fallout," could have stated his thesis in a single sentence: "Writing on a word processor makes it very hard to stop editing and revising long enough to write a readable sentence." Instead, his essay consists of a long series of false starts by which he demonstrates the ease and the temptation of revising sentences on a word processor. The cumulative effect of all of the examples makes his thesis vivid, believable, and funny.

How Many Examples Are Enough?

It would make every writer's job much easier if there were a single, simple answer to the question of how many examples to use. Instead, the answer is "enough," "enough to persuade the reader," "enough to convince the reader." Sometimes one

---

* From *The View from 80* by Malcolm Cowley. Copyright © 1980 by Malcolm Cowley. Reprinted by permission of Viking Penguin Inc.

fully developed example might be enough. The advertisements for organizations such as Save the Children often tell the story of a specific child in need of food and shelter. The single example, accompanied with a photograph, is enough to persuade many people to sponsor a child. Tom Wolfe in the opening paragraphs of his essay "A Sunday Kind of Love" focuses on one example: two teenagers lost in a kiss at 8:45 A.M. in a New York City subway station on a weekday. That example of "love at rush hour" set against the swirl of hurrying people with "no time" for such behavior represents the type of experience normally set apart for Sundays in New York.

Other times you might need to use many examples. In "Cut," for instance, Bob Greene writes about how being "cut" from the junior high school basketball team changed his life. To support his thesis and extend it beyond his own personal experience, Greene includes the stories of four other men who had similar experiences. But why four examples? Why not three or five or seven? There is nothing magical about the number four—Greene might have used four because he had space for four—but the four give authority to Greene's assertion, or at least they create the illusion of authority. To prove the validity of Greene's thesis would require a proper statistical sample. Only then could it be said with certainty that the experience of being "cut" makes men superachievers later in life. In most writing situations, however, such thoroughness is not needed. If the examples are well chosen and relevant, the reader is likely to accept your assertions.

Where Can You Find Examples?

Unfortunately, finding examples to use is generally not an easy matter. Even when you are narrating an experience that happened to you or describing something that you saw or presenting a personal opinion, you will have to spend some time remembering the events, sorting out the details of the experience, or deciding which examples best support what you believe. If you are presenting information about a subject outside of yourself, your problems are even greater. No matter how much you once knew about a subject, you forget specific details. Remember all the studying you did for a history course—all the dates, names, theories, and interpretations that you had on instant recall the day of the examination? A semester or a year later, how much can you remember? If the subject is totally new, you will have to gather examples from sources outside of yourself.

When you think about researching a subject, you might think only of going to a library to look up your topic in the card catalog or in a periodical index. Certainly the writers of many essays in this text researched their subjects in this way. However, as the six examples in this chapter show, you do not necessarily have to find your examples or information in printed sources. Your memories, your experiences, and your observations can be good places to begin. In writing "Computer Fallout," Russell Baker found a ready source of examples in his own experiences with writing on a word processor. Similarly, Anna Quindlen drew upon her thirty-four years of experience with her last name to write "The Name Is Mine." Tom Wolfe, in "A Sunday Kind of Love," describes what he witnessed in a subway station on his way to work one morning.

The experiences of other people can also be excellent sources of information. The examples of college slang in William Safire's "Words for Nerds" come from students at a number of eastern colleges and universities. Given the short-lived nature of such words, the library would probably not be a good place to look for examples of similar expressions used at your school. Like Safire, you would want fellow students to supplement your own careful listening. Finally, Bob Greene's "Cut" recounts the experiences of five men who were "cut" from athletic teams when they were young. Again, library research would not produce the examples that Greene needed.

Sample Student Essay

EXAMPLE

Charles Jenkins chose to write an essay that added to the examples of campus slang William Safire had compiled in "Words for Nerds." His earlier draft appears below.

EARLIER DRAFT

```
          Some Examples of Campus Slang

''How'd ya do on the exam?'' ''I aced it. How about
you?'' ''I bombed it, big time. I think I'll just bag
my class and go crash.'' Confused? Does it sound like a
foreign language? No, it is still English, but with
frequent interjections of college slang found on many
campuses such as here at the University of Delaware.
Campus slang, in itself, is nothing new, but is a
constantly changing phenomenon. Old expressions fade
away and new ones rise to take their places just as new
students replace old students. Now it is time for some
translations. ''Acing'' an exam or ''getting an ace''
is a reference to getting an A on that exam. On the
other hand, ''bombing'' or ''bombing, big time'' evokes
images of a disaster or failure, and that is precisely
what it means, to fail or fail miserably. Slang on
campus, however, is not limited to exams. ''Bagging''
class is today's form of yesterday's practice of
''cutting'' class. After a student has ''bagged'' or
''cut'' his class, he is likely to go ''crash.'' To
''crash'' is to go back to the dorm and sleep.
''Crashing'' could be a reference to the sound made
when a tired student flops into bed after a tough day;
it is unclear. The surface has been barely scratched in
campus slang; a full exposition would take much longer,
but at least you won't be totally in the dark.
```

When Charles came to revise his essay, he had his instructor's comments and the reactions of several classmates. Everyone had agreed that he had chosen good examples and, by using them in an imagined dialogue, had caught his readers' attention. Charles was troubled by his final sentence, but was not sure how else to conclude. After the class had discussed slang and how quickly it changes, he found an idea for a new concluding sentence—one that was more in keeping with the tone he had established. Charles changed several sentences to avoid empty generalizations and clichés—phrases such as "old expressions fade away," "surface barely scratched," and "won't be totally in the dark." In the time between drafts, Charles found another example to add as well. The revision follows:

REVISED DRAFT

Some Strange New Words on Campus

```
''How'd ya do on the exam?''
''I aced it. How about you?''
''I bombed it, big time. I think I'll just bag my
classes and go crash.''
    Confused? Does it sound like a foreign language?
No, it is still English, but with frequent
interjections of college slang found on many campuses
such as here at the University of Delaware. Campus
slang, in itself, is nothing new, but it is a
constantly changing phenomenon. Now it is time for a
translation. The phrase ''acing an exam'' or ''getting
an ace'' is today's campus terminology for getting an
A. On the other hand, ''bombing'' or ''bombing, big
time'' evokes images of a disaster or a failure, and
that is precisely what it means, to fail or fail
miserably. Campus slang, however, is not limited to
exams. ''Bagging'' class is today's term for
yesterday's practice of ''cutting'' class. After a
student has ''bagged'' his classes, he is likely to go
''crash.'' To ''crash'' is to go back to the dorm and
sleep. ''Crashing'' might be a reference to the sound
made when a tired student flops into bed after a tough
day. Even the social life on campus is not immune to
the use of slang. Consider the word ''scope,'' a
shortened form of ''telescope.'' ''Scope'' can be used
```

```
as either a noun or a verb. To ''scope'' is to spend
time gazing longingly at members of the opposite sex.
As a noun, it is most often used to refer to the one
person, who after many hours of ''scoping,'' you find
especially enchanting. If you don't understand all
these strange new words, don't worry—they will soon be
as obsolete as ''cool'' and ''peachy keen.''
```

Some Things to Remember

1. Use examples—effective writing depends upon them.
2. The number of examples necessarily varies. Sometimes one will do; sometimes you will need many. If your want your readers to do or to believe something, you will need to supply some evidence to gain their support or confidence.
3. Since you can never remember everything you once knew, you need to go outside of your own memory to gather examples and illustrations. In short, finding examples often requires some type of research.
4. Choose examples that are relevant and accurate. Quality is more important than quantity. Make sure your examples support your argument or illustrate the points you are trying to make. If you use an outside authority—either an oral or a printed source—make sure that the source is knowledgeable and reliable. Remember also to document your use of those sources.

A Sunday Kind of Love

TOM WOLFE

Tom Wolfe was born in Richmond, Virginia, in 1931 and received a Ph.D. in American Studies from Yale in 1957. When he joined the staff of the New York Herald Tribune's Sunday magazine, New York, *in 1962, he developed the flamboyant style and interest in new trends in popular culture that have become his trademark. His books include* The Kandy-Kolored Tangerine-Flake Streamline Baby *(1965),* The Electric Kool-Aid Acid Test *(1968),* Mauve Gloves & Madmen, Clutter & Vine *(1976),* From Bauhaus to Our House *(1981), and* The Purple Decades *(1983). In 1987 he published his first novel,* The Bonfire of the Vanities, *made into a movie in 1990.* The Right Stuff *(1979), a history of the early space program, won the American Book Award. Much of Wolfe's writing has appeared in* Esquire, Harper's, *and* Rolling Stone. *In these paragraphs from the beginning of his essay "A Sunday Kind of Love," originally published in the* New York Herald's *Sunday magazine section, Wolfe describes two kids lost in a kiss at 8:45 on a weekday morning during the subway rush hour. What could be more improbable in a city where real love has to wait until Sunday?*

1   LOVE? Attar of libido in the air! It is 8:45 A.M. Thursday morning in the IRT subway station at 50th Street and Broadway and already two kids are hung up in a kind of herringbone weave of arms and legs, which proves, one has to admit, that love is not *confined* to Sunday in New York. Still, the odds! All the faces come popping in clots out of the Seventh Avenue local, past the King Size Ice Cream machine, and the turnstiles start whacking away as if the world were breaking up on the reefs. Four steps past the turnstiles everybody is already backed up haunch to paunch for the climb up the ramp and the stairs to the surface, a great funnel of flesh, wool, felt, leather, rubber and steaming alumicron, with the blood squeezing through everybody's old sclerotic arteries in hopped-up spurts from too much coffee and the effort of surfacing from the subway at the

rush hour. Yet there on the landing are a boy and a girl, both about eighteen, in one of those utter, My Sin, backbreaking embraces.

He envelops her not only with his arms but with his chest, which has the American teen-ager concave shape to it. She has her head cocked at a 90-degree angle and they both have their eyes pressed shut for all they are worth and some incredibly feverish action going with each other's mouths. All round them, tens, scores, it seems like hundreds, of faces and bodies are perspiring, trooping and bellying up the stairs with arteriosclerotic grimaces past a showcase full of such novel items as Joy Buzzers, Squirting Nickels, Finger Rats, Scary Tarantulas and spoons with realistic dead flies on them, past Fred's barbershop, which is just off the landing and has glossy photographs of young men with the kind of baroque haircuts one can get in there, and up onto 50th Street into a madhouse of traffic and shops with weird lingerie and gray hair-dyeing displays in the windows, signs for free teacup readings and a pool-playing match between the Playboy Bunnies and Downey's Showgirls, and then everybody pounds on toward the Time-Life Building, the Brill Building or NBC.

The boy and the girl just keep on writhing in their embroilment. Her hand is sliding up the back of his neck, which he turns when her fingers wander into the intricate formal gardens of his Chicago Boxcar hairdo at the base of the skull. The turn causes his face to start to mash in the ciliated hull of her beehive hairdo, and so she rolls her head 180 degrees to the other side, using their mouths for the pivot. But aside from good hair grooming, they are oblivious to everything but each other. Everybody gives them a once-over. Disgusting! Amusing! How touching! A few kids pass by and say things like "Swing it, baby." But the great majority in that heaving funnel up the stairs seem to be as much astounded as anything else. The vision of love at rush hour cannot strike anyone exactly as romance. It is a feat, like a fat man crossing the English Channel in a barrel. It is an earnest accomplishment against the tide. It is a piece of slightly gross heroics, after the manner of those knobby, varicose old men who come out from some place in baggy shorts every year and run through the streets of Boston in the Marathon race. And somehow that is the gaffe against love all week long in New York, for everybody, not just two kids writhing under their coiffures in the 50th Street subway station; too hurried, too crowded, too hard, and no time for dalliance. Which explains why the real thing in New York is, as it says in the song, a Sunday kind of love.

QUESTIONS ON SUBJECT AND PURPOSE

1. What is so unusual about the kiss that Wolfe witnesses? Why write about such a seemingly ordinary event?
2. How does the setting influence Wolfe's reaction to the kiss?
3. Characterize Wolfe's attitude or tone in the selection. For example, does he seem to be offended by such a public display of affection? Does he seem to be amused?

QUESTIONS ON STRATEGY AND AUDIENCE

1. What type of detail does Wolfe notice? In the scene? In the crowd? In the two teenagers?
2. Speculate on how Wolfe gathered all the details. Did he remember everything he saw? Did he stop to take notes?
3. What expectations does Wolfe seem to have about his audience? What evidence (setting, detail, subject, language) can you cite to support your argument?

QUESTIONS ON VOCABULARY AND STYLE

1. How is the selection both formal and informal at the same time? Why mix informal language with such unusual word choices (for example, "attar of libido" in paragraph 1)?
2. Wolfe has a fondness for the exclamation mark. How often does he use it in this passage? What is the effect of such a device?
3. Find some examples of parallelism in the selection. Why does Wolfe use parallelism?
4. Be able to define the following words: *attar* (paragraph 1), *libido* (1), *sclerotic* (1), *embroilment* (3), *ciliated* (3), *gaffe* (3), *coiffures* (3), *dalliance* (3).

WRITING SUGGESTIONS

1. Sit somewhere public and people-watch. You might try a cafeteria or a street or even a part of your campus. Watch for typical behavior that seems unusual in its context. Describe what you see in a paragraph. Remember to focus on a single example. Watch for other people's reactions to what you see.

2. Are you ever offended by what people do in public? Write an essay explaining why a certain activity or behavior is inappropriate in a public place. Be sure to use specific examples.

   Prewriting:

   a. Select a public place where you can observe people. Make a list of unusual activities and behavior that you observe.

   b. Ask friends and relatives for examples of public behavior to which they object.

   c. Check to see if your college prohibits any particular types of public behavior.

   Rewriting:

   a. Ask friends or classmates to read your essay. How do they react to your examples? Use their reactions to rethink your choice of examples.

   b. Remember that several important, developed examples are more effective than a series of silly or unrealistic examples. Did you adequately develop your examples? Are they realistic or true?

3. Can two young (and unmarried) people kiss in public anywhere in the world? Are such displays of public affection acceptable? Select several cultures or countries and research the problem. In an essay complete with examples and appropriate documentation, present your findings to an audience of American college students.

Computer Fallout

RUSSELL BAKER

Born in Virginia, in 1925, Russell Baker received a B.A. from Johns Hopkins University in 1947. He began his journalistic career with the Baltimore Sun. *In 1962 he began his "Observer" column for the* Times, *and he received the Pulitzer Prize in 1979 for distinguished commentary. Baker's most recent collections of essays are* Poor Russell's Almanac *(1972),* So This Is Depravity *(1980),* The Rescue of Miss Yaskell and Other Pipe Dreams *(1983), and* There's a Country in My Cellar *(1990), all of which demonstrate his ability to use humor to puncture the solemnities of politicians, social theorists, and abusers of the English language. His autobiography,* Growing Up *(1982), won Baker a second Pulitzer. He published a second autobiography,* The Good Life, *in 1989. In "Computer Fallout," published in* The New York Times Magazine, *Baker makes vivid the temptations of revising prose on a word processor.*

1   THE WONDERFUL THING about writing with a computer instead of a typewriter or a lead pencil is that it's so easy to rewrite that you can make each sentence almost perfect before moving on to the next sentence.

2   An impressive aspect of using a computer to write with

3   One of the plusses about a computer on which to write

4   Happily, the computer is a marked improvement over both the typewriter and the lead pencil for purposes of literary composition, due to the ease with which rewriting can be effectuated, thus enabling

5   What a marked improvement the computer is for the writer over the typewriter and lead pencil

6   The typewriter and lead pencil were good enough in their day, but if Shakespeare had been able to access a computer with a good writing program

7   If writing friends scoff when you sit down at the computer and say, "The lead pencil was good enough for Shakespeare

One of the drawbacks of having a computer on which to write is the ease and rapidity with which the writing can be done, thus leading to the inclusion of many superfluous terms like "lead pencil," when the single word "pencil" would be completely, entirely and utterly adequate.   *8*

The ease with which one can rewrite on a computer gives it an advantage over such writing instruments as the pencil and typewriter by enabling the writer to turn an awkward and graceless sentence into one that is practically perfect, although it   *9*

The writer's eternal quest for the practically perfect sentence may be ending at last, thanks to the computer's gift of editing ease and swiftness to those confronting awkward, formless, nasty, illiterate sentences such as   *10*

Man's quest is eternal, but what specifically is it that he quests, and why does he   *11*

Mankind's quest is   *12*

Man's and woman's quest   *13*

Mankind's and womankind's quest   *14*

Humanity's quest for the perfect writing device   *15*

Eternal has been humanity's quest   *16*

Eternal have been many of humanity's quests   *17*

From the earliest cave writing, eternal has been the quest for a device that will forever prevent writers from using the word "quest," particularly when modified by such adjectives as "eternal," "endless," "tireless" and   *18*

Many people are amazed at the ease   *19*

Many persons are amazed by the ease   *20*

Lots of people are astounded when they see the nearly perfect sentences I write since upgrading my writing instrumentation from pencil and typewriter to   *21*

Listen, folks, there's nothing to writing almost perfect sentences with ease and rapidity provided you've given up the old horse-and-buggy writing mentality that says Shakespeare couldn't have written those great plays if he had enjoyed the convenience of electronic compositional instrumentation.   *22*

Folks, have you ever realized that there's nothing to writing almost   *23*

24   Have you ever stopped to think, folks, that maybe Shakespeare could have written even better if

25   To be or not to be, that is the central focus of the inquiry.

26   In the intrapersonal relationships played out within the mind as to the relative merits of continuing to exist as opposed to not continuing to exist

27   Live or die, a choice as ancient as humanities' eternal quest, is a tough choice which has confounded mankind as well as womankind ever since the option of dreaming was first perceived as a potentially negating effect of the quiescence assumed to be obtainable through the latter course of action.

28   I'm sick and tired of Luddites saying pencils and typewriters are just as good as computers for writing nearly perfect sentences when they—the Luddites, that is—have never experienced the swiftness and ease of computer writing which makes it possible to compose almost perfect sentences in practically no time at

29   Folks, are you sick and tired of

30   Are you, dear reader

31   Good reader, are you

32   A lot of you nice folks out there are probably just as sick and tired as I am of hearing people say they are sick and tired of this and that and

33   Listen, people, I'm just as sick and tired as you are of having writers and TV commercial performers who oil me in cornpone politician prose addressed to "you nice folks out

34   A curious feature of computers, as opposed to pencils and typewriters, is that when you ought to be writing something more interesting than a nearly perfect sentence

35   Since it is easier to revise and edit with a computer than with a typewriter or pencil, this amazing machine makes it very hard to stop editing and revising long enough to write a readable sentence, much less an entire newspaper column.

QUESTIONS ON SUBJECT AND PURPOSE

1. What is the subject of Baker's essay? In what way is the essay itself an example of "computer fallout"?

2. Why does Baker cast his message in this particular form? Why not write a more conventional essay?

3. What exactly do the examples that form the body of the essay prove?

QUESTIONS ON STRATEGY AND AUDIENCE

1. What structure, if any, is there to Baker's essay? Is the structure effective?

2. Does Baker attempt to make transitions from one example to another? If so, how are transitions made?

3. Does this essay seem to follow the rules for good writing that you have learned? Explain why or why not.

4. Who is Baker's audience? How might he want you to respond to the essay? Is he warning against using a word processor?

QUESTIONS ON VOCABULARY AND STYLE

1. Try to characterize his tone in the essay. Is he serious? humorous? How exactly do you know?

2. What allusions or clichés appear in Baker's essay? Check the Glossary at the back of this book for definitions of both terms.

3. Be able to define each of the following words or terms: *effectuated* (paragraph 4), *superfluous* (8), *quiescence* (27), *Luddites* (28).

WRITING SUGGESTIONS

1. Write a paragraph discussing the purpose of revision. Using Baker's essay as an example, you can address the issues of how much revision is necessary, what the goals of revision are, or what can happen if you allow too much time for revising. For some additional information you might also read Peter Elbow's "Quick Revising" (Chapter 6). Obviously you can draw upon your own experience in revising as well.

2. Choose an item that is intended to make life easier, more efficient, or more interesting. The item should be either totally worthless or absolutely indispensable. In an essay support your

position about the value of this item by using examples. Do not try, however, to imitate Baker's essay.

Prewriting:

a. When you are watching television or reading magazines, look for advertisements of products intended to make your life easier (a vegetable slicer, a sweater vacuum, a paring knife that can cut nails). Make a list of such devices.

b. Spend some time thinking about an object that is absolutely indispensable to daily life. What things do you use every day?

c. Once you have chosen your subject, do the following: make a list of instances when the item either failed or worked brilliantly; decide why you bought the item in the first place; think about what your audience already knows about this object (if it is widely advertised or commonly owned, your audience will understand your essay more easily).

Rewriting:

a. Choosing a structure can be tricky, especially since you probably do not want to imitate Baker's. Remember to introduce the object about which you are writing early in the essay—this is not a mystery the reader is supposed to solve. You might begin by quoting some of the advertising phrases associated with a particularly popular item.

b. Notice that Baker does not describe a computer or a word processor. He focuses instead on the results of using one. Depending upon what you are writing about, you might also be able to concentrate on results only, without actually describing the item and how it works. Rethink your descriptive strategies in the essay.

c. Find some friends who are willing to read your essay. Ask them if the paper is clear. What do they think your purpose was? Does their understanding agree with your original intention? If not, change your essay.

3. Some simple, everyday inventions/devices have become so essential in our lives that it is difficult to imagine what life was like without them. Select such an object, and research its invention/discovery/origin and subsequent success. You might

consider writing either a traditional college research paper or a feature article for a popular magazine.

As a way of stimulating your thinking, you might consider the following possible subjects:

a. Nylon stockings or panty hose

b. Ball point pens

c. Athletic shoes

d. Portable radios

e. Digital watches

f. Hand-held calculators

Cut

BOB GREENE

Bob Greene was born in Columbus, Ohio, in 1947 and received a B.J. from Northwestern University in 1969. He was a reporter and later a columnist for the Chicago Sun-Times *from 1969 to 1978, then began a syndicated column for the* Chicago Tribune. *Greene has been a contributing editor for* Esquire *with his column "American Beat" and a contributing correspondent for "ABC News Nightline." His books include* We Didn't Have None of Them Fat Funky Angels on the Wall of Heartbreak Hotel, and Other Reports from America *(1971),* Running: A Nixon-McGovern Campaign Journal *(1973),* Billion Dollar Baby *(1974),* Johnny Deadline, Reporter: The Best of Bob Greene *(1976),* American Beat *(1983),* Good Morning, Merry Sunshine: A Father's Journal of His Child's First Year *(1984),* Cheeseburger: The Best of Bob Greene *(1985), and* Be True to Your School: A Diary of 1964 *(1987). His most recent book,* Homecoming: When the Soldiers Returned From Vietnam *(1989), is a collection of 200 letters written by veterans. In this essay from* Esquire, *Greene relates the stories of five successful men who shared the experience of being "cut from the team." Does being "cut," Greene wonders, make you a superachiever later in life?*

Exemplification

1   I REMEMBER VIVIDLY the last time I cried. I was twelve years old, in the seventh grade, and I had tried out for the junior high school basketball team. I walked into the gymnasium; there was a piece of paper tacked to the bulletin board.

2   It was a cut list. The seventh-grade coach had put it up on the board. The boys whose names were on the list were still on the team; they were welcome to keep coming to practices. The boys whose names were not on the list had been cut; their presence was no longer desired. My name was not on the list.

3   I had not known the cut was coming that day. I stood and stared at the list. The coach had not composed it with a great deal of subtlety; the names of the very best athletes were at the

58

top of the sheet of paper, and the other members of the squad were listed in what appeared to be a descending order of talent. I kept looking at the bottom of the list, hoping against hope that my name would miraculously appear there if I looked hard enough.

I held myself together as I walked out of the gym and out of the school, but when I got home I began to sob. I couldn't stop. For the first time in my life, I had been told officially that I wasn't good enough. Athletics meant everything to boys that age; if you were on the team, even a substitute, it put you in the desirable group. If you weren't on the team, you might as well not be alive.

I had tried desperately in practice, but the coach never seemed to notice. It didn't matter how hard I was willing to work; he didn't want me there. I knew that when I went to school the next morning I would have to face the boys who had not been cut—the boys whose names were on the list, who were still on the team, who had been judged worthy while I had been judged unworthy.

All these years later, I remember it as if I were still standing right there in the gym. And a curious thing has happened: in traveling around the country, I have found that an inordinately large proportion of successful men share that same memory— the memory of being cut from a sports team as a boy.

I don't know how the mind works in matters like this; I don't know what went on in my head following that day when I was cut. But I know that my ambition has been enormous ever since then; I know that for all of my life since that day, I have done more work than I had to be doing, taken more assignments than I had to be taking, put in more hours than I had to be spending. I don't know if all of that came from a determination never to allow myself to be cut again—never to allow someone to tell me that I'm not good enough again— but I know it's there. And apparently it's there in a lot of other men, too.

Bob Graham, thirty-six, is a partner with the Jenner & Block law firm in Chicago. "When I was sixteen, baseball was my whole life," he said. "I had gone to a relatively small high school, and I had been on the team. But then my family moved, and I was going to a much bigger high school. All during the winter months I told everyone that I was a ballplayer. When spring came, of course I went out for the team.

9   "The cut list went up. I did not make the team. Reading that cut list is one of the clearest things I have in my memory. I wanted not to believe it, but there it was.

10   "I went home and told my father about it. He suggested that maybe I should talk to the coach. So I did. I pleaded to be put back on the team. He said there was nothing he could do; he said he didn't have enough room.

11   "I know for a fact that it altered my perception of myself. My view of myself was knocked down; my self-esteem was lowered. I felt so embarrassed; my whole life up to that point had revolved around sports, and particularly around playing baseball. That was the group I wanted to be in—the guys on the baseball team. And I was told that I wasn't good enough to be one of them.

12   "I know now that it changed me. I found out, even though I couldn't articulate it at the time, that there would be times in my life when certain people would be in a position to say 'You're not good enough' to me. I did not want that to happen ever again.

13   "It seems obvious to me now that being cut was what started me in determining that my success would always be based on my own abilities, and not on someone else's perceptions. Since then I've always been something of an overachiever; when I came to the law firm I was very aggressive in trying to run my own cases right away, to be the lead lawyer in the cases with which I was involved. I made partner at thirty-one; I never wanted to be left behind.

14   "Looking back, maybe it shouldn't have been that important. It was only baseball. You pass that by. Here I am. That coach is probably still there, still a high school baseball coach, still cutting boys off the baseball team every year. I wonder how many hundreds of boys he's cut in his life?"

15   MAURICE MCGRATH is senior vice-president of Genstar Mortgage Corporation, a mortgage banking firm in Glendale,

California. "I'm forty-seven years old, and I was fourteen when it happened to me, and I still feel something when I think about it," he said.

"I was in the eighth grade. I went to St. Philip's School in Pasadena. I went out for the baseball team, and one day at practice the coach came over to me. He was an Occidental College student who had been hired as the eighth-grade coach. 16

"He said, 'You're no good.' Those were his words. I asked him why he was saying that. He said, 'You can't hit the ball. I don't want you here.' I didn't know what to do, so I went over and sat off to the side, watching the others practice. The coach said I should leave the practice field. He said that I wasn't on the team, and that I didn't belong there anymore. 17

"I was outwardly stoic about it. I didn't want anyone to see how I felt. I didn't want to show that it hurt. But oh, did it hurt. All my friends played baseball after school every day. My best friend was the pitcher on the team. After I got whittled down by the coach, I would hear the other boys talking in class about what they were going to do at practice after school. I knew that I'd just have to go home. 18

"I guess you make your mind up never to allow yourself to be hurt like that again. In some way I must have been saying to myself, 'I'll play the game better.' Not the sports game, but anything I tried. I must have been saying, 'If I have to, I'll sit on the bench, but I'll be part of the team.' 19

"I try to make my own kids believe that, too. I try to tell them that they should show that they're a little bit better than the rest. I tell them to think of themselves as better. Who cares what anyone else thinks? You know, I can almost hear that coach saying the words. 'You're no good.'" 20

Author MALCOLM MACPHERSON (*The Blood of His Servants*), forty, lives in New York. "It happened to me in the ninth grade, at the Yalesville School in Yalesville, Connecticut," he said. "Both of my parents had just been killed in a car crash, and as you can imagine, it was a very difficult time in my life. I went out for the baseball team, and I did pretty well in practice. 21

"But in the first game I clutched. I was playing second base; the batter hit a pop-up, and I moved back to catch it. I can see 22 it now. I felt dizzy as I looked up at the ball. It was like I was moving in slow motion, but the ball was going at regular speed. I couldn't get out of the way of my own feet. The ball dropped to the ground. I didn't catch it.

23   "The next day at practice, the coach read off the lineup. I wasn't on it. I was off the squad.

24   "I remember what I did: I walked. It was a cold spring afternoon, and the ground was wet, and I just walked. I was living with an aunt and uncle, and I didn't want to go home. I just wanted to walk forever.

25   "It drove my opinion of myself right into a tunnel. Right into a cave. And when I came out of the cave, something inside of me wanted to make sure in one manner or another that I would never again be told I wasn't good enough.

26   "I will confess that my ambition, to this day, is out of control. It's like a fire. I think the fire would have pretty much stayed in control if I hadn't been cut from that team. But that got it going. You don't slice ambition two ways; it's either there or it isn't. Those of us who went through something like that always know that we have to catch the ball. We'd rather die than have the ball fall at our feet.

27   "Once that fire is started in us, it never gets extinguished, until we die or have heart attacks or something. Sometimes I wonder about the home-run hitters; the guys who never even had to worry about being cut. They may have gotten the applause and the attention back then, but I wonder if they ever got the fire. I doubt it. I think maybe you have to get kicked in the teeth to get the fire started.

28   "You can tell the effect of something like that by examining the trail you've left in your life, and tracing it backward. It's almost like being a junkie with a need for success. You get attention and applause and you like it, but you never quite trust it. Because you know that back then you were good enough if only they would have given you a chance. You don't trust what you achieve, because you're afraid that someone will take it away from you. You know that it can happen; it already did.

29   "So you try to show people how good you are. Maybe you don't go out and become Dan Rather; maybe you just end up owning the Pontiac dealership in your town. But it's your deal-

ership, and you're the top man, and every day you're showing people that you're good enough.

DAN RATHER, fifty-two, is anchor of the CBS *Evening News.* 30
"When I was thirteen, I had rheumatic fever," he said. "I became extremely skinny and extremely weak, but I still went out for the seventh-grade baseball team at Alexander Hamilton Junior High School in Houston.

"The school was small enough that there was no cut as 31
such; you were supposed to figure out that you weren't good enough, and quit. Game after game I sat at the end of the bench, hoping that maybe this was the time I would get in. The coach never even looked at me; I might as well have been invisible.

"I told my mother about it. Her advice was not to quit. So 32
I went to practice very day, and I tried to do well so that the coach would be impressed. He never even knew I was there. At home in my room I would fantasize that there was a big game, and the three guys in front of me would all get hurt, and the coach would turn to me and put me in, and I would make the winning hit. But then there'd be another game, and the late innings would come, and if we were way ahead I'd keep hoping that this was the game when the coach would put me in. He never did.

"When you're that age, you're looking for someone to tell 33
you you're okay. Your sense of self-esteem is just being formed. And what that experience that baseball season did was make me think that perhaps I wasn't okay.

"In the last game of the season something terrible hap- 34
pened. It was the last of the ninth inning, there were two outs, and there were two strikes on the batter. And the coach turned to me and told me to go out to right field.

"It was a totally humiliating thing for him to do. For him 35
to put me in for one pitch, the last pitch of the season, in front of all the other boys on the team . . . I stood out there for that one pitch, and I just wanted to sink into the ground and disappear. Looking back on it, it was an extremely unkind thing for him to have done. That was nearly forty years ago, and I don't know why the memory should be so vivid now; I've never

known if the coach was purposely making fun of me—and if he was, why a grown man would do that to a thirteen-year-old boy.

36 "I'm not a psychologist. I don't know if a man can point to one event in his life and say that that's the thing that made him the way he is. But when you're that age, and you're searching for your own identity, and all you want is to be told that you're all right . . . I wish I understood it better, but I know the feeling is still there."

QUESTIONS ON SUBJECT AND PURPOSE

1. Greene's "cuts" all refer to not making an athletic team. What other kinds of "cuts" can you experience?

2. It is always risky to speculate on an author's purpose, but why would Greene write about this? Why reveal to everyone something that hurt so much?

3. How might Greene have gone about gathering examples of other men's similar experiences? Why would they be willing to contribute? Would everyone who has been cut be so candid?

4. What can be said in the coaches' defense? Should everyone who tries out be automatically guaranteed a place on the team?

QUESTIONS ON STRATEGY AND AUDIENCE

1. Greene structures his essay in an unusual way. How can the essay be divided? Why give a series of examples of other men who were "cut"?

2. How many examples are enough? What if Greene had used two examples? Eight examples? How would either extreme have influenced your reaction as a reader?

3. Greene does not provide a final concluding paragraph. Why?

4. Are you skeptical after you have finished the essay? Does everyone react to being cut in the same way? What would it take to convince you that these reactions are typical?

QUESTIONS ON VOCABULARY AND STYLE

1. How would you characterize the tone of Greene's essay? How is it achieved? Through language? Sentence structure? Paragraphing?

2. Why does Greene allow each man to tell his own story? Why not just summarize their experiences? Each story is enclosed in quotation marks. Do you think that these were the exact words of each man? Why?

3. What do *inordinately* (paragraph 6) and *stoic* (18) mean?

WRITING SUGGESTIONS

1. What is it like to "make the team"? Remember a time when you were chosen and others were not. How did it feel? What are the benefits of "making it"? In a paragraph describe a similar experience when you were a part of a team, an organization, a fraternity or sorority—or when you won a prize or were elected to an office.

2. Describe a similar experience you have had. It might have happened in an academic course during your school years, in a school or community activity, in athletics, in music or dance lessons. We can be "cut" from almost anything. Remember to make your narrative vivid through the use of detail. Try to show the reader what happened and how you felt.

Prewriting:

a. Make a list of some possible events about which to write.

b. Select one of those events and brainstorm. Jot down whatever you remember about the event and your reactions to it. Do not worry about writing complete sentences.

c. Use the details generated from your brainstorm in your essay. Do not try to include every detail, but select those that seem the most revealing. Always ask yourself, how important is this detail?

Rewriting:

a. Remember that in writing about yourself it is especially important to keep your readers interested. They need to feel how significant this experience was. Do not just *tell* them; *show* them. One way to do this is to dramatize the experience. Did you?

65

  b. Look carefully at your introduction. Do you begin in a vivid way? Does it make your reader want to keep reading? Test it by asking friends or relatives to read just the opening paragraphs.

  c. How effective is your conclusion? Do you just stop? Do you just repeat in slightly altered words what you said in your introduction? Try to find another possible ending.

3. Check the validity of Greene's argument. What can you find in your library about the psychological effects of such vivid rejections? A reference librarian can help you start your search for information. Use that research in an essay about the positive or negative effects of such an experience. Remember to document your sources. You might write your paper in one of the following forms (each of which has a slightly different audience):

  a. A conventional research paper for a college course.

  b. An article for a popular magazine (for example, *Esquire, Ms., Cosmopolitan*).

  c. A feature article for your school's newspaper.

Words for Nerds

WILLIAM SAFIRE

William Safire was born in New York City in 1929 and attended Syracuse University for two years before becoming a war correspondent for WNBC and the Armed Forces Radio Network. Safire wrote speeches for Richard Nixon and in 1968 was appointed special assistant to the president. In 1974 Safire began a political column for The New York Times *and later the column "On Language" for* The New York Times Magazine. *His investigation of Bert Lance (an assistant to President Carter) won him a Pulitzer Prize in 1978. His works include the political thriller* Full Disclosure *(1977), a collection of political writings (Safire's* Washington, *1980), collections from his language columns,* On Language *(1980),* What's the Good Word? *(1982),* Take My Word for It *(1986),* You Could Look It Up *(1989), and* Language Maven Strikes Again *(1990). In 1987 he published* Freedom, *a historical novel about Abraham Lincoln and the Civil War. For a* New York Times Magazine *column on campus slang, Safire uses a wide range of college informants, whom he refers to in the article as "The Lexicographic Irregulars." Not only is "campusese" always changing, but, as Safire's examples show, it varies widely from one campus to another.*

"Collegians now register for 'guts,'" writes Faith Heisler of the University of Pennsylvania," . . . to lessen the necessity to become 'throats.'" 1

This prime example of campusese, instantly understandable to any college student, was submitted in response to a query in this space for a current review of the slang that has replaced the hip expressions of yesteryear. 2

Remember "snap course," the subject you took for a breather? That is called a "gut course" today, presumably because you know the answers in your intestines, and has been growing in use since the early fifties. Variations include the middle western "cake course" (from "a piece of cake," or "easy") and the Californian "mick course" (not an ethnic slur, but a derivation of "Mickey Mouse," or "inconsequential"). 3

67

4   Examples of gut courses—where "gut gunners" get an "easy Ace" (A) as opposed to a "Hook" (C) or "Flag" (F)—are on the analogy of "Rocks for Jocks," a generation-old put-down of a geology course attended by athletes. More recent examples are astronomy's "Stars for Studs," art's "Nudes for Dudes," psychology's "Nuts and Sluts," European civilization's "Plato to NATO," anthropology's "Monkeys to Junkies," and comparative religion's "Gods for Clods." Students of linguistics engage in "Blabs in Labs." Courses on the art of film are referred to as "Monday Night at the Movies," music appreciation is "Clapping for Credit," and any science course aimed at liberal arts students includes a technocrat's derogation of the generalist as "Physics for Poets."

5   Students take these courses to avoid becoming "throats," which is the term for what used to be called "grinds," which in turn replaced "bookworms." "The term 'throat,'" explains Mitchel A. Baum of the University of Pennsylvania, "is short for 'cutthroat' and refers to a person who wants an A at any cost and who would dilute your standardized solution of hydrochloric acid if given half a chance. At Penn, these students are often called 'premeds,' regardless of their postcollege plans."

6   Other replacements of "grind" are "squid" (an ink squirter), "pencil geek," "spider," "cereb," and "grub." "'Grub' is often used as a verb as well," writes Philip Frayne of Columbia University, "as in 'He's in the library grubbing for a history exam.'" At Yale, the grind is a "weenie"—not "wienie," as spelled here not long ago—and at Harvard, the excessively studious student is derided as a "wonk," which Amy Berman, Harvard '79, fancifully suggests may be "know" spelled backward. (In British slang, "wonky" means "unsteady.") At some southern colleges, such people are "gomes," which Sean Finnell describes as "those who carry a calculator hooked onto their pants belt or, off campus, wear black socks with loafers and shorts (sorry, Dad). The derivation of this word undoubtedly comes from 'Gomer,' as in 'Gomer Pyle.'"

7   "Here at MIT," observes Robert van der Heide, "we refer to someone who studies too much as a 'tool.' At MIT, 'nerd' is spelled 'gnurd.' There is a distinction between gnurds and tools. Tools study all the time, perhaps to get into med school. Gnurds

study all the time because they like to. Gnurds are a subset of tools." (Not so at Colgate, reports Mathi Fuchs, where a tool is one who exploits others.)

"Nerd," no matter how spelled, is a big word with the youthful set.   *8*

Its origin is probably in a forties variation of "nuts"—as in "nerts to you"—and a "nert" became a "nerd," probably influenced by a rhyming scatological word. Like so many campusisms, the noun is turned into a verb with the addition of "out." "At Brown," writes Alison Kane, "the sons and daughters of the previous generation of 'bookworms' are called 'nerds' instead of 'grinds.' Rather than 'grind away' at their books, they prefer to 'nerd out.'"   *9*

What about "cramming?" That word is still used a lot ("alot," on campus, is one word), though a variation exists. "Staying awake the whole night through to 'cram' is called 'pulling an all-nighter,'" writes Susan Chumsky of Penn, noting: "An 'all-nighter' is never 'spent,' never 'had,' but only 'pulled.'"   *10*

New terms for "cramming" are "shedding" (from "woodshed"), "speeding," and "heavy booking" or "megabooking." At schools of architecture, "charretting" is used. "'Charretting' (to describe pulling an all-nighter)," write Carey Reilly and Peter Fein of Yale, "comes from the French word for cart. A cart was used to collect the architectural drawings of a student in any atelier of the Ecole des Beaux-Arts in Paris, mostly between 1860 and 1930. The word has come to mean the harried period in which a student's drawings are completed, or simply working all night to complete the next day's assignment." (Professor Susan Fiske of Carnegie-Mellon spells it "charette," which is the spelling *Webster's Third New International Dictionary* prefers, but ascribes it to a drawing tool.)   *11*

In the event that the all-night pullers do not succeed in passing the exam, their reaction is vividly described in an "out" verb used at Cornell, situated high above Cayuga's waters. "One threatens to 'gorge out,'" testifies Michele Cusack, "which does not refer to eating three banana splits (that's 'pigging out'), but to jumping off one of the many scenic bridges on campus."   *12*

Other schools prefer "veg out," soft *g*, or to turn into a vegetable after one "blows off," or fails.

13   A traditional, generation-spanning campus activity is vomiting. Accordingly, students have their own terms for the habit. In my college days, "upchuck" was the preferred euphemism, and since then the alliterative "losing your lunch" and the debonair "tossing your cookies" have been in use. Today the activity—usually from an introduction to overindulgence in alcohol by a "pin," or an innocent with a weak stomach—has upchucked the verb "to boot." The origin of "booting" may be to use your shoe as a receptacle, but that is speculative. Mathew Shapiro of Columbia submits the most descriptive: "Praying to the Great White Porcelain God (kneeling required)."

14   " 'Power' is a common prefix at Dartmouth," reports Rick Jones, "e.g., 'power book' or 'power boot.' " A "tool" or "grind" is sometimes called a "power tool" or an "auger"—a boring tool. The "Power Tower" at many schools is the administration building.

15   Whatever happened to "Big Man on Campus?" He's gone—sometimes remembered only in acronym form, as "bee-moc"—though Anne Griffin says he is called a "politico" at the University of Virginia, and J. Barrett Hickman recalls a Hamilton College usage of "Young God." Nobody remembers what a "co-ed" is, though the term is sometimes used now to refer to men who attend colleges that formerly catered to women. A "stud"—the horse-breeding term used recently to admire sexual prowess—is now a derogation of BMOC.

16   Remember the pleasures of cutting classes? " 'Cutting' is practically never used anymore," says Audrey Ziss at Skidmore. "The new terminology is 'bucking.' " This newly favored verb is not to be confused with the sixties favorite, "to bust"—to arrest. Today, with sit-ins and other demonstrations only dimly remembered, a "bust" is no longer a police raid and "busting" is not a dreaded activity. "One is busted on the basketball court when one's shot is blocked," explains Bob Torres of New Brunswick, illustrating "busted's" new meaning of being bested. "One is busted in conversation by snappy rejoinder. 'Busting GQ' means to dress in high fashion. . . . GQ refers to *Gentlemen's*

Quarterly, the men's fashion magazine. Hence one has out-dressed the exemplar when one 'busts GQ.'"

The term for "farewell," which was the inane "bye now" 17
a generation ago, is "later," from "see you later," but pro-nounced "lay-tah." Parents are "rents," reflecting a tendency to clip a syllable rather than any gratitude for payments of up-keep. Pizza has been shortened to "tza," pronounced "za." Nancy Pines of Mount Holyoke reports: "You guys want to go in on a za?" Reply: "Intense!" For years, the most common intensifying adjective was "terrific" or "cosmic;" it is somehow fitting that the leading intensifier has become "intense." Its only competition at the moment is "flaming," as in "flaming youth."

A word that kept cropping up in this rewarding response 18
by the Lexicographic Irregulars was "random." My happiest days at Syracuse U. were spent just strolling about, determined to be aimless, and that wandering wonderment now has a verb: to random. The word, normally an adjective meaning "hap-hazard," is also a college noun that Edward Fitzgerald of MIT interprets as "a person who does not belong on our dormitory floor," or, by extension, a welcome foreigner.

We'd better conclude this megabooking before some Young 19
God gorges out. Lay-tah.

QUESTIONS ON SUBJECT AND PURPOSE

1. What is slang? Check a dictionary for a definition. In what way are these examples of slang?
2. How does slang get invented? Why is it used so much?
3. What subjects or activities lend themselves best to slang?
4. Why would a reader—especially someone not currently at col-lege—be interested in reading an article such as this?

QUESTIONS ON STRATEGY AND AUDIENCE

1. How does Safire structure his essay? Is there a distinct tran-sition from section to section?
2. How effective is Safire's introduction? His conclusion? Why does he begin and end the way he does?
3. What assumptions does Safire seem to make about his audi-

ence? Can you point to specific remarks or passages that support your conclusion?

QUESTIONS ON VOCABULARY AND STYLE

1. How would you characterize the tone of Safire's essay? What is the result of mixing formal words—such as those listed in question 3, below—with campus slang?
2. Safire's essay was originally written for a newspaper. How does that seem to have influenced the essay's structure or style?
3. Be able to define the following words: *technocrat* (paragraph 4), *derogation* (4), *scatological* (9), *atelier* (11), *harried* (11), *euphemism* (13), *alliterative* (13), *debonair* (13), *acronym* (15).

WRITING SUGGESTIONS

1. Compile some examples of campus slang used at your school. Ask your friends and classmates for examples. Spend some time listening and talking to people. Once you have gathered a range of examples, select the best—maybe three or four words—and write a paragraph explaining them.
2. If you have gathered a particularly good range of examples, write an essay guide to your school's slang. You might write for one of the following audiences:
   a. Your fellow students. Such a guide might appear in your campus newspaper or magazine.
   b. Parents. The school administration has decided to send home a brochure to help parents understand their children's new vocabulary.
   c. Local residents. The editor of the town newspaper is interested in an article on the new campus slang. Remember that the majority of the newspaper's readers are neither students nor parents of students.

   Prewriting:
   a. Use the two strategies described in Writing Suggestion 1 to gather examples.
   b. Once you have eight or ten possible words or phrases, ask your friends to review the list and to contribute additional usages.

c. Your essay will be more effective if your examples are fresh. No one wants to read about words that have been used for years. Test your words by checking them in dictionaries of slang available in your library. If they are listed, they probably are too old to be valuable.

Rewriting:

a. Have you adequately defined each word and phrase? Have you given sample sentences showing how each is used?

b. If possible, ask several older people to read your essay to see if they are familiar with any of these expressions.

c. Many readers might feel that Safire's ending is too "cute." Do not just imitate what he has done. Try to find another way of ending your essay.

3. Select a particular period in time—the 1950s, the 1960s, or the 1970s, for example—and compile examples of slang then common. You might ask your older brothers or sisters, your parents, or your grandparents for contributions. Magazines and books published during those years are also helpful. Write an essay guide for those words.

The Name Is Mine

ANNA QUINDLEN

Born in 1953, Anna Quindlen attended Barnard College in New York City. She reported for the New York Post *and then moved to* The New York Times *to write a weekly column, "About New York." In order to raise her two children, she quit her full-time position as deputy metropolitan editor for the* Times. *Several freelance essays she wrote for the* Times' *"Her's" column brought her offers from rival newspapers. The* Times *responded by inviting her to create her weekly "Life in the 30's" which appears in some thirty additional newspapers. Her first book,* Living out Loud *(1988), is a compilation of sixty-five essays from that column, most of which are humorous and reflective accounts of everyday happenings in the life of a woman, mother, and wife. This essay first appeared in "Life in the 30's." Quindlen remembers why she did not take her husband's name when they married. "This is a story about a name," she writes. "The name is mine. I was given it at birth, and I have never changed it, although I married."*

1   I AM ON THE TELEPHONE to the emergency room of the local hospital. My elder son is getting stitches in his palm, and I have called to make myself feel better, because I am at home, waiting, and my husband is there, holding him. I am 34 years old, and I am crying like a child, making a slippery mess of my face. "Mrs. Krovatin?" says the nurse, and for the first time in my life I answer "Yes."

2   This is a story about a name. The name is mine. I was given it at birth, and I have never changed it, although I married. I could come up with lots of reasons why. It was a political decision, a simple statement that I was somebody and not an adjunct of anybody, especially a husband. As a friend of mine told her horrified mother, "He didn't adopt me, he married me."

3   It was a professional and a personal decision, too. I grew up with an ugly dog of a name, one I came to love because I thought it was weird and unlovable. Amid the Debbies and

74

Kathys of my childhood, I had a first name only my grand-mothers had and a last name that began with a strange letter. "Sorry, the letters I, O, Q, U, V, X, Y and Z are not available," the catalogues said about monogrammed key rings and cocktail napkins. Seeing my name in black on white at the top of a good story, suddenly it wasn't an ugly dog anymore.

But neither of these are honest reasons, because they as- 4 sume rational consideration, and it so happens that when it came to changing my name, there was no consideration, ra-tional or otherwise. It was mine. It belonged to me. I don't even share a checking account with my husband. Damned if I was going to be hidden beneath the umbrella of his identity.

It seemed like a simple decision. But nowadays I think the 5 only simple decisions are whether to have grilled cheese or tuna fish for lunch. Last week, my older child wanted an explanation of why he, his dad and his brother have one name, and I have another.

My answer was long, philosophical and rambling—that is 6 to say, unsatisfactory. What's in a name? I could have said disingenuously. But I was talking to a person who had just spent three torturous, exhilarating years learning names for things, and I wanted to communicate to him that mine meant some-thing quite special to me, had seemed as form-fitting as my skin, and as painful to remove. Personal identity and independence, however, were not what he was looking for; he just wanted to make sure I was one of them. And I am—and then again, I am not. When I made this decision, I was part of a couple. Now, there are two me's, the me who is the individual and the me who is part of a family of four, a family of four in which, in a small way, I am left out.

A wise friend who finds herself in the same fix says she 7 never wants to change her name, only to have a slightly dif-ferent identity as a family member, an identity for pediatricians' offices and parent-teacher conferences. She also says that the entire situation reminds her of the women's movement as a whole. We did these things as individuals, made these decisions about ourselves and what we wanted to be and do. And they were good decisions, the right decisions. But we based them on individual choice, not on group dynamics. We thought in terms of our sense of ourselves, not our relationships with others.

8   Some people found alternative solutions: hyphenated names, merged names, matriarchal names for the girls and patriarchal ones for the boys, one name at work and another at home. I did not like those choices; I thought they were middle grounds, and I didn't live much in the middle ground at the time. I was once slightly disdainful of women who went all the way and changed their names. But I now know too many smart, independent, terrific women who have the same last names as their husbands to be disdainful anymore. (Besides, if I made this decision as part of a feminist world view, it seems dishonest to turn around and trash other women for deciding as they did.)

9   I made my choice. I haven't changed my mind. I've just changed my life. Sometimes I feel like one of those worms I used to hear about in biology, the ones that, chopped in half, walked off in different directions. My name works fine for one half, not quite as well for the other. I would never give it up. Except for that one morning when I talked to the nurse at the hospital, I always answer the question "Mrs. Krovatin?" with "No, this is Mr. Krovatin's wife." It's just that I understand the down side now.

10   When I decided not to disappear beneath my husband's umbrella, it did not occur to me that I would be the only one left outside. It did not occur to me that I would ever care—not enough to change, just enough to think about the things we do on our own and what they mean when we aren't on our own anymore.

QUESTIONS ON SUBJECT AND PURPOSE

1. Why did Quindlen not change her last name when she married?

2. How does she feel about her decision now?

3. Since Quindlen does not plan to change her name, what purpose might she have in writing the essay?

QUESTIONS ON STRATEGY AND AUDIENCE

1. The essay could begin at the second paragraph. Why might Quindlen have chosen to begin the essay with the telephone call experience?
2. In paragraph 9, Quindlen returns to the incident at the hospital. How does this device help hold the essay together?
3. The essay appeared in a column headed "Life in the 30's." How might that affect the nature of the audience who might read the essay?

QUESTIONS ON VOCABULARY AND STYLE

1. At the beginning of paragraphs 2 and 9, Quindlen uses three very short simple sentences in a row. Why?
2. Twice in the essay (paragraphs 4 and 10), Quindlen refers to coming under her husband's "umbrella." What is the effect of such an image?
3. Be able to define the following words: *disingenuously* (paragraph 6) and *disdainful* (8).

WRITING SUGGESTIONS

1. In a paragraph explore the meaning that you find in your name. You can choose your first or last name, or even a nickname. How does that name define you?
2. In paragraph 6, Quindlen remarks, "there are two me's, the me who is the individual and the me who is part of a family of four. . . ." Everyone experiences such moments of awareness. Think about those times when you have been "two," and in an essay explore the dilemma posed by being an individual and, at the same time, a part of a larger whole.

Prewriting:

  a. Make a list of relationships that might have produced similar experiences (you and your family, you and your friends, you and a social group).
  b. Select one of those relationships and freewrite about it, trying to focus on a significant and specific decision you made.

   c. Remember that the experience will have to be narrated in a time sequence, either starting with the decision and then tracing out the consequences or starting with the consequences and then flashing back to the decision.

Rewriting:

   a. Try, if you have not already done so, to imitate Quindlen's strategy of "hooking" the reader into the essay.

   b. Experiment with a different time sequence (as described in c above) for your essay. Does the other sequence work any more effectively?

   c. Try to find someone to read your essay—a friend, roommate, classmate, or tutor in a writing center. Ask your reader for some constructive criticism and then listen to what you hear.

3. How widespread and recent is the phenomenon of women keeping their maiden names? Research the problem through periodical sources in your college's library and through interviews. Then, using that research, write an essay for one of the following audiences:

   a. An article intended for a male audience

   b. An article intended for an unmarried female audience who might be considering such a decision

   c. A traditional research paper for a college course

A Writer's Revision Process: Yumbo

ANDREW WARD

Andrew Ward, author, humorist, and essayist, was born in Chicago, Illinois, in 1946. He was educated at Oberlin College and the Rhode Island School of Design. Following his graduation, he worked as a photographer for the Ford Foundation in New Delhi, India, from 1968 to 1970. After two years as a free-lance writer and photographer, he took a position as an art teacher at a private school in Connecticut where he taught until 1974. His books include Fits and Starts: The Premature Memoirs of Andrew Ward *(1978), for which he was awarded an Atlantic Grant from* The Atlantic; Bits and Pieces *(1980), a book of essays and parodies;* The Blood Seed: A Novel of India *(1985); and* A Cry of Absence: The True Story of a Father's Search For His Kidnapped Children *(1988). His work has appeared in magazines such as* Redbook, Fantasy and Science Fiction, Horizon, American Heritage, *and* Inquiry.

On revising, Ward observes: "I make it a practice to retain just about every scrap of discarded material: partially, no doubt, out of some touching concern for my biographers, but ostensibly, at least, out of my continuing need to reassure myself that I haven't lost my touch. After I've gone over draft after draft of some perfectly simple little paragraph, and find myself still dissatisfied, I pluck out a file on an earlier essay and reassure myself with all the early attempts I had to make to sound fluent, poised, and casual."

The selection reproduced here from The Atlantic *is the first paragraph from the short essay "Yumbo" named after a ham and cheese sandwich once sold by Burger King. The essay reflects on how restaurants have "lately taken to treating us all as if we were children" by turning ordinary food into something "festive."*

REVISED DRAFT*

I WAS SITTING at an inn with Kelly Susan, my ten-year-old niece, when she was handed the children's menu. It was printed in gay pastels on construction paper and gave her a choice of a Ferdinand Burger, a Freddie the Fish Stick, or a Porky Pig Sandwich. Like most children's menus, it first anthropomorphized the ingredients and then killed them off. As Kelly read it her eyes grew large, and in them I could see gentle Ferdinand being led away to the stockyard, Freddie gasping at the end of a hook, Porky stuttering his entreaties as the ax descended. Kelly Susan, alone in her family, is a resolute vegetarian and has already faced up to the dread that whispers to us as we slice our steaks. She wound up ordering a cheese sandwich, but the children's menu had ruined her appetite, and she spent the meal picking at her food.

QUESTIONS FOR DISCUSSION

1. How effective does this paragraph seem as an introduction? Does it catch your interest? Why or why not?
2. How does Ward seem to feel about children's menus? About vegetarianism? Does anything in the paragraph reveal his attitudes and values?
3. How does Ward use parallel structure in his paragraph?
4. Be able to define the following words: *anthropomorphize, entreaties,* and *resolute.*

EARLIER DRAFT

I WAS SITTING with my ten-year-old niece this weekend when she was handed the children's menu. It gave her the choice of a Ferdinand Burger, a Freddie the Fish Stick, a Porky Pig Sandwich, and something called a College Boy, which was a grilled cheese sandwich. Like most children's menus it made the mistake of reminding Kelly Susan, a devout vegetarian by her own choosing, that Ferdinand had been led off to the meatyards,

---

* Bar indicates areas of major revision.

Freddie the Fish had been caught on a hook, Porky Pig had stuttered his entreaties as the ax descended. Kelly wound up ordering the College Boy, but the children's menu had ruined her appetite and she wound up picking at her food.

QUESTIONS ON THE REVISION

1. In the earlier draft Ward includes the name of the cheese sandwich (College Boy), but in the final draft he omits it. Why?

2. Writers frequently revise to make word choices more precise and vivid. Which changes seem to have been made for that reason?

3. In the earlier draft, Ward observes, "it made the mistake of reminding," but he deletes that remark in the final version. Why? What replaces that evaluative comment?

4. What is the difference between a "devout" vegetarian and a "resolute" one? Why change the word?

WRITING SUGGESTIONS

1. The tendency for restaurants to use special names for items on their menus is not limited to those intended for children. Visit one or more local restaurants and notice the menus. What special terms are used? In a paragraph report your findings. Focus your paragraph around either a particular restaurant or a particular pattern that you see occurring in several restaurants.

2. Later in his essay Ward remarks that restaurants give names to sandwiches (for example, Whopper, Big Mac, Triple-R Burger) to "convert an essentially bleak industry, mass-marketed fast foods, into something festive." The idea of assigning names to products is not unique to the fast-food industry. Choose another industry that uses special names, and in an essay analyze those names and the reasons why they might have been chosen. Some possibilities include:

   a. Automobiles

   b. Breakfast cereals

   c. Musical groups (for example, heavy metal, country, reggae bands)

d. Cosmetics

e. Candy bars

Prewriting:

a. Once you have chosen a possible subject, make a list of the names currently in use. Do not rely on just your memory; try to locate advertisements in magazines.

b. Look for characteristics that the names have in common. What associations do those names have? In what way are those associations appropriate? Make a list of the characteristics. Then try to construct a classification scheme.

c. Remember that your essay will not be just a collection of examples. You need to analyze the information that you have gathered. Make a brief outline of your paper, and be sure to include some analysis under each subsection.

Rewriting:

a. Your essay needs to have a clear, explicit thesis and a clear, explicit structure. Using a colored pen, underline your thesis statement and the topic sentence (or the subject) of each paragraph.

b. Have you included enough examples? Do not generalize based on just one or two examples. Remember that readers need specific, relevant information.

c. Carefully examine each sentence in your essay. Is each a complete sentence? Have you used a variety of sentence structures and lengths?

3. Companies spend large amounts of money trying to find the "right" name for a particular product. Expand your topic from suggestion 2 to include library research. Business, marketing, and advertising magazines are good sources for information. Be sure to document your sources.

TWO

Narration

When a friend asks, "What did you do last night?" you reply with a narrative: "After the chemistry midterm was over at 8:30, we went to Shakey's for pizza. Then we stopped at the bowling alley for a couple of games, and about 11 we split up and I went back to the dorm for some serious sleeping." A narrative is a story, and all stories, whether they are personal narratives, or novels, or histories, have the same essential ingredients: a series of events arranged in a chosen order and told by a narrator for some particular purpose. Your reply, for example, exhibits all four elements: a series of events (the four things you did last evening) arranged in an order (chronological) and told by a narrator ("I," a first-person narrator) for some particular purpose (to answer your friend's question).

Any type of writing can and does use narration; it is not something found only in personal experience essays or fiction. Narration can also be used to provide evidence in an argument. Bob Greene in "Cut" (Chapter 1) groups five personal narrative examples to support his assertion that being cut from an athletic team can make you a superachiever in life. Narration can also be found mixed with description in William Least Heat-Moon's "Nameless, Tennessee" (Chapter 3) or underlying a persuasive essay in Richard Rodriguez's "None of This Is Fair" (Chapter 9). In fact, there are examples of narration in the readings found in every chapter of this text.

What Do You Include in a Narrative?

No one, probably not even your mother, wants to hear everything you did today. Readers, like listeners, want you to exercise selection, for some things are more important or interesting than others. Historians have to select out of a mass of data what they will include and emphasize. They cannot tell the whole story, for if they did, the reader would get entangled in trivia, and the significant shape and meaning of the narrative would be lost. Even in personal experiences you condense and select. Generally you need to pare away, to cut out the unnecessary and the uninteresting. What you include depends, of course, on what happened and, more importantly, upon the purpose or meaning that you are trying to convey.

How Do You Structure a Narrative?

Time structures all narratives, although events do not always need to be arranged in chronological order. A narrative can begin at one point in time and then "flash back" to an earlier action or event. Langston Hughes's "Salvation" is told by a narrator looking back at an experience that occurred when he was thirteen, although the story itself is told in the order in which it happened. The most typical inversion is to begin at the end of the narrative and then to move backward in time to explain how that end was reached. Two cautions are obvious: first, do not switch time too frequently, especially in short papers; second, make sure that the switches are clearly marked for your reader.

Remember as well that you control where your narrative begins and ends. For example, the experience that E. B. White narrates in "Once More to the Lake" began when he and his son arrived at the lake and ended with their departure. The essay, however, begins with a flashback to his first summer at the lake thirty-seven years earlier. It ends as he watches his son pull on his cold, soggy bathing suit. The essay builds to that single moment of insight, and so that scene serves as the appropriate end of the narrative. It would have been anticlimactic for White to have added another paragraph detailing their final departure from the lake. Do not feel the need to "finish" the story if, in fact, you have achieved your purpose. Try to build to a climactic moment and end there.

Writers frequently change or modify an actual personal experience in order to tell the story more effectively, heighten the tension, or make their purpose clearer. In her essay "On Keeping a Notebook" (Chapter 6), Joan Didion remarks:

> I tell what some would call lies. "That's simply not true," the members of my family frequently tell me when they come up against my memory of a shared event. "The party was *not* for you, the spider was *not* a black widow, *it wasn't that way at all.*" Very likely they are right, for not only have I always had trouble distinguishing between what happened and what merely might have happened, but I remain unconvinced that the distinction, for my purposes, matters.

Whenever you recall an experience, even if it just happened last week, you do not necessarily remember it exactly as it happened. The value of a personal narrative does not rest in accuracy to the original experience. It does not matter, for example, whether the scene with sister Monroe in the Christian Methodist Episcopal Church occurred exactly as Maya Angelou describes it years later. What does matter is that it could have happened and that it is faithful to the purpose Angelou intends.

How Are Narratives Told?

Two things are especially important in relating your narrative. First, you need to choose a point of view from which to tell the story. Personal experience narratives, such as those by Hughes, Angelou, and White, are generally told in the first person: the narrator is an actor in the story. Historical narratives and narratives used as illustrations in a larger piece of writing are generally told in the third person. The historian, for example, is outside the narrative and provides an objective view of the actions described. Point of view can vary in one other way. The narrator can reveal only his or her own thoughts (and so use what is known as the limited point of view), or the narrator can reveal what anyone else in the narrative thinks or feels (and so use the omniscient, or all-knowing, point of view).

Second, you need to decide whether you are going to "show" or "tell" or mix the two. You "show" in a narrative by dramatizing a scene and creating dialogue. Hughes re-creates his experience for the reader by showing what happened and by recording some of the conversation that took place the night he was "saved from sin." The other option is "telling," that is, summarizing what happened. E. B. White tells the reader what he experienced and how he felt. He never dramatizes a particular scene and he never uses dialogue. Showing makes a narrative more vivid, for it allows the reader to experience the scene directly. Telling, on the other hand, allows you to include a greater number of events and details. Either way, selectivity is necessary. Hughes does not dramatize all of the events that happened; White does not summarize day-to-day activities. Each writer selects those moments which best give shape and significance to the experience.

What Do You Write About
If Nothing Ever Happened to You?

It is easy to assume that the only things worth writing about are once-in-a-lifetime experiences—a heroic or death-defying act, a personal tragedy, an Olympic medal–winning performance. But a good personal experience narrative does not need to be based on an extraordinary experience. In fact, ordinary experiences, because they are about things familiar to every reader, are the best sources for personal narratives. There is nothing extraordinary, for example, about the events related in Langston Hughes's "Salvation," even though Hughes's experience was a turning point in his life. Sister Monroe's unintentionally comic performance in Maya Angelou's narrative was actually only one of several similar performances that Angelou relates in the first part of her autobiography *I Know Why the Caged Bird Sings*. E. B. White's return to the lake where he summered as a child, and even his feelings as he watches his son, are ordinary experiences shared and understood by every parent revisiting the past.

The secret to writing a good personal experience narrative lies in two areas. First, you must tell your story artfully. Following the advice outlined in this introduction is a good way to ensure that your narrative will be constructed as effectively as possible. Just telling what happened is not enough, though, for you must do a second, equally important thing: you must reveal a purpose in your tale. Purposes can be many. You might offer insight into human behavior or motivation; you might mark a significant moment in your life; you might reveal an awareness of what it is to be young and to have dreams; you might reflect on the precariousness of life and inevitability of change and decay. What is important is that your narrative have a point, a reason for being, and that you make the reason clear to your reader.

Sample Student Essay

NARRATION

Hope Zucker decided to write about a powerful childhood memory—a pair of red shoes that became her "ruby slippers" and the key to the Land of Oz.

EARLIER DRAFT

My New Shoes

When you are four years old anything longer than five minutes feels like eternity, so when the clerk told me and my mom that it would take three to four weeks for my new shoes to arrive, I was almost in tears. Since seeing *The Wizard of Oz*, I had thought of little else other than owning a pair of ruby slippers. My dreams were full of spinning houses, little munchkins, flying monkeys, and talking lions. All I wanted was to be Dorothy, and the shoe store had made a promise to find me a pair of red mary-janes which would hopefully take me to Munchkin Land and Oz.

For the next three weeks I made all the preparations I could think of in order to become Dorothy. It did not matter how convincing Judy Garland was because I knew in my heart that I was the true Dorothy. I sang ''Somewhere Over the Rainbow'' day and night, and I played dress up with an old light blue checked dress of my mother's. I even went as far as to carry my dog in a basket, but that did not work out too well. I had my mom braid my long brown hair, and after I insisted, she tied a light blue ribbon around each braid. I skipped wherever I went, and I even went as far as coloring part of our driveway with chalk to create my very own yellow brick road.

The only thing missing to my new persona was my ruby slippers. After my mother explained to me that three weeks really was not that far off in the future, I decided to help the store in their search for my red mary-janes. For a month I called the store everyday when I got home from preschool. Mr. Rogers and Big Bird could wait because there was nothing in the whole wide world that was more important than my red patent leather shoes. By the end of the month, the nice little old ladies at the store knew me by name and thought that I was the cutest child. Lucky for them, they did not have to put up with me.

Finally, after what seemed like years, the lady on the other side of the phone said that yes, my shiny red shoes had arrived. Now I had only to plead with my mother to get her to make a special trip into the city. After a few days of delay and a great deal of futile temper tantrums, my mom took me to the store. I could hardly contain my excitement. During the ride, I practiced the one and only line that only the real Dorothy could say, ''There's no place like home.'' And of course, I clicked my beat up boondockers three times each time I recited my part. It was all practice for the real thing.

As we pulled into the parking lot, all the little old ladies inside the store waved to me as if they had been expecting me for days. I finally got to see my shoes, and they were as perfect as I knew they'd be. I was practically jumping out of my seat when she began to remove the stiff tissue paper surrounding my shoes, so rather than wait for her to fit my little feet into my slippers, I grabbed them from her and did it myself. They were the prettiest pair of shoes any girl could have!

For the next few weeks I was Dorothy and I'd stop everyone I'd see in order to prove it by tapping my heels together and saying, ''There's no place like home.'' But soon my feet grew too big for my ruby slippers, and as I graduated into the next larger size, I no longer wanted to be Dorothy. As I grew up, so did my dreams. Cinderella, now she was someone to be! Yet,

once again that phase, like the phases I am going
through now, passed fairly quickly.

Hope made enough copies of her essay so that the whole class could read and then discuss it. After reading her essay to the class, Hope asked her classmates for their reactions. Several students suggested that she tighten her narrative, eliminating those details that were not essential to the story. Most of their suggestions were centered in paragraphs 4 and 5. "Why mention Mr. Rogers and Big Bird?" someone asked. "I didn't want you to have to wait several days to pick them up, and I didn't want to be reminded of your temper," commented another. When Hope came to revise her draft, she used this advice. She also eliminated a number of cliches and made a significant change in the ending of the paper. Notice how much more effective the final version is as the result of these minor revisions.

REVISED DRAFT

The Ruby Slippers

To a four-year old, anything longer than five minutes feels like eternity, so when the clerk told me and my mom that it would take three to four weeks for my new shoes to arrive, I was almost in tears. Since seeing *The Wizard of Oz*, I had thought of little else other than owning a pair of ruby slippers. My dreams were full of spinning houses, little munchkins, flying monkeys, and talking lions. All I wanted was to be Dorothy, and the shoe store had made a promise to find me a pair of red mary-janes which would hopefully take me to Munchkin Land and Oz.

For the next three weeks I made all the preparations I could think of in order to become Dorothy. It did not matter how convincing Judy Garland was because I knew in my heart that I was the true Dorothy. I sang ''Somewhere Over the Rainbow'' day and night, and I played dress up with an old light blue checked dress of my mother's. I even went as far as to carry my dog in a basket. My mom braided my long brown hair, and after I insisted, she tied a light blue ribbon around each braid. I skipped everywhere I went and colored part of our driveway with chalk to create my very own yellow brick road.

The only thing missing was my ruby slippers. After my mother explained that three weeks really was not that far off, I decided to help the store in their search for my red mary-janes. For a month I called the store everyday when I got home from preschool. By the end of the month, the ladies at the store knew me by name.

Finally, the woman on the other end of the phone said that yes, my shiny red shoes had arrived. I could hardly contain my excitement. During the ride, I practiced the one line that only the real Dorothy could say, ''There's no place like home.'' And of course, I clicked my beat up loafers three times each time I recited that line. It was all practice for the real thing.

As we pulled into the parking lot, all the ladies inside the store waved to me as if they had been expecting me. I finally got to see my shoes, and they were as perfect as I had imagined. I was practically jumping out of my seat when she began to remove the stiff tissue paper surrounding my shoes, so rather than wait for her to fit my little feet into my slippers, I grabbed them from her and did it myself. They were the prettiest pair of shoes any girl could have!

For the next few weeks I was Dorothy and I'd stop everyone I'd see in order to prove it by tapping my heels together and saying, ''There's no place like home.'' But soon my feet grew too big for my ruby slippers, and as I graduated into the next larger size, I no longer wanted to be Dorothy. As I grew up, so did my dreams.

Some Things to Remember

1. Decide first why you are telling the reader *this* story. You must have a purpose clearly in mind.
2. Choose an illustration, event, or experience that can be cov-

ered adequately within the space limitations you face. Do not try to narrate the whole of World War II in an essay!

3. Decide on which point of view you will use. Do you want to be a part of the narrative or an objective observer? Which is more appropriate for your purpose?

4. Keeping your purpose in mind, select those details or events which seem the most important or the most revealing.

5. Arrange those details in an order—either a strict chronological one or one that employs a flashback. Remember to keep your verb tenses consistent and to signal any switches in time.

6. Remember the differences between showing and telling. Which method will be better for your narrative?

Salvation

LANGSTON HUGHES

Langston Hughes (1902–1967) was born in Joplin, Missouri, and spent most of his childhood in Lawrence, Kansas. He attended high school in Cleveland, Ohio, where he first began to read and to write poetry. In 1921, he enrolled in Columbia University, where he studied for one year and published many of his early poems. Hughes then abandoned his studies to work at various odd jobs in New York and to travel abroad. When he returned to the States, he continued to work on poems he had begun while at school and, in 1926, published his first volume, entitled The Weary Blues *(1926). This book won him critical acclaim and launched his successful career as a poet. Hughes was granted a scholarship to Lincoln University in Pennsylvania, where he graduated in 1929. By 1930, he had won several awards for his poetry and become an important member of the literary circle that helped form the Harlem Renaissance. Among his writings are* Not Without Laughter *(1930),* The Ways of White Folks *(1940),* Simple Speaks His Mind *(1950), and* Selected Poems *(1959). Hughes was also a gifted prose writer, as this famous selection from* The Big Sea: An Autobiography *(1940) reveals: ''I was saved from sin when I was going on thirteen.''*

I WAS SAVED FROM SIN when I was going on thirteen. But not really saved. It happened like this. There was a big revival at my Auntie Reed's church. Every night for weeks there had been much preaching, singing, praying, and shouting, and some very hardened sinners had been brought to Christ, and the membership of the church had grown by leaps and bounds. Then just before the revival ended, they held a special meeting for children, ''to bring the young lambs to the fold.'' My aunt spoke of it for days ahead. That night I was escorted to the front row and placed on the mourners' bench with all the other young sinners, who had not yet been brought to Jesus.

My aunt told me that when you were saved you saw a light, and something happened to you inside! And Jesus came into your life! And God was with you from then on! She said you could see and hear and feel Jesus in your soul. I believed her. I had heard a great many old people say the same thing and it seemed to me they ought to know. So I sat there calmly in the hot, crowded church, waiting for Jesus to come to me.

3   The preacher preached a wonderful rhythmical sermon, all moans and shouts and lonely cries and dire pictures of hell, and then he sang a song about the ninety and nine safe in the fold, but one little lamb was left out in the cold. Then he said: "Won't you come? Won't you come to Jesus? Young lambs, won't you come?" And he held out his arms to all us young sinners there on the mourners' bench. And the little girls cried. And some of them jumped up and went to Jesus right away. But most of us just sat there.

4   A great many old people came and knelt around us and prayed, old women with jet-black faces and braided hair, old men with work-gnarled hands. And the church sang a song about the lower lights are burning, some poor sinners to be saved. And the whole building rocked with prayer and song.

5   Still I kept waiting to *see* Jesus.

6   Finally all the young people had gone to the altar and were saved, but one boy and me. He was a rounder's son named Westley. Westley and I were surrounded by sisters and deacons praying. It was very hot in the church, and getting late now. Finally Westley said to me in a whisper: "God damn! I'm tired o' sitting here. Let's get up and be saved." So he got up and was saved.

7   Then I was left all alone on the mourner's bench. My aunt came and knelt at my knees and cried, while prayers and song swirled all around me in the little church. The whole congregation prayed for me alone, in a mighty wail of moans and voices. And I kept waiting serenely for Jesus, waiting, waiting— but he didn't come. I wanted to see him, but nothing happened to me. Nothing! I wanted something to happen to me, but nothing happened.

8   I hear the songs and the minister saying: "Why don't you come? My dear child, why don't you come to Jesus? Jesus is waiting for you. He wants you. Why don't you come? Sister Reed, what is this child's name?"

"Langston," my aunt sobbed.   9

"Langston, why don't you come? Why don't you come and   10
be saved? Oh, Lamb of God! Why don't you come?"

Now it was really getting late. I began to be ashamed of   11
myself, holding everything up so long. I began to wonder what
God thought about Westley, who certainly hadn't seen Jesus
either, but who was now sitting proudly on the platform, swinging his knickerbockered legs and grinning down at me, surrounded by deacons and old women on their knees praying.
God had not struck Westley dead for taking his name in vain
or for lying in the temple. So I decided that maybe to save
further trouble, I'd better lie, too, and say that Jesus had come,
and get up and be saved.

So I got up.   12

Suddenly the whole room broke into a sea of shouting, as   13
they saw me rise. Waves of rejoicing swept the place. Women
leaped in the air. My aunt threw her arms around me. The
minister took me by the hand and led me to the platform.

When things quieted down, in a hushed silence, punctuated   14
by a few ecstatic "Amens," all the new young lambs were
blessed in the name of God. Then joyous singing filled the room.

That night, for the last time in my life but one—for I was   15
a big boy twelve years old—I cried. I cried, in bed alone, and
couldn't stop. I buried my head under the quilts, but my aunt
heard me. She woke up and told my uncle I was crying because
the Holy Ghost had come into my life, and because I had seen
Jesus. But I was really crying because I couldn't bear to tell her
that I had lied, that I had deceived everybody in the church,
that I hadn't seen Jesus, and that now I didn't believe there
was a Jesus any more, since he didn't come to help me.

QUESTIONS ON SUBJECT AND PURPOSE

1. Who narrates the story? From what point in time is it told?

2. What does the narrator expect to happen when he is to be
   saved? What does happen?

3. Why does the narrator cry at the end of the story?

4. What was Hughes's attitude toward his experience when it
   first happened? At the time he originally wrote this selection?
   How does the opening sentence reflect that change in attitude?

QUESTIONS ON STRATEGY AND AUDIENCE

1. Why not tell the story in the present tense? How would that change the story?

2. How much dialogue is used in the narration? Why not use more?

3. Why does Hughes blend telling with showing in the story?

4. How much time is represented by the events in the story? Where does Hughes compress the time in his narrative? Why does he do so?

QUESTIONS ON VOCABULARY AND STYLE

1. What is the effect of the short paragraphs (5, 9, and 12)? How does Hughes use paragraphing to help shape his story?

2. How much description does Hughes include in his narrative? What types of details does he single out?

3. What is the effect of the exclamation marks used in paragraph 2?

4. Try to identify or explain the following phrases: *the ninety and nine safe in the fold* (paragraph 3), *the lower lights are burning* (4), *a rounder's son* (6), *knickerbockered legs* (11).

WRITING SUGGESTIONS

1. We have all been disappointed by something or someone in our life. Single out a particular event from your life. Spend some time trying to remember what happened and exactly how you felt. In a paragraph or an essay, narrate that experience. Remember that you need to make your reader understand how you felt and what it all meant to you. Try using some dialogue.

2. Have you ever experienced anything that changed your life? It does not need to be a dramatic change—just a conviction that you will never do *that* again or that you will *always* do that again. In a paragraph or an essay, narrate your experience.

Prewriting:

a. Divide your prewriting sessions for this paper into a series of activities done on different days. On day one, concentrate just on making a list of possible vivid experiences—a near miss, a careless moment, a time you were caught, a stupid choice.

b. On day two, spend a half an hour freewriting about two of the events from your list. Try to do one writing in the morning and one in the afternoon. Do not worry about writing complete, correct sentences. Do not stop during the writing.

c. On day three, spend an hour thinking about one of the two events. Jot down as much detail as you can remember.

d. On day four, write a draft of the essay, using the details gathered from the activities above.

Rewriting:

a. A successful narrative has a shape and a purpose. You do not need to include everything that happened, just those events relevant to the experience and its effect on you. Look again at the narratives included in this chapter. Notice what they include and exclude. Does your narrative show the same economy?

b. Did you use any dialogue? Sparing use will probably make your narrative more vivid—that is, it will show rather than tell.

c. Is the order of events clear to the reader? Is the story told in a strict chronological order? Did you use flashbacks? Think about other possible arrangements for your narrative.

3. Two recent U.S. presidents have described themselves as "born-again" Christians. Exactly what does that phrase mean? Research the origins of the term and the growth of such belief in America today. Write an essay relating your findings. Remember to cite references where necessary.

Sister Monroe

MAYA ANGELOU

Maya Angelou was born Marguerita Johnson in St. Louis, Missouri, in 1928. She was raised in rural Stamps, Arkansas. She served as a coordinator for the Southern Christian Leadership Conference at the request of Martin Luther King, Jr. Her most significant writings have been her series of five autobiographical works: I Know Why the Caged Bird Sings *(1970),* Gather Together in My Name *(1974),* Singin' and Swingin' and Gettin' Merry like Christmas *(1976),* The Heart of a Woman *(1981), and* All God's Children Need Travelin' Shoes *(1987), a record of her visit to Ghana from 1962 to 1964. Her latest books have been two collections of poetry,* Now Sheeba Sings the Song *(1987) and* I Shall Not Be Moved *(1990). In this passage from the first of her memoirs, Angelou recalls how Sister Monroe ''got the spirit'' one Sunday morning at the Christian Methodist Episcopal Church.*

1   IN THE CHRISTIAN Methodist Episcopal Church the children's section was on the right, cater-cornered from the pew that held those ominous women called the Mothers of the Church. In the young people's section the benches were placed close together, and when a child's legs no longer comfortably fitted in the narrow space, it was an indication to the elders that that person could now move into the intermediate area (center church). Bailey and I were allowed to sit with the other children only when there were informal meetings, church socials or the like. But on the Sundays when Reverend Thomas preached, it was ordained that we occupy the first row, called the mourners' bench. I thought we were placed in front because Momma was proud of us, but Bailey assured me that she just wanted to keep her grandchildren under her thumb and eye.

2   Reverend Thomas took his text from Deuteronomy. And I was stretched between loathing his voice and wanting to listen to the sermon. Deuteronomy was my favorite book in the Bible. The laws were so absolute, so clearly set down, that I knew if

98

a person truly wanted to avoid hell and brimstone, and being roasted forever in the devil's fire, all she had to do was memorize Deuteronomy and follow its teaching, word for word. I also liked the way the word rolled off the tongue.

Bailey and I sat alone on the front bench, the wooden slats pressing hard on our behinds and the backs of our thighs. I would have wriggled just a bit, but each time I looked over at Momma, she seemed to threaten, "Move and I'll tear you up," so, obedient to the unvoiced command, I sat still. The church ladies were warming up behind me with a few hallelujahs and praise the Lords and Amens, and the preacher hadn't really moved into the meat of the sermon. 3

It was going to be a hot service. 4

On my way into church, I saw Sister Monroe, her open-faced gold crown glinting when she opened her mouth to return a neighborly greeting. She lived in the country and couldn't get to church every Sunday, so she made up for her absences by shouting so hard when she did make it that she shook the whole church. As soon as she took her seat, all the ushers would move to her side of the church because it took three women and sometimes a man or two to hold her. 5

Once she hadn't been to church for a few months (she had taken off to have a child), she got the spirit and started shouting, throwing her arms around and jerking her body, so that the ushers went over to hold her down, but she tore herself away from them and ran up to the pulpit. She stood in front of the altar, shaking like a freshly caught trout. She screamed at Reverend Taylor. "Preach it. I say, preach it." Naturally he kept on preaching as if she wasn't standing there telling him what to do. Then she screamed an extremely fierce "I said, preach it" and stepped up on the altar. The Reverend kept on throwing out phrases like home-run balls and Sister Monroe made a quick break and grasped for him. For just a second, everything and everyone in the church except Reverend Taylor and Sister Monroe hung loose like stockings on a washline. Then she caught the minister by the sleeve of his jacket and his coattail, then she rocked him from side to side. 6

I have to say this for our minister, he never stopped giving us the lesson. The usher board made its way to the pulpit, going 7 up both aisles with a little more haste than is customarily seen in church. Truth to tell, they fairly ran to the minister's aid. Then two of the deacons, in their shiny Sunday suits, joined the ladies in white on the pulpit, and each time they pried Sister Monroe loose from the preacher he took another deep breath and kept on preaching, and Sister Monroe grabbed him in another place, and more firmly. Reverend Taylor was helping his rescuers as much as possible by jumping around when he got a chance. His voice at one point got so low it sounded like a roll of thunder, then Sister Monroe's "Preach it" cut through the roar, and we all wondered (I did, in any case) if it would ever end. Would they go on forever, or get tired out at last like a game of blindman's bluff that lasted too long, with nobody caring who was "it"?

8   I'll never know what might have happened, because magically the pandemonium spread. The spirit infused Deacon Jackson and Sister Willson, the chairman of the usher board, at the same time. Deacon Jackson, a tall, thin, quiet man, who was also a part-time Sunday school teacher, gave a scream like a falling tree, leaned back on thin air and punched Reverend Taylor on the arm. It must have hurt as much as it caught the Reverend unawares. There was a moment's break in the rolling sounds and Reverend Taylor jerked around surprised, and hauled off and punched Deacon Jackson. In the same second Sister Willson caught his tie, looped it over her fist a few times, and pressed down on him. There wasn't time to laugh or cry before all three of them were down on the floor behind the altar. Their legs spiked out like kindling wood.

9   Sister Monroe, who had been the cause of all the excitement, walked off the dais, cool and spent, and raised her flinty voice in the hymn, "I came to Jesus, as I was, worried, wounded, and sad, I found in Him a resting place and He has made me glad."

10   The minister took advantage of already being on the floor and asked in a choky little voice if the church would kneel with him to offer a prayer of thanksgiving. He said we had been visited with a mighty spirit, and let the whole church say Amen.

11   On the next Sunday, he took his text from the eighteenth chapter of the Gospel according to St. Luke, and talked quietly

but seriously about the Pharisees, who prayed in the streets so that the public would be impressed with their religious devotion. I doubt that anyone got the message—certainly not those to whom it was directed. The deacon board, however, did appropriate funds for him to buy a new suit. The other was a total loss.

QUESTIONS ON SUBJECT AND PURPOSE

1. Who is the narrator? How old does she seem to be? How do you know?

2. Why does Sister Monroe behave as she does?

3. How does the section on the narrator and Bailey act as a preface to the story of Sister Monroe? Is it relevant, for example, that the narrator's favorite book of the Bible is Deuteronomy?

QUESTIONS ON STRATEGY AND AUDIENCE

1. Part of the art of narration is knowing what events to select. Look carefully at Angelou's story of Sister Monroe (paragraphs 5 to 9). What events does she choose to include in her narrative?

2. How is Sister Monroe described? Make a list of all of the physical particulars we are given about her. How, other than direct description, is Sister Monroe revealed to the reader?

3. What shift occurs between paragraph 5 and 6? Did you notice it the first time you read the selection?

QUESTIONS ON VOCABULARY AND STYLE

1. Other than a few words uttered by Sister Monroe, Angelou uses no other dialogue in the selection. How, then, is the story told? What advantage does this method have?

2. Writing humor is never easy. Having a funny situation is essential, but, in addition, the story must be told in the right way. (Remember how people can ruin a good joke?) How does Angelou's language and style contribute to the humor in the selection?

3. How effective are the following images:
    a. "She stood in front of the altar, shaking like a freshly caught trout" (paragraph 6).

b. "The Reverend kept on throwing out phrases like home-run balls" (6).

c. "Everyone in the church . . . hung loose like stockings on a washline" (6).

d. "Their legs spiked out like kindling wood" (8).

WRITING SUGGESTIONS

1. Everyone has experienced a funny, embarrassing moment—maybe it happened to you or maybe you just witnessed it. In a paragraph narrate the incident.

2. Select a "first" from your experience—your first day in junior high school, your first date, your first time driving a car, your first day at college. Recreate that first. Do not just include a chronology of everything that happened. Focus your narrative around a significant feature of that first experience, whether funny or serious.

Prewriting:

   a. Several days before your essay is due, set aside an hour to comb your memories for some significant "firsts." Make a list of possibilities, jotting down whatever details you remember. Let the list rest for a day before looking at it again.

   b. Scan your list and select the most promising item. For another hour jot down randomly whatever you remember. Focus on re-creating the event in your memory. One detail often triggers others. Do not try to write yet; just gather details.

   c. Remember that your narrative needs to hinge on a significant feature—it can be an insight (such as in Hughes's "Salvation" or White's "Once More to the Lake") or a serious or comic pattern (as in "Sister Monroe"). Write down an explicit statement of what it is you want to reveal in your narrative. Use that statement to decide what details to include and what to exclude.

Rewriting:

   a. After a draft is completed, go back and look at the purpose statement you wrote in prewriting. Carefully test each detail you included to see if it relates to that intended purpose. Omit any irrelevant or inappropriate details.

b. Look at your conclusion. How did you end? Did you lead up to a climactic moment, or did you end with a flat conclusion ("And so you can see why this experience was important to me")? Compare how the writers in this chapter end their narratives.

3. Religious experiences are not always as physical as Sister Monroe's. Select a prominent historical or contemporary figure who has had an experience—a conversion, a miracle, a vision. Research the story, and in a narrative retell the story. Remember to document your sources.

On Being Chased

ANNIE DILLARD

Born in Pittsburgh in 1945, Annie Dillard received an M.A. in English from Hollins College in Virginia. A poet, essayist, and novelist, she served as a contributing editor of Harper's *for a number of years, and her work has appeared in* American Scholar, Harper's, *and* The Atlantic. *Her books include the Pulitzer Prize-winning* Pilgrim at Tinker Creek *(1974),* Tickets for a Prayer Wheel *(1974),* Holy the Firm *(1977),* Teaching a Stone to Talk *(1982),* Living by Fiction *(1982),* Encounters with Chinese Writers *(1984),* An American Childhood *(1987), and* The Writing Life *(1989). She has also co-edited* The Best American Essays *(1988).* An American Childhood, *the book in which this essay originally appeared as a chapter, is a memoir of her childhood, chronicling her intellectual and moral development in vivid language and images. In ''On Being Chased,'' Dillard describes how at the age of seven she discovered an adult who knew ''what I thought only children who trained at football knew: that you have to fling yourself at what you're doing, you have to point yourself, forget yourself, aim, dive.''*

1 SOME BOYS TAUGHT ME to play football. This was fine sport. You thought up a new strategy for every play and whispered it to the others. You went out for a pass, fooling everyone. Best, you got to throw yourself mightily at someone's running legs. Either you brought him down or you hit the ground flat out on your chin, with your arms empty before you. It was all or nothing. If you hesitated in fear, you would miss and get hurt: you would take a hard fall while the kid got away, or you would get kicked in the face while the kid got away. But if you flung yourself wholeheartedly at the back of his knees—if you gathered and joined body and soul and pointed them diving fearlessly—then you likely wouldn't get hurt, and you'd stop the ball. Your fate, and your team's score, depended on your concentration and courage. Nothing girls did could compare with it.

Boys welcomed me at baseball, too, for I had, through en- 2
thusiastic practice, what was weirdly known as a boy's arm. In
winter, in the snow, there was neither baseball nor football, so
the boys and I threw snowballs at passing cars. I got in trouble
throwing snowballs, and have seldom been happier since.

On one weekday morning after Christmas, six inches of new 3
snow had just fallen. We were standing up to our boot tops in
snow on a front yard on trafficked Reynolds Street, waiting for
cars. The cars traveled Reynolds Street slowly and evenly; they
were targets all but wrapped in red ribbons, cream puffs. We
couldn't miss.

I was seven; the boys were eight, nine, and ten. The oldest 4
two Fahey boys were there—Mikey and Peter—polite blond
boys who lived near me on Lloyd Street, and who already had
four brothers and sisters. My parents approved Mikey and Peter
Fahey. Chickie McBride was there, a tough kid, and Billy Paul
and Mackie Kean too, from across Reynolds, where the boys
grew up dark and furious, grew up skinny, knowing, and
skilled. We had all drifted from our houses that morning looking
for action, and had found it here on Reynolds Street.

It was cloudy but cold. The cars' tires laid behind them on 5
the snowy street a complex trail of beige chunks like crenellated
castle walls. I had stepped on some earlier; they squeaked. We
could have wished for more traffic. When a car came, we all
popped it one. In the intervals between cars we reverted to the
natural solitude of children.

I started making an iceball—a perfect iceball, from perfectly 6
white snow, perfectly spherical, and squeezed perfectly trans-
lucent so no snow remained all the way through. (The Fahey
boys and I considered it unfair actually to throw an iceball at
somebody, but it had been known to happen.)

I had just embarked on the iceball project when we heard 7
tire chains come clanking from afar. A black Buick was moving
toward us down the street. We all spread out, banged together
some regular snowballs, took aim, and, when the Buick drew
nigh, fired.

A soft snowball hit the driver's windshield right before the 8
driver's face. It made a smashed star with a hump in the middle.

105

9   Often, of course, we hit our target, but this time, the only time in all of life, the car pulled over and stopped. Its wide black door opened; a man got out of it, running. He didn't even close the car door.

10   He ran after us, and we ran away from him, up the snowy Reynolds sidewalk. At the corner, I looked back; incredibly, he was still after us. He was in city clothes: a suit and tie, street shoes. Any normal adult would have quit, having sprung us into flight and made his point. This man was gaining on us. He was a thin man, all action. All of a sudden, we were running for our lives.

11   Wordless, we split up. We were on our turf; we could lose ourselves in the neighborhood backyards, everyone for himself. I paused and considered. Everyone had vanished except Mikey Fahey, who was just rounding the corner of a yellow brick house. Poor Mikey, I trailed him. The driver of the Buick sensibly picked the two of us to follow. The man apparently had all day.

12   He chased Mikey and me around the yellow house and up a backyard path we knew by heart: under a low tree, up a bank, through a hedge, down some snowy steps, and across the grocery store's delivery driveway. We smashed through a gap in another hedge, entered a scruffy backyard and ran around its back porch and tight between houses to Edgerton Avenue; we ran across Edgerton to an alley and up our own sliding woodpile to the Halls' front yard; he kept coming. We ran up Lloyd Street and wound through mazy backyards toward the steep hilltop at Willard and Lang.

13   He chased us silently, block after block. He chased us silently over picket fences, through thorny hedges, between houses, around garbage cans, and across streets. Every time I glanced back, choking for breath, I expected he would have quit. He must have been as breathless as we were. His jacket strained over his body. It was an immense discovery, pounding into my hot head with every sliding, joyous step, that this ordinary adult evidently knew what I thought only children who trained at football knew: that you have to fling yourself at what you're doing, you have to point yourself, forget yourself, aim, dive.

14   Mikey and I had nowhere to go, in our own neighborhood

or out of it, but away from this man who was chasing us. He impelled us forward; we compelled him to follow our route. The air was cold; every breath tore my throat. We kept running, block after block; we kept improvising, backyard after backyard, running a frantic course and choosing it simultaneously, failing always to find small places or hard places to slow him down, and discovering always, exhilarated, dismayed, that only bare speed could save us—for he would never give up, this man—and we were losing speed.

He chased us through the backyard labyrinths of ten blocks *15* before he caught us by our jackets. He caught us and we all stopped.

We three stood staggering, half blinded, coughing, in an *16* obscure hilltop backyard: a man in his twenties, a boy, a girl. He had released our jackets, our pursuer, our captor, our hero: he knew we weren't going anywhere. We all played by the rules. Mikey and I unzipped our jackets. I pulled off my sopping mittens. Our tracks multiplied in the backyard's new snow. We had been breaking new snow all morning. We didn't look at each other. I was cherishing my excitement. The man's lower pants legs were wet; his cuffs were full of snow, and there was a prow of snow beneath them on his shoes and socks. Some trees bordered the little flat backyard, some messy winter trees. There was no one around: a clearing in a grove, and we the only players.

It was a long time before he could speak. I had some dif- *17* ficulty at first recalling why we were there. My lips felt swollen; I couldn't see out of the sides of my eyes; I kept coughing.

"You stupid kids," he began perfunctorily. *18*

We listened perfunctorily indeed, if we listened at all, for *19* the chewing out was redundant, a mere formality, and beside the point. The point was that he had chased us passionately without giving up, and so he had caught us. Now he came down to earth. I wanted the glory to last forever.

But how could the glory have lasted forever? We could have *20* run through every backyard in North America until we got to Panama. But when he trapped us at the lip of the Panama Canal, what precisely could he have done to prolong the drama of the chase and cap its glory? I brooded about this for the next few

107

years. He could only have fried Mikey Fahey and me in boiling oil, say, or dismembered us piecemeal, or staked us to anthills. None of which I really wanted, and none of which any adult was likely to do, even in the spirit of fun. He could only chew us out there in the Panamanian jungle, after months or years of exalting pursuit. He could only begin, "You stupid kids," and continue in his ordinary Pittsburgh accent with his normal righteous anger and the usual common sense.

21   If in that snowy backyard the driver of the black Buick had cut off our heads, Mikey's and mine, I would have died happy, for nothing has required so much of me since as being chased all over Pittsburgh in the middle of winter—running terrified, exhausted—by this sainted, skinny, furious red-headed man who wished to have a word with us. I don't know how he found his way back to his car.

QUESTIONS ON SUBJECT AND PURPOSE

1. In what sense is the chase for Dillard a "glory" she wanted to "last forever" (paragraph 19)?
2. What is unexpected about the driver's behavior?
3. How does Dillard feel about her pursuer?

QUESTIONS ON STRATEGY AND AUDIENCE

1. How do the first two paragraphs of the essay serve as an introduction to the episode with the snowballs and the chase?
2. When and how does Dillard describe the man?
3. What expectations could Dillard have of her readers?

QUESTIONS ON VOCABULARY AND STYLE

1. What is particularly appropriate about the one-sentence description of the man's legs (paragraph 16): "The man's lower pants legs were wet; his cuffs were full of snow, and there was a prow of snow beneath them on his shoes and socks"?
2. Be prepared to discuss the effect created by each of the following sentences:
   a. "The cars' tires laid behind them on the snowy street a

complex trail of beige chunks like crenellated castle walls"
(paragraph 5).

   b. "He could only begin, 'You stupid kids,' and continue in
his ordinary Pittsburgh accent with his normal righteous
anger and the usual common sense" (paragraph 20).

3. Be able to define the following words: *crenellated* (paragraph
5), *reverted* (5), *nigh* (7), *prow* (16), *perfunctorily* (18).

WRITING SUGGESTIONS

1. Chases are always exciting—whether we are a participant or
an observer (think how many films feature chase sequences).
In a paragraph, narrate a chase that you remember from your
childhood.

2. Select a remembered experience from your past, preferably an
experience other than a chase. In an essay, recreate that experience for your readers. Remember that the experience must
have a central focus or a reason why you are retelling it.

Prewriting:

   a. Over a period of a day or two, keep a list of possible experiences about which you might write.

   b. For each of the most promising possibilities, finish the following sentence: "The significance of this experience
was. . . ."

   c. Select two of those experiences and freewrite for 15 minutes
about each.

Rewriting:

   a. Remember that a narrative must have a beginning, middle,
and end. Check your narrative to make sure that you come
to the climactic moment in the story and then immediately
conclude. Compare your ending to those used in the readings in this chapter.

   b. Try changing the time sequence of your narrative. If you
told the story in chronological order, try using a flashback
to begin the story. If you began with a flashback, try a strict
chronological order. Which seems to work better?

   c. Remember to keep descriptive details to an effective minimum. Too much description slows down the story. Go

through your narrative and underline all of the instances in which you described something. Are there too many?

3. To what extent do all autobiographical memoirs tell a similar story? In your college's library, find four books similar to Dillard's *An American Childhood*—that is, books that record childhood years. Read all four, and then in an essay using these four as examples discuss the similarities that all of them share. To what extent are childhood memories universal rather than unique?

The Death of the Moth

VIRGINIA WOOLF

Born in London and educated at home, Virginia Woolf (1882–1941) is generally regarded as one of the finest writers of the twentieth century. A novelist, essayist, and critic, she was a member of the Bloomsbury group—a circle of artists and writers, including John Maynard Keynes, Lytton Strachey, Vanessa and Clive Bell, and E. M. Forster, active in London from about 1906 to the early 1930s. She and her husband Leonard Woolf founded the Hogarth Press, which published books by her and other members of the Bloomsbury group. Her novels include The Voyage Out *(1915),* Jacob's Room *(1922),* Mrs. Dalloway *(1925),* To the Lighthouse *(1927),* Orlando *(1928), and* The Waves *(1931). Woolf's essays and reviews have been collected in works such as* The Common Reader *(1925, 1932) and a four-volume* Collected Essays *(1967). In "The Death of the Moth," originally collected posthumously in* The Death of the Moth and Other Essays *(1942), Woolf watches a moth, "a tiny bead of pure life," struggle with death.*

MOTHS THAT FLY BY DAY are not properly to be called moths; they do not excite that pleasant sense of dark autumn nights and ivy-blossom which the commonest yellow underwing asleep in the shadow of the curtain never fails to rouse in us. They are hybrid creatures, neither gay like butterflies nor sombre like their own species. Nevertheless the present specimen, with his narrow hay-coloured wings, fringed with a tassel of the same colour, seemed to be content with life. It was a pleasant morning, mid-September, mild, benignant, yet with a keener breath than that of the summer months. The plough was already scoring the field opposite the window, and where the share had been, the earth was pressed flat and gleamed with moisture. Such vigour came rolling in from the fields and the down beyond that it was difficult to keep the eyes strictly turned upon the book. The rooks too were keeping one of their annual festivities; soaring round the tree-tops until it looked as if a vast net with thousands of black knots in it has been cast up into the air; which, after a few moments sank slowly down upon the trees until every twig seemed to have a knot at the end of it. Then, suddenly, the net would be thrown into the air again in a wider circle this time, with the utmost clamour and vociferation, as though to be thrown into the air and settle slowly down upon the tree-tops were a tremendously exciting experience.

2   The same energy which inspired the rooks, the ploughmen, the horses, and even, it seemed, the lean bare-backed downs, sent the moth fluttering from side to side of his square of the window-pane. One could not help watching him. One was, indeed, conscious of a queer feeling of pity for him. The possibilities of pleasure seemed that morning so enormous and so various that to have only a moth's part in life, and a day moth's at that, appeared a hard fate, and his zest in enjoying his meagre opportunities to the full, pathetic. He flew vigorously to one corner of his compartment, and, after waiting there a second, flew across to the other. What remained for him but to fly to a third corner and then to a fourth? That was all he could do, in spite of the size of the downs, the width of the sky, the far-off smoke of houses, and the romantic voice, now and then, of a steamer out at sea. What he could do he did. Watching him, it seemed as if a fibre, very thin but pure, of the enormous energy of the world had been thrust into his frail and diminutive body. As often as he crossed the pane, I could fancy that a thread of vital light became visible. He was little or nothing but life.

3   Yet, because he was so small, and so simple a form of the energy that was rolling in at the open window and driving its way through so many narrow and intricate corridors in my own brain and in those of other human beings, there was something marvelous as well as pathetic about him. It was as if someone had taken a tiny bead of pure life and decking it as lightly as possible with down and feathers, had set it dancing and zigzagging to show us the true nature of life. Thus displayed one could not get over the strangeness of it. One is apt to forget all about life, seeing it humped and bossed and garnished and cumbered so that it has to move with the greatest circumspection and dignity. Again, the thought of all that life might have been

112

had he been born in any other shape caused one to view his simple activities with a kind of pity.

After a time, tired by his dancing apparently, he settled on 4 the window ledge in the sun, and the queer spectacle being at an end, I forgot about him. Then, looking up, my eye was caught by him. He was trying to resume his dancing, but seemed either so stiff or so awkward that he could only flutter to the bottom of the window-pane; and when he tried to fly across it he failed. Being intent on other matters I watched these futile attempts for a time without thinking, unconsciously waiting for him to resume his flight, as one waits for a machine, that has stopped momentarily, to start again without considering the reason for its failure. After perhaps a seventh attempt he slipped from the wooden ledge and fell, fluttering his wings, on to his back on the window-sill. The helplessness of his attitude roused me. It flashed upon me that he was in difficulties; he could no longer raise himself; his legs struggled vainly. But, as I stretched out a pencil, meaning to help him to right himself, it came over me that the failure and awkwardness were the approach of death. I laid the pencil down again.

The legs agitated themselves once more. I looked as if for 5 the enemy against which he struggled. I looked out of doors. What had happened there? Presumably it was midday, and work in the fields had stopped. Stillness and quiet had replaced the previous animation. The birds had taken themselves off to feed in the brooks. The horses stood still. Yet the power was there all the same, massed outside indifferent, impersonal, not attending to anything in particular. Somehow it was opposed to the little hay-coloured moth. It was useless to try to do anything. One could only watch the extraordinary efforts made by those tiny legs against an oncoming doom which could, had it chosen, have submerged an entire city, not merely a city, but masses of human beings; nothing, I knew, had any chance against death. Nevertheless after a pause of exhaustion the legs fluttered again. It was superb this last protest, and so frantic that he succeeded at last in righting himself. One's sympathies, of course, were all on the side of life. Also, when there was nobody to care or to know, this gigantic effort on the part of an insignificant little moth, against a power of such magnitude, to retain what no one else valued or desired to keep, moved one strangely. Again, somehow, one saw life, a pure bead. I lifted the pencil again, useless though I knew it to be. But even as I did so, the unmistakable tokens of death showed themselves. The body relaxed, and instantly grew stiff. The struggle was over. The insignificant little creature now knew death. As I looked at the dead moth, this minute wayside triumph of so great a force over so mean an antagonist filled me with wonder. Just as life had been strange a few minutes before, so death was now as strange. The moth having righted himself now lay most decently and uncomplainingly composed. O yes, he seemed to say, death is stronger than I am.

QUESTIONS ON SUBJECT AND PURPOSE

1. What does Woolf see in the moth fluttering at the window?
2. How much time elapses in the narrative? Why is time important?
3. Why should the death of the moth be interesting to a reader?

QUESTIONS ON STRATEGY AND AUDIENCE

1. What does Woolf see outside of the window? How is that scene connected with the moth?
2. What is "superb" about the moth's final struggle to right itself before dying?
3. How, as a reader, do you react to the title "The Death of the Moth"? Does the title seem effective?

QUESTIONS ON VOCABULARY AND STYLE

1. In what sense does the plow "score" the field?
2. Woolf switches pronouns (from "I" to "one") at several points in the essay. Why?
3. Be prepared to define the following words: *benignant* (paragraph 1), *down* (1), *clamour* (1), *vociferation* (1), *cumbered* (2), *antagonist* (5).

WRITING SUGGESTIONS

1. Choose another instance in which something in the natural world demonstrates a fundamental truth about all living things. In a paragraph, explore that similarity.

2. The seemingly insignificant can always contain or reflect a universal truth or principle. Choose an event and explore in an essay how it reveals a lesson to us all.

Prewriting:

a. Make a list of possible subjects. Be sure to include both happenings in nature and predictable, common events in human behavior.

b. Next to each possible subject, list the truth or principle that is revealed. Try then to freewrite for a few minutes about each possible subject.

c. Remember that you are narrating the event. It must have a beginning, middle, and end. Be sure to structure the event so that it has the shape necessary for a story.

Rewriting:

a. Make sure that you do not reveal the truth or principle too early or too often in the narrative. While you are not trying to write a mystery, you also should not overstress the "lesson" that you see.

b. Look at each detail in the descriptions you have written. Underline each and ask yourself how each relates to the story you are telling.

c. Remember to catch your reader's attention in the first paragraph. Look closely at your introduction. Ask a friend to read it. Does your friend want to keep reading?

3. Read each of the six selections in the chapter. Then using these six as examples of effective narrative writing, write an essay aimed at freshman English students describing how to write a narrative.

Once More to the Lake

E. B. WHITE

Elwyn Brooks White (1899–1985) was born in Mount Vernon, New York, and received a B.A. from Cornell in 1921. His freshman English teacher was William Strunk, whose Elements of Style *White revised in 1959 and made into a textbook classic. In 1925 White began writing for* The New Yorker *and was one of the mainstays of that magazine, his precise, ironic, nostalgic prose style closely associated with its own. From 1937 to 1943, he also wrote the column ''One Man's Meat'' for* Harper's. *His books include the children's classic* Charlotte's Web *(1952),* The Second Tree From the Corner *(1954),* The Essays of E. B. White *(1977), and* The Poems and Sketches of E. B. White *(1981). White was awarded the Presidential Medal of Freedom in 1963 and a special Pulitzer Prize for his work as a whole in 1978. In ''Once More to the Lake'' White revisits the lake in Maine where he summered as a child. Taking his son with him, White discovers that their identities merge: ''I began to sustain the illusion that he was I, and therefore, by simple transposition, that I was my father.''*

1   ONE SUMMER along about 1904, my father rented a camp on a lake in Maine and took us all there for the month of August. We all got ringworm from some kittens and had to rub Pond's Extract on our arms and legs night and morning, and my father rolled over in a canoe with all his clothes on; but outside of that the vacation was a success and from then on none of us ever thought there was any place in the world like that lake in Maine. We returned summer after summer—always on August 1st for one month. I have since become a salt-water man, but sometimes in summer there are days when the restlessness of the tides and the fearful cold of the sea water and the incessant wind that blows across the afternoon and into the evening make me wish for the placidity of a lake in the woods. A few weeks ago this feeling got so strong I bought myself a couple of bass hooks and a spinner and returned to the lake where we used to go, for a week's fishing and to revisit old haunts.

I took along my son, who had never had any fresh water   *2*
up his nose and who had seen lily pads only from train windows. On the journey over to the lake I began to wonder what
it would be like. I wondered how time would have marred this
unique, this holy spot—the coves and streams, the hills that
the sun set behind, the camps and the paths behind the camps.
I was sure that the tarred road would have found it out and I
wondered in what other ways it would be desolated. It is strange
how much you can remember about places like that once you
allow your mind to return into the grooves that lead back. You
remember one thing, and that suddenly reminds you of another
thing. I guess I remembered clearest of all the early mornings,
when the lake was cool and motionless, remembered how the
bedroom smelled of the lumber it was made of and of the wet
woods whose scent entered through the screen. The partitions
in the camp were thin and did not extend clear to the top of
the rooms, and as I was always the first up I would dress softly
so as not to wake the others, and sneak out into the sweet
outdoors and start out in the canoe, keeping close along the
shore in the long shadows of the pines. I remembered being
very careful never to rub my paddle against the gunwale for
fear of disturbing the stillness of the cathedral.

The lake had never been what you would call a wild lake.   *3*
There were cottages sprinkled around the shores, and it was in
farming country although the shores of the lake were quite
heavily wooded. Some of the cottages were owned by nearby
farmers, and you would live at the shore and eat your meals
at the farmhouse. That's what our family did. But although it
wasn't wild, it was a fairly large and undisturbed lake and there
were places in it which, to a child at least, seemed infinitely
remote and primeval.

I was right about the tar: it led to within half a mile of the   *4*
shore. But when I got back there, with my boy, and we settled
into a camp near a farmhouse and into the kind of summertime
I had known, I could tell that it was going to be pretty much
the same as it had been before—I knew it, lying in bed the first
morning, smelling the bedroom, and hearing the boy sneak
quietly out and go off along the shore in a boat. I began to
sustain the illusion that he was I, and therefore, by simple trans-

position, that I was my father. This sensation persisted, kept cropping up all the time we were there. It was not an entirely new feeling, but in this setting it grew much stronger. I seemed to be living a dual existence. I would be in the middle of some simple act, I would be picking up a bait box or laying down a table fork, or I would be saying something, and suddenly it would be not I but my father who was saying the words or making the gesture. It gave me a creepy sensation.

5   We went fishing the first morning. I felt the same damp moss covering the worms in the bait can, and saw the dragonfly alight on the tip of my rod as it hovered a few inches from the surface of the water. It was the arrival of this fly that convinced me beyond any doubt that everything was as it always had been, that the years were a mirage and there had been no years. The small waves were the same, chucking the rowboat under the chin as we fished at anchor, and the boat was the same boat, the same color green and the ribs broken in the same places, and under the floor-boards the same fresh-water leavings and debris—the dead helgramite, the wisps of moss, the rusty discarded fishhook, the dried blood from yesterday's catch. We stared silently at the tips of our rods, at the dragonflies that came and went. I lowered the tip of mine into the water, tentatively, pensively dislodging the fly, which darted two feet away, poised, darted two feet back, and came to rest again a little farther up the rod. There had been no years between the ducking of this dragonfly and the other one—the one that was part of memory. I looked at the boy, who was silently watching his fly, and it was my hands that held his rod, my eyes watching. I felt dizzy and didn't know which rod I was at the end of.

6   We caught two bass, hauling them in briskly as though they were mackerel, pulling them over the side of the boat in a businesslike manner without any landing net, and stunning them with a blow on the back of the head. When we got back for a swim before lunch, the lake was exactly where we had left it, the same number of inches from the dock, and there was only the merest suggestion of a breeze. This seemed an utterly enchanted sea, this lake you could leave to its own devices for a few hours and come back to, and find that it had not stirred, this constant and trustworthy body of water. In the shallows,

the dark, water-soaked sticks and twigs, smooth and old, were undulating in clusters on the bottom against the clean ribbed sand, and the track of the mussel was plain. A school of minnows swam by, each minnow with its small individual shadow, doubling the attendance, so clear and sharp in the sunlight. Some of the other campers were in swimming, along the shore, one of them with a cake of soap, and the water felt thin and clear and unsubstantial. Over the years there had been this person with the cake of soap, this cultist, and here he was. There had been no years.

Up to the farmhouse to dinner through the teeming, dusty field, the road under our sneakers was only a two-track road. The middle track was missing, the one with the marks of the hooves and splotches of dried, flaky manure. There had always been three tracks to choose from in choosing which track to walk in; now the choice was narrowed down to two. For a moment I missed terribly the middle alternative. But the way led past the tennis court, and something about the way it lay there in the sun reassured me; the tape had loosened along the backline, the alleys were green with plantains and other weeds, and the net (installed in June and removed in September) sagged in the dry noon, and the whole place steamed with midday heat and hunger and emptiness. There was a choice of pie for dessert, and one was blueberry and one was apple, and the waitresses were the same country girls, there having been no passage of time, only the illusion of it as in a dropped curtain—the waitresses were still fifteen; their hair had been washed, that was the only difference—they had been to the movies and seen the pretty girls with the clean hair.

Summertime, oh summertime, pattern of life indelible, the fadeproof lake, the woods unshatterable, the pasture with the sweetfern and the juniper forever and ever, summer without end; this was the background, and the life along the shore was the design, the cottages with their innocent and tranquil design, their tiny docks with the flagpole and the American flag floating against the white clouds in the blue sky, the little paths over the roots of the trees leading from camp to camp and the paths leading back to the outhouses and the can of lime for sprinkling, and at the souvenir counters at the store the miniature birch-bark canoes and the post cards that showed things looking a little better than they looked. This was the American family at play, escaping the city heat, wondering whether the newcomers in the camp at the head of the cove were "common" or "nice," wondering whether it was true that the people who drove up for Sunday dinner at the farmhouse were turned away because there wasn't enough chicken.

9   It seemed to me, as I kept remembering all this, that those times and those summers had been infinitely precious and worth saving. There had been jollity and peace and goodness. The arriving (at the beginning of August) had been so big a business in itself, at the railway station the farm wagon drawn up, the first smell of the pine-laden air, the first glimpse of the smiling farmer, and the great importance of the trunks and your father's enormous authority in such matters, and the feel of the wagon under you for the long ten-mile haul, and at the top of the last long hill catching the first view of the lake after eleven months of not seeing this cherished body of water. The shouts and cries of the other campers when they saw you, and the trunks to be unpacked, to give up their rich burden. (Arriving was less exciting nowadays, when you sneaked up in your car and parked it under a tree near the camp and took out the bags and in five minutes it was all over, no fuss, no loud wonderful fuss about trunks.)

10   Peace and goodness and jollity. The only thing that was wrong now, really, was the sound of the place, an unfamiliar nervous sound of the outboard motors. This was the note that jarred, the one thing that would sometimes break the illusion and set the years moving. In those other summertimes all motors were inboard; and when they were at a little distance, the noise they made was a sedative, an ingredient of summer sleep. They were one-cylinder and two-cylinder engines, and some were make-and-break and some were jump-spark, but they all made a sleepy sound across the lake. The one-lungers throbbed and fluttered, and the twin-cylinder ones purred and purred, and that was a quiet sound too. But now the campers all had outboards. In the daytime, in the hot mornings, these motors made a petulant, irritable sound; at night, in the still evening when the afterglow lit the water, they whined about one's ears

120

like mosquitoes. My boy loved our rented outboard, and his great desire was to achieve singlehanded mastery over it, and authority, and he soon learned the trick of choking it a little (but not too much), and the adjustment of the needle valve. Watching him I would remember the things you could do with the old one-cylinder engine with the heavy flywheel, how you could have it eating out of your hand if you got really close to it spiritually. Motor boats in those days didn't have clutches, and you would make a landing by shutting off the motor at the proper time and coasting in with a dead rudder. But there was a way of reversing them, if you learned the trick, by cutting the switch and putting it on again exactly on the final dying revolution of the flywheel, so that it would kick back against compression and begin reversing. Approaching a dock in a strong following breeze, it was difficult to slow up sufficiently by the ordinary coasting method, and if a boy felt he had complete mastery over his motor, he was tempted to keep it running beyond its time and then reverse it a few feet from the dock. It took a cool nerve, because if you threw the switch a twentieth of a second too soon you would catch the flywheel when it still has speed enough to go up past center, and the boat would leap ahead, charging bull-fashion at the dock.

We had a good week at the camp. The bass were biting   *11* well and the sun shone endlessly, day after day. We would be tired at night and lie down in the accumulated heat of the little bedrooms after the long hot day and the breeze would stir almost imperceptibly outside and the smell of the swamp drift in through the rusty screens. Sleep would come easily and in the morning the red squirrel would be on the roof, tapping out his gay routine. I kept remembering everything, lying in bed in the mornings—the small steamboat that had a long rounded stern like the lip of a Ubangi, and how quietly she ran on the moonlight sails, when the older boys played their mandolins and the girls sang and we ate doughnuts dipped in sugar, and how sweet the music was on the water in the shining night, and what it had felt like to think about girls then. After breakfast we would go up to the store and the things were in the same place—the minnows in a bottle, the plugs and spinners disarranged and pawed over by the youngsters from the boys' camp, the fig newtons and the Beeman's gum. Outside, the road was tarred and cars stood in front of the store. Inside, all was just as it had always been, except that there was more Coca Cola and not so much Moxie and root beer and birch beer and sarsaparilla. We would walk out with a bottle of pop apiece and sometimes the pop would backfire up our noses and hurt. We explored the streams, quietly, where the turtles slid off the sunny logs and dug their way into the soft bottom; and we lay on the town wharf and fed worms to the tame bass. Everywhere we went I had trouble making out which was I, the one walking at my side, the one walking in my pants.

12 One afternoon while we were there at that lake a thunderstorm came up. It was like the revival of an old melodrama that I had seen long ago with childish awe. The second-act climax of the drama of the electrical disturbance over a lake in America had not changed in any important respect. This was the big scene, still the big scene. The whole thing was so familiar, the first feeling of oppression and heat and a general air around camp of not wanting to go very far away. In midafternoon (it was all the same) a curious darkening of the sky, and a lull in everything that had made life tick; and then the way the boats suddenly swung the other way at their moorings with the coming of a breeze out of the new quarter, and the premonitory rumble. Then the kettle drum, then the snare, then the bass drum and cymbals, then crackling light against the dark, and the gods grinning and licking their chops in the hills. Afterward the calm, the rain steadily rustling in the calm lake, the return of light and hope and spirits, and the campers running out in joy and relief to go swimming in the rain, their bright cries perpetuating the deathless joke about how they were getting simply drenched, and the children screaming with delight at the new sensation of bathing in the rain, and the joke about getting drenched linking the generations in a strong indestructible chain. And the comedian who waded in carrying an umbrella.

13 When the others went swimming my son said he was going in too. He pulled his dripping trunks from the line where they had hung all through the shower, and wrung them out. Languidly, and with no thought of going in, I watched him, his

hard little body, skinny and bare, saw him wince slightly as he pulled up around his vitals the small, soggy, icy garment. As he buckled the swollen belt suddenly my groin felt the chill of death.

QUESTIONS ON SUBJECT AND PURPOSE

1. Why does White go "once more" to the lake?
2. In what ways does White's son remind him of himself as a child? Make a list of the similarities he notices.
3. What is the meaning of the final sentence? Why does he feel "the chill of death"?
4. White's essay has achieved the status of a classic. Unquestionably White is an excellent writer, but surely the popularity of the essay depends upon something more. What else might account for that popularity?

QUESTIONS ON STRATEGY AND AUDIENCE

1. How does White structure his narrative? What events does he choose to highlight?
2. No narrative can record everything, and this is certainly not an hour-by-hour account of what happened. What does White ignore? Why, for example, does he end his narrative before the end of the actual experience (that is, leaving the lake)?
3. Why is his son never described?
4. What assumptions does White make about his audience?

QUESTIONS ON VOCABULARY AND STYLE

1. At several points White has trouble distinguishing between who is the son and who is the father. Select one of those scenes and examine how White describes the moment. How does the prose capture that confusion?
2. Can you find examples of figurative language—similes and metaphors, for example—in White's essay? Make a list.
3. Be able to define the following words: *placidity* (paragraph 1), *gunwale* (2), *primeval* (3), *teeming* (7), *premonitory* (12), *languidly* (13).

123

WRITING SUGGESTIONS

1. In the second paragraph, White observes: "It is strange how much you can remember about places like that once you allow your mind to return into the grooves that lead back. You remember one thing, and that suddenly reminds you of another thing." Try what he suggests. Pick a particular event you remember from your childhood. Make a list of what you remember. Then in a paragraph, narrate your experience. Do not try to make it seem significant or earthshaking. Just try to make it vivid and interesting.

2. Look for a moment or an experience in your memories that brought an insight. Suddenly you saw or you understood or you knew. Narrate the experience but build to the moment of your understanding.

Prewriting:

   a. Make a list of your most powerful memories. Just list the events first. Later go back and make notes on each one.

   b. Select a promising event. Set aside an hour to think about what happened. Try to remember what happened just before and just after. Who else was there? What were you wearing?

   c. Complete the following sentence: "The insight that I am trying to reveal is ———." Use that statement to check over your prewriting notes.

   d. Study White's essay or Hughes's as possible structural models.

Rewriting:

   a. Once your draft is finished, set it aside for at least a day. When you look at it again, check every detail against the purpose statement you wrote as a prewriting activity.

   b. Check to make sure you have used vivid verbs and concrete nouns. Do not overuse adjectives or adverbs.

   c. Just as the ending of a narrative should come to a climatic end, so its introduction ought to plunge the reader into the experience. Check to make sure you begin and end quickly and definitely.

3. What is your earliest memory? What factors control that aspect of our memories? Is it possible to remember events that took

place before you could talk? What kinds of early memories are most easily recalled? In a research paper provide some answers to these questions. Since memory plays such a significant role in everyone's life, you can assume that any audience will be interested in opinions that scientists now hold of this subject. You might prepare your paper in one of the following formats:

a. A traditional research paper for a college course
b. A feature article for a popular magazine.

Be sure to document your sources.

A Writer's Revision Process:
Up, Up, and Away

SUSAN ALLEN TOTH

Born in Ames, Iowa, in 1940, Susan Allen Toth graduated from Smith College and Berkeley and received a Ph.D. from the University of Minnesota in 1969. She taught English at San Francisco State College and is currently a professor at Macalester College in Minnesota. Toth has contributed articles and stories to McCall's, Harper's, Cosmopolitan, Redbook, Ms., *and* Great River Review *and has written two memoirs—*Blooming: A Small Town Girlhood *(1981) and* Ivy Days: Making My Way Out East *(1984). Her most recent book is* How to Prepare for Your High School Reunion and Other Midlife Musings, *a collection of personal essays about the large and small problems of adult life.*

Of revising, Toth notes: "I do like to revise. I do a great deal of prewriting in my head—when gardening, putting away the dishes, taking a walk. I let the ideas slosh around. When I sit down to write, my first draft is usually very close to my final draft. The real difficulty for me takes place in my head before I write that first draft. After that is finished I try to wait at least a day before coming back in cold blood to revise. I spend a lot of time revising sentence rhythms and trying to find the right word."

The selection reprinted here is from the "Up, Up and Away" chapter in Ivy Days: Making My Way Out East *(1984), an autobiographical account of Toth's undergraduate years at Smith College. In this passage a small-town girl explores the "Big City"—Boston.*

REVISED DRAFT*

1   BUT WHEN I FINALLY GOT to Boston, I arrived on a bus. From the time I came to Smith, I was headed for Boston. When I read in high school about America's literary heritage, I focused on

---

* Bars indicate areas of major revision.

New England: Hawthorne, not Willa Cather; Thoreau, not Sinclair Lewis; Millay, not Edgar Lee Masters. In high-school history, I learned that Boston was where America had started; I had once waded across the springs of the Mississippi at Lake Itasca, and now I wanted to see the beginning of the Revolution at Boston Harbor.

As I debated my selection of a college, my mother urged   *2*
Radcliffe and I leaned toward Smith. Although I wanted to be close to Boston—and on the map, Northampton seemed close—I was afraid of leaping right into it. I did not want to live in a big city. I was not even comfortable in Des Moines. So I settled on Smith, thinking that I could of course get to know Boston on weekends, day trips, vacations.

Once rooted in Northampton, however, I found Boston impossibly far away. I seldom had a weekend free from the pressures of tests and papers, or the subtler pressures of social life. When did I first see Boston? Was it my freshman year when I went to visit a friend at Radcliffe, stayed in her dorm, and ventured down a few of the streets around Harvard Square? Was it my sophomore year when Sophie and I took a two-hour, bumpy bus ride, spent a night in the Y.W.C.A., and window-shopped among the expensive shoe stores and dress shops on Boylston Street? On one of my two or three trips in those freshman and sophomore years, I rode the M.T.A., sampled German sausages in a dark beer-washed cellar, and walked in awe through the Museum of Fine Arts. I loved it all.

Most of all, I reveled in Filene's basement. My freshman   *4*
roommate, Alice, from Framingham, had told me about Filene's, a landmark as notable as the Old North Church. Already an obsessive bargain-hunter from my early days of allowance-stretching, I had practiced my skills only in the relatively small confines of Des Moines' Younkers. Once I walked down the steep basement stairs into Filene's acres of bargains, my horizons suddenly expanded. As I wandered from bin to bin, tantalized by torn-out labels I couldn't quite decipher, I felt as if the inexhaustible wealth and resources of a glamorous city had been called here for my personal advantage. If I didn't feel at home on the streets of Boston, here I was an experienced hand. I snatched a crumpled blouse from another shopper's reach,

and jostled my way to the mirror. Identifying it with Boston, I took Filene's to my heart.

5   These brief excursions into the Big City whetted my appetite for more. During my sophomore year, I began to think about the possibility of spending a summer there. Shouldn't I get some job experience besides my internship at the *Ames Daily Tribune?* Could I justify the expense of a shared apartment in Boston by some kind of work in publishing? Miss Bailey, Head of Scholarships and Student Aid, agreed that I could; she would waive the requirement that I earn at least $300 during the summer toward my college expenses. Soon my friend Molly O'Brien and I began talking about living together in Boston. When Molly's best friend, Katie Hill, heard about it, she immediately decided she wanted to join us. With uncertain expectations, we all began sending out job applications, I in publishing, Molly in art-related fields, Katie in summer teaching. To our surprise, we all succeeded. Smith, Katie said, sometimes paid off. Although *The Atlantic*, Houghton Mifflin, Little, Brown, and the Boston *Globe* decided they didn't want me, the *Harvard Business Review* invited me for an interview. Would I like to serve as a vacation replacement, partly in subscriptions and circulation, partly in editorial, wherever they were shorthanded? I would indeed. Did I like Smith? I did. Did I know Art Simpkins, the college business manager, who had been the editor's best man? Sort of. Had I ever met the editor's son, Jack, who was a freshman at Amherst? I hadn't. But I was eager and anxious to please. I mentioned the thrill of learning about publishing by working on a Harvard magazine. I was hired.

QUESTIONS FOR DISCUSSION

1. What do Boston and New England mean to Toth? Why do they remind her of Hawthorne, Thoreau, and Millay rather than Cather, Lewis, and Masters?

2. Why would anyone write an autobiography? Why would anyone read one?

3. How does Toth seem to select details? Study the visits to Boston (paragraph 3), or Filene's (paragraph 4), or the job inter-

view (paragraph 5). Out of everything that might have been included, why select these details?

4. In the final version, Toth split one paragraph into two (see Question 3 on the draft, below). Could she also have split paragraph 5 into two? Where would the split have come? What does that change suggest about paragraphing?

5. How many examples of parallel structure can you find in this selection? How does it help to organize paragraphs?

6. Be able to define the following words: *reveled* (paragraph 4), *tantalized* (4), *decipher* (4), *jostled* (4), *whetted* (5).

EARLIER DRAFT

But when I finally got to Boston, I took the bus. From the time I arrived at Smith, I knew Boston hovered at the edge of my dreams. When I read about America's literary heritage in high school, I focused on New England: Hawthorne, not Mark Twain; Thoreau, not Sinclair Lewis; Millay, not Edgar Lee Masters, seemed hallowed by time and tradition. Even my child's pack of "Authors" cards had bearded and imposing Bostonian faces. In American history, I learned that Boston was where it had all started; I had once waded across the springs of the Mississippi at Lake Itasca, and now I wanted to see where democracy had poured from the waters of Boston Harbor.

As I debated my selection of a college, my mother urged Radcliffe and I leaned towards Smith. Although I wanted to be close to Boston—and somehow on the map, Northampton seemed close—I was afraid of leaping right into it. I did not want to live in the heart of a big city. I was not even comfortable in Des Moines. So I settled on Smith, thinking that I could of course get to know Boston on weekends, day trips, perhaps some vacations. Once rooted in Northampton, however, Boston seemed impossibly far away. I do not remember when I first saw Boston. My memories are still in a romantic tangle. I seldom had a weekend free from the pressures of looming tests and papers, or the subtler pressures of my erratic social life. Was it my freshman year when I went to visit my Ames friend at Radcliffe, stayed in her dorm, and first ventured down a few of the

~~When I first saw Boston. My memories are still in a ~~ *hopelessly* ~~ tangle.~~

(13)

As I debated my selection of ~~an~~ a ¢ollege, my~~n~~ mother urged Radcliffe
and I leaned towards Smith. Although I wanted to be close to Boston—~~n~~and
somehow on the map, Northampton seemed close—I was afraid of leaping right
into it. I did not want to live in ~~the heart of~~ a big city. I was not
even comfor~~t~~able in Des Moines.~~x~~ So I settled on Smith, ~~xx~~ thinking that
I could of course get to know Boston on weekends, day trips, perhaps
some vacations. ¶ Once ~~rxin~~ rooted in N⸱rthampton, however, */I found*/ Boston ~~seemed~~
~~I do not remember when I first saw the city.~~
impossibly far away. I seldom ~~had~~ had a weekend free from the pressures
or
⁶f looming tests and papers,/~~sometimes~~ the subtler pressures of my ~~—~~
When did I first see Boston?
social life. ╱ Was it my freshman year when I went to visit ~~my Ames~~ friend
a
I~~—~~ at Radcliffe, stayed in her dorm, and ∆ventured down a few of the ╱side *winding*
~~admiring not only the coffeeshops but the lean, tweedy look of the Harvard men?~~
streets around Harvard Square~~?~~, Was it my sophomore year when Sophie and
a
I took ~~that~~ two-hour, bumpy bus ride, ~~to Bos k spent nights in~~
wistfully peered all morning into *dress shops, and boutiques*
the Y.W⸱C.A., ~~and looked in~~ the windows of expensive shoe stores, on
knew
Boylston Street? ~~I remember the astonishing green of the Boston Public~~
color gratuitously added to
~~Garden? XXXXX looked just like/Robert McCloskey's pictures in Make Way~~
On one of my two or three trips in those freshman and sophomore years, I
~~For Ducklings. X~~ rode the M.T.A., ~~my first subway,~~ sampled ~~German cooking~~ *German sausages*
in a dark, beer-washed cellar~~x~~,~~—~~ and walked in awe through the Fine A~~r~~ts
I loved it all. *of*
Museum. ╱ It ~~was all wonderful, a city that seemed to offer quaintness and~~
~~sophistication,~~ *ancient brick townhouses* ~~Jazzier boutiques~~
~~urban excitement, tradition, and much absorbed, intellectual excitement and~~
~~impeccable~~
~~clothing men.~~

Most of all, I revelled in Filene's basement. My ~~xx~~ freshman roommate
from Framingham,
Alice, had told me about Filene's, ~~where she occasionally shopped, and other~~
→ *a landmark evidently as notable as the Old North*
~~—~~ to ~~not to miss it when I got to Boston.~~ Already *Church.*
an obsessive ~~bxg~~ bargain-hunter from my early days of allowance-stretching,
only practiced
~~I~~ I had ~~learned~~ my skills in the relatively small confines of

First draft of a page of Susan Allen Toth's
Up, Up, and Away

side streets around Harvard Square, admiring not only the coffeeshops but the lean, tweedy look of the Harvard men? Was
it my sophomore year when Sophie and I took that two-hour,
bumpy bus ride to Boston, spent a night in the Y.W.C.A., and
wistfully peered all morning into the windows of expensive
shoe stores, dress shops, and boutiques on Boylston Street? I
know the astonishing green of the Boston Public Garden looked
just like color gratuitously added to Robert McCloskey's pictures
in *Make Way for Ducklings*. On one of my two or three trips in
those freshman and sophomore years, I rode the M.T.A., my
first subway, sampled German cooking in a dark, beer-washed
cellar, and walked in awe through the Fine Arts Museum. It
was all wonderful, a city that seemed to offer quaintness and
urban excitement, tradition and real stores, intellectual excitement and exciting men.

Most of all, I revelled in Filene's basement. My freshman   3
roommate Alice had told me about Filene's, where she occasionally shopped, and other girls told me to be sure not to miss
it when I got to Boston. Already an obsessive bargain-hunter
from my early days of allowance-stretching, in fact, I had
learned my skills in the relatively small confines of Des Moines'
Younkers' after-Christmas clearances. Once Sophie guided me
down the steep basement stairs into Filene's acres of bargains,
my horizons suddenly expanded. As I excitedly wandered from
bin to bin, tantalized by torn-out labels I couldn't quite decipher, I felt as if the inexhaustible wealth and resources of a
glamorous city had been culled for my personal advantage right
here in a tousled heap of lacy underpants, or a rack of imperfect
cashmere sweaters, or even a pile of Filene's unbelievably cheap
"discontinued" hair-brushes. The smartly dressed women I had
seen on Boylston Street wore clothes just like this; if I shopped
long enough in Filene's, I would look like them too. After years
of ferreting out bargains in odd corners of Younkers, I was offered nothing but bargains with everything "regular priced"
already discounted. If I couldn't quite feel at home on the streets
of Boston, here I was an experienced hand, grabbing for a crumpled blouse just as another shopper reached for it too, clutching
my pile of acquisitions, jostling my way to the mirror. Somehow
identifying it with Boston, I took Filene's to my heart.

4   These brief excursions into The Big City whetted my appetite for more. Sometime during my sophomore year, I began to think about the possibility of spending a summer there. Shouldn't I get some job experience besides the *Ames Daily Tribune?* Could I justify the expense of a shared apartment in Boston by the prestige of some kind of work in publishing? Miss Bailey, head of Scholarships, agreed that I could; she would waive the requirement that I earn at least $300 during the summer towards my college expenses. Soon Molly O'Brien, my friend down the hall, who was a year ahead of me, and I began talking seriously about living together in Boston. When Molly's best friend, Katie Hill, heard about it, she immediately decided she wanted to join us. With high expectations, we all began sending out job applications, me in publishing, Molly in art-related fields, Katie in summer teaching. Astonishingly, we all succeeded. Although *The Atlantic,* Houghton Mifflin, Little Brown, and the Boston *Globe* politely decided they didn't need me, the *Harvard Business Review* invited me for an interview. Would I like to serve as a vacation replacement, partly in subscriptions and circulation, partly in editorial, wherever they were shorthanded? I would indeed. Did I like Smith? Had I ever met the editor's son, Jack, who was a freshman at Amherst? I hadn't. But I was eager and anxious to please. I mentioned the unimagined thrill of working on a Harvard magazine, one whose circulation, as the editor had told me, included the highest-placed executives in the country. I was hired.

QUESTIONS ON THE REVISION

1. A large number of changes in descriptive detail are made in what became paragraph 3 in the final version. Make a list of what Toth added and what she deleted. Do you see any general principle that accounts for those changes?

2. Toth also makes changes in the description of the basement at Filene's (paragraph 4) and in the account of the interview at the *Harvard Business Review* (paragraph 5). Make a list of the changes made in both passages.

3. Toth splits the second paragraph in the first draft into two paragraphs (numbered 2 and 3 in the final version). Why?

How can one paragraph be split into two without making a change in the opening sentences?

4. Why might Toth have made the following changes from one draft to another?

   a. Deletion of the sentence referring to the game of "Authors."

   b. Deletion of the reference to the Boston Public Garden.

WRITING SUGGESTIONS

1. Formulate a thesis about one strategy Toth used in her revision. In a paragraph support your thesis with evidence from the two versions.

2. Coming to college, whether you are eighteen or thirty-eight, can have its scary moments. Focus on one particular moment in your first few days as a college student—your first night in the dorm, your first college class, your first meal in the dining hall, your first walk through a sea of unfamiliar faces. In an essay make that experience vivid to your reader.

Prewriting:

   a. Try brainstorming about your memories of those first few days. Jot down notes on everything that you can remember.

   b. Look back over your notes. Do you see a particular experience that seems more vivid or significant than the others? Try freewriting about that experience. Do not worry about developing a story or pattern.

   c. Remember that you will have to re-create that experience for your reader. You cannot just tell your reader what happened and what you felt; you will have to show it. Review the introduction to Chapter 2 on writing narratives.

Rewriting:

   a. Complete the following sentence: "My purpose in this essay is to ———." Then look through your essay again. Is everything in your essay consistent with that statement?

   b. Check to make sure that you have used vivid verbs and concrete nouns. Do not overuse adjectives and adverbs.

   c. Did you use any dialogue? Using dialogue is a good way of showing rather than telling.

133

3. What types of support services are available to help freshmen adjust to college life—either as new students or as returning adults? Using research, write a paper intended for incoming students, detailing where they can turn for help.

THREE

Description

You have bought a car—your first—and understandably you can hardly wait to tell your friends. "What does it look like?" they ask and you modestly reply, "A silver-gray '68 VW Beetle with red racing stripes and a sunroof." What you have done is provide a description; you have given your listeners enough information to allow them to form a mental picture of your new (and used) car. Like narration, description is an everyday activity. You describe to a friend what cooked snails really taste like, how your favorite perfume smells, how your body feels when you have a fever, how a local rock band sounded last night. Description re-creates sense impressions, ideas, and feelings by translating them into words.

That translation is not always easy. For one thing, when you have a first-hand experience, all of your senses are working at the same time: you see, taste, smell, feel, hear; you experience feelings and have thoughts about the experience. When you convey that experience to a reader or a listener, you can only record one sense impression at a time. Furthermore, sometimes it is difficult to find an adequate translation for a particular sense impression—how do you describe the smell of musk perfume or the taste of freshly squeezed orange juice? On the other hand, the translation into words offers two distinct advantages: first, ideally it isolates the most important aspects of the experience, ruling out anything else that might distract your reader's attention; second, it makes those experiences more permanent. Sensory impressions decay in seconds, but written descriptions survive indefinitely.

Consider, for example, how precisely James Agee re-creates for the reader the experience of men watering their lawns on summer evenings, evoking sight, sound, and touch:

> The hoses were attached at spigots that stood out of the brick foundations of the houses. The nozzles were variously set but usually so there was a long sweet stream of spray, the nozzle wet in the hand, the water trickling the right forearm and the peeled-back cuff, and the water whishing out a long loose and low-curved cone, and so gentle a sound. First an insane noise of violence in the nozzle, then the still irregular sound of adjustment, then the smoothing into steadiness and a pitch as accurately tuned to the size and style of stream as any violin. So many qualities of sound out of one hose: so many choral differences out of those several hoses that were in earshot. Out of any one hose, the almost dead silence of the release, and the short still arch of the separate big drops, silent as a held breath, and the only noise the flattering noise on leaves and the slapped grass at the fall of each big drop. That, and the intense hiss with the intense stream; that, and that same intensity not growing less but growing more quiet and delicate with the turn of the nozzle, up to that extreme tender whisper when the water was just a wide bell of film.*

Traditionally, descriptions are divided into two categories: objective and subjective. In objective description you record details without making any personal evaluation or reaction. The first half of Roger Angell's description of a baseball is purely objective in recording weight, dimensions, colors, and materials. The ultimate in objective description is found in scientific prose such as you might find in a science textbook.

Few descriptions outside of science writing, however, are completely objective. Instead of trying to include every detail, writers choose details carefully. That process of selection is determined by the writer's purpose and by the impression that the writer wants to create. For example, when Scott Momaday in "The Way to Rainy Mountain" describes the plains of Oklahoma in late summer, he offers his readers a perspective of what he sees: "The grass turns brittle and brown, and it cracks beneath your feet. . . . At a distance in July or August the steaming

---

* James Agee, "Knoxville: Summer 1915," from *A Death in the Family* (New York: Bantam Books). First published in 1957.

foliage seems almost to writhe in fire." Not everyone looking at that landscape would have "seen" what Momaday saw.

In subjective description, you are free to interpret the details for your reader; your reactions and descriptions can be emotional and value loaded. When Gretel Ehrlich in "A River's Route" describes the river as a "white chute tumbling over soft folds of conglomerate rock—brown bellies," the reader immediately knows that this is not the type of description that would be found in a geology textbook.

Descriptions serve a variety of purposes, but in every case it is important to make that purpose clear to your reader. Sometimes description is done solely to record the facts, as in Angell's description of the baseball, or to evoke an atmosphere, as in Agee's description of watering a lawn with a hose and nozzle. More often, description is used as support for other purposes. Gretel Ehrlich, in describing her journey to the source of the river, is not trying to describe accurately a landscape. Instead, she uses description to emphasize the oneness that links people and nature.

How Do You Describe an Object or a Place?

The first task in writing a description is to decide what you want to describe. As in every other writing task, making a good choice means that the act of writing will be easier and probably more successful. Before you begin, keep two things in mind: first, there is rarely any point in describing a common object or place—something every reader has seen—unless you do it in a fresh and perceptive way. Roger Angell describes a baseball, but he does so by dissecting it, giving a series of facts about its composition. All of Agee's readers had probably watered a lawn using a hose and nozzle and had seen, felt, and heard what he describes, but after reading his description, what they are left with is a sense of vividness—this passage evokes or re-creates in our minds a mental picture of that activity.

Second, remember that your description needs to create a focused impression. To do that, you need to select details which contribute to your purpose. That will give you a way of deciding which details out of the many available are relevant. Details in a description must be carefully chosen and arranged; otherwise, your reader will be overwhelmed or bored by the accumulation of detail.

How Do You Describe a Person?

Before you begin to describe a person, remember an experience that everyone has had. You have read a novel and then seen a film or a made-for-television version, and the two experiences did not mesh. The characters, you are convinced, just did not *look* like the actors and actresses: "She was thinner and blond" or "He was all wrong—not big enough, not rugged enough." Any time you read a narrative that contains a character—either real or fictional—you form a mental picture of the person, and that picture is generally not based upon any physical description that the author has provided. In fact, in many narratives, authors provide only minimal description of the people involved. For example, if you look closely at William Allen White's description of his daughter Mary, you will find only a few physical details: she was dressed in "khakis," a "little figure" with a "strong, muscular body," a "long pig-tail," and a "red hair ribbon." Of the Thurmond Watts family in William Least Heat-Moon's "Nameless, Tennessee," you are told even less: Thurmond himself is "tall" and "thin"; but his wife Miss Ginny, his sister-in-law Marilyn, and his daughter Hilda are not physically described at all. In both narratives, however, you get a vivid image of the people being described.

Fictional characters or real people are created or revealed primarily through ways other than direct physical description. What a person does or says, for example, also reveals personality. The reader sees Mary in White's portrait of his daughter through what she does; the ways in which she behaves; the things, people, and values important to her. Those details recreate Mary White for the reader, and finally, they are the things most important about her. The Wattses, in Least Heat-Moon's narrative, are revealed by how they react, what they say, how their speech sounds, what they consider to be important. These are the key factors in re-creating Least Heat-Moon's experience for the reader.

In fact, descriptions of people should not try to be verbal portraits recording physical attributes in photographic detail. Words finally are never as efficient in doing that as photographs. If the objective in describing a person is not photographic accuracy, what then is it? Go back to the advice offered earlier in this introduction: decide first what impression you want to create in your reader. Why are you describing this person? What is it about this person that is worth describing? In all likelihood the answer will be something other than physical attributes. Once you know what that something is, you can then choose those details which best reveal or display the person.

How Do You Organize a Description?

You have found a subject; you have studied it—either first-hand or in memory; you have decided upon a reason for describing this particular subject; you have selected details which contribute to that reason or purpose. Now you need to organize your paragraph or essay. Descriptions, like narratives, have principles of order, although the principles vary depending upon what sense impressions are involved. When the primary descriptive emphasis is on seeing, the most obvious organization is spatial—moving from front to back, side to side, outside to inside, top to bottom, general to specific. The description moves as a camera would. Roger Angell's description of a baseball moves outward from the cork nucleus, through the layers of rubber, wool yarn, and rubber cement, to the cowhide exterior.

Other sense experiences might be arranged in order of importance, from the most obvious to the least—the loudest noise at the concert, the most pervasive odor in the restaurant—or even in chronological order. Agee's description of the sound water makes as it surges through a nozzle follows a chronological sequence from turning on the water through adjusting the nozzle from "separate big drops" through "a wide bell of film."

Does Description Mean Lots of Adjectives and Adverbs?

Remember that one-sentence description of your car: "A silver-gray '68 VW Beetle with red racing stripes and a sunroof." Your audience would have no trouble creating a vivid mental picture from that little bit of information, because it has seen VW Beetles before. The noun provides the primary image. The only two adjectives describe color. The point is that you can create an image without providing a mountain of adjectives and adverbs—just as you imagine what a character looks like without being told. When Scott Momaday writes of his grandmother, he does not describe what she looked like. Instead, he sees her in "postures that were peculiar to her": "standing at the wood stove on a winter morning and turning meat in a great iron skillet; sitting at the south window, bent above her beadwork, and afterwards, when her vision failed, looking down for a long time into the fold of her hands; going out upon a cane, very slowly as she did when the weight of age came upon her; praying." One of the greatest dangers in writing a description lies in trying to describe too much, trying to qualify every noun with at least one adjective and every verb with an adverb. Precise, vivid nouns and verbs will do most of the work for you.

Sample Student Essay

DESCRIPTION

Nadine Resnick chose to describe her favorite childhood toy—
a stuffed doll she had named Natalie.

EARLIER DRAFT

Pretty in Pink

Standing in the middle of the aisle, staring up at
the world as most children in nursery school do,
something pink caught my eye. Just like Rapunzel in her
high tower, there was a girl inside a cardboard and
plastic prison atop a high shelf smiled down at me. I
pointed to the doll and brought her home with me that
same day. Somehow I knew that she was special.

She was named Natalie. I do not know why, but the
name just seemed perfect, like the rest of her. Natalie
was less than twelve inches tall and wore a pink
outfit. Her hands and grimacing face were made of
plastic while the rest of her body was stuffed with
love. She had brown eyes and brown hair, just like me,
which peeked through her burgundy and pink-flowered
bonnet. Perhaps the most unusual feature about her was
that my mom had tattooed my name on her large bottom so
that if Natalie ever strayed from me at nursery school
or at the supermarket, she would be able to find me.

There was some kind of magic about Natalie's face.
I think it was her grin from ear to ear. Even if I had
played with her until she was so dirty that most of her
facial features were hidden, Natalie's never-ending
smile usually shown through. When I neglected her for
days to play with some new toy and then later returned,
her friendly smirk was still there. When I was left
home alone for a few hours, her smile assured me that I
need not be afraid. Natalie's bright smile also cheered

141

me up when I was sick or had a bad day. And she always
had enough hugs for me.

As I was growing up, Natalie and her beaming face
could usually be found somewhere in my room—on my bed,
in her carriage, hiding under a pile a junk, and later
piled in my closet with the rest of my other dolls and
stuffed animals. When I got older, I foolishly decided
that I no longer needed such childish toys. So I put
Natalie and the rest of my stuffed animals in a large
black plastic bag in a dark corner of the basement. I
now realize that the basement really is not an
honorable place for someone who has meant so much to
me. But, I will bet that she is still smiling anyway.

Nadine had a chance to read her essay to a small group of
classmates during a collaborative editing session. Everyone
liked the essay and most of their suggested changes were fairly
minor. For example, several people objected to her choice of
the words "grimaced" and "smirk," feeling that such words
were not appropriate choices for a lovable doll. Another student, however, suggested a revision in the final paragraph. "It
seems like you put her farther and farther away from you as
you got older. Why don't you emphasize that distancing by
having it occur in stages?" he commented. When Nadine rewrote her essay, she made a number of minor changes in the
first three paragraphs and then followed her classmate's idea
in the fourth paragraph.

REVISED DRAFT

Natalie

Standing in the store's aisle, staring up at the
world as most pre-school children do, something pink
caught my eye. Just like Rapunzel in her high tower, a
girl trapped inside a cardboard and plastic prison atop
a high shelf smiled down at me. I pointed to the doll
and brought her home with me that same day. Somehow I
knew that she was special.

She was named Natalie. I do not know why, but the

142

name just seemed perfect, like the rest of her. Natalie was less than twelve inches tall and wore a pink outfit. Her hands and smiling face were made of plastic while the rest of her body was plumply stuffed. Just like me, she had brown eyes and brown hair which peeked through her burgundy and pink-flowered bonnet. Perhaps her most unusual feature was my name tattooed on her bottom so that if Natalie every strayed from me at nursery school or at the supermarket, she would be able to find me.

Natalie's face had a certain glow, some kind of magic. I think it was her grin from ear to ear. After I had played with her, no matter how dirty her face was, Natalie's never-ending smile still beamed through. When I neglected her for days to play with some new toy and then later returned, her friendly grin was still there. Years later, when I was old enough to be left home alone for a few hours, her smile assured me that I need not be afraid. Natalie's bright smile also cheered me up when I was sick or had a bad day. And she always had enough hugs for me.

As I was growing up, Natalie and her beaming face could usually be found somewhere in my room. However, she seemed to move further away from me as I got older. Natalie no longer slept with me; she slept in her own carriage. Then she rested on a high shelf across my room. Later she made her way into my closet with the rest of the dolls and stuffed animals that I had outgrown. Eventually, I decided that I no longer needed such childish toys, so I put Natalie and my other stuffed animals in a large black plastic bag in a dark cellar corner. Even though I abandoned her, I am sure that Natalie is still smiling at me today.

Some Things to Remember

1. Choose your subject carefully, making sure that you have a specific reason or purpose in mind for whatever you describe.
2. Study or observe your subject—try to see it or experience it in a fresh way. Gather details; make a list; use all your senses.

3. Use your purpose as a way of deciding which details ought to be included and which excluded.

4. Choose a pattern of organization to focus your reader's attention.

5. Use precise, vivid nouns and verbs, as well as adjectives and adverbs, to create your descriptions.

A Baseball

ROGER ANGELL

Roger Angell was born in New York in 1920 and received a B.A. from Harvard in 1942. From 1947 to 1956 he was a contributor to Holiday, *then became a fiction editor for* The New Yorker, *where his columns on baseball appear several times a year. Angell has been called "baseball's most articulate fan" and in 1980 won the George Polk Award for commentary. His books include* The Stone Arbor and Other Stories *(1966),* A Day in the Life of Roger Angell *(1970),* The Summer Game *(1972),* Five Seasons: A Baseball Companion *(1977), and* Late Innings: A New Baseball Companion *(1982).* Baseball *(1984) was a joint project combining Walter Iooss's photographs with Angell's essays. Angell's most recent book is* Season Ticket: The Baseball Companion *(1988). Angell's writing combines scientific objectivity and poetic sensitivity, qualities that can be seen in this opening paragraph from his book* Five Seasons. *Angell "sees" a baseball in two distinctly different ways.*

IT WEIGHS JUST FIVE OUNCES and measures between 2.86 and 2.94 inches in diameter. It is made of a composition-cork nucleus encased in two thin layers of rubber, one black and one red, surrounded by 121 yards of tightly wrapped blue-gray wool yarn, 45 yards of white wool yarn, 53 more yards of blue-gray wool yarn, 150 yards of fine cotton yarn, a coat of rubber cement, and a cowhide (formerly horsehide) exterior, which is held together with 216 slightly raised red cotton stitches. Printed certifications, endorsements, and outdoor advertising spherically attest to its authenticity. Like most institutions, it is considered inferior in its present form to its ancient archetypes, and in this case the complaint is probably justified; on occasion in recent years it has actually been known to come apart under the demands of its brief but rigorous active career. Baseballs are assembled and hand-stitched in Taiwan (before this year the work was done in Haiti, and before 1973 in Chicopee, Massachusetts), and contemporary pitchers claim that there is a tangible variation in the size and feel of the balls that now come into play in a single game; a true peewee is treasured by hurlers, and its departure from the premises, by fair means or foul, is secretly mourned. But never mind: any baseball is beautiful. No other small package comes as close to the ideal in design and utility. It is a perfect object for a man's hand. Pick it up and it instantly suggests its purpose; it is meant to be thrown a considerable distance—thrown hard and with precision. Its feel and heft are the beginning of the sport's critical dimensions; if it were a fraction of an inch larger or smaller, a few centigrams heavier or lighter, the game of baseball would be utterly different.

QUESTIONS ON SUBJECT AND PURPOSE

1. Every adult has surely "seen" a baseball. Why then describe one? How does Angell's description differ from what you might expect?
2. Does it make any sense to say, as Angell does, that if a baseball were any larger or smaller the game would be "utterly different"? What might that statement mean?
3. Could you make the same claim for a football, a softball, a basketball, a soccer ball? Is there anything special about a baseball?

QUESTIONS ON STRATEGY AND AUDIENCE

1. How does Angell structure his paragraph?
2. How effective are the opening sentences? Do they catch your attention? Why or why not?
3. This selection is the first paragraph in Angell's *Five Seasons: A Baseball Companion*. Why begin a book about baseball with a description of the ball?

QUESTIONS ON VOCABULARY AND STYLE

1. What types of transitional devices does Angell use to hold his paragraph together?
2. What might Angell mean by the sentence: "Printed certifi-

cations, endorsements, and outdoor advertising spherically attest to its authenticity"?

3. Be able to define the following words: *archetype, tangible, heft.*

WRITING SUGGESTIONS

1. Generally there is no good reason to describe an everyday object in photographic detail. On the other hand, sometimes you can see the ordinary in a new and fresh way. Select something you own, something ordinary, and describe it in a paragraph. Do not try to "photograph" the object verbally; try instead to see it in a fresh way.

2. Select a drawer in your desk, dresser, or kitchen or your wallet or purse. Catalog its contents. Look at what you see. What do those things reveal about you? Using descriptive detail, write an essay about what you find—both literally and figuratively. Remember that you must also catch and hold your reader's interest.

Prewriting:

a. In all likelihood you cannot include everything you find in your essay. Arrange the items on a table or desk. Complete the following sentence for each item: "What is revealing/interesting about this item is _____."

b. Once you have a list of sentences, group the items on the basis of what they reveal. Eliminate any items that do not fit into the pattern you plan to develop.

c. Unless you have a thesis that holds the items together, your essay will probably just become a list—"Here are some things that I found." Before you begin your paper, write a thesis sentence that reflects your purpose. Eliminate any items from your list that do not fit the pattern you plan to develop.

Rewriting:

a. Everyone could write an essay on this topic. What makes yours particularly interesting? What might make a reader want to read it? Answer that last question in one sentence.

b. Test your essay for reader interest by asking a classmate or roommate to read it. Use this reaction as a guide to possible revision.

147

c. Remember that your introduction will be especially crucial. Look at what you have written. Do you start with something that will catch your reader's interest? Does your introduction provoke curiosity? Startle? Establish a common ground ("That is exactly like me!")?

3. Angell obviously researched the composition of a baseball—what it was made of, how many yards of what color yarn. Do the same for any common object. Find out how it is made; how many are made annually; how it is sold; how people who use it feel about it. In an essay describe your findings.

Mary White

WILLIAM ALLEN WHITE

William Allen White (1868–1944) was born and died in Emporia, Kansas. He is recognized as one of the most important political journalists of turn-of-the-century America. White grew up in the frontier town of El Dorado, Kansas, where his father was a doctor and store-keeper, active in Democratic politics. He attended the College of Emporia and the University of Kansas, holding various newspaper jobs. He worked on the editorial staff of the Kansas City Journal *and* The Kansas City Star. *In 1895, he bought the* Emporia Gazette *and served as its editor, writing stinging political attacks that brought him much political influence and notoriety. White was a prodigious writer who produced several collections of essays on politics and economics, political biographies, novels, and innumerable magazine articles. In 1922, he won a Pulitzer Prize for his editorial "To an Anxious Friend," a defense of American journalistic freedom. Among White's better-known works are* The Court of Boyville, *a collection of stories (1899); the novels* A Certain Rich Man *(1909) and* In the Heart of a Fool *(1918); and the Pulitzer-Prize–winning* The Autobiography of William Allen White, *published posthumously in 1946. The death of his sixteen-year-old daughter Mary in 1921 prompted his most frequently reprinted editorial, "Mary White," a loving tribute that immortalized her.*

THE ASSOCIATED PRESS reports carrying the news of Mary White's death declared that it came as the result of a fall from a horse. How she would have hooted at that! She never fell from a horse in her life. Horses have fallen on her and with her—"I'm always trying to hold'em in my lap," she used to say. But she was proud of few things, and one was that she could ride anything that had four legs and hair. Her death resulted not from a fall, but from a blow on the head which fractured her skull, and the blow came from the limb of an overhanging tree on the parking.

The last hour of her life was typical of its happiness. She came home from a day's work at school, topped off by a hard grind with the copy on the High School Annual, and felt that a ride would refresh her. She climbed into her khakis, chattering to her mother about the work she was doing, and hurried to get her horse and be out on the dirt roads for the country air and the radiant green fields of the spring. As she rode through the town on an easy gallop she kept waving at passers-by. She knew everyone in town. For a decade the little figure with the long pig-tail and the red hair ribbon has been familiar on the streets of Emporia, and she got in the way of speaking to those who nodded at her. She passed the Kerrs, walking the horse, in front of the Normal Library, and waved at them; passed another friend a few hundred feet further on, and waved at her. The horse was walking and as she turned into North Merchant street she took off her cowboy hat, and the horse swung into a lope. She passed the Tripletts and waved her cowboy hat at them, still moving gaily north on Merchant street. A Gazette carrier passed—a High School boy friend—and she waved at him but with her bridle hand: the horse veered quickly, plunged into the parking where the low-hanging limb faced her, and while she still looked back waving, the blow came. But she did not fall from the horse; she slipped off, dazed a bit, staggered and fell in a faint. She never quite recovered consciousness.

3   But she did not fall from the horse, neither was she riding fast. A year or so ago she used to go like the wind. But that habit was broken, and she used the horse to get into the open to get fresh, hard exercise, and to work off a certain surplus energy that welled up in her and needed a physical outlet. That need has been in her heart for years. It was back of the impulse that kept the dauntless, little brown-clad figure on the streets and country roads of this community and built into a strong, muscular body what had been a frail and sickly frame during the first years of her life. But the riding gave her more than a body. It released a gay and hardy soul. She was the happiest thing in the world. And she was happy because she was enlarging her horizon. She came to know all sorts and conditions of men; Charley O'Brien, the traffic cop, was one of her best friends. W. L. Holtz, the Latin teacher, was another. Tom O'Connor, farmer-politician, and Rev. J. H. J. Rice, preacher and police judge, and Frank Beach, music master, were her

special friends; and all the girls, black and white, above the track and below the track, in Pepville and Stringtown, were among her acquaintances. And she brought home riotous stories of her adventures. She loved to rollick; persiflage was her natural expression at home. Her humor was a continual bubble of joy. She seemed to think in hyperbole and metaphor. She was mischievous without malice, as full of faults as an old shoe. No angel was Mary White, but an easy girl to live with, for she never nursed a grouch five minutes in her life.

With all her eagerness for the out-of-doors, she loved books.   4 On her table when she left her room were a book on Conrad, one by Galsworthy, "Creative Chemistry" by E. E. Slosson, and a Kipling book. She read Mark Twain, Dickens and Kipling before she was 10—all of their writings. Wells and Arnold Bennett particularly amused and diverted her. She was entered as a student in Wellesley in 1922; was assistant editor of the High School Annual this year, and in line for election to the editorship of the Annual next year. She was a member of the executive committee of the High School Y.W.C.A.

Within the last two years she had begun to be moved by   5 an ambition to draw. She began as most children do by scribbling in her school books, funny pictures. She bought cartoon magazines and took a course—rather casually, naturally, for she was, after all, a child with no strong purposes—and this year she tasted the first fruits of success by having her pictures accepted by the High School Annual. But the thrill of delight she got when Mr. Ecord, of the Normal Annual, asked her to do the cartooning for that book this spring, was too beautiful for words. She fell to her work with all her enthusiastic heart. Her drawings were accepted, and her pride—always repressed by a lively sense of the ridiculousness of the figure she was cutting—was a really gorgeous thing to see. No successful artist ever drank a deeper draught of satisfaction than she took from the little fame her work was getting among her schoolfellows. In her glory, she almost forgot her horse—but never her car.

For she used the car as a jitney bus. It was her social life.   6 She never had a "party" in all her nearly seventeen years— wouldn't have one; but she never drove a block in the car in her life that she didn't begin to fill the car with pick-ups! Everybody rode with Mary White—white and black, old and young, rich and poor, men and women. She liked nothing better than to fill the car full of long-legged High School boys and an occasional girl, and parade the town. She never had a "date," nor went to a dance, except once with her brother, Bill, and the "boy proposition" didn't interest her—yet. But young people— great spring-breaking, varnish-cracking, fender-bending, door-sagging carloads of "kids"— gave her great pleasure. Her zests were keen. But the most fun she ever had in her life was acting as chairman of the committee that got up the big turkey dinner for the poor folks at the county home; scores of pies, gallons of slaw; jam, cakes, preserves, oranges and a wilderness of turkey were loaded in the car and taken to the country home. And, being of a practical turn of mind, she risked her own Christmas dinner by staying to see that the poor folks actually got it all. Not that she was a cynic; she just disliked to tempt folks. While there she found a blind colored uncle, very old, who could do nothing but make rag rugs, and she rustled up from her school friends rags enough to keep him busy for a season. The last engagement she tried to make was to take the guests at the country home out for a car ride. And the last endeavor of her life was to try to get a rest room for colored girls in the High School. She found one girl reading in the toilet, because there was no better place for a colored girl to loaf, and it inflamed her sense of injustice and she became a nagging harpie to those who, she thought, could remedy the evil. The poor she had always with her, and was glad of it. She hungered and thirsted for righteousness; and was the most impious creature in the world. She joined the Congregational Church without consulting her parents; not particularly for her soul's good. She never had a thrill of piety in her life, and would have hooted at a "testimony." But even as a little child she felt the church was an agency for helping people to more of life's abundance, and she wanted to help. She never wanted help for herself. Clothes meant little to her. It was a fight to get a new rig on her; but eventually a harder fight to get off. She never wore a jewel and had no ring but her High School class ring, and never asked for anything but a wrist watch. She refused to have her hair up; though she was nearly 17. "Mother," she protested, "you don't know how much I get by with, in my braided pigtails that I could not, with my hair up." Above every other passion of her life was her passion not to grow up, to be a child. The tom-boy in her which was big, seemed to loath to be put away forever in skirts. She was a Peter Pan, who refused to grow up.

Her funeral yesterday at the Congregational Church was as she would have wished it; no singing, no flowers save the big bunch of red roses from her Brother Bill's Harvard classmen— Heavens, how proud that would have made her! and the red roses from the Gazette force—in vases at her head and feet. A short prayer, Paul's beautiful essay on "Love" from the Thirteenth Chapter of First Corinthians, some remarks about her democratic spirit by her friend, John H. J. Rice, pastor and police judge, which she would have deprecated if she could, a prayer sent down for her by her friend, Carl Nau, and opening the service the slow, poignant movement from Beethoven's Moonlight Sonata, which she loved, and closing the service a cutting from the joyously melancholy first movement of Tschaikowski's Pathetic Symphony, which she liked to hear in certain moods on the phonograph; then the Lord's Prayer by her friends in the High School. 7

That was all. 8

For her pallbearers only her friends were chosen; her Latin teacher—W. L. Holtz; her High School principal, Rice Brown; her doctor, Frank Foncannon; her friend, W. W. Finney; her pal at the Gazette office, Walter Hughes; and her brother Bill. It would have made her smile to know that her friend, Charley O'Brien, the traffic cop, had been transferred from Sixth and Commercial to the corner near the church to direct her friends who came to bid her goodbye. 9

A rift in the clouds in a gray day threw a shaft of sunlight upon her coffin as her nervous, energetic little body sank to its last sleep. But the soul of her, the glowing, gorgeous, fervent soul of her, surely was flaming in eager joy upon some other dawn. 10

QUESTIONS ON SUBJECT AND PURPOSE

1. Why might White have chosen to write about the accidental death of his young daughter?

2. What do Mary's interests reveal about her? What kind of a person was she?

3. How does White blend telling and showing in his essay (see "How Are Narratives Told?" in the introduction to Chapter 2)? How does that help him shape his tribute?

QUESTIONS ON STRATEGY AND AUDIENCE

1. How much physical description does White give of his daughter? What physical details does he focus on? Why these?

2. What other details does White use to describe his daughter? How do you get a sense of her personality?

3. Why does White begin as he does? Why in the second paragraph does he trace her final ride in such detail?

4. How does White structure his essay?

QUESTIONS ON VOCABULARY AND STYLE

1. What is the effect of the inverted sentence at the end of paragraph 3?

2. What is the effect of the single three-word paragraph (8): "That was all"?

3. Be able to define the following words: *lope* (paragraph 2), *rollick* (3), *persiflage* (3), *hyperbole* (3), *jitney* (6), *deprecated* (7), *fervent* (10).

WRITING SUGGESTIONS

1. In a paragraph try to "capture" your best friend or your roommate or your greatest rival. Remember to select details that reveal personality; remember to keep a central focus.

2. Writing about a close friend or a relative is never easy. You know too much; you cannot be objective enough. When you have lost that person, it is even more difficult. Still, writing about the person is a way to order your experience, record your grief, and remember and memorialize your friend or relative. If you have had such an experience, try a tribute similar to White's.

Prewriting:

a. Spend some time thinking about possible subjects. Once you have made a choice, try freewriting for twenty minutes. Write whatever comes to mind about the person and your feelings.

b. Finish the following sentence: "What I want the reader to know about this person is _____." Use that statement as a way of testing every detail you decide to include.

c. Do not try to describe the person photographically. Select details that reveal personality, that reveal the qualities about the person that you wish to emphasize. Check every detail.

Rewriting:

a. Ask a friend or a classmate to read your essay. Once your reader has finished, ask her or him to finish the test sentence you wrote in item b above. Does your reader see the same purpose as you did?

b. Look carefully at the structure of your essay. What type of structure did you use? Is it chronological? Would it be better to start with a flashback? Force yourself to jot down an outline of an alternate structure.

3. Select a famous young person who has died. Research the story to find details about the person's life and values. Using your research, write a sympathetic tribute.

Nameless, Tennessee

WILLIAM LEAST HEAT-MOON

William Least Heat-Moon is the tribal name of part-Sioux William Trogdon. Born in Missouri in 1939, he earned a Ph.D. in English from the University of Missouri in 1973. His best-selling Blue Highways: A Journey into America *(1982) is the account of his 14,000-mile journey through American backroads in a converted van called "Ghost Dancing." The book is noted for its detailed and sensitive descriptions of the lesser-known areas of America. In 1985, an 11-cassette set of Least Heat-Moon's reading of* Blue Highways *was released. Most recently he wrote the introduction to* American Roads *(1989), a collection of photographs by Winston Swift Boyer. In this chapter from* Blue Highways, *he describes his experiences at a general store in Nameless, Tennessee, where he meets Thurmond and Virginia Watts, living in a world seemingly untouched by time.*

1   NAMELESS, TENNESSEE, was a town of maybe ninety people if you pushed it, a dozen houses along the road, a couple of barns, same number of churches, a general merchandise store selling Fire Chief gasoline, and a community center with a lighted volleyball court. Behind the center was an open-roof, rusting metal privy with PAINT ME on the door, in the hollow of a nearby oak lay a full pint of Jack Daniel's Black Label. From the houses, the odor of coal smoke.

2   Next to a red tobacco barn stood the general merchandise with a poster of Senator Albert Gore, Jr., smiling from the window. I knocked. The door opened partway. A tall, thin man said, "Closed up. For good," and started to shut the door.

3   "Don't want to buy anything. Just a question for Mr. Thurmond Watts."

4   The man peered through the slight opening. He looked me over. "What question would that be?"

5   "If this is Nameless, Tennessee, could he tell me how it got that name?"

The man turned back into the store and called out, "Miss 6
Ginny! Somebody here wants to know how Nameless come to
be Nameless."

Miss Ginny edged to the door and looked me and my truck 7
over. Clearly, she didn't approve. She said, "You know as well
as I do, Thurmond. Don't keep him on the stoop in the damp
to tell him." Miss Ginny, I found out, was Mrs. Virginia Watts,
Thurmond's wife.

I stepped in and they both began telling the story, adding 8
a detail here, the other correcting a fact there, both smiling at
the foolishness of it all. It seems the hilltop settlement went for
years without a name. Then one day the Post Office Department
told the people if they wanted mail up on the mountain they
would have to give the place a name you could properly address
a letter to. The community met; there were only a handful, but
they commenced debating. Some wanted patriotic names, some
names from nature, one man recommended in all seriousness
his own name. They couldn't agree, and they ran out of names
to argue about. Finally, a fellow tired of the talk; he didn't like
the mail he received anyway. "Forget the durn Post Office," he
said. "This here's a nameless place if I ever seen one, so leave
it be." And that's just what they did.

Watts pointed out the window. "We used to have signs on 9
the road, but the Halloween boys keep tearin' them down."

"You think Nameless is a funny name," Miss Ginny said. 10
"I see it plain in your eyes. Well, you take yourself up north a
piece to Difficult or Defeated or Shake Rag. Now them are silly
names."

The old store, lighted only by three fifty-watt bulbs, smelled 11
of coal oil and baking bread. In the middle of the rectangular
room, where the oak floor sagged a little, stood an iron stove.
To the right was a wooden table with an unfinished game of
checkers and a stool made from an apple-tree stump. On shelves
around the walls sat earthen jugs with corncob stoppers, a few
canned goods, and some of the two thousand old clocks and
clockworks Thurmond Watts owned. Only one was ticking, the
others he just looked at. I asked how long he'd been in the
store.

"Thirty-five years, but we closed the first day of the year. 12

We're hopin' to sell it to a churchly couple. Upright people. No athians.''

13   "Did you build this store?"

14   "I built this one, but it's the third general store on the ground. I fear it'll be the last. I take no pleasure in that. Once you could come in here for a gallon of paint, a pickle, a pair of shoes, and a can of corn."

15   "Or horehound candy," Miss Ginny said. "Or corsets and salves. We had cough syrups and all that for the body. In season, we'd buy and sell blackberries and walnuts and chestnuts, before the blight got them. And outside, Thurmond milled corn and sharpened plows. Even shoed a horse sometimes."

16   "We could fix up a horse or a man or a baby," Watts said.

17   "Thurmond, tell him we had a doctor on the ridge in them days."

18   "We had a doctor on the ridge in them days. As good as any doctor alivin'. He'd cut a crooked toenail or deliver a woman. Dead these last years."

19   "I got some bad ham meat one day," Miss Ginny said, "and took to vomitin.' All day, all night. Hangin' on the drop edge of yonder. I said to Thurmond, "Thurmond, unless you want shut of me, call the doctor.'"

20   "I studied on it," Watts said.

21   "You never did. You got him right now. He come over and put three drops of iodeen in half a glass of well water. I drank it down and the vomitin' stopped with the last swallow. Would you think iodeen could do that?"

22   "He put Miss Ginny on one teaspoon of spirits of ammonia in well water for her nerves. Ain't nothin' works better for her to this day."

23   "Calms me like the hand of the Lord."

24   Hilda, the Wattses' daughter, came out of the backroom. "I remember him," she said. "I was just a baby. Y'all were talkin' to him, and he lifted me up on the counter and gave me a stick of Juicy Fruit and a piece of cheese."

25   "Knew the old medicines," Watts said. "Only drugstore he needed was a good kitchen cabinet. None of them anteebeeotics that hit you worsen your ailment. Forgotten lore now, the old medicines, because they ain't profit in iodeen."

Miss Ginny started back to the side room where she and 26
her sister Marilyn were taking apart a duck-down mattress to
make bolsters. She stopped at the window for another look at
Ghost Dancing. "How do you sleep in that thing? Ain't you all
cramped and cold?"

"How does the clam sleep in his shell?" Watts said in my 27
defense.

"Thurmond, get the boy a piece of buttermilk pie afore he 28
goes on."

"Hilda, get some buttermilk pie." He looked at me. "You 29
like good music?" I said I did. He cranked up an old Edison
phonograph, the kind with the big morning-glory blossom for
a speaker, and put on a wax cylinder. "This will by 'My Mother's Prayer,'" he said.

While I ate buttermilk pie, Watts served as disc jockey of 30
Nameless, Tennessee. "Here's 'Mountain Rose.'" It was one of
those moments that you know at the time will stay with you
to the grave: the sweet pie, the gaunt man playing the old music,
the coals in the stove glowing orange, the scent of kerosene
and hot bread. "Here's 'Evening Rhapsody.'" The music was
so heavily romantic we both laughed. I thought: It is for this I
have come.

Feathered over and giggling, Miss Ginny stepped from the 31
side room. She knew she was a sight. "Thurmond, give him
some lunch. Still looks hungry."

Hilda pulled food off the woodstove in the backroom: 32
home-butchered and canned whole-hog sausage, home-
canned June apples, turnip greens, cole slaw, potatoes, stuffing,
hot cornbread. All delicious.

Watts and Hilda sat and talked while I ate. "Wish you would 33
join me."

"We've ate," Watts said. "Cain't beat a woodstove for fla- 34
vorful cookin.'"

He told me he was raised in a one-hundred-fifty-year-old 35
cabin still standing in one of the hollows. "How many's left,"
he said, "that grew up in a log cabin? I ain't the last surely, but
I must be climbin' on the list."

Hilda cleared the table. "You Watts ladies know how to 36
cook."

159

37   "She's in nursin' school at Tennessee Tech. I went over for one of them football games last year there at Coevul." To say *Cookeville*, you let the word collapse in upon itself so that it comes out "Coevul."

38   "Do you like football?" I asked.

39   "Don't know. I was so high up in that stadium, I never opened my eyes."

40   Watts went to the back and returned with a fat spiral notebook that he set on the table. His expression had changed. "Miss Ginny's *Deathbook*."

41   The thing startled me. Was it something I was supposed to sign? He opened it but said nothing. There were scads of names written in a tidy hand over pages incised to crinkliness by a ballpoint. Chronologically, the names had piled up: Wives, grandparents, a stillborn infant, relatives, friends close and distant. Names, names. After each, the date of the unknown finally known and transcribed. The last entry bore yesterday's date.

42   "She's wrote out twenty years' worth. Ever day she listens to the hospital report on the radio and puts the names in. Folks come by to check a date. Or they just turn through the books. Read them like a scrapbook."

43   Hilda said, "Like Saint Peter at the gates inscribin' the names."

44   Watts took my arm. "Come along," He led me to the fruit cellar under the store. As we went down, he said, "Always take a newborn baby upstairs afore you take him downstairs, otherwise you'll incline him downwards."

45   The cellar was dry and full of cobwebs and jar after jar of home-canned food, the bottles organized as a shopkeeper would: sausage, pumpkin, sweet pickles, tomatoes, corn relish, blackberries, peppers, squash, jellies. He held a hand out toward the dusty bottles. "Our tomorrows."

46   Upstairs again, he said, "Hope to sell the store to the right folk. I see now, though, it'll be somebody offen the ridge. I've studied on it, and maybe it's the end of our place." He stirred the coals. "This store could give a comfortable livin', but not likely get your rich. But just gettin' by is dice rollin' to people nowadays. I never did see my day guaranteed."

47   When it was time to go, Watts said, "If you find anyone

160

along your ways wants a good store—on the road to Cordell
Hull Lake—tell them about us."

I said I would. Miss Ginny and Hilda and Marilyn came out   48
to say goodbye. It was cold and drizzling again. "Weather to
give a man the weary dismals," Watts grumbled. "Where you
headed from here?"

"I don't know."   49

"Cain't get lost then."   50

Miss Ginny looked again at my rig. It had worried her from   51
the first as it had my mother. "I hope you don't get yourself
kilt in that durn thing gallivantin' around the country."

"Come back when the hills dry off," Watts said. "We'll go   52
lookin for some of them round rocks all sparkly inside."

I though a moment. "Geodes?"   53

"Them's the ones. The country's properly full of them."   54

QUESTIONS ON SUBJECT AND PURPOSE

1. At one point in the narrative (paragraph 30), Least Heat-Moon
   remarks, "I thought: It is for this I have come." What does he
   seem to be suggesting? What is the "this" that he finds in
   Nameless (paragraph 40)?

2. Why do "Miss Ginny's *Deathbook*" (paragraph 40) and the
   "fruit cellar" (44) seem appropriate details?

3. What might have attracted Least Heat-Moon to this place and
   these people? What does he want you to sense? Is there anything in his description and narrative that suggests how he
   feels about Nameless?

QUESTIONS ON STRATEGY AND AUDIENCE

1. After you have read the selection, describe each member of
   the Watts family. Describe the exterior and interior of their
   store. Then carefully go through the selection and see how
   many specific descriptive details Least Heat-Moon uses. List
   them.

2. What devices other than direct description does Least Heat-
   Moon use to create the sense of place and personality? Make
   a list and be prepared to tell how those devices work.

3. How is the narrative arranged? Is the order just spatial and
   chronological?

161

4. This selection is taken from *Blue Highways: A Journey into America*, a bestseller for nearly a year. Why would a travel narrative—full of stories such as this—be so appealing to an American audience?

QUESTIONS ON VOCABULARY AND STYLE

1. Least Heat-Moon attempts to reproduce the pronunciation of some words—for example, *athians* (paragraph 12), *iodeen* (21), and *anteebeeotics* (25). Make a list of all such phonetic spellings. Why does Least Heat-Moon do this? Do you think he captures all of the Wattses' accent or just some part of it? Is the device effective?

2. Examine how Least Heat-Moon uses dialogue in his description. How are the Wattses revealed by what they say? How much of what was actually said during the visit is recorded? Can you find specific points in the story where Least Heat-Moon obviously omits dialogue?

3. Try to define or explain the following words and phrases: *horehound candy* (paragraph 15), *bolsters* (26), *buttermilk pie* (28), *incised to crinkliness by a ballpoint* (41), *weary dismals* (48), *gallivantin' around* (51).

WRITING SUGGESTIONS

1. Choose a campus building or a location that has acquired a strange or vivid name (for example, the cafeteria in the Student Center known as "The Scrounge"). In a paragraph describe the place to a friend who has never seen it.

2. Look for an unusual place in town (a barber shop or hair salon, a food co-op, a pool hall, a diner). In an essay describe the place for your reader. You might think of your essay as a feature article for next Sunday's local newspaper. Include descriptions of people and dialogue to help catch the right tone.

Prewriting:

a. Take a walk and make a list of possible places.

b. Visit one or more of them and take notes on what you see. Imagine yourself as a newspaper reporter. If people are present, try to write down exactly what they say.

c. Decide on a particular quality or feeling or idea that you want to convey about this place. Write a statement of purpose.

d. Do not "overpeople" your description. Do not try to describe every character completely. Reveal personality through significant detail and dialogue.

Rewriting:

a. Check to make sure that you have made effective use of verbs and nouns. Do not rely on adjectives and adverbs to do the work of description.

b. Using your statement of purpose, check every detail that you included in your essay. Does it belong? Does it relate to that stated purpose?

3. Least Heat-Moon is fascinated by unusual names, and often drives considerable distances to visit towns with names such as Dime Box, Hungry Horse, Liberty Bond, Ninety-Six, and Tuba City. Choose an unusual place name (town, river, subdivision, topographical feature) from your home state and research the origin of the name. A reference librarian can show you how to locate source materials. If possible, you could contact your local historical society or public library for help or interview some knowledgeable local residents. Using your research, write an essay about how that name was chosen. Remember to document your sources.

A River's Route

GRETEL EHRLICH

Gretel Ehrlich was born in Santa Barbara, California, and educated at Bennington College, the New School of Social Research, and the UCLA Film School. A poet, film editor, novelist, and essayist, Ehrlich has contributed to Harper's *since 1985. Her work includes two books of poetry,* Geode Rock Body *(1970) and* To Touch the Water *(1981); a collection of essays,* The Solace of Open Spaces *(1985); a book of short stories, bound back-to-back with a collection by Edward Hoagland, entitled* City Tales/Wyoming Stories *(1986); and a novel about a Japanese internment camp during World War II,* Heart Mountain *(1988). In 1976, Ehrlich visited Wyoming on a Public Broadcasting System assignment to film sheep ranchers in the Big Horn Mountains. She moved there a few years later, gave up city life, and learned sheepherding. "A River's Route" was first published in the introduction to the Sierra Club's wilderness wall calendar in 1989. In her search for the river's origin, Ehrlich discovers far more than a literal spring, for she finds that "to trace the history of a river, or a raindrop . . . is also to trace the history of the soul, the history of the mind descending and arising in the body."*

1   IT'S MORNING in the Absaroka Mountains. The word *absaroka* means "raven" in the Crow language, though I've seen no ravens in three days. Last night I slept with my head butted against an Englemann spruce, and on waking the limbs looked like hundreds of arms swinging in a circle. The trunk is bigger than an elephant's leg, bigger than my torso. I stick my nose against the bark. Tiny opals of sap stick to my cheeks and the bark breaks up, textured: red and gray, coarse and smooth, wet and flaked.

2   A tree is an aerial garden, a botanical migration from the sea, from those earliest plants, the seaweeds; it is a purchase on crumbled rock, on ground. The human, standing, is only a different upsweep and articulation of cells. How tree-like we are, how human the tree.

3   But I've come here to seek out the source of a river, and

as we make the daylong ascent from a verdant valley, I think about walking and wilderness. We use the word "wilderness," but perhaps we mean wildness. Isn't that why I've come here? In wilderness, I seek the wildness in myself—and in so doing, come on the wildness everywhere around me because, being part of nature, I'm cut from the same cloth.

Following the coastline of a lake, I watch how wind picks up water in dark blasts and drops it again. Ducks glide in Vs away from me, out onto the fractured, darkening mirror. I stop. A hatch of mayflies powders the air and the archaic, straight-winged dragonflies hang, blunt-nosed, above me. A friend talks about aquatic bugs: water beetles, spinners, assassin bugs, and one that hatches, mates, and dies in a total life-span of two hours. At the end of the meadow, the lake drains into a fast-moving creek. I quicken my pace and trudge upward. Walking is also an ambulation of mind. The human armor of bones rattles, fat rolls, and inside this durable, fleshy prison of mine, I make a beeline toward otherness, lightness, or, maybe like a moth, toward flame. 4

Somewhere along the trail I laugh out loud. How shell-like the body seems suddenly—not fleshy at all, but inhuman and hard. And farther up, I step out of my body though I'm still held fast by something, but what? I don't know. 5

How foolish the preparations for wilderness trips seem now. We pore over our maps, chart our expeditions. We "gear up" at trailheads with pitons and crampons, horsepacks and back-packs, fly rods and cameras, forgetting the meaning of simply going, of lifting thought-covers, of disburdenment. I look up from these thoughts. A blue heron rises from a gravel bar and glides behind a gray screen of dead trees, appears in an opening where an avalanche downed pines, and lands again on water. 6

I stop to eat lunch. Ralph Waldo Emerson wrote, "The Gautama said that the first men ate the earth and found it sweet." I eat baloney and cheese and think about eating the earth. It's another way of framing our wonder in which the width of the mouth stands for the generous palate of consciousness. I cleanse my palate with miner's lettuce and stream water and try to imagine what kinds of sweetness the earth provides: the taste of glacial flour, or the mineral taste of basalt, the fresh and foul 7 bouquets of rivers, the desiccated, stinging flavor of a snow-storm—like eating red ants, my friend says.

8   As I begin to walk again it occurs to me that this notion of "eating the earth" is not about gluttony, hedonism, or sin, but, rather, unconditional love. Everywhere I look I see the possibility of love. To find wildness, I must first offer myself up, accept all that comes before me: a bullfrog breathing hard on a rock; moose tracks under elk scats; a cloud that looks like a clothespin; a seep of water from a high cirque, black on brown rock, draining down from the brain of the world.

9   At tree line, birdsong stops. I'm lifted into another move-ment of music, one with no particular notes, only windsounds becoming watersounds, becoming windsounds. Above, a corn-ice crowns a ridge and melts into a teal and turquoise lake, like a bladder leaking its wine.

10   On top of Marston Pass I'm in a ruck of steep valleys and gray, treeless peaks. The alpine carpet, studded with red paint-brush and alpine buttercups, gives way to rock. Now all the way across a vertiginous valley, I see where water oozes from moss and mud, how, at its source, it quickly becomes something else.

11   Emerson also said: "Every natural fact is an emanation, and that from which it emanates is an emanation also, and from every emanation is a new emanation." The ooze, the source of a great river, is now a white chute tumbling over soft folds of conglomerate rock—brown bellies. Now wind tears at it, throwing sheets of water to another part of the mountainside; soft earth gives way under my feet, clouds spill upward and spit rain. Isn't everything redolent with loss, with momentary ra-diance, a coming to different ground? Stone basins catch the waterfall, spill it again, like thoughts strung together, laddered down.

12   I see where meltwater is split by a rock—half going west to the Pacific, the other going east to the Atlantic, for this is the Continental Divide. Down the other side the air I gulp feels softer. Ice spans and tunnels the creek, then, when night comes but before the full moon, falling stars have the same look as that white chute of water, falling against the rock of night.

13   To rise above tree line is to go above thought and after, the

descent back into birdsong, bog orchids, willows, and firs, is to sink into the preliterate parts of ourselves. It is to forget discontent, undisciplined needs. Here the world is only space, raw loneliness, green valleys hung vertically. Losing myself to it— if I can—I do not fall . . . or, if I do, I'm only another cataract of water.

Wildness has no conditions, no sure routes, no peaks or 14 goals, no source that is not instantly becoming something more than itself, then letting go of that, always becoming. It cannot be stripped of its complexity by CAT scan or telescope. Rather, it is a many-pointed truth, almost a bluntness, a sudden essence like the wild strawberries strung along the ground on scarlet runners under my feet. Wildness is source and fruition at once, as if every river circled round, the mouth eating the tail—and the tail, the source.

Now I am camped among trees again. Four yearling moose, 15 their chestnut coats shiny from a summer's diet of willow shoots, tramp past my bedroll and drink from a spring that issues sulfurous water. The ooze, the white chute, the narrow stream—now almost a river—joins this small spring and slows into skinny oxbows and deep pools before breaking again on rock, a stepladder of sequined riffles.

To trace the history of a river, or a raindrop, as John Muir 16 would have done, is also to trace the history of the soul, the history of the mind descending and arising in the body. In both, we constantly seek and stumble on divinity, which, like the cornice feeding the lake and the spring becoming a waterfall, feeds, spills, falls, and feeds itself over and over again.

QUESTIONS ON SUBJECT AND PURPOSE

1. Literally, what event does Ehrlich describe in the essay?

2. How does this description differ from what you might expect in a description of a journey?

3. What purpose might Ehrlich have in writing the essay?

QUESTIONS ON STRATEGY AND AUDIENCE

1. How does the metaphor of a "journey" or a search for origins structure the essay?

2. What is the difference between "wilderness" and "wildness"? Check the two words in a dictionary.

3. This essay appeared in a Sierra Club wilderness wall calendar. How might the place of publication influence the essay?

QUESTIONS ON VOCABULARY AND STYLE

1. As Ehrlich makes her way up and then back down the mountain, how does her description of the river (and the bodies of water along the way) change?

2. In what possible way does anyone "eat the earth" (paragraphs 7 and 8)?

3. Be prepared to define the following words: *purchase* (paragraph 2), *articulation* (2), *verdant* (3), *ambulation* (4), *disburdenment* (6), *palate* (7), *desiccated* (7), *hedonism* (8), *cirque* (8), *cornice* (9), *teal* (9), *ruck* (10), *vertiginous* (10), *emanation* (11), *redolent* (11), *yearling* (15), *oxbow* (15), *riffle* (15).

WRITING SUGGESTIONS

1. Look around your room, refrigerator, apartment, home, or yard and find a living or organic object. In a paragraph, describe what you see. Spend time "seeing" and studying the object before you begin to write.

2. Nature can be seen and interpreted in many ways. Select a landscape or a natural event and in an essay describe it to your reader in such a way as to reveal a significance other than just scientific or photographic reality.

   Prewriting:

   a. Make a list of possible subjects—a thunderstorm, a park, a hurricane, a clear night, a fog, a bed of flowers. Try to select something that you can directly experience.

   b. Next to each subject, write down what you see as "revealed" in each—for example, indifference, benevolence, or hostility toward man.

   c. Select two of the most promising subjects and make a list of possible descriptive details to use. Remember that each detail needs to be connected with the significance that you are trying to convey.

Rewriting:

a. Check to make sure that you have used vivid nouns and verbs to carry most of the descriptive burden. Do not use too many adjectives and adverbs.

b. Go through your essay and underline every descriptive detail. Are there too many? Are you trying to make the reader see too much? Are all of the details related to the significance that you are trying to reveal.

c. Have you been too heavy-handed in emphasizing the significance that you see? Remember you are trying to reveal significance, you are not lecturing your reader on the significance.

3. Read each of the six selections in this chapter. Then using the six as examples of descriptive writing, write an essay telling a reader how to write a description. You might imagine that your essay will be distributed in freshman English classes this semester as a guide to writing a descriptive essay.

The Inheritance of Tools

SCOTT RUSSELL SANDERS

Born in Memphis, Tennessee, in 1945, Sanders graduated from Brown University and received a Ph.D. from Cambridge University. Currently a professor of English at Indiana University, Sanders is a novelist, an essayist, a science fiction writer, and a teller of tales. His diverse accomplishments include D. H. Lawrence: The World of Five Novels *(1974);* Wilderness Plots: Tales about the Settlement of the American Land *(1983);* Fetching the Dead *(1984), a collection of stories;* Stone Country *(1985);* Hear the Wind Blow: American Folksongs Retold *(1985); and a number of novels for children and adolescents including* Bad Man Ballad *(1986),* The Engineer of Beasts *(1988), and* Aurora Means Dawn *(1989). In 1987 he wrote* The Paradise of Bombs, *an autobiographical work about his own spiritual growth and his appreciation of nature and family, despite having grown up on a weapons storage base. In this personal essay, occasioned by his father's death, Sanders explores the "inheritance" that adheres to four tools passed through four generations of his family.*

1   AT JUST ABOUT THE HOUR when my father died, soon after dawn one February morning when ice coated the windows like cataracts, I banged my thumb with a hammer. Naturally I swore at the hammer, the reckless thing, and in the moment of swearing I thought of what my father would say: "If you'd try hitting the nail it would go in a whole lot faster. Don't you know your thumb's not as hard as that hammer?" We both were doing carpentry that day, but far apart. He was building cupboards at my brother's place in Oklahoma; I was at home in Indiana putting up a wall in the basement to make a bedroom for my daughter. By the time my mother called with news of his death—the long distance wires whittling her voice until it seemed too thin to bear the weight of what she had to say— my thumb was swollen. A week or so later a white scar in the shape of a crescent moon began to show above the cuticle, and

month by month it rose across the pink sky of my thumbnail. It took the better part of a year for the scar to disappear, and every time I noticed it I thought of my father.

The hammer had belonged to him, and to his father before him. The three of us have used it to build houses and barns and chicken coops, to upholster chairs and crack walnuts, to make doll furniture and book shelves and jewelry boxes. The head is scratched and pockmarked, like an old plowshare that has been working rocky fields, and it gives off the sort of dull sheen you see on fast creek water in the shade. It is a finishing hammer, about the weight of a bread loaf, too light, really, for framing walls, too heavy for cabinetwork, with a curved claw for pulling nails, a rounded head for pounding, a fluted neck for looks, and a hickory handle for strength.

The present handle is my third one, bought from a lumberyard in Tennessee down the road from where my brother and I were helping my father build his retirement house. I broke the previous one by trying to pull sixteen-penny nails out of floor joists—a foolish thing to do with a finishing hammer, as my father pointed out. "You ever hear of a crowbar?" he said. No telling how many handles he and my grandfather had gone through before me. My grandfather used to cut down hickory trees on his farm, saw them into slabs, cure the planks in his hayloft, and carve handles with a drawknife. The grain in hickory is crooked and knotty, and therefore rough, hard to split, like the grain in the two men who owned this hammer before me.

After proposing marriage to a neighbor girl, my grandfather used this hammer to build a house for his bride on a stretch of river bottom in northern Mississippi. The lumber for the place, like the hickory for the handle, was cut on his own land. By the day of the wedding he had not quite finished the house, and so right after the ceremony he took his wife home and put her to work. My grandmother had worn her Sunday dress for the wedding, with a fringe of lace tacked on around the hem in honor of the occasion. She removed this lace and folded it away before going out to help my grandfather nail siding on the house. "There she was in her good dress," he told me some fifty-odd years after that wedding day, "holding up them long

171

pieces of clapboard while I hammered, and together we got the place covered up before dark.'' As the family grew to four, six, eight, and eventually thirteen, my grandfather used this hammer to enlarge his house room by room, like a chambered nautilus expanding his shell.

5   By and by the hammer was passed along to my father. One day he was up on the roof of our pony barn nailing shingles with it, when I stepped out the kitchen door to call him for supper. Before I could yell, something about the sight of him straddling the spine of that roof and swinging the hammer caught my eye and made me hold my tongue. I was five or six years old, and the world's commonplaces were still news to me. He would pull a nail from the pouch at his waist, bring the hammer down, and a moment later the *thunk* of the blow would reach my ears. And that is what had stopped me in my tracks and stilled my tongue, that momentary gap between seeing and hearing the blow. Instead of yelling from the kitchen door, I ran to the barn and climbed two rungs up the ladder—as far as I was allowed to go—and spoke quietly to my father. On our walk to the house he explained that sound takes time to make its way through air. Suddenly the world seemed larger, the air more dense, if sound could be held back like any ordinary traveler.

6   By the time I started using this hammer, at about the age when I discovered the speed of sound, it already contained houses and mysteries for me. The smooth handle was one my grandfather had made. In those days I needed both hands to swing it. My father would start a nail in a scrap of wood, and I would pound away until I bent it over.

7   ''Looks like you got ahold of some of those rubber nails,'' he would tell me. ''Here, let me see if I can find you some stiff ones.'' And he would rummage in a drawer until he came up with a fistful of more cooperative nails. ''Look at the head,'' he would tell me. ''Don't look at your hands, don't look at the hammer. Just look at the head of that nail and pretty soon you'll learn to hit it square.''

8   Pretty soon I did learn. While he worked in the garage cutting dovetail joints for a drawer or skinning a deer or tuning an engine, I would hammer nails. I made innocent blocks of

wood look like porcupines. He did not talk much in the midst of his tools, but he kept up a nearly ceaseless humming, slipping in and out of a dozen tunes in an afternoon, often running back over the same stretch of melody again and again, as if searching for a way out. When the humming did cease, I knew he was faced with a task requiring great delicacy or concentration, and I took care not to distract him.

He kept scraps of wood in a cardboard box—the ends of two-by-fours, slabs of shelving and plywood, odd pieces of molding—and everything in it was fair game. I nailed scraps together to fashion what I called boats or houses, but the results usually bore only faint resemblance to the visions I carried in my head. I would hold up these constructions to show my father, and he would turn them over in his hands admiringly, speculating about what they might be. My cobbled-together guitars might have been alien spaceships, my barns might have been models of Aztec temples, each wooden contraption might have been anything but what I had set out to make. ₉

Now and again I would feel the need to have a chunk of wood shaped or shortened before I riddled it with nails, and I would clamp it in a vise and scrape at it with a handsaw. My father would let me lacerate the board until my arm gave out, and then he would wrap his hand around mine and help me finish the cut, showing me how to use my thumb to guide the blade, how to pull back on the saw to keep it from binding, how to let my shoulder do the work. ₁₀

"Don't force it," he would say, "just drag it easy and give the teeth a chance to bite." ₁₁

As the saw teeth bit down, the wood released its smell, each kind with its own fragrance, oak or walnut or cherry or pine— usually pine because it was the softest, easiest for a child to work. No matter how weathered and gray the board, no matter how warped and cracked, inside there was this smell waiting, as of something freshly baked. I gathered every smidgen of sawdust and stored it away in coffee cans, which I kept in a drawer of the workbench. When I did not feel like hammering nails I would dump my sawdust on the concrete floor of the garage and landscape it into highways and farms and towns, running miniature cars and trucks along miniature roads. Looming as ₁₂

huge as a colossus, my father worked over and around me, now and again bending down to inspect my work, careful not to trample my creations. It was a landscape that smelled dizzyingly of wood. Even after a bath my skin would carry the smell, and so would my father's hair, when he lifted me for a bedtime hug.

13　I tell these things not only from memory but also from recent observation, because my own son now turns blocks of wood into nailed porcupines, dumps cans full of sawdust at my feet and sculpts highways on the floor. He learns how to swing a hammer from the elbow instead of the wrist, how to lay his thumb beside the blade to guide a saw, how to tap a chisel with a wooden mallet, how to mark a hole with an awl before starting a drill bit. My daughter did the same before him, and even now, on the brink of teenage aloofness, she will occasionally drag out my box of wood scraps and carpenter something. So I have seen my apprenticeship to wood and tools reenacted in each of my children, as my father saw his own apprenticeship renewed in me.

14　The saw I use belonged to him, as did my level and both of my squares, and all four tools had belonged to his father. The blade of the saw is the bluish color of gun barrels, and the maple handle, dark from the sweat of hands, is inscribed with curving leaf designs. The level is a shaft of walnut two feet long, edged with brass and pierced by three round windows in which air bubbles float in oil-filled tubes of glass. The middle window serves for testing if a surface is horizontal, the others for testing if a surface is plumb or vertical. My grandfather used to carry this level on the gun-rack behind the seat in his pickup, and when I rode with him I would turn around to watch the bubbles dance. The larger of the two squares is called a framing square, a flat steel elbow, so beat up and tarnished you can barely make out the rows of numbers that show how to figure the cuts on rafters. The smaller one is called a try square, for marking right angles, with a blued steel blade for the shank and a brass-faced block of cherry for the head.

15　I was taught early on that a saw is not to be used apart from a square: "If you're going to cut a piece of wood," my father insisted, "you owe it to the tree to cut it straight."

Long before studying geometry, I learned there is a mystical 16
virtue in right angles. There is an unspoken morality in seeking
the level and the plumb. A house will stand, a table will bear
weight, the sides of a box will hold together only if the joints
are square and the members upright. When the bubble is lined
up between two marks etched in the glass tube of a level, you
have aligned yourself with the forces that hold the universe
together. When you miter the corners of a picture frame, each
angle must be exactly forty-five degrees, as they are in the perfect triangles of Pythagoras, not a degree more or less. Otherwise
the frame will hang crookedly, as if ashamed of itself and of its
maker. No matter if the joints you are cutting do not show.
Even if you are butting two pieces of wood together inside a
cabinet, where not one except a wrecking crew will ever see
them, you must take pains to insure that the ends are square
and the studs are plumb.

I took pains over the wall I was building on the day my 17
father died. Not long after that wall was finished—paneled with
tongue-and-groove boards of yellow pine, the nail holes filled
with putty and the wood all stained and sealed—I came close
to wrecking it one afternoon when my daughter ran howling
up the stairs to announce that her gerbils had escaped from
their cage and were hiding in my brand new wall. She could
hear them scratching and squeaking behind her bed. Impossible! I said. How on earth could they get inside my drum-tight
wall? Through the heating vent, she answered. I went downstairs, pressed my ear to the honey-colored wood, and heard
the *scritch scritch* of tiny feet.

"What can we do?" my daughter wailed. "They'll starve 18
to death, they'll die of thirst, they'll suffocate."

"Hold on," I shouted, "I'll think of something." 19

While I thought and she fretted, the radio on her bedside 20
table delivered us the headlines. Several thousand people had
died in a city in India from a poisonous cloud that had leaked
overnight from a chemical plant. A nuclear-powered submarine
had been launched. Rioting continued in South Africa. An airplane had been hijacked in the Mediterranean. Authorities cal-
culated that several thousand homeless people slept on the
streets within sight of the Washington Monument. I felt my

usual helplessness in face of all these calamities. But here was my daughter weeping because her gerbils were holed up in a wall. This calamity I could handle.

21   "Don't worry," I told her. "We'll set food and water by the heating vent and lure them out. And if that doesn't do the trick, I'll tear the wall apart until we find them."

22   She stopped crying and gazed as me. "You'd really tear it apart? Just for my gerbils? The *wall*?" Astonishment slowed her down only for a second, however, before she ran to the workbench and began tugging at drawers, saying, "Let's see, what'll we need? Crowbar. Hammer. Chisels. I hope we don't have to use them—but just in case."

23   We didn't need the wrecking tools. I never had to assault my handsome wall, because the gerbils eventually came out to nibble at a dish of popcorn. But for several hours I studied the tongue-and-groove skin I had nailed up on the day of my father's death, considering where to begin prying. There were no gaps in that wall, no crooked joints.

24   I had botched a great many pieces of wood before I mastered the right angle with a saw, botched even more before I learned to miter a joint. The knowledge of these things resides in my hands and eyes and the webwork of muscles, not in the tools. There are machines for sale—powered miter boxes and radial-arm saws, for instance—that will enable any casual soul to cut proper angles in boards. The skill is invested in the gadget instead of the person who uses it, and this is what distinguishes a machine from a tool. If I had to earn my keep by making furniture or building houses, I suppose I would buy powered saws and pneumatic nailers; the need for speed would drive me to it. But since I carpenter only for my own pleasure or to help neighbors or to remake the house around the ears of my family, I stick with hand tools. Most of the ones I own were given to me by my father, who also taught me how to wield them. The tools in my work-bench are a double inheritance, for each hammer and level and saw is wrapped in a cloud of knowing.

25   All of these tools are a pleasure to look at and to hold. Merchants would never paste NEW NEW NEW! signs on them in stores. Their designs are old because they work, because they

serve their purpose well. Like folksongs and aphorisms and the grainy bits of language, these tools have been pared down to essentials. I look at my claw hammer, the distillation of a hundred generations of carpenters, and consider that it holds up well beside those other classics—Greek vases, Gregorian chants, *Don Quixote*, barbed fish hooks, candles, spoons. Knowledge of hammering stretches back to the earliest humans who squatted beside fires chipping flints. Anthropologists have a lovely name for those unworked rocks that served as the earliest hammers. *Dawn stones*, they are called. Their only qualification for the work, aside from hardness, is that they fit the hand. Our ancestors used them for grinding corn, tapping awls, smashing bones. From dawn stones to this claw hammer is a great leap in time, but no great distance in design or imagination.

On that iced-over February morning when I smashed my thumb 26
with the hammer, I was down in the basement framing the wall that my daughter's gerbils would later hide in. I was thinking of my father, as I always did whenever I built anything, thinking how he would have gone about the work, hearing in memory what he would have said about the wisdom of hitting the nail instead of my thumb. I had the studs and plates nailed together all square and trim, and was lifting the wall into place when the phone rang upstairs. My wife answered, and in a moment she came to the basement door and called down softly to me. The stillness in her voice made me drop the framed wall and hurry upstairs. She told me my father was dead. Then I heard the details over the phone from my mother. Building a set of cupboards for my brother in Oklahoma, he had knocked off work early the previous afternoon because of cramps in his stomach. Early this morning, on his way into the kitchen of my brother's trailer, maybe going for a glass of water, so early that no one else was awake, he slumped down on the linoleum and his heart quit.

For several hours I paced around inside my house, upstairs 27
and down, in and out of every room, looking for the right door to open and knowing there was no such door. My wife and children followed me and wrapped me in arms and backed away again, circling and staring as if I were on fire. Where was

177

the door, the door, the door? I kept wondering. My smashed thumb turned purple and throbbed, making me furious. I wanted to cut if off and rush outside and scrape away the snow and hack a hole in the frozen earth and bury the shameful thing.

28   I went down into the basement, opened a drawer in my workbench, and stared at the ranks of chisels and knives. Oiled and sharp, as my father would have kept them, they gleamed at me like teeth. I took up a clasp knife, pried out the longest blade and tested the edge on the hair of my forearm. A tuft came away cleanly, and I saw my father testing the sharpness of tools on his own skin, the blades of axes and knives and gouges and hoes, saw the red hair shaved off in patches from his arms and the backs of his hands. "That will cut bear," he would say. He never cut a bear with his blades, now my blades, but he cut deer, dirt, wood. I closed the knife and put it away. Then I took up the hammer and went back to work on my daughter's wall, snugging the bottom plate against a chalkline on the floor, shimming the top plate against the joists overhead, plumbing the studs with my level, making sure before I drove the first nail that every line was square and true.

QUESTIONS ON SUBJECT AND PURPOSE

1. What is the subject of Sanders's essay? Is it tools? His father's death?
2. Is Sanders's father or grandfather (or his children) ever described in the story? How are they revealed to the reader?
3. What "door" (paragraph 27) is Sanders searching for?
4. What exactly has Sanders inherited from his father?

QUESTIONS ON STRATEGY AND AUDIENCE

1. How does Sanders use time to structure his essay? Is the story told in chronological order?
2. What is the function of each of the following episodes or events in the essay?
   a. The sore thumb
   b. "A mystical virtue in right angles" (paragraph 16)
   c. The wall he was building

3. What expectations does Sanders seem to have about his audience?

QUESTIONS ON VOCABULARY AND STYLE

1. How much dialogue does Sanders use in the story? What does the dialogue contribute?
2. Throughout the essay, Sanders makes use of many effective similes and metaphors. Make a list of six such devices. What does each contribute to the essay? How fresh and arresting are these images?
3. Be able to define each of the following words or phrases: *plowshare* (paragraph 2), *sixteen-penny nails* (3), *chambered nautilus* (4), *rummage* (7), *lacerate* (10), *smidgen* (12), *plumb* (14), *miter* (24), *aphorisms* (25), *shimming* (28).

WRITING SUGGESTIONS

1. Study the childhood scenes or episodes that Sanders includes in his essay—for example, calling his father to supper (paragraph 5), hammering nails (6–9), landscaping with sawdust (12). Notice how Sanders re-creates sensory experiences. Then in a paragraph re-create a similar experience from your childhood. Remember to evoke sensory impressions for your reader—a sight, a sound, a smell, a touch.
2. Think about a skill, talent, or even a habit that you have learned from or share with a family member. In addition to the ability or trait, what else have you "inherited"? How does it affect your life? In an essay describe the inheritance and its effect on you.

Prewriting:

a. Divide a piece of paper into two columns. In the left-hand column, make a list of possible subjects. Work on the list over a period of several days. In the space to the right of this list jot down the significance that you see in such an inheritance.

b. Select one of the items from your list and freewrite for 15 minutes. Concentrate on the significance of this ability or trait in your life. How has it shaped or altered your life, your perceptions? Reread what you have just written. Then freewrite for another 15 minutes.

179

c. Like Sanders, you will be dealing with two "times" in the essay—your childhood and your present. Notice how Sanders manipulates time in his essay. He does not narrate the story in a strict chronological sequence. Experiment with time as an organizational strategy in your essay. Outline two or more structures for the essay.

Rewriting:

a. Check your essay to see if you have used vivid verbs and concrete nouns. Watch that you do not overwork adjectives and adverbs.

b. Did you include dialogue in your essay? If not, try adding some. Remember, though, that dialogue slows the pace of a story. Do not overuse it.

c. Look carefully at your conclusion. You want to end forcefully; you want to emphasize the significance of your inheritance. Reread your essay several times and then try freewriting a new conclusion. Try for a completely new ending. If you are using a peer reader, ask that reader to judge both conclusions.

3. The passing on of traditional crafts or skills is an important part of cultural tradition. Choose a society that interests you, and find a particular craft that is preserved from one generation to another. It might also be something that has been preserved in your family's religious or ethnic heritage. In a research paper, document the nature of the craft and the methods by which the culture ensures its transmission. What is important about this craft? What does it represent to that society? Why bother to preserve it?

A Writer's Revision Process:
The Way to Rainy Mountain

N. SCOTT MOMADAY

N(avarre) Scott Momaday was born in Lawton, Oklahoma, in 1934. He earned a B.A. from the University of New Mexico and a Ph.D. in English from Stanford University. A professor of English, artist, editor, poet, and novelist, N. Scott Momaday is a frequent contributor to The New York Times *and other periodicals. His work includes a book of Kiowa Indian folktales,* The Journey of Tai-me *(1967), which he revised as* The Way to Rainy Mountain *(1969); the Pulitzer Prize-winning novel,* House Made of Dawn *(1968);* Angle of Geese and Other Poems *(1974); a children's book,* The Gourd Dancer *(1976), which he illustrated himself; a book of tribal tales, childhood memories, and genealogies,* The Names: A Memoir *(1976); and* The Ancient Child *(1989). He also edited* The Complete Poems of Frederick Goddard Tuckerman *(1965) and* American Indian Authors *(1971). This essay originally appeared in the magazine* The Reporter *in 1967, but Momaday revised it and used it as the introduction to his book* The Way to Rainy Mountain. *Returning to Oklahoma to visit the grave of his grandmother, Momaday uses the occasion to reflect upon the migration of his people, the Kiowas, from the high country of western Montana to the plains of Oklahoma. "To look upon that landscape in the early morning," writes Momaday, "with the sun at your back, is to lose the sense of proportion. Your imagination comes to life, and this, you think, is where Creation was begun."*

REVISED DRAFT

A SINGLE KNOLL rises out of the plain in Oklahoma, north and   1
west of the Wichita Range. For my people, the Kiowas, it is an
old landmark, and they gave it the name Rainy Mountain. The
hardest weather in the world is there. Winter brings blizzards,
hot tornadic winds arise in the spring, and in summer the prairie
is an anvil's edge. The grass turns brittle and brown, and it

cracks beneath your feet. There are green belts along the rivers and creeks, linear groves of hickory and pecan, willow and witch hazel. At a distance in July or August the steaming foliage seems almost to writhe in fire. Great green and yellow grasshoppers are everywhere in the tall grass, popping up like corn to sting the flesh, and tortoises crawl about on the red earth, going nowhere in the plenty of time. Loneliness is an aspect of the land. All things in the plain are isolate; there is no confusion of objects in the eye, but one hill or one tree or one man. To look upon that landscape in the early morning, with the sun at your back, is to lose the sense of proportion. Your imagination comes to life, and this, you think, is where Creation was begun.

2   I returned to Rainy Mountain in July. My grandmother had died in the spring, and I wanted to be at her grave. She had lived to be very old and at last infirm. Her only living daughter was with her when she died, and I was told that in death her face was that of a child.

3   I like to think of her as a child. When she was born, the Kiowas were living the last great moment of their history. For more than a hundred years they had controlled the open range from the Smoky Hill River to the Red, from the headwaters of the Canadian to the fork of the Arkansas and Cimarron. In alliance with the Comanches, they had ruled the whole of the southern Plains. War was their sacred business, and they were among the finest horsemen the world has ever known. But warfare for the Kiowas was preeminently a matter of disposition rather than of survival, and they never understood the grim, unrelenting advance of the U.S. Cavalry. When at last, divided and ill-provisioned, they were driven onto the Staked Plains in the cold rains of autumn, they fell into panic. In Palo Duro Canyon they abandoned their crucial stores to pillage and had nothing then but their lives. In order to save themselves, they surrendered to the soldiers at Fort Sill and were imprisoned in the old stone corral that now stands as a military museum. My grandmother was spared the humiliation of those high gray walls by eight or ten years, but she must have known from birth the affliction of defeat, the dark brooding of old warriors.

4   Her name was Aho, and she belonged to the last culture to

evolve in North America. Her forebears came down from the high country in western Montana nearly three centuries ago. They were a mountain people, a mysterious tribe of hunters whose language has never been positively classified in any major group. In the late seventeenth century they began a long migration to the south and east. It was a journey toward the dawn, and it led to a golden age. Along the way the Kiowas were befriended by the Crows, who gave them the culture and religion of the Plains. They acquired horses, and their ancient nomadic spirit was suddenly free of the ground. They acquired Tai-me, the sacred Sun Dance doll, from that moment the object and symbol of their worship, and so shared in the divinity of the sun. Not least, they acquired the sense of destiny, therefore courage and pride. When they entered upon the southern Plains they had been transformed. No longer were they slaves to the simple necessity of survival; they were a lordly and dangerous society of fighters and thieves, hunters and priests of the sun. According to their origin myth, they entered the world through a hollow log. From one point of view, their migration was the fruit of an old prophecy, for indeed they emerged from a sunless world.

Although my grandmother lived out her long life in the 5 shadow of Rainy Mountain, the immense landscape of the continental interior lay like memory in her blood. She could tell of the Crows, whom she had never seen, and of the Black Hills, where she had never been. I wanted to see in reality what she had seen more perfectly in the mind's eye, and traveled fifteen hundred miles to begin my pilgrimage.

Yellowstone, it seemed to me, was the top of the world, a 6 region of deep lakes and dark timber, canyons and waterfalls. But, beautiful as it is, one might have the sense of confinement there. The skyline in all directions is close at hand, the high wall of the woods and deep cleavages of shade. There is a perfect freedom in the mountains, but it belongs to the eagle and the elk, the badger and the bear. The Kiowas reckoned their stature by the distance they could see, and they were bent and blind in the wilderness.

Descending eastward, the highland meadows are a stairway 7

183

to the plain. In July the inland slope of the Rockies is luxuriant with flax and buckwheat, stonecrop and larkspur. The earth unfolds and the limit of the land recedes. Clusters of trees, and animals grazing far in the distance, cause the vision to reach away and wonder to build upon the mind. The sun follows a longer course in the day, and the sky is immense beyond all comparison. The great billowing clouds that sail upon it are shadows that move upon the grain like water, dividing light. Farther down, in the land of the Crows and Blackfeet, the plain is yellow. Sweet clover takes hold of the hills and bends upon itself to cover and seal the soil. There the Kiowas paused on their way; they had come to the place where they must change their lives. The sun is at home on the plains. Precisely there does it have the certain character of a god. When the Kiowas came to the land of the Crows, they could see the dark lees of the hills at dawn across the Bighorn River, the profusion of light on the grain shelves, the oldest deity ranging after the solstices. Not yet would they veer southward to the caldron of the land that lay below; they must wean their blood from the northern winter and hold the mountains a while longer in their view. They bore Tai-me in procession to the east.

8   A dark mist lay over the Black Hills, and the land was like iron. At the top of a ridge I caught sight of Devil's Tower up-thrust against the gray sky as if in the birth of time the core of the earth had broken through its crust and the motion of the world was begun. There are things in nature that engender an awful quiet in the heart of man; Devil's Tower is one of them. Two centuries ago, because they could not do otherwise, the Kiowas made a legend at the base of the rock. My grandmother said:

Eight children were there at play, seven sisters and their brother. Suddenly the boy was struck dumb; he trembled and began to run upon his hands and feet. His fingers became claws, and his body was covered with fur. Directly there was a bear where the boy had been. The sisters were terrified; they ran, and the bear after them. They came to the stump of a great tree, and the tree spoke to them. It bade them climb upon it, and as they did so it began to rise into the air. The bear came to kill them, but they were just beyond its reach. It

184

reared against the tree and scored the bark all around with its claws.
The seven sisters were borne into the sky, and they became the stars
of the Big Dipper.

From that moment, and so long as the legend lives, the Kiowas
have kinsmen in the night sky. Whatever they were in the
mountains, they could be no more. However tenuous their well-
being, however much they had suffered and would suffer again,
they had found a way out of the wilderness.

My grandmother had a reverence for the sun, a holy regard   *9*
that now is all but gone out of mankind. There was a wariness
in her, and an ancient awe. She was a Christian in her later
years, but she had come a long way about, and she never forgot
her birthright. As a child she had been to the Sun Dances; she
had taken part in those annual rites, and by them she had
learned the restoration of her people in the presence of Tai-me.
She was about seven when the last Kiowa Sun Dance was held
in 1887 on the Washita River above Rainy Mountain Creek.
The buffalo were gone. In order to consummate the ancient
sacrifice—to impale the head of a buffalo bull upon the medicine tree—a delegation of old men journeyed into Texas, there
to beg and barter for an animal from the Goodnight herd. She
was ten when the Kiowas came together for the last time as a
living Sun Dance culture. They could find no buffalo; they had
to hang an old hide from the sacred tree. Before the dance could
begin, a company of soldiers rode out from Fort Sill under orders
to disperse the tribe. Forbidden without cause the essential act
of their faith, having seen the wild herds slaughtered and left
to rot upon the ground, the Kiowas backed away forever from
the medicine tree. That was July 20, 1890, at the great bend of
the Washita. My grandmother was there. Without bitterness,
and for as long as she lived, she bore a vision of deicide.

Now that I can have her only in memory, I see my grand-   *10*
mother in the several postures that were peculiar to her: standing at the wood stove on a winter morning and turning meat
in a great iron skillet; sitting at the south window, bent above
her beadwork, and afterwards, when her vision failed, looking
down for a long time into the fold of her hands; going out upon
a cane, very slowly as she did when the weight of age came

upon her; praying. I remember her most often at prayer. She made long, rambling prayers out of suffering and hope, having seen many things. I was never sure that I had the right to hear, so exclusive were they of all mere custom and company. The last time I saw her she prayed standing by the side of her bed at night, naked to the waist, the light of a kerosene lamp moving upon her dark skin. Her long, black hair, always drawn and braided in the day, lay upon her shoulders and against her breasts like a shawl. I do not speak Kiowa, and I never understood her prayers, but there was something inherently sad in the sound, some merest hesitation upon the syllables of sorrow. She began in a high and descending pitch, exhausting her breath to silence; then again and again—and always the same intensity of effort, of something that is, and is not, like urgency in the human voice. Transported so in the dancing light among the shadows of her room, she seemed beyond the reach of time. But that was illusion; I think I knew then that I should not see her again.

11   Houses are like sentinels in the plain, old keepers of the weather watch. There, in a very little while, wood takes on the appearance of great age. All colors wear soon away in the wind and rain, and then the wood is burned gray and the grain appears and the nails turn red with rust. The windowpanes are black and opaque; you imagine there is nothing within, and indeed there are many ghosts, bones given up to the land. They stand here and there against the sky, and you approach them for a longer time than you expect. They belong in the distance; it is their domain.

12   Once there was a lot of sound in my grandmother's house, a lot of coming and going, feasting and talk. The summers there were full of excitement and reunion. The Kiowas are a summer people; they abide the cold and keep to themselves, but when the season turns and the land becomes warm and vital they cannot hold still; an old love of going returns upon them. The aged visitors who came to my grandmother's house when I was a child were made of lean and leather, and they bore themselves upright. They wore great black hats and bright ample shirts that shook in the wind. They rubbed fat upon their hair and wound their braids with strips of colored cloth. Some of them painted

their faces and carried the scars of old and cherished enmities. They were an old council of warlords, come to remind and be reminded of who they were. Their wives and daughters served them well. The women might indulge themselves; gossip was at once the mark and compensation of their servitude. They made loud and elaborate talk among themselves, full of jest and gesture, fright and false alarm. They went abroad in fringed and flowered shawls, bright beadwork and German silver. They were at home in the kitchen, and they prepared meals that were banquets.

There were frequent prayer meetings, and great nocturnal *13* feasts. When I was a child I played with my cousins outside, where the lamplight fell upon the ground and the singing of the old people rose up around us and carried away into the darkness. There were a lot of good things to eat, a lot of laughter and surprise. And afterwards, when the quiet returned, I lay down with my grandmother and could hear the frogs away by the river and feel the motion of the air.

Now there is a funeral silence in the rooms, the endless *14* wake of some final word. The walls have closed in upon my grandmother's house. When I returned to it in mourning, I saw for the first time in my life how small it was. It was late at night, and there was a white moon, nearly full. I sat for a long time on the stone steps by the kitchen door. From there I could see out across the land; I could see the long row of trees by the creek, the low light upon the rolling plains, and the stars of the Big Dipper. Once I looked at the moon and caught sight of a strange thing. A cricket had perched upon the handrail, only a few inches away from me. My line of vision was such that the creature filled the moon like a fossil. It had gone there, I thought, to live and die, for there, of all places, was its small definition made whole and eternal. A warm wind rose up and purled like the longing within me.

The next morning I awoke at dawn and went out on the *15* dirt road to Rainy Mountain. It was already hot, and the grasshoppers began to fill the air. Still, it was early in the morning, and the birds sang out of the shadows. The long yellow grass on the mountain shone in the bright light, and a scissortail hied above the land. There, where it ought to be, at the end of a long and legendary way, was my grandmother's grave. Here and there on the dark stones were ancestral names. Looking back once, I saw the mountain and came away.

QUESTIONS FOR DISCUSSION

1. What event triggers Momaday's essay?
2. How many "journeys" are involved in Momaday's story?
3. Why might Momaday have titled the essay "The Way to Rainy Mountain"? Why not, for example, refer more specifically to the event that has brought him back?
4. Why might Momaday retell the legend of the "seven sisters" (paragraph 8)? How does that fit into his essay?
5. How much descriptive detail does Momaday give of his grandmother? Go through the essay and isolate each physical detail the reader is given.
6. What expectations might Momaday have of his audience? How might those expectations affect the essay?
7. Be prepared to define the following words: *knoll* (paragraph 1), *writhe* (1), *pillage* (3), *nomadic* (4), *luxuriant* (7), *lees* (7), *solstices* (7), *veer* (7), *tenuous* (8), *deicide* (9), *enmities* (12), *purled* (14), *hied* (15).

NOTE ON EARLIER DRAFT

Between the first appearance of "The Way to Rainy Mountain" in the magazine *The Reporter* in January 1967 and its publication as part of *The Way to Rainy Mountain* (Albuquerque: Univ. of New Mexico Press, 1969), Momaday made one major change. He added what are now paragraphs 6 and 7.

QUESTIONS ON THE REVISION

1. Why might Momaday have decided to add paragraphs 6 and 7? What do they contribute to the essay?
2. What is the effect of these other minor changes that Momaday made?

  a. Final: "They were driven onto the Staked Plains in the cold rains of autumn" (paragraph 3).

  Earlier: "They were driven onto the Staked Plains in the cold of autumn."

  b. Final: "As a child she had been to the Sun Dances; she had taken part in those annual rites" (paragraph 9).

  Earlier: "As a child she had been to the Sun Dances; she had taken part in that annual rite."

  c. Final: "In order to consummate the ancient sacrifice—to impale the head of a buffalo bull upon the medicine tree" (paragraph 9).

  Earlier: "In order to consummate the ancient sacrifice—to impale the head of a buffalo bull upon the Tai-me tree."

WRITING SUGGESTIONS

1. In a substantial paragraph analyze the effects that Momaday achieved by adding paragraphs 6 and 7 to the essay.

2. Momaday once told an interviewer: "I believe that the Indian has an understanding of the physical world and of the earth as a spiritual entity that is his, very much his own. The non-Indian can benefit a good deal by having that perception revealed to him." What do such perceptions reveal to the non-Indian?

Prewriting:

  a. Reread Momaday's essay carefully, looking for evidence of how he perceives the physical world. How does he describe the physical world? What does he seem to "see" in nature? How does his "seeing" differ from that of a scientist?

  b. On the basis of what he says, try to finish the following sentence, "Momaday sees nature as . . . "

  c. Brainstorm about the possible benefits to you from seeing things as Momaday sees them. Try to list a number of possibilities. What might you do differently?

Rewriting:

  a. Look carefully at how you have structured the body of your essay. Probably you either began with the most significant point or ended with it. Would the essay work better if the order were changed?

189

b. Look again at your introduction. Have you begun with something that might catch your reader's attention? Try to avoid beginning with just a thesis statement.

c. Carefully examine every sentence in your essay. Is each a complete sentence? Do the sentences have some variety in both structure and length?

3. Observation of the natural world is central to both Gretel Ehrlich in "A River's Route" (Chapter 3) and Momaday. Compare and contrast how these two writers see the natural world. You can extend your research beyond these two selections by reading other books by the two writers. See the biographical headnotes to each selection for references to their other books.

FOUR

Division
and
Classification

Division and classification are closely related methods of analysis, but you can remember the difference by asking yourself whether you are analyzing a single thing or analyzing two or more things. Division occurs when a single subject is subdivided or dissected into its parts. To list the ingredients in a can of soup or a box of cereal is to perform a division. The key to division is that you begin with a single thing. Gail Sheehy in "Predictable Crises in Adulthood" uses division to mark off six stages that typically occur in the lives of every adult between the ages of eighteen and fifty. Sheehy is not classifying the lives of many adults; she is dividing adulthood in a series of subdivisions or periods. Division is used to show the components of a larger subject; it helps the reader understand a complex whole by considering it in smaller units.

Classification, instead of starting with a single subject and then subdividing it into smaller units, begins with two or more items which are then grouped or classified into categories. Newspapers, for example, contain "classifieds" in which advertisements for the same type of goods or services are grouped or classified together. A classification must have at least two categories. Depending upon how many items you start with and how different they are, you can end up having quite a few categories. You probably remember in at least rough form the taxonomic classification you learned in high school biology. It begins by setting up as many as five kingdoms (animals, plants, monera, fungi, and protista) and then moves downward to increasingly narrower categories (phylum or division, class, order, family, genus, species). Most classifications outside of the sciences are not as precisely and hierarchically defined. Mary Mebane in "Shades of Black," for example, classifies black people on the basis of their skin color ranging from almost white to what she calls "black black." Mebane establishes a classification, not a division, for she starts with many people and then separates them into groups on the basis of a particular feature.

How Do You Choose a Subject?

In choosing your subject for either division or classification, be sure to avoid the obvious approach to the obvious subject. Every teacher has read at some point a classification essay placing teachers into three groups based solely on the grade level at which they teach: elementary school teachers teach in elementary school, middle school teachers teach in middle school, and high school teachers teach in high school. Although the classification is complete and accurate, such a subject and approach are likely to lead you into writing that is boring and simply not worth either your time or your reader's. No subject is inherently bad, but if you choose to write about something common, you need to find an interesting angle from which to approach it. Before you begin to write, answer two questions: first, what is your purpose? and second, will your reader learn something or be entertained by what you plan to write?

How Do You Divide or Classify a Subject?

Since both division and classification involve separation into parts—either dividing a whole into pieces or sorting many things into related groups or categories—you have to find ways in which to divide or group. Those ways can be objective and formal, such as the classification schemes used by biologists, or subjective and informal like Susan Allen Toth's scheme in "Cinematypes." Either way, several things are particularly important.

First, you subdivide or categorize for a reason or a purpose, and your division or classification should be made with that end in mind. Bernard R. Berelson in the "The Value of Children: A Taxonomical Essay," places people's reasons for wanting children into six categories: biological, cultural, political, economic, familial, and personal. His purpose is to explain to the reader the various factors that motivate people to *want* children. The six categories represent the spectrum of reasons why adults *want* children. Berelson does not include, for example, a category labeled "accidental," for such a heading would lie outside of and be irrelevant to his stated purpose.

Second, your division or classification must be complete—you cannot omit pieces or leave items unclassified. How complete your classification needs to be depends upon your purpose. Given the limited purpose that Toth has, it is sufficient to offer just three types of dates. They do not represent all possible dates, but in the comic context of Toth's essay, the three are enough to establish her point. Berelson, on the other hand, sets out to be exhaustive, to isolate all of the reasons people at any time or in any place have wanted children. As a result, he has to include some categories that are essentially irrelevant for most Americans. For example, probably few if any Americans ever want children because of political reasons, that is, because their government encourages them to do so. But in some societies at certain periods of time political reasons have been important. Therefore, Berelson must include that category as well.

Third, the categories or subdivisions you establish need to be parallel in form. In mathematical terms, the categories should share a lowest common denominator. A simple and fairly effective test for parallelism is to see whether your categories are all phrased in similar grammatical terms. Berelson, for example, defines his categories (the reasons for wanting children) in exactly parallel form:

the biological
the cultural
the political
the economic

the familial

the personal

    personal power

    personal competence

    personal status

    personal extension

    personal experience

    personal pleasure

For this reason you should not establish a catch-all category which you label something like "other." When Berelson is finished with his classification scheme, no reasons for wanting children are left unaccounted for; everything fits into one of the six subdivisions.

Finally, your categories or subdivisions should be mutually exclusive; that is, items should belong in only one category. Toth's "cinematypes" cannot be mistaken for one another.

How Do You Structure a Division or Classification Essay?

The body of a division or classification essay will have as many parts as you have subdivisions or categories. Each subdivision or category will probably be treated in a single paragraph or in a group of related paragraphs. Toth, for example, uses a very symmetrical form in her essay: she organizes "Cinematypes" around the three different men with whom she has gone to the movies, treating each date in three paragraphs. Not every essay will be so evenly and perfectly divided. The central portion of Sheehy's "Predictable Crises of Adulthood" covers the six stages of adulthood in sections of varying length.

Once you have decided how many subdivisions or categories you will have and how long each one will be, you still have to decide in what order to arrange those parts or categories. Sometimes you must devise your own order. Toth, for example, could have arranged her "cinematypes" in any order. Nothing in the material itself determines the sequence. However, not all divisions or classifications have the same flexibility in their arrangement. Some invite, or imply, or even demand a particular order. Because she is tracing the chronological development of adults, Sheehy has a built-in order that she has to follow. Her essay would not have made sense if she organized her division in any other way. Similarly, if you were classifying films using the ratings established by the motion pictures industry, you would essentially have to follow the G, PG, PG13, R, NC-17, and X sequence. Although you could begin at either end, it would not make sense to begin with any of the four middle categories.

Having an order underlying your division or classification can be a great help for both you and your reader. It allows you to know where to place each section, dictating the order you will follow. It gives your reader a clear sense of direction. Berelson, for example, in "The Value of Children: A Taxonomical Essay," arranges his reasons why people have children in an order that "starts with chemistry and proceeds to spirit." That is, he deals first with the biological reasons for wanting children and moves finally to the most spiritual of reasons—love.

Sample Student Essay

DIVISION AND CLASSIFICATION

April Lavallee found a subject to divide in another course she was taking. Notice how the division is similar to, but not identical with, a process analysis. April's purpose is not to tell the reader how memory works—such a subject would probably be too complicated for a short paper. Instead, April uses the accepted three-part division of memory to show why we remember some things but not others.

EARLIER DRAFT

Improving Your Memory

While attempting to memorize chapter upon chapter of unlearned material the night before a test, what college student would not want to learn more about the workings of our memory system with the hope, perhaps, of shortening the duration of time required to learn a unit of material? The first step in the process of increasing memory is to learn more about the workings and structures of our memory systems. Although controversial, the information-processing model of memory described here is a widely accepted model of our memory system and its components. This model breaks our memory down into three principal storage structures, each corresponding to a stage of processing of a stimulus. Information about a particular stimulus is entered, or registered, in the first of these structures, known as the Sensory Register, by means of one or more of the five senses. It is held here very briefly—for approximately 250 msec to 2 seconds—in raw sensory form, and eventually decays and vanishes completely. Once recognized, information can pass to the next storage structure—the Short-Term Memory (STM). Information is stored here not as raw sensory data, but as familiar recognizable patterns. By the use of rehearsal, information may be retained here for much

```
longer than in the Sensory Register, but without the
use of this, the information decays just as in the
Sensory Register. Another limitation, in addition to
time, on STM is the amount of material which can be
stored at one time in STM, even with the help of
rehearsal. The generally accepted number of items which
can be held in STM is approximately seven, varying by
two depending upon the individual. According to this
model, increased repetition leads the information to
storage in long—term memory, the third of the storage
structures. This structure is relatively permanent and
contains all of our knowledge about the world. Any
limit on the amount of material this structure is
capable of holding has not been established and is
seemingly nonexistent, seeing that the amount that we
can learn appears to be unlimited. Learning of material
such as this can aid the diligent student in perfecting
memory strategies designed to enhance his memory
capabilities.
```

The strength of April's essay is that it has specific information to convey, information April had available because she was also taking a psychology course that semester. When her classmates had a chance to read her opening sentences on a mimeographed handout, several were anxious to read on— "anything to help with studying," remarked one student. But as soon as April heard that response, she realized a problem. Her opening sentences and her title seem to promise advice on how to improve memory. In fact, the essay analyzes the three divisions that constitute memory. As a result of the students' responses, April decided to rewrite her introduction and conclusion to reflect her real subject. In the process of revising, April decided as well to emphasize the three-part division of memory even more by introducing paragraph divisions into her paper.

REVISED DRAFT

```
              The Structure of Memory

     George Washington was our first President; the
  North defeated the South in the Civil War; the Japanese
```

197

bombed Pearl Harbor during World War II; and the whale is the largest living mammal. These statements have nothing in common except that practically every American knows them. Although they are unimportant to our everyday lives, we can remember facts such as these, but we cannot remember where our keys are when we are late for work. We can recite the Pledge of Allegiance, but we cannot remember the seven digits the telephone operator just gave us. Why is this?

The information-processing model used to describe how our memories work helps explain phenomena such as these. This model defines three principal storage structures, each of which corresponds to a stage in the processing of a stimulus. Information is first entered or registered by means of one or more of the five senses in the Sensory Register. It is held here briefly—for approximately 250 msec to 2 seconds—in raw sensory form, and eventually decays and vanishes completely.

Once the information is recognized it can pass to the next storage structure—the Short-Term Memory (STM). Information is stored here as familiar, recognizable patterns. By the use of rehearsal (forced recall and repetition), information can be retained here for much longer than the Sensory Register. Without rehearsal, though, the information decays just as it does in the Sensory Register. Another limitation, in addition to time, on STM is the amount of material that can be stored here at one time, even with the help of rehearsal. The generally accepted number of items that can be held in STM is seven, plus or minus two depending on the individual.

With increased repetition, information is transferred from STM to Long-Term Memory (LTM), the third of the storage structures. This structure is relatively permanent and contains all of our knowledge about the world. Apparently LTM is unlimited in the amount of information it can hold. The secret to remembering is to get the information into LTM, so next time pay attention and rehearse that telephone number or the location of your keys and sunglasses. Then you won't forget.

Some Things to Remember

1. In choosing a subject for division or classification ask yourself: first, what is my purpose? and second, will my reader learn something or be entertained by my paper?

2. Remember that your subdivision or classification should reflect your purpose—that is, the number of categories or parts is related to what you are trying to do.

3. Make sure that your division or classification is complete. Do not omit any pieces or items. Everything should be accounted for.

4. Take care that the parts or categories be phrased in parallel form.

5. Avoid a category labeled something such as "other" or "miscellaneous."

6. Remember to make your categories or subdivisions mutually exclusive.

7. Once your have established your subdivisions, check to see whether there is an order implied or demanded by your subject.

8. As you move from one subdivision to another, provide markers for the reader so that the parts are clearly labeled.

Everyday Drugs

ADAM SMITH

Adam Smith is the pseudonym of George J. W. Goodman. He was born in 1930 in St. Louis, Missouri, and earned a B.A. from Harvard in 1952, then studied as a Rhodes Scholar at Oxford. Smith has worked as a reporter for Collier's *and* Barron's *associate editor for* Time *and* Fortune, *editor for* Institutional Investor, *contributing editor and vice-president of* New York, *and occasional columnist for* Newsweek. *In 1969, he won the G. M. Loeb Award for his business writing. He was a commentator for* NBC News *and since 1984, he has been host and editor-in-chief of* Adam Smith's Money World. *His books include* The Bubble Makers *(1955),* A Killing in the Market *(1958),* The Wheeler Dealers *(1959),* The Money Game *(1968),* Supermoney *(1972),* Powers of Mind *(1975),* Paper Money *(1981), and* The Roaring Eighties *(1988). Smith has a talent for making business writing lively and entertaining. He has also written the screenplays for* The Wheeler Dealers *(1963) and* The Americanization of Emily *(1964). In this selection from* Powers of Mind, *Smith points to some powerful drugs that are a part of many Americans' everyday diet. "In our society," Smith notes, "there are some drugs we think of as okay drugs, and other drugs make us gasp."*

1 AMERICANS TAKE XANTHINES at the rate of 100 *billion* doses per year. Xanthines are alkaloids which stimulate portions of the cerebral cortex. They give you a "more rapid and clearer flow of thought, allay drowsiness . . . motor activity is increased. There is a keener appreciation of sensory stimuli, and reaction time to them is diminished." This description, again from the pharmacology textbook, is similar to descriptions of cocaine and amphetamine. Of course, the xanthine addict pays a price. He is, says Sir Clifford Allbutt, Regius Professor of Medicine at Cambridge, "subject to fits of agitation and depression; he loses color and has a haggard appearance. The appetite falls off; the heart suffers; it palpitates, or it intermits. As with other such agents, a renewed dose of the poison gives temporary relief, but at the cost of the misery."

Xanthines are generally taken orally through "aqueous ex- 2 tracts" of the plants that produce these alkaloids, either in seeds or leaves. In the United States the three most common methylated xanthines taken are called caffeine, theophyline, and theobromine. The seeds of *Coffea arabica* contain caffeine, the leaves of *Thea sinensis* contain caffeine and theophylline, and the seeds of *Theobroma cacao* contain caffeine and theobromine. In America the three are known as "coffee," "tea" and "cocoa," and they are consumed daily, at the rate of billions of pounds a year. They are generally drunk as hot drinks, but Americans also drink cold drinks containing caffeine from the nuts of the tree *Cola acuminata.* The original drinks ended in the word "cola," but now there are many "colas" which do not bear that name in the title. The early ads for Coca-Cola said it gave you a lift.

Coffee, tea, cocoa and cola drinks are all drugs. Caffeine is 3 a central nervous system stimulant, theophylline less so, and theobromine hardly at all. All xanthines increase the production of urine. Xanthines act on smooth muscles—relaxing, for example, especially in the case of theophylline, bronchi that may have been constricted. LIke the salicylates—aspirin—xanthines can cause stomach irritation. Caffeine can cause sleeplessness, and researchers have found that it causes chromosome breaks.

Maxwell House, meet the Regius Professor of Medicine. Is 4 the stuff good to the last drop, or another dose of the poison? Is it a food, to be sold in supermarkets, or a stimulant to the central nervous system like the amphetamines? "The popularity of the xanthine beverages depends on their stimulant action, although most people are unaware of any stimulation," says the giant pharmacology text.

It is surprising to find substances we think of so cheerfully, 5 perkin' in the pot, listed as drugs. That's the point. In our society, there are some drugs we think of as okay drugs, and other drugs make us gasp. A coffee drinker who drinks coffee all day and cannot function without it is just a heavy coffee drinker, but someone using a non-okay drug is a "drug user" or an "addict."

QUESTIONS ON SUBJECT AND PURPOSE

1. What are xanthines?
2. Why does Smith wait so long to identify the three most commonly used "methylated xanthines"?
3. Is there any shift in Smith's approach to his subject? Characterize any changes you see.

QUESTIONS ON STRATEGY AND AUDIENCE

1. How does Smith structure this selection? Look at both how individual paragraphs are put together and how the group of paragraphs as a whole is structured.
2. Why does Smith have a quotation from Sir Clifford Allbutt? What does it add to his argument? Why quote from a pharmacology textbook?
3. What assumptions does Smith have about his audience? How do those assumptions help shape his remarks?

QUESTIONS ON VOCABULARY AND STYLE

1. Why does Smith use the pharmacological terminology? Why the Latin identifications?
2. What is the effect of mixing scientific terminology with such informal words as *stuff* (paragraph 4), *perkin'* (5), and *okay* (5)?
3. Be able to define the following words: *alkaloids* (paragraph 1), *cerebral cortex* (1), *amphetamine* (1), *haggard* (1), *palpitates* (1), *aqueous* (2), *bronchi* (3), *salicylates* (3).

WRITING SUGGESTIONS

1. Smith does not rigidly classify xanthines, but instead divides them into the three most commonly used forms. Select a common food or beverage and subdivide it into its constituent parts. Contents labels on packages are always a good place to start. Present your subdivision in a paragraph.
2. Americans exhibit widely differing attitudes toward the food they eat, in large part because they have the greatest choice of any people in the world. Some eat regularly at fast-food restaurants; others consume only health foods. In an essay,

classify the American eater. Remember that you should probably have four to six categories.

Prewriting:

a. Establish, through observation, the range of alternatives.
Visit a supermarket and a health food store. Consult the
Yellow Pages for a listing of restaurants. Check food mag-
azines at the local newsstand: Jot down your impressions.
Make sure, though, that you look at food from a variety of
viewpoints. Do not focus just on what appeals to you.

b. Interview someone who has strong feelings about food or
whose food habits are strikingly different from your own.

c. Check back over the list of things to remember at the end
of the introduction to this chapter. Keep that advice in mind
as you plan your essay.

Rewriting:

a. Look at the subheads used in the essays by Sheehy and
Berelson. Did you use a similar strategy to organize your
essay?

b. Since classification essays involve a series of pieces, it is
important to provide adequate links between those sections. Look carefully at how you made the transitions from
one category to another. Compare your links to those used
by Sheehy and Berelson.

c. Are your categories phrased in parallel form? On a separate
sheet of paper, make a short outline of what you have written.

d. Find a peer reader and ask for an honest reaction to your
paper, its organization, and its interest.

3. Americans have become increasingly concerned about the additives put into food. Research the nature of food additives.
How many are there? What do they do? Develop a classification scheme to explain the largest groups or subdivisions.
Be sure to use examples and document your sources.

Cinematypes

SUSAN ALLEN TOTH

Toth's "Up, Up, and Away" is included in Chapter 2, and bio-
graphical information can be found there. In "Cinematypes," orig-
inally published in Harper's, *Toth classifies the men who take her*
to movies: Aaron likes art films; Pete, films with redeeming social
value; and Sam, movies that are entertaining. But her own passion,
Toth confesses, is for Technicolor musicals and films in which "the
men and women always like each other."

1   AARON TAKES ME only to art films. That's what I call them, anyway: strange movies with vague poetic images I don't always
understand. Long dreamy movies about a distant Technicolor
past, even longer black-and-white movies about the general
meaninglessness of life. We do not go unless at least one rep-
utable critic has found the cinematography superb. We went
to the *The Devil's Eye,* and Aaron turned to me in the middle
and said, "My God, this is *funny.*" I do not think he was pleased.

2   When Aaron and I go to the movies, we drive our cars
separately and meet by the box office. Inside the theater he sits
tentatively in his seat, ready to move if he can't see well, poised
to leave if the film is disappointing. He leans away from me,
careful not to touch the bare flesh of his arm against the bare
flesh of mine. Sometimes he leans so far I am afraid he may be
touching the woman on his other side. If the movie is very good,
he leans forward, too, peering between the heads of the couple
in front of us. The light from the screen bounces off his glasses;
he gleams with intensity, sitting there on the edge of his seat,
watching the screen. Once I tapped him on the arm so I could
whisper a comment in his ear. He jumped.

3   After *Belle de Jour* Aaron said he wanted to ask me if he
could stay overnight. "But I can't," he shook his head mourn-
fully before I had a chance to answer, "because I know I never
sleep well in strange beds." Then he apologized for asking. "It's
just that after a film like that," he said, "I feel the need to assert
myself."

Pete takes me only to movies that he thinks have redeeming   4
social value. He doesn't call them "films". They tend to be about
poverty, war, injustice, political corruption, struggling unions
in the 1930s, and the military-industrial complex. Pete doesn't
like propaganda movies, though, and he doesn't like to be too
depressed, either. We stayed away from *The Sorrow and the Pity;*
it would be, he said, just too much. Besides, he assured me,
things are never that hopeless. So most of the movies we see
are made in Hollywood. Because they are always topical, these
movies offer what Pete calls "food for thought." When we saw
Coming Home, Pete's jaw set so firmly with the first half-hour
that I knew we would end up at Poppin' Fresh Pies afterward.

When Pete and I go to the movies, we take turns driving   5
so no one owes anyone else anything. We leave the car far from
the theater so we don't have to pay for parking space. If it's
raining or snowing, Pete offers to let me off at the door, but I
can tell he'll feel better if I go with him while he finds a spot,
so we share the walk too. Inside the theater Pete will hold my
hand when I get scared if I ask him. He puts my hand firmly
on his knee and covers it completely with his own hand. His
knee never twitches. After a while, when the scary part is past,
he loosens his hand slightly and I know that is a signal to take
mine away. He sits companionably close, letting his jacket just
touch my sweater, but he does not infringe. He thinks I ought
to know he is there if I need him.

One night, after *The China Syndrome,* I asked Pete if he   6
wouldn't like to stay for a second drink, even though it was
past midnight. He thought a while about that, considering my
offer from all possible angles, but finally he said no. Relationships today, he said, have a tendency to move too quickly.

Sam likes movies that are entertaining. By that he means   7
movies that Will Jones in the *Minneapolis Tribune* loved and
either *Time* or *Newsweek* rather liked; also movies that do not
have sappy love stories, are not musicals, do not have subtitles,
and will not force him to think. He does not go to movies to
think. He liked *California Suite* and *The Seduction of Joe Tynan,*
though the plots, he said, could have been zippier. He saw it
all coming too far in advance, and that took the fun out. He

205

doesn't like to know what is going to happen. "I just want my brain to be tickled," he says. It is very hard for me to pick out movies for Sam.

8   When Sam takes me to the movies, he pays for everything. He thinks that's what a man ought to do. But I buy my own popcorn, because he doesn't approve of it; the grease might smear his flannel slacks. Inside the theater, Sam makes himself comfortable. He takes of his jacket, puts one arm around me, and all during the movie he plays with my hand, stroking my palm, beating a small tattoo on my wrist. Although he watches the movie intently, his body operates on instinct. Once I inclined my head and kissed him lightly just behind his ear. He beat a faster tattoo on my wrist, quick and musical, but he didn't look away from the screen.

9   When Sam takes me home from the movies, he stands outside my door and kisses me long and hard. He would like to come in, he says regretfully, but his steady girlfriend in Duluth wouldn't like it. When the *Tribune* gives a movie four stars, he has to save it to see with her. Otherwise her feelings might be hurt.

10   I go to some movies by myself. On rainy Sunday afternoons I often sneak into a revival house or a college auditorium for old Technicolor musicals, *Kiss Me Kate, Seven Brides for Seven Brothers, Calamity Jane,* even once, *The Sound of Music.* Wearing saggy jeans so I can prop my feet on the seat in front, I sit toward the rear where no one can see me. I eat large handfuls of popcorn with double butter. Once the movie starts, I feel completely at home. Howard Keel and I are old friends; I grin back at him on the screen. I know the sound tracks by heart. Sometimes when I get really carried away I hum along with Kathryn Grayson, remembering how I once thought I would fill out a formal like that. I am rather glad now I never did. Skirts whirl, feet tap, acrobatic young men perform impossible feats, and then the camera dissolves into a dream sequence I know I can comfortably follow. It is not, thank God, Bergman.

11   If I can't find an old musical, I settle for Hepburn and Tracy, vintage Grant or Gable, on adventurous days Claudette Colbert or James Stewart. Before I buy my ticket I make sure it will all

end happily. If necessary, I ask the girl at the box office. I have never seen *Stella Dallas* or *Intermezzo*. Over the years I have developed other peccadilloes: I will, for example, see anything that is redeemed by Thelma Ritter. At the end of *Daddy Long Legs* I wait happily for the scene when Fred Clark, no longer angry, at last pours Thelma a convivial drink. They smile at each other, I smile at them, I feel they are smiling at me. In the movies I go to by myself, the men and women always like each other.

QUESTIONS ON SUBJECT AND PURPOSE

1. Characterize each of Toth's cinematypes. How is each type revealed?

2. What types of movies does Toth go to alone? What common characteristics do they have?

3. Why does Toth end with the remark: "In the movies I go to by myself, the men and women always like each other"?

QUESTIONS ON STRATEGY AND AUDIENCE

1. Why does Toth begin as she does? Why not give an introductory paragraph? What would be the effect of such a paragraph?

2. Why does Toth end each of the three narrative "types" with a comment on the male-female relationship?

3. Does Toth's essay capture your interest? It is, after all, one person's experiences with three types of film-watchers. Why should we as readers be interested in the essay?

QUESTIONS ON VOCABULARY AND STYLE

1. How does Toth use parallel structures in her essay? How many different types of parallelism can you find? How does each function?

2. How would you characterize the tone of Toth's essay? How is it achieved? Be able to point to at least three different devices or techniques.

3. Be able to define the following words: *tattoo* (paragraph 8), *peccadilloes* (11), *convivial* (11).

WRITING SUGGESTIONS

1. Select a common subject and make a classification scheme. Keep it fairly simple—people who can regularly be found in the cafeteria, types of roommates, types of blind dates. In a paragraph or two present your scheme and give an example of each category.

2. Make a list of a dozen recent films. Check it against newspapers and magazines to make sure that your list is fairly representative. Then, using the list, devise a scheme of classification that includes the films currently being released. You could also do the same thing with books. You might consider writing for one of the following publications:

   a. local newspaper

   b. campus newspaper

   c. national news magazine such as *Time* or *Newsweek*

Prewriting:

   a. Check a metropolitan newspaper. If necessary, do so in your campus library. Most Friday, Saturday, or Sunday editions include brief reviews of the new films. That will help you construct your scheme.

   b. Talk to relatives and friends about recent films as well. That will give you an additional body of information.

   c. Write the relevant pieces of information about each film on index cards. Sort the cards into as many categories as seem appropriate. Remember, however, that you do not want twelve categories, each of which contains a single example. Try to create a scheme that contains three to six categories.

Rewriting:

   a. Look again at how you organized your classification scheme. Why begin with that category? Why end with that one? Complete the following: ''The ordering principle in my essay is _____.''

   b. Since your reader will not have seen every one of these films, you will have to summarize each in a sentence or two. On the other hand, your essay should not consist just of summaries of the films. Make a copy of your paper and highlight in colored pen all of the sentences that summarize plot. Then look at what remains. Have you defined and analyzed the categories as well?

c. Find a peer reader and ask for some honest criticism. Did the reader find the essay interesting? Is the scheme too obvious? Are there enough examples to explain your categories?

3. Find a list of the most popular something, for example, books or films or music. *The Book of Lists* is a good source for such lists, and it can be found in almost any library. Using the list, devise a scheme of classification. Make sure that your categories are clear and separate. Use examples to make the classification vivid and interesting.

Predictable Crises of Adulthood

GAIL SHEEHY

Born in 1937 in Mamaroneck, New York, Gail Sheehy graduated from the University of Vermont with a double major in English and home economics and did graduate study in journalism at Columbia University. She worked as a filmstrip editor, a fashion editor, a feature writer for the New York Herald Tribune, *and a contributing editor for* New York *magazine. She has also contributed articles to* Cosmopolitan, McCall's, Glamour, Good Housekeeping, London Sunday Telegraph, Paris Match, *and* The New York Times Magazine. *Her work includes a novel about the breakup of a marriage,* Lovesounds *(1970);* Panthermania: The Clash of Black Against Black in One American City *(1971);* Speed Is of the Essence *(1971), a collection of articles originally published in* New York *magazine;* Hustling: Prostitution in Our Wide Open Society *(1973);* Passages: The Predictable Crises of Adult Life *(1976);* Pathfinders *(1981);* The Spirit of Survival *(1986);* Character: America's Search for Leadership *(1988), a study of presidential candidates; and* The Man Who Changed the World: The Lives of Mikhail S. Gorbachev *(1990). The following selection is taken from the second chapter of* Passages, *a best-selling book which describes six different stages in adult life. "With each passage from one stage of human growth to the next . . . ," Sheehy writes, "we are left exposed and vulnerable—but also yeasty and embryonic again, capable of stretching in ways we hadn't known before."*

1   WE ARE NOT UNLIKE a particularly hardy crustacean. The lobster grows by developing and shedding a series of hard, protective shells. Each time it expands from within, the confining shell must be sloughed off. It is left exposed and vulnerable until, in time, a new covering grows to replace the old.

2   With each passage from one stage of human growth to the next we, too, must shed a protective structure. We are left exposed and vulnerable—but also yeasty and embryonic again, capable of stretching in ways we hadn't known before. These

sheddings may take several years or more. Coming out of each passage, though, we enter a longer and more stable period in which we can expect relative tranquillity and a sense of equilibrium regained. . . .

As we shall see, each person engages the steps of development in his or her own characteristic *step-style*. Some people never complete the whole sequence. And none of us "solves" with one step—by jumping out of the parental home into a job or marriage, for example—the problems in separating from the caregivers of childhood. Nor do we "achieve" autonomy once and for all by converting our dreams into concrete goals, even when we attain those goals. The central issues or tasks of one period are never fully completed, tied up, and cast aside. But when they lose their primacy and the current life structure has served its purpose, we are ready to move on to the next period.

Can one catch up? What might look to others like listlessness, contrariness, a maddening refusal to face up to an obvious task may be a person's own unique detour that will bring him out later on the other side. Developmental gains won can later be lost—and rewon. It's plausible, though it can't be proven, that the mastery of one set of tasks fortifies us for the next period and the next set of challenges. But it's important not to think too mechanistically. Machines work by units. The bureaucracy (supposedly) works step by step. Human beings, thank God, have an individual inner dynamic that can never be precisely coded.

Although I have indicated the ages when Americans are likely to go through each stage, and the differences between men and women where they are striking, do not take the ages too seriously. The stages are the thing, and most particularly the sequence.

Here is the briefest outline of the developmental ladder.

Pulling Up Roots

Before 18, the motto is loud and clear: "I have to get away from my parents." But the words are seldom connected to action. Generally still safely part of our families, even if away at school, we feel our autonomy to be subject to erosion from moment to moment.

8   After 18, we begin Pulling Up Roots in earnest. College, military service, and short-term travels are all customary vehicles our society provides for the first round trips between family and a base of one's own. In the attempt to separate our view of the world from our family's view, despite vigorous protestations to the contrary—"I know exactly what I want!"—we cast about for any beliefs we can call our own. And in the process of testing those beliefs we are often drawn to fads, preferably those most mysterious and inaccessible to our parents.

9   Whatever tentative memberships we try out in the world, the fear haunts us that we are really kids who cannot take care of ourselves. We cover that fear with acts of defiance and mimicked confidence. For allies to replace our parents, we turn to our contemporaries. They become conspirators. So long as their perspective meshes with our own, they are able to substitute for the sanctuary of the family. But that doesn't last very long. And the instant they diverge from the shaky ideals of "our group," they are seen as betrayers. Rebounds to the family are common between the ages of 18 and 22.

10   The tasks of this passage are to locate ourselves in a peer group role, a sex role, an anticipated occupation, an ideology or world view. As a result, we gather the impetus to leave home physically and the identity to *begin* leaving home emotionally.

11   Even as one part of us seeks to be an individual, another part longs to restore the safety and comfort of merging with another. Thus one of the most popular myths of this passage is: We can piggyback our development by attaching to a Stronger One. But people who marry during this time often prolong financial and emotional ties to the family and relatives that impede them from becoming self-sufficient.

12   A stormy passage through the Pulling Up Roots years will probably facilitate the normal progression of the adult life cycle. If one doesn't have an identity crisis at this point, it will erupt during a later transition, when the penalties may be harder to bear.

The Trying Twenties

13   The Trying Twenties confront us with the question of how to take hold in the adult world. Our focus shifts from the interior

turmoils of late adolescence—"Who am I?" "What is truth?"—
and we become almost totally preoccupied with working out
the externals. "How do I put my aspirations into effect?" "What
is the best way to start?" "Where do I go?" "Who can help
me?" "How did *you* do it?"

In this period, which is longer and more stable compared   14
with the passage that leads to it, the tasks are as enormous as
they are exhilarating: To shape a Dream, that vision of ourselves
which will generate energy, aliveness, and hope. To prepare for
a lifework. To find a mentor if possible. And to form the capacity
for intimacy, without losing in the process whatever consistency
of self we have thus far mustered. The first test structure must
be erected around the life we choose to try.

Doing what we "should" is the most pervasive theme of   15
the twenties. The "shoulds" are largely defined by family
models, the press of the culture, or the prejudices of our peers.
If the prevailing cultural instructions are that one should get
married and settle down behind one's own door, a nuclear
family is born. If instead the peers insist that one should do
one's own thing, the 25-year-old is likely to harness himself
onto a Harley-Davidson and burn up Route 66 in the commitment to have no commitments.

One of the terrifying aspects of the twenties is the inner   16
conviction that the choices we make are irrevocable. It is largely
a false fear. Change is quite possible, and some alteration of our
original choices is probably inevitable.

Two impulses, as always, are at work. One is to build a firm,   17
safe structure for the future by making strong commitments, to
"be set." Yet people who slip into a ready-made form without
much self-examination are likely to find themselves *locked in.*

The other urge is to explore and experiment, keeping any   18
structure tentative and therefore easily reversible. Taken to the
extreme, these are people who skip from one trial job and one
limited personal encounter to another, spending their twenties
in the *transient* state.

Although the choices of our twenties are not irrevocable,   19
they do set in motion a Life Pattern. Some of us follow the
locked-in pattern, others the transient pattern, the wunderkind
pattern, the caregiver pattern, and there are a number of others.

213

Such patterns strongly influence the particular questions raised for each person during each passage. . . .

20   Buoyed by powerful illusions and belief in the power of the will, we commonly insist in our twenties that what we have chosen to do is the one true course in life. Our backs go up at the merest hint that we are like our parents, that two decades of parental training might be reflected in our current actions and attitudes.

21   "Not me," is the motto, "I'm different."

Catch-30

22   Impatient with devoting ourselves to the "shoulds," a new vitality springs from within as we approach 30. Men and women alike speak of feeling too narrow and restricted. They blame all sorts of things, but what the restrictions boil down to are the outgrowth of career and personal choices of the twenties. They may have been choices perfectly suited to that stage. But now the fit feels different. Some inner aspect that was left out is striving to be taken into account. Important new choices must be made, and commitments altered or deepened. The work involves great change, turmoil, and often crisis—a simultaneous feeling of rock bottom and the urge to bust out.

23   One common response is the tearing up of the life we spent most of our twenties putting together. It may mean striking out on a secondary road toward a new vision or converting a dream of "running for president" into a more realistic goal. The single person feels a push to find a partner. The woman who was previously content at home with children chafes to venture into the world. The childless couple reconsiders children. And almost everyone who is married, especially those married for seven years, feels a discontent.

24   If the discontent doesn't lead to a divorce, it will, or should, call for a serious review of the marriage and of each partner's aspirations in their Catch-30 condition. The gist of that condition was expressed by a 29-year-old associate with a Wall Street law firm:

25   "I'm considering leaving the firm. I've been there four years now; I'm getting good feedback, but I have no clients of my own. I feel weak. If I wait much longer, it will be too late, too

close to that fateful time of decision on whether or not to become a partner. I'm success-oriented. But the concept of being 55 years old and stuck in a monotonous job drives me wild. It drives me crazy now, just a little bit. I'd say that 85 percent of the time I thoroughly enjoy my work. But when I get a screwball case, I come away from court saying, 'What am I doing here?' It's a *visceral* reaction that I'm wasting my time. I'm trying to find some way to make a social contribution or a slot in city government. I keep saying, 'There's something more.'"

Besides the push to broaden himself professionally, there is 26 a wish to expand his personal life. He wants two or three more children. "The concept of a home has become very meaningful to me, a place to get away from troubles and relax. I love my son in a way I could not have anticipated. I never could live alone."

Consumed with the work of making his own critical life- 27 steering decisions, he demonstrates the essential shift at this age: an absolute requirement to be more self-concerned. The self has new value now that his competency has been proved.

His wife is struggling with her own age-30 priorities. She 28 wants to go to law school, but he wants more children. If she is going to stay home, she wants him to make more time for the family instead of taking on even wider professional commitments. His view of the bind, of what he would most like from his wife, is this:

"I'd like not to be bothered. It sounds cruel, but I'd like not 29 to have to worry about what she's going to do next week. Which is why I've told her several times that I think she should do something. Go back to school and get a degree in social work or geography or whatever. Hopefully that would fulfill her, and then I wouldn't have to worry about her line of problems. I want her to be decisive about herself."

The trouble with his advice to his wife is that it comes out 30 of concern with *his* convenience, rather than with *her* development. She quickly picks up on this lack of goodwill: He is trying to dispose of her. At the same time, he refuses her the same latitude to be "selfish" in making an independent decision to broaden her own horizons. Both perceive a lack of mutuality. And that is what Catch-30 is all about for the couple.

215

Rooting and Extending

31   Life becomes less provisional, more rational and orderly in the early thirties. We begin to settle down in the full sense. Most of us begin putting down roots and sending out new shoots. People buy houses and become very earnest about climbing career ladders. Men in particular concern themselves with "making it." Satisfaction with marriage generally goes downhill in the thirties (for those who have remained together) compared with the highly valued, vision-supporting marriage of the twenties. This coincides with the couple's reduced social life outside the family and the in-turned focus on raising their children.

The Deadline Decade

32   In the middle of the thirties we come upon a crossroads. We have reached the halfway mark. Yet even as we are reaching our prime, we begin to see there is a place where it finishes. Time starts to squeeze.

33   The loss of youth, the faltering of physical powers we have always taken for granted, the fading purpose of stereotyped roles by which we have thus far identified ourselves, the spiritual dilemma of having no absolute answers—any or all of these shocks can give this passage the character of crisis. Such thoughts usher in a decade between 35 and 45 that can be called the Deadline Decade. It is a time of both danger and opportunity. All of us have the chance to rework the narrow identity by which we defined ourselves in the first half of life. And those of us who make the most of the opportunity will have a full-out authenticity crisis.

34   To come through this authenticity crisis, we must reexamine our purposes and reevaluate how to spend our resources from now on. "Why am I doing all this? What do I really believe in?" No matter what we have been doing, there will be parts of ourselves that have been suppressed and now need to find expression. "Bad" feelings will demand acknowledgment along with the good.

35   It is frightening to step off onto the treacherous footbridge leading to the second half of life. We can't take everything with us on this journey through uncertainty. Along the way, we

discover that we are alone. We no longer have to ask permission because we are the providers of our own safety. We must learn to give ourselves permission. We stumble upon feminine or masculine aspects of our natures that up to this time have usually been masked. There is grieving to be done because an old self is dying. By taking in our suppressed and even our unwanted parts, we prepare at the gut level for the reintegration of an identity that is ours and ours alone—not some artificial form put together to please the culture or our mates. It is a dark passage at the beginning. But by disassembling ourselves, we can glimpse the light and gather our parts into a renewal.

Women sense this inner crossroads earlier than men do. 36 The time pinch often prompts a woman to stop and take an all-points survey at age 35. Whatever options she has already played out, she feels a "my last chance" urgency to review those options she has set aside and those that aging and biology will close off in the *now foreseeable* future. For all her qualms and confusion about where to start looking for a new future, she usually enjoys an exhilaration of release. Assertiveness begins rising. There are so many firsts ahead.

Men, too, feel the time push in the mid-thirties. Most men 37 respond by pressing down harder on the career accelerator. It's "my last chance" to pull away from the pack. It is no longer enough to be the loyal junior executive, the promising young novelist, the lawyer who does a little *pro bono* work on the side. He wants now to become part of top management, to be recognized as an established writer, or an active politician with his own legislative program. With some chagrin, he discovers that he has been too anxious to please and too vulnerable to criticism. He wants to put together his own ship.

During this period of intense concentration on external advancement, it is common for men to be unaware of the more 38 difficult, gut issues that are propelling them forward. The survey that was neglected at 35 becomes a crucible at 40. Whatever rung of achievement he has reached, the man of 40 usually feels stale, restless, burdened, and unappreciated. He worries about his health. He wonders, "Is this all there is?" He may make a series of departures from well established lifelong base lines, including marriage. More and more men are seeking second careers in midlife. Some become self-destructive. And many men in their forties experience a major shift of emphasis away from pouring all their energies into their own advancement. A more tender, feeling side comes into play. They become interested in developing an ethical self.

Renewal or Resignation

39   Somewhere in the mid-forties, equilibrium is regained. A new stability is achieved, which may be more or less satisfying.

40   If one has refused to budge through the midlife transition, the sense of staleness will calcify into resignation. One by one, the safety and supports will be withdrawn from the person who is standing still. Parents will become children; children will become strangers; a mate will grow away or go away; the career will become just a job—and each of these events will be felt as an abandonment. The crisis will probably emerge again around 50. And although its wallop will be greater, the jolt may be just what is needed to prod the resigned middle-ager toward seeking revitalization.

41   On the other hand . . .

42   If we have confronted ourselves in the middle passage and found a renewal of purpose around which we are eager to build a more authentic life structure, these may well be the best years. Personal happiness takes a sharp turn upward for partners who can now accept the fact: "I cannot expect *anyone* to fully understand me." Parents can be forgiven for the burdens of our childhood. Children can be let go without leaving us in collapsed silence. At 50, there is a new warmth and mellowing. Friends become more important than ever, but so does privacy. Since it is so often proclaimed by people past midlife, the motto of this stage might be "No more bullshit."

QUESTIONS ON SUBJECT AND PURPOSE

1. In what senses are these crises "predictable"? What does that word suggest?

2. How sharply drawn—and how ironclad—are Sheehy's divisions? Why?

3. What purpose might Sheehy have in writing?

QUESTIONS ON STRATEGY AND AUDIENCE

1. What is the effect of subdividing the text by using headings?
2. Why might Sheehy choose to use "we" instead of "one" or "he" or "she"?
3. How precisely can you define Sheehy's audience? What features of the selection suggest that definition?

QUESTIONS ON VOCABULARY AND STYLE

1. Why might Sheehy begin with the analogy to the lobster? What is appropriate about that analogy?
2. Why might Sheehy "quote" the response of a 29-year-old in paragraphs 25, 26, and 29?
3. Be prepared to define the following words: *sloughed* (1), *autonomy* (3), *impetus* (10), *wunderkind* (19), *chafes* (23), *visceral* (25), *"pro bono"* (37), *chagrin* (37), *calcify* (40).

WRITING SUGGESTIONS

1. Natural processes, such as the stages of development or of a life cycle, are good examples of how division differs from classification. You are subdividing a whole into a series of parts rather than taking many things and separating them into categories. Select any natural process—perhaps from a course that you are studying this semester or term—and describe in a substantial paragraph or two the various stages or subdivisions in the process.
2. Sheehy begins her division with those older than 18. Drawing on your own life experiences, and those of your friends, construct a division that covers the teenage years. What subdivisions seem common to Americans between the ages of 13 and 18? Write to a teenage audience.

Prewriting:

   a. Take six sheets of blank paper, and on the top of each, write a different age. Then on the page below, list everything that you can think of that happened to you during that year. Work on your sheets over a several-day period.
   b. Brainstorm with a friend or two about the significant moments or events that occurred during those years. Take

notes. Do you see any general patterns beginning to emerge?

c. Reread the Sheehy article. Notice how she establishes her subdivisions, how she characterizes each. As you plan your subdivisions, ask yourself if you have provided similar significant generalizations about each stage.

Rewriting:

a. Look back over your notes from your brainstorming session. Did anyone say something that might be quoted? Notice how Sheehy uses quotations in her text. Try the same device in yours.

b. As a rule of thumb, try for no more than three subdivisions. Remember that Sheehy covered 30 to 35 years in six stages.

c. Look at your introduction. Have you tried to catch your reader's interest? Or have you written a standard thesis introduction ("Teenagers pass through three distinct stages on their way to adulthood")? How would *Time* or *Newsweek* begin a story on this topic?

3. Sheehy stops her division with those aged 50. Obviously, though, adults must continue to develop and change until death. Drawing upon published research and interviews with those over 50, write an essay in which you identify the stages through which mature Americans pass. You might write to an audience of younger people who need to understand the stages through which their parents and grandparents are passing.

Shades of Black

MARY MEBANE

Mary Elizabeth Mebane, novelist, teacher, and civil rights activist, was born in 1933 in Durham, North Carolina. Her father was a farmer, her mother a factory laborer. She received her education at North Carolina State College and at the University of North Carolina, where she earned both her master's and doctoral degrees. Her work has been anthologized in A Galaxy of Black Writers *(1970) and* The Eloquence of Protest *(1972). A play,* Take A Sad Song, *was first produced in 1975. Her writings deal mainly with the black experience in the South and the new consciousness that was born during the years of the civil rights movement. Mebane said: "It is my belief that the black folk are the most creative, viable people that America has produced. They just don't know it." Mebane's most recent and widely acclaimed books are her autobiographies entitled* Mary *(1981) and* Mary, Wayfarer *(1983). Prejudice comes in many forms, and in this selection from* Mary, *Mebane recounts her experiences as a "dark, but not too dark" college student.*

DURING MY FIRST WEEK of classes as a freshman, I was stopped one day in the hall by the chairman's wife, who was indistinguishable in color from a white woman. She wanted to see me, she said.

This woman had no official position on the faculty, except that she was an instructor in English; nevertheless, her summons had to be obeyed. In the segregated world there were (and remain) gross abuses of authority because those at the pinnacle, and even their spouses, felt that the people "under" them had no recourse except to submit—and they were right except that sometimes a black who got sick and tired of it would go to the whites and complain. This course of action was severely condemned by the blacks, but an interesting thing happened—such action always got positive results. Power was thought of in negative terms: I can deny someone something, I can strike at someone who can't strike back, I can ride someone down; that proves I am powerful. The concept of power as a force for good, for affirmative response to people or situations, was not in evidence.

3   When I went to her office, she greeted me with a big smile. "You know," she said, "you made the highest mark on the verbal part of the examination." She was referring to the examination that the entire freshman class took upon entering the college. I looked at her but I didn't feel warmth, for in spite of her smile her eyes and tone of voice were saying, "How could this black-skinned girl score higher on the verbal than some of the students who've had more advantages than she? It must be some sort of fluke. Let me talk to her." I felt it, but I managed to smile my thanks and back off. For here at North Carolina College at Durham, as it had been since the beginning, social class and color were the primary criteria used in determining status on the campus.

4   First came the children of doctors, lawyers, and college teachers. Next came the children of public-school teachers, businessmen, and anybody else who had access to more money than the poor black working class. After that came the bulk of the student population, the children of the working class, most of whom were the first in their families to go beyond high school. The attitude toward them was: You're here because we need the numbers, but in all other things defer to your betters.

5   The faculty assumed that light-skinned students were more intelligent, and they were always a bit nonplussed when a dark-skinned student did well, especially if she was a girl. They had reason to be appalled when they discovered that I planned to do not only well but better than my light-skinned peers.

6   I don't know whether African men recently transported to the New World considered themselves handsome or, more important, whether they considered African women beautiful in comparison with Native American Indian women or immigrant European women. It is a question that I have never heard raised or seen research on. If African men considered African women beautiful, just when their shift in interest away from black black women occurred might prove to be an interesting topic for researchers. But one thing I know for sure: by the twentieth cen-

tury, really black skin on a woman was considered ugly in this country. This was particularly true among those who were exposed to college.

Hazel, who was light brown, used to say to me, "You are *dark*, but not *too* dark." The saved commiserating with the damned. I had the feeling that if nature had painted one more brushstroke on me, I'd have had to kill myself.   7

Black skin was to be disguised at all costs. Since a black face is rather hard to disguise, many women took refuge in ludicrous makeup. Mrs. Burry, one of my teachers in elementary school, used white face powder. But she neglected to powder her neck and arms, and even the black on her face gleamed through the white, giving her an eerie appearance. But she did the best she could.   8

I observed all through elementary and high school that for various entertainments the girls were placed on the stage in order of color. And very black ones didn't get into the front row. If they were past caramel-brown, to the back row they would go. And nobody questioned the justice of these decisions—neither the students nor the teachers.   9

One of the teachers at Wildwood School, who was from the Deep South and was just as black as she could be, had been a strict enforcer of these standards. That was another irony—that someone who had been judged outside the realm of beauty herself because of her skin tones should have adopted them so wholeheartedly and applied them herself without question.   10

One girl stymied that teacher, though. Ruby, a black cherry of a girl, not only got off the back row but off the front row as well, to stand alone at stage center. She could outsing, outdance, and outdeclaim everyone else, and talent proved triumphant over pigmentation. But the May Queen and her Court (and in high school, Miss Wildwood) were always chosen from among the lighter ones.   11

When I was a freshman in high school, it became clear that a light-skinned sophomore girl named Rose was going to get the "best girl scholar" prize for the next three years, and there was nothing I could do about it, even though I knew I was the better. Rose was caramel-colored and had shoulder-length hair. She was highly favored by the science and math teacher, who   12 figured the averages. I wasn't. There was only one prize. There-fore, Rose would get it until she graduated. I was one year behind her, and I would not get it until after she graduated.

13   To be held in such low esteem was painful. It was difficult not to feel that I had been cheated out of the medal, which I felt that, in a fair competition, I perhaps would have won. Being unable to protest or do anything about it was a traumatic ex-perience for me. From then on I instinctively tended to avoid the college-exposed dark-skinned male, knowing that when he looked at me he saw himself and, most of the time, his mother and sister as well, and since he had rejected his blackness, he had rejected theirs and mine.

14   Oddly enough, the lighter-skinned black male did not seem to feel so much prejudice toward the black black woman. It was no accident, I felt, that Mr. Harrison, the eighth-grade teacher, who was reddish-yellow himself, once protested to the science and math teacher about the fact that he always assigned sweeping duties to Doris and Ruby Lee, two black black girls. Mr. Harrison said to them one day, right in the other teacher's presence, "You must be some bad girls. Every day I come down here ya'll are sweeping." The science and math teacher got the point and didn't ask them to sweep anymore.

15   Uneducated black males, too, sometimes related very well to the black black woman. They had been less firmly indoctri-nated by the white society around them and were more securely rooted in their own culture.

16   Because of the stigma attached to having dark skin, a black black woman had to do many things to find a place for herself. One possibility was to attach herself to a light-skinned woman, hoping that some of the magic would rub off on her. A second was to make herself sexually available, hoping to attract a mate. Third, she could resign herself to a more chaste life-style—either (for the professional woman) teaching and work in established churches or (for the uneducated woman) domestic work and zealous service in the Holy and Sanctified churches.

17   Even as a young girl, Lucy had chosen the first route. Lucy was short, skinny, short-haired, and black black, and thus un-acceptable. So she made her choice. She selected Patricia, the lightest-skinned girl in the school, as her friend, and followed

her around. Patricia and her friends barely tolerated Lucy, but Lucy smiled and doggedly hung on, hoping that some who noticed Patricia might notice her, too. Though I felt shame for her behavior, even then I understood.

As is often the case of the victim agreeing with and adopting the attitudes of oppressor, so I have seen it with black black women. I have seen them adopt the oppressor's attitude that they are nothing but "sex machines," and their supposedly superior sexual performance becomes their sole reason for being and for esteeming themselves. Such women learn early that in order to make themselves attractive to men they have somehow to shift the emphasis from physical beauty to some other area— usually sexual performance. Their constant talk is of their desirability and their ability to gratify a man sexually. 18

I knew two such women well—both of them black black. To hear their endless talk of sexual conquests was very sad. I have never seen the category that these women fall into described anywhere. It is not that of promiscuity or nymphomania. It is the category of total self-rejection: "Since I am black, I am ugly, I am nobody. I will perform on the level that they have assigned to me." Such women are the pitiful results of what not only white America but also, and more important, black America has done to them. 19

Some, not taking the sexuality route but still accepting black society's view of their worthlessness, swing all the way across to intense religiosity. Some are staunch, fervent workers in the more traditional Southern churches—Baptist and Methodist— and others are leaders and ministers in the lower status, more evangelical Holiness sects. 20

Another avenue open to the black black woman is excellence in a career. Since in the South the field most accessible to such women is education, a great many of them prepared to become teachers. But here, too, the black black woman had problems. Grades weren't given to her lightly in school, nor were promotions on the job. Consequently, she had to prepare especially well. She had to pass examinations with flying colors or be left behind; she knew that she would receive no special consideration. She had to be overqualified for a job because otherwise she didn't stand a chance of getting it—and she was 21 competing only with other blacks. She had to have something to back her up: not charm, not personality—but training.

22   The black black woman's training would pay off in the 1970's. With the arrival of integration the black black woman would find, paradoxically enough, that her skin color in an integrated situation was not the handicap it had been in an all-black situation. But it wasn't until the middle and late 1960s, when the post-1945 generation of black males arrived on college campuses, that I noticed any change in the situation at all. *He* wore an afro and *she* wore an afro, and sometimes the only way you could tell them apart was when his afro was taller than hers. Black had become beautiful, and the really black girl was often selected as queen of various campus activities. It was then that the dread I felt at dealing with the college-educated black male began to ease. Even now, though, when I have occasion to engage in any type of transaction with a college-educated black man, I gauge his age. If I guess he was born after 1945, I feel confident that the transaction will turn out all right. If he probably was born before 1945, my stomach tightens, I find myself taking shallow breaths, and I try to state my business and escape as soon as possible.

QUESTIONS ON SUBJECT AND PURPOSE

1. What kinds of prejudice and discrimination did Mebane encounter? What were the reasons for that discrimination?
2. How does Mebane mix personal experience with commentary on human behavior? Does the mixture seem to work? What does it add to the selection?
3. What is Mebane's purpose in writing?

QUESTIONS ON STRATEGY AND AUDIENCE

1. How is classification used in the selection? How many classifications are made?
2. How is the selection structured? Make a sketchy outline of the organization. What does it reveal?
3. How does Mebane use examples in her classification scheme? Are there examples for all of the categories? Why or why not?

QUESTIONS ON VOCABULARY AND STYLE

1. How does Mebane describe the shades of black? What types of adjectives, for example, does she use?
2. What is the difference between "established churches" and "Holy and Sanctified churches" (paragraph 16)? Why does Mebane use the capital letters?
3. Be able to define the following words: *fluke* (paragraph 3), *nonplussed* (5), *commiserate* (7), *stymied* (11), *traumatic* (13), *indoctrinated* (15), *chaste* (16), *staunch* (20).

WRITING SUGGESTIONS

1. In a paragraph classify the most obvious prejudices people have. These do not need to be based on color or race—it could be appearance, social or economic class, intelligence, social behavior. Limit your classification to two or three major topics.
2. Have you or a friend ever been classified by someone and discriminated against as a result? In an essay use your experience to show how and why that classification was made. If you have not had this experience, turn the question around. Have you ever classified someone and discriminated against that person as a result?

Prewriting:

a. If you have encountered discrimination, you will probably have a wide range of experiences from which to draw. If you have not, you will need to examine closely your own behavior. Either way, make a list of possible experiences.

b. Remember that prejudices are based on stereotypes that distort, reduce, ridicule. Your essay should expose the inadequacies of such ways of thinking; it should not celebrate any form of discrimination.

c. Once you have gathered examples, you must decide which ones you will include. As you saw in Chapter 1, sometimes one well-developed, appropriate example is enough; other times, a number of examples are necessary. Do not try to include every experience. Decide which ones on your list seem most promising.

d. Try freewriting about each of the examples. Set each of those freewritings aside until it is time to assemble a draft of the complete essay.

227

Rewriting:

a. Remember that your examples should reveal the discrimination at work. Do not just tell your readers; show them. Look carefully at your draft to see if you have made the examples dramatic and vivid enough.

b. In drawing upon your experiences in this way, your essay will probably make use of narrative as well as classification strategies. Look back through Chapter 2 to review the principles of effective narration. See how closely you followed that advice.

c. Once you have a draft of our essay, spend some time re-reading and studying Mebane's essay. Notice how she tells her story, how she reveals prejudice, how she makes transitions from one aspect of the topic to another.

3. Research the problems encountered in interracial, interreligious, or intercultural marriages. What types of prejudice do people encounter? Have they changed in recent years? Classify those problems. You might write to a special audience—for example, couples planning such a marriage.

Faces of the Enemy

SAM KEEN

Sam Keen was raised in Maryville, Tennessee, and graduated from Princeton with a Ph.D. in philosophy. A free-lance writer and lecturer, he was a contributing editor at Psychology Today *and a professor of philosophy at Princeton Theological Seminary and Louisville Presbyterian Seminary, and the Director of the theological program at Esalen Institute, Big Sur, California. He is sometimes called a "vagabond philosopher" because his writing frequently blends psychology, philosophy, and theology. His work includes* Gabriel Marcel *(1967);* Apology for Wonder, *a book about why we remain religious (1969); a collection of personal essays,* To a Dancing God *(1970);* Voices and Visions, *a collection of interviews with various philosophers about the state of contemporary life (1974);* Beginnings Without End *(1976); a co-authored book,* Life Maps: Conversations on the Journey of Faith *(1978); a book about the causes and solutions for a basic human "emotion," boredom,* What to Do When You're Bored and Blue *(1980);* The Passionate Life: Stages of Loving *(1983);* Faces of the Enemy *(1985), made into an award-winning television program which he narrated; and a co-authored book,* Your Mythic Journey *(1989). In* Faces of the Enemy, *he blends psychology and sociology to discuss how paranoia and the "hostile imagination" cast our enemies into stereotypical images of evil. This essay, which first appeared in* Esquire *in 1985, is a synopsis of his book by the same name. "Wars come and go," writes Keen, "the images we use to dehumanize our enemies remain strangely the same."*

THE WORLD, as always, is debating the issues of war and peace. *1* Conservatives believe safety lies in more arms and increased firepower. Liberals place their trust in disarmament and a nuclear freeze. I suggest we will be saved by neither fire nor ice, that the solutions being offered by the political right and left miss the mark. Our problem lies not in our technology, but in our minds, in our ancient tendency to create our enemies in our own imagination.

2   Our best hope for avoiding war is to understand the psychology of this enmity, the ways in which our mind works to produce our habits of paranoia, projection, and the making of propaganda. How do we create our enemies and turn the world into a killing ground?

3   We first need to answer some inevitable objections, raised by the advocates of power politics, who say: "You can't psychologize political conflict. You can't solve the problem of war by studying perception. We don't *create* enemies. There are real aggressors—Hitler, Stalin, Qaddafi."

4   True: There are always political, economic, and territorial causes of war. Wars come and go; the images we use to dehumanize our enemies remain strangely the same. The unchanging projections of the hostile imagination are continually imposed onto changing historical circumstances. Not that the enemy is innocent of these projections—as popular wisdom has it, paranoids sometimes have *real* enemies. Nevertheless, to understand the hostile imagination we need to temporarily ignore the question of guilt and innocence. Our quest is for an understanding of the unchanging images we place on the enemy.

The Enemy as Created by Paranoia

5   Paranoia is not an occasional individual pathology, but rather it is the human condition. History shows us that, with few exceptions, social cohesion within tribes is maintained by paranoia: when we do not have enemies, we invent them. The group identity of a people depends on division between insiders and outsiders, us and them, the tribe and the enemy.

6   The first meaning of *the enemy* is simply the stranger, the alien. The bond of tribal membership is maintained by projecting hostile and divisive emotions upon the outsider. Paranoia forms the mold from which we create enemies.

7   In the paranoid imagination, *alien* means the same as *evil*, while the tribe itself is defined as good: a single network of malevolent intent stretches over the rest of the world. "They" are out to get "us." All occurrences prove the basic assumption that an outside power is conspiring against the community.

The Enemy as Enemy of God

In the language of rhetoric, every war is a crusade, a "just"   *8*
war, a battle between good and evil. Warfare is a ritual in which
the sacred blood of our heroes is sacrificed to destroy the enemies of God.

We like to think that theocracies and holy wars ended with   *9*
the coming of the Industrial Revolution and the emergence of
secular cultures in the West. Yet in World War I the kaiser was
pictured as the devil; in World War II both Germany and the
U.S. proclaimed *Gott mit uns,* "In God We Trust"; each accused
the other of being Christ-killers. Sophisticated politicians may
insist that the conflict between the U.S. and the USSR is a matter
of pragmatic power politics, but theological dimensions have
not disappeared. President Reagan warns us against "the aggressive impulses of an evil empire" and asks us to "pray for
the salvation of all those who live in totalitarian darkness, pray
they will discover the joy of knowing God."

By picturing the enemy as the enemy of God we convert   *10*
the guilt associated with murder into pride. A warrior who kills
such an enemy strikes a blow for truth and goodness. Remorse
isn't necessary. The warrior engaged in righteous battle against
the enemies of God may even see himself as a priest, saving his
enemy from the grip of evil by killing him.

The Enemy as Barbarian

The enemy not only is a demon but is also a destroyer of culture.   *11*
If he is human at all, he is brutish, dumb, and cruel, lower on
the scale of evolution than The People. To the Greeks he was
a barbarian. To the Americans he was, most recently, a "gook"
or "slant." To the South African he is a black or "colored."

The barbarian theme was used widely in World War II prop-   *12*
aganda by all participants. Nazi anti-semitic tracts contrasted
the sunny, healthy Aryan with the inferior, dark, and contaminated races—Jews, Gypsies, Eastern Europeans. American soldiers were pictured as Chicago-style gangsters. Blacks were portrayed as quasi-gorillas despoiling the artistic achievements of
European civilization. One poster used in Holland warned the
Dutch that their supposed "liberators" were a mélange of KKK,

231

jazz-crazed blacks, convicts, hangmen, and mad bombers. In turn, the U.S. frequently pictured the Germans as a Nazi horde of dark monsters on a mindless rampage.

13   The image of the barbarian represents a force to be feared: power without intelligence, matter without mind, an enemy that must be conquered by culture. The warrior who defeats the barbarian is a culture hero, keeping the dark powers in abeyance.

The Enemy as Rapist

14   Associated with the enemy as barbarian is the image of the enemy as rapist, the destroyer of motherhood.

15   As rapist, the enemy is lust defiling innocence. He is according to Nazi propaganda the Jew who lurks in the shadows waiting to seduce Aryan girls. Or in the propaganda of the Ku Klux Klan he is the black man with an insatiable lust for white women. In American war posters he is the Jap carrying away the naked Occidental woman.

16   The portrait of the enemy as rapist, destroyer of the madonna, warns us of danger and awakens our pornographic imagination by reminding us of the enticement of rape. The appeal to sexual adventure is a sine qua non in motivating men to go to war: To the warrior belong the spoils, and chief among the spoils are the enemy's women.

The Enemy as Beast, Insect, Reptile

17   The power of bestial images to degrade is rooted in the neurotic structure of the hostile imagination. Karen Horney has shown that neurosis always involves a movement between glorified and degraded images of the self. In warfare we act out a mass neurosis whereby we glorify ourselves as agents of God and project our feelings of degradation and impotence upon the enemy. We are suprahuman; therefore they must be subhuman. By destroying the bestial and contaminated enemy we can gain immortality, escape evil, transcend decay and death.

The Enemy as Death

In the iconography of propaganda, the enemy is the bringer of *18* death. He is Death riding on a bomb, the Grim Reaper cutting down youth in its prime. His face is stripped of flesh, his body a dangling skeleton.

War is an irrational ritual. Generation after generation we *19* sacrifice our substance in a vain effort to kill some essential enemy. Now he wears an American or Soviet face. A moment ago he was a Nazi, a Jew, a Moslem, a Christian, a pagan. But the true face of the enemy, as Saint Paul said, is Death itself. The unconscious power that motivates us to fight for Peace, kill for Life, is the magical assumption that if we can destroy this particular enemy we can defeat Death.

Lying within each of us is the desire for immortality. And *20* because this near-instinctive desire for immortality is balanced by the precariously repressed fear that death might really eradicate all traces of our existence, we will go to any extreme to reassure ourselves. By submitting to the divine ordeal of war, in which we are willing to die or kill the enemy who *is* Death, we affirm our own deathlessness.

The Reluctant Killers

It is easy to despair when we look at the human genius for *21* creating enemies in the image of our own disowned vices. When we add our mass paranoia and projection to our constantly progressing weapons technology, it seems we are doomed to destroy ourselves.

But the persistent archetypal images of the enemy may *22* point in a more hopeful direction. We demean our enemies not because we are instinctively sadistic, but because it is difficult for us to kill others whom we recognize as fully human beings. Our natural empathy, our instinct for compassion, is strong: society does what it must to attempt to overcome the moral imperative that forbids us from killing.

Even so, the effort is successful only for a minority. In spite *23* of our best propaganda, few men and women will actually try to kill an enemy. In his book *Men Against Fire,* Brigadier General

233

S.L.A. Marshall presents the results of his study of American soldiers under fire during World War II. He discovered that *in combat* the percentage of men who would fire their rifle at the enemy *even once* did not rise above 25 percent, and the more usual figure was 15 percent. He further discovered that the fear of killing was every bit as strong as the fear of dying.

24   If it is difficult to mold men into killers, we may still hope to transform our efforts from fighting an outward enemy to doing battle with our own paranoia. Our true war is our struggle against the antagonistic mind. Our true enemy is our propensity to make enemies. The highest form of moral courage requires us to look at ourselves from another perspective, to repent, and to reown our own shadows. True self-knowledge introduces self-doubt into our minds. And self-doubt is a healthy counterbalance to the dogmatic, self-righteous certainty that governs political rhetoric and behavior; it is, therefore, the beginning of compassion.

QUESTIONS ON SUBJECT AND PURPOSE

1. According to Keen, why do we give "faces" to our enemies?
2. What characteristics do all of the "faces" share?
3. Why might Keen be writing about this subject? What might he hope to accomplish?

QUESTIONS ON STRATEGY AND AUDIENCE

1. Into how many categories does Keen classify the images that we create of our enemies?
2. How are those categories ordered or arranged?
3. Obviously Keen's essay has the greatest meaning when a nation is at war. However, what other possible applications might his audience find in this essay?

QUESTIONS ON VOCABULARY AND STYLE

1. Why might Keen have used the word "face" rather than "image"?
2. Keen's essay contains quite a few words that readers might need to check in a dictionary. On the other hand, the essay is

still informal in tone and quite readable. What does this mixture suggest about Keen's sense of his readers?

3. Be prepared to define the following words: *enmity* (1), *paranoia* (2), *pathology* (5), *divisive* (6), *malevolent* (7), *theocracies* (9), *totalitarian* (9), *despoiling* (12), *melange* (12), *rampage* (12), *abeyance* (13), *defiling* (15), *insatiable* (15), *sine qua non* (16), *bestial* (17), *neurosis* (17), *iconography* (18), *eradicate* (19), *archetypal* (22), *demean* (22), *propensity* (24)

WRITING SUGGESTIONS

1. The "them-us" distinction takes many forms, not all of which have as serious a significance as those about which Keen writes. For example, rivalries between schools or between town and campus are frequently seen in similar terms or images. In a paragraph discuss the characteristics of this "them-us" distinction as it applies to a campus or community rivalry. What are the "faces" given to "them"?

2. The "them-us" distinction underlies all forms of prejudice and bigotry as well. Select a common form of prejudice (such as one based on race, religion, nationality, gender, age, sexual orientation, physical or mental characteristics) and classify the types of "faces" that are assigned to that group. Like Keen, do not be afraid to analyze why such "faces" get created.

Prewriting:

a. Brainstorm for a possible topic. Spend some time just making a list of possibilities. Add to your list over a three-day period.

b. Rule off a sheet of paper into six equal blocks. Down the left-hand margin list your possible topics. Then in the five blocks running from left to right, list the various categories that each topic suggests.

c. Examine your grid carefully. How many categories or subdivisions have you established for each topic? Remember that you ought to have at least three. Check to make sure that the categories are parallel in form.

Rewriting:

a. Look carefully at your introduction. Do you attempt to catch your reader's attention? Reread the body of your

235

essay several times. Now freewrite a new introduction to your paper. Imagine that your article will appear in a magazine, so work to grab and hold your reader's interest.

b. Have you provided enough examples and details for each category? Remember that your paragraphs need to be developed. No body paragraph in this type of essay should be only two or three sentences in length.

c. Look back at how you arranged the parts in your classification scheme. Is this the best order? How did you decide which parts to place first and last? The order should be a conscious decision on your part. Make a copy of your paper, cut it apart, and rearrange the body paragraphs. Experiment—even if you decide to stay with your original plan.

3. Your college or university library should have a number of books that reproduce propaganda art especially from World War I or II. Study the "faces" by which the "enemy" was depicted and then in an essay classify the images that were most common.

The Value of Children: A Taxonomical Essay

BERNARD R. BERELSON

Bernard R. Berelson (1912–1979) was born on Spokane, Washington, educated at Whitman College and the University of Washington, and received a Ph.D. from the University of Chicago. He divided his time between the academic world and the world of international development assistance. In 1962, he joined the Population Council, eventually serving as its president until his retirement in 1974. Berelson published extensively on population policy and the prospects for fertility declines in developing countries. Among his dozen books are Voting *(1954), a study of opinion formation in a presidential campaign;* Graduate Education in the United States *(1960); and* Human Behavior *(1964). Berelson's concern with population policy is obvious in this essay reprinted from the* Annual Report *of the* Population Council. *Using a clear scheme of classification, Berelson analyzes the reasons why people want children.*

WHY DO PEOPLE want children? It is a simple question to ask, perhaps an impossible one to answer.

Throughout most of human history, the question never seemed to need a reply. These years, however, the question has a new tone. It is being asked in a nonrhetorical way because of three revolutions in thought and behavior that characterize the latter decades of the twentieth century: the vital revolution in which lower death rates have given rise to the population problem and raise new issues about human fertility; the sexual revolution from reproduction; and the women's revolution, in which childbearing and -rearing no longer are being accepted as the only or even the primary roles of half the human race. Accordingly, for about the first time, the question of why people want children now can be asked, so to speak, with a straight face.

3   "Why" questions of this kind, with simple surfaces but profound depths, are not answered or settled; they are ventilated, explicated, clarified. Anything as complex as the motives for having children can be classified in various ways, and any such taxonomy has an arbitrary character to it. This one starts with chemistry and proceeds to spirit.

The Biological

4   Do people innately want children for some built-in reason of physiology? Is there anything to maternal instinct, or parental instinct? Or is biology satisfied with the sex instinct as the way to assure continuity?

5   In psychoanalytic thought there is talk of the "child-wish," the "instinctual drive of physiological cause," "the innate femaleness of the girl direct(ing) her development toward motherhood," and the wanting of children as "the essence of her self-realization," indicating normality. From the experimental literature, there is some evidence that man, like other animals, is innately attracted to the quality of "babyishness."

6   If the young and adults of several species are compared for differences in bodily and facial features, it will be seen readily that the nature of the difference is apparently the same almost throughout the phylogenetic scale. Limbs are shorter and much heavier in proportion to the torso in babies than in adults. Also, the head is proportionately much larger in relation to the body than is the case with adults. On the face itself, the forehead is more prominent and bulbous; the eyes large and perhaps located as far down as below the middle of the face, because of the large forehead. In addition, the cheeks may be round and protruding. In many species there is also a greater degree of overall fatness in contrast to normal adult bodies. . . . In man, as in other animals, social prescriptions and customs are not the sole or even primary factors that guarantee the rearing and protection of babies. This seems to indicate that the biologically rooted releaser of babyishness may have promoted infant care in primitive man before societies ever were formed, just as it appears to do in many animal

species. Thus this releaser may have a high survival value for the species of man.*

In the human species the question of social and personal 7 motivation distinctively arises, but that does not necessarily mean that the biology is completely obliterated. In animals the instinct to reproduce appears to be all; in humans is it something?

The Cultural

Whatever the biological answer, people do not want all the 8 children they physically can have—no society, hardly any woman. Everywhere social traditions and social pressures enforce a certain conformity to the approved childbearing pattern, whether large numbers of children in Africa or small numbers in Eastern Europe. People want children because that is "the thing to do"—culturally sanctioned and institutionally supported, hence about as natural as any social behavior can be.

Such social expectations, expressed by everyone toward 9 everyone, are extremely strong in influencing behavior even on such an important element in life as childbearing and on whether the outcome is two children or six. In most human societies, the thing to do gets done, for social rewards and punishments are among the most powerful. Whether they produce lots of children or few and whether the matter is fully conscious or not, the cultural norms are all the more effective if, as often, they are rationalized as the will of God or the hand of fate.

The Political

The cultural shades off into political considerations: reproduc- 10 tion for the purposes of a higher authority. In a way, the human responsibility to perpetuate the species is the grandest such expression—the human family pitted politically against fauna and flora—and there always might be people who partly rationalize their own childbearing as a contribution to that lofty

* Eckhard H. Hess, "Ethology and Developmental Psychology," in Paul H. Musser, ed., *Carmichael's Manual of Child Psychology*, Vol. 1 (New York: Wiley, 1970), pp. 20–21.

end. Beneath that, however, there are political units for whom collective childbearing is or has been explicitly encouraged as a demographic duty—countries concerned with national glory or competitive political position; governments concerned with the supply of workers and soldiers; churches concerned with propagation of the faith or their relative strength; ethnic minorities concerned with their political power; linguistic communities competing for position; clans and tribes concerned over their relative status within a larger setting. In ancient Rome, according to the Oxford English Dictionary, the proletariat—from the root *proles,* for progeny—were "the lowest class of the community, regarded as contributing nothing to the state but offspring": and a proletaire was "one who served the state not with his property but only with his offspring." The world has changed since then, but not all the way.

The Economic

11 As the "new home economics" is reminding us in its current attention to the microeconomics of fertility, children are economically valuable. Not that that would come as a surprise to the poor peasant who consciously acts on the premise, but it is clear that some people want children or not for economic reasons.

12 Start with the obvious case of economic returns from children that appears to be characteristic of the rural poor. To some extent, that accounts for their generally higher fertility than that of their urban and wealthier counterparts: labor in the fields; hunting, fishing, animal care; help in the home and with the younger children; dowry and "bride-wealth"; support in later life (the individualized system of social security).

13 The economics of the case carries through on the negative side as well. It is not publicly comfortable to think of children as another consumer durable, but sometimes that is precisely the way parents do think of them, before conception: another child or a trip to Europe; a birth deferred in favor of a new car, the nth child requiring more expenditure on education or housing. But observe the special characteristics of children viewed as consumer durables: they come only in whole units; they are

not rentable or returnable or exchangeable or available on trial; they cannot be evaluated quickly; they do not come in several competing brands or products; their quality cannot be pretested before delivery; they usually are not available for appraisal in large numbers in one's personal experience; they themselves participate actively in the household's decisions. And in the broad view, both societies and families tend to choose standard of living over number of children when the opportunity presents itself.

The Familial

In some societies people want children for what might be called familial reasons: to extend the family line or the family name; to propitiate the ancestors; to enable the proper functioning of religious rituals involving the family (e.g., the Hindu son needed to light the father's funeral pyre, the Jewish son needed to say Kaddish for the dead father). Such reasons may seem thin in the modern, secularized society but they have been and are powerful indeed in other places.   14

In addition, one class of family reasons shares a border with the following category, namely, having children in order to maintain or improve a marriage: to hold the husband or occupy the wife; to repair or rejuvenate their marriage; to increase the number of children on the assumption that family happiness lies that way. The point is underlined by its converse: in some societies the failure to bear children (or males) is a threat to the marriage and a ready cause for divorce.   15

Beyond all that is the profound significance of children to the very institution of the family itself. To many people, husband and wife alone do not seem a proper family—they need children to enrich the circle, to validate its family character, to gather the redemptive influence of offspring. Children need the family, but the family seems also to need children, as the social institution uniquely available, at least in principle, for security, comfort, assurance, and direction in a changing, often hostile, world. To most people, such a home base, in the literal sense, needs more than one person for sustenance and in generational extension.   16

The Personal

17 Up to here the reasons for wanting children primarily refer to instrumental benefits. Now we come to a variety of reasons for wanting children that are supposed to bring direct personal benefits.

18 *Personal Power.* As noted, having children sometimes gives one parent power over the other. More than that, it gives the parents power over the child(ren)—in many cases, perhaps most, about as much effective power as they ever will have the opportunity of exercising on an individual basis. They are looked up to by the child(ren), literally and figuratively, and rarely does that happen otherwise. Beyond that, having children is involved in a wider circle of power:

19 In most simple societies the lines of kinship are the lines of political power, social prestige and economic aggrandizement. The more children a man has, the more successful marriage alliances he can arrange, increasing his own power and influence by linking himself to men of greater power or to men who will be his supporters. . . . In primitive and peasant societies, the man with few children is the man of minor influence and the childless man is virtually a social nonentity*

20 *Personal Competence.* Becoming a parent demonstrates competence in an essential human role. Men and women who are closed off from other demonstrations of competence, through lack of talent or educational opportunity or social status, still have this central one. For males, parenthood is thought to show virility, potency, *machismo*. For females it demonstrates fecundity, itself so critical to an acceptable life in many societies.

21 *Personal Status.* Everywhere parenthood confers status. It is an accomplishment open to all, or virtually all, and realized by the overwhelming majority of adult humankind. Indeed, achieving parenthood surely must be one of the two most sig-

---

* Burton Benedict, ''Population Regulation in Primitive Societies,'' in Anthony Ellison, *Population Control* (London: Penguin, 1970), pp. 176–77.

nificant events in one's life—that and being born in the first place. In many societies, then and only then is one considered a real man or a real woman.

Childbearing is one of the few ways in which the poor can   *22* compete with the rich. Life cannot make the poor man prosperous in material goods and services but it easily can make him rich with children. He cannot have as much of anything else worth having, except sex, which itself typically means children in such societies. Even so, the poor still are deprived by the arithmetic; they have only two or three times as many children as the rich whereas the rich have at least forty times the income of the poor.

Personal Extension. Beyond the family line, wanting children   *23* is a way to reach for personal immortality—for most people, the only way available. It is a way to extend oneself indefinitely into the future. And short of that, there is simply the physical and psychological extension of oneself in the children, here and now—a kind of narcissism: there they are and they are mine (or like me).

Look in thy glass and tell the face thou viewest,   *24*
Now is the time that face should form another;
But if thou live, remember'd not to be,
Die single, and thine image dies with thee.
    —*Shakespeare's Sonnets, III*

Personal Experience. Among all the activities of life, parent-   *25* hood is a unique experience. It is a part of life, or personal growth, that simply cannot be experienced in any other way and hence is literally an indispensable element of the full life. The experience has many profound facets: the deep curiosity as to how the child will turn out; the renewal of self in the second chance; the reliving of one's own childhood; the redemptive opportunity; the challenge to shape another human being; the sheer creativity and self-realization involved. For a large proportion of the world's women, there was and probably still is nothing else for the grown female to do with her time and energy, as society defines her role. And for many women, it might be the most emotional and spiritual experience they ever have and perhaps the most gratifying as well.

26   *Personal Pleasure.* Last, but one hopes not least, in the list of reasons for wanting children is the altruistic pleasure of having them, caring for them, watching them grow, shaping them, being with them, enjoying them. This reason comes last on the list but it is typically the first one mentioned in the casual inquiry: "because I like children." Even this reason has its dark side, as with parents who live through their children, often to the latter's distaste and disadvantage. But that should not obscure a fundamental reason for wanting children: love.

27   There are, in short, many reasons for wanting children. Taken together, they must be among the most compelling motivations in human behavior: culturally imposed, institutionally reinforced, psychologically welcome.

QUESTIONS ON SUBJECT AND PURPOSE

1. What is "the value of children"? How many different values does Berelson cite?
2. Berelson gives positive, negative, and neutral reasons for wanting children. Is the overall effect of the essay positive, negative, or neutral?
3. Which of Berelson's reasons seem most relevant in American society today? Which seem least relevant?

QUESTIONS ON STRATEGY AND AUDIENCE

1. How does Berelson organize his classification? Can you find an explicit statement of organization?
2. Could the classification have been organized in a different way? Would that have changed the essay in any way?
3. How effective is Berelson's introduction? His conclusion? Suggest other ways in which the essay could have begun or ended.

QUESTIONS ON VOCABULARY AND STYLE

1. Berelson asks a number of rhetorical questions (see Glossary). Why does he ask them? Does he answer them? Does he "ventilate," "explicate," and "clarify" them (paragraph 3)?

2. Describe the tone of Berelson's essay—what does he sound like? Be prepared to support your statement with some specific illustrations from the text.

3. Be able to define the following words: *taxonomy* (paragraph 3), *physiology* (4), *phylogenetic* (6), *bulbous* (6), *sanctioned* (8), *fauna and flora* (10), *demographic* (10), *consumer durable* (13), *propitiate* (14), *sustenance* (16), *aggrandizement* (19), *nonentity* (19), *"machismo"* (20), *fecundity* (20), *narcissism* (23).

WRITING SUGGESTIONS

1. Why do you want or not want to have children? Classify your reasons in a paragraph. Focus on two or three reasons at most and be sure to have some logical order to your arrangement. You might try writing to a specific audience—for example, your fiancé or your parents.

2. Why do people in the United States go to college? In an essay classify the reasons why people make this decision. Remember that you are not just dealing with the reasons why *you* are going; you are analyzing the reasons (and values) of an entire nation.

Prewriting:

a. Interview twenty fellow students, asking their reasons for attending college. Try to get a broad spectrum of different ages, different social and economic backgrounds, different majors. Include some who are paying for their own education and some who have come back to school after years at home or in the job market. Do not ask just your freshman English classmates.

b. Analyze your own reasons. Make a list. Decide which seem to be the most important reasons, which the least.

c. If your instructor approves the use of outside sources, you can search for additional information from your college's library or admissions office. Studies are done each year on entering freshmen to assess, among other things, what they see as important about a college education.

Rewriting:

a. Look carefully at the organizational principle you have used in the body of your essay. How did you decide which ex-

245

ample to put first? Which last? Try reordering the body of your paper.

b. Does each paragraph include an explicit statement of focus/ topic? Make a copy of your paper and underline those statements. Using a pen of another color, mark transitions to see if they are always present.

c. Try for an interesting title. If you started with something like "The Reasons for Going to College" or "The Value of College: A Taxonomical Essay," try again.

3. Berelson gives very few specific examples to support his classification of values. Research one of his values and find an example or examples of societies that have seen children in this way. You might want to focus on the political, economic, or familial categories.

A Writer's Revision Process: E Pluribus Onion

JAMES VILLAS

James Villas was born in Charlotte, North Carolina, in 1938. He left college teaching of comparative literature and Romance languages to become a food writer, and is now food and wine editor of Town and Country *magazine. His essays have appeared in a variety of magazines including* Esquire, Cuisine, Bon Appetit, *and* Gourmet. *He is the author of* American Taste: A Celebration of Gastronomy Coast to Coast *(1982), a selection of essays celebrating the best of native American cooking;* James Villas's The Town and Country Cookbook *(1985);* James Villas's Country Cooking *(1988); and* Villas at Table: A Passion For Food and Drink *(1988).*

On revising, Villas writes: "I think I did four different drafts of the piece, and this specimen shows as well as any what hell I go through getting a story into shape. Not just the language and style but the never-ending research."

This selection reproduces the introductory paragraphs from an essay that appeared in the January 1985 issue of Town and Country, *a magazine that characterizes itself as appealing to "upper-income Americans." In that issue, Villas's essay was accompanied by a color photograph of a roasted onion and twelve recipes for dishes using other members of the* Allium *genus.*

REVISED DRAFT*

WHEN THE MOST sagacious of Victorian culinarians, Mrs. Beeton, spoke rather cryptically of "the alliaceous tribe," she was referring to none other than the ancient and noble members of the lily family known in kitchens round the world as the onion,   *1*

* Bars indicate areas of major revision.

247

scallion, leek, shallot, chive, and garlic. I don't suppose it really matters that many cooks today are hardly aware of the close affinity the common bulb onion we take so much for granted has with these other vegetables of the *Allium* genus, but it does bother me how Americans underestimate the versatility of the onion and how so few give a second thought to exploiting the potential of its aromatic relatives. More often than not, the onion itself is considered no more than a flavoring agent to soups, stews, stocks, sauces, salads, and sandwiches. Though I'd be the last to deny that nothing awakens the gustatory senses or inspires the soul like the aroma of onions simmering in a lusty stew or the crunch of a few sweet, odoriferous slices on a juicy hamburger, it would be nice to see the onion highlighted in ways other than the all-too-familiar fried rings and creamed preparations.

2 As for scallions, about the only time you encounter these peppery "green onions" is when they are mixed into Oriental food, added to a plate of *nouvelle cuisine* for garnish, or added raw to salads for zest. And how many cooks can taste the delicate but distinctive difference between genuine shallots and tiny yellow onions? The only people who've learned about the many uses of fresh chives are those who grow them, and the social status of leeks is still so dubious in this country that the likelihood of finding an ample fresh supply in the supermarket is about as remote in most areas as spotting a bunch of fresh sorrel. Fortunately, garlic as a seasoning has gained wider acceptance in our cookery over the past few decade (there's even an annual garlic festival every June near San Francisco), but only now are adventurous chefs learning about the gustatory advantages of baking, roasting, and braising whole cloves of this deceptively sweet member of the onion family.

3 The bulb onion predates recorded history but was most likely first cultivated in central Asia. We know it was a favorite vegetable in Mesopotamia around 2400 B.C., and various works of art and temple decorations testify to its popularity in ancient Egypt. Whether Alexander the Great introduced the onion to Europe is debatable, but it's certain that by 500 B.C. the Greeks had incorporated the bulb in their sophisticated style of cooking

(Hippocrates believed the onion to be good for sight) and that during the Roman Empire its abundance was such that onions (all except the highly prized sweet specimens from Pompeii) were distributed widely as food for the poor. The lofty role of the onion in Chinese cookery can be traced at least back to the time of Marco Polo, while the earliest medieval tomes of Britain and western Europe illustrate its importance both as a seasoning for many dishes and as a medicament for all ills. Cortés found many types of onions in Mexico, and it is said that Père Marquette, while exploring Michigan in 1624, was literally saved from starvation by nourishing himself on the vegetable whose odor the Indians of the region called *chicago*! Ironically, it does seem that the onion commanded more creative attention in Colonial America and throughout the nineteenth century than in present-day kitchens, but, with the exception of such enlightened early volumes as *The Joy of Cooking* (which originally included recipes for onion pie, glazed onions, onion shortcake, and onion soufflé), it can hardly be said that this fragrant globe has enjoyed much glory in this country throughout the twentieth century.

QUESTIONS FOR DISCUSSION

1. What is Villas's thesis in this selection? Put it into a sentence of your own.

2. What is the function of each of the three paragraphs? Why does Villas survey the history of the onion in the third paragraph?

3. What does the title "E Pluribus Onion" mean? Where else does part of that phrase occur? Does that seem like an appropriate title?

4. What expectations does Villas seem to have about his audience? How can you tell?

5. Be able to define the following words: *sagacious* (paragraph 1), *culinarians* (1), *cryptically* (1), *affinity* (1), *gustatory* (1), *odoriferous* (1), *nouvelle cuisine* (2), *dubious* (2), *sorrel* (2), *tomes* (3), *medicament* (3), *soufflé* (3).

EARLIER DRAFT

The Fragrant Family of Gastronomy

1 WHEN THAT MOST sagacious of British food writers, Mrs. Beeton, spoke of "the alliaceous tribe," she was referring to none other than the ancient and noble members of the lily family known in serious kitchens round the world as the onion, scallion, leek, shallot, chive, and garlic. Of course most cooks today are still unaware of the close affinity the common bulb onion has with these other vegetables of the *Allium* genus, and it does bother me considerably that people take the onion so much for granted and that few give so much as a second thought to exploiting the potential of its aromatic relatives. More often than not the odoriferous onion is considered no more than a flavoring agent to soups, stews, stocks, sauces, salads, and sandwiches, and, with the exceptions of fried onion rings and creamed onions, is rarely allowed to stand on its own merit. When do you ever see scallions (or green onions) except chopped up and added to salads for zest, and who but the most knowledgeable chef ever goes to the trouble to track down fresh chives or genuine shallots? In this country the only people who've learned about the many uses of fresh chives are those who grow them, and even our most respected cookbook writers treat leeks as if they were as rare as fresh sorrel. Garlic has gained wide acceptance in our cookery over the past few decades, but only now are adventurous chefs learning about the gustatory advantages of baking, roasting, and braising whole cloves of this deceptively sweet member of the onion family.

2 The onion itself predates recorded history but was most likely first cultivated in Central Asia. We know it was a favorite vegetable in Mesopotamia around 2400 B.C., and its popularity in ancient Egypt is attested to in various works of art and temple decorations. Whether Alexander the Great introduced the onion to Europe is debatable, but it's certain that by 500 B.C. the Greeks had incorporated the bulb in their sophisticated style of cooking and that it was later distributed widely as food for the poor during the Roman Empire. By the time of Marco Polo, numerous varieties of onions were being cultivated in China, while the earliest western European tomes testify to its impor-

tance in medieval and Elizabethan kitchens. Cortés found all types of onions in Mexico, and it is said that Pére Marquette, while exploring Michigan in 1624, was literally saved from starvation by nourishing himself on a vegetable the odor of which the Indians of the region called *chicago*! Ironically, the onion figures much more importantly in Colonial American kitchens than in our present-day cookery, and even in the early 1900s, classic volumes like *The Joy of Cooking* were including recipes for onion pie, glazed onions, onion shortcake, and onion soufflé.

QUESTIONS ON THE REVISION

1. Villas expanded the first paragraph of the earlier draft, making it into two separate paragraphs. What does he add? Does the division into two seem more effective?
2. Which title do you like better? Why?
3. Villas expanded the final sentence considerably. What did he add? Are the changes appropriate?
4. What is the effect of each of the following minor changes:
    a. "British food writers" changed to "Victorian culinarians"
    b. The addition of the first-person ("I") references in the first paragraph
    c. The addition of the parenthetical references to Hippocrates and the "sweet specimens from Pompeii" in the last paragraph
    d. "Cortés found all types of onions" changed to "Cortés found many types of onions"
5. Does there seem to be any general principle behind the revisions? Do they have anything in common?

WRITING SUGGESTIONS

1. Condense Villas's paragraphs into a single one. Try to preserve his ideas, but paraphrase them in your own words and write for a more general audience. The point is to encourage the reader to experiment with onions.
2. In an essay celebrate the virtues of your favorite fruit, vege-

table, or starch. Like Villas, mix personal experience with some research.

Prewriting:

a. Remember that the assignment specifies fruit, vegetable, or starch. It should be something that could be served in a variety of ways. Do not choose a particular dish (sundaes, pizza, french fries). Make a list of possible subjects, drawing upon your own favorite foods.

b. What does your audience already know about the subject? You must present more information than just the obvious. Find an encyclopedia article on your subject. You might be able to include details about its history, its varieties, and its popularity.

c. Remember that you are not writing an encyclopedia article. An encyclopedia merely gives information. Your essay should celebrate the virtues of your subject. On a separate sheet of paper, list the objectives that the two different types of writing might have.

Rewriting:

a. Find a peer reader. Ask that reader if he or she finds your essay interesting and informative. Encourage an honest response, and then act on that response.

b. Check your word choice. You are writing to a general audience—one that may have only some familiarity with your subject and with cooking. Be careful though to avoid technical terms or jargon that might not be understood by your reader.

c. What one part of your essay gave you the most trouble? Go back and work only on that area.

3. The fruits and vegetables we eat today—and the animals raised for meat—are the products of special cultivation and breeding techniques designed to develop them for better yield. Select a particular food and research its history. Where did it originate? How has it developed? How have its uses changed over the years?

FIVE

Comparison
and
Contrast

Whenever you decide between two alternatives, you make a comparison and contrast. Which portable cassette player is the better value or has the more attractive set of features? Which professor's section of introductory sociology should you register for in the spring semester? In both cases you make the decision by comparing alternatives on a series of relevant points and then deciding which has the greater advantages.

In comparison and contrast, subjects are set in opposition in order to reveal their similarities and differences. Comparison involves finding similarities between two or more things, people, or ideas; contrast involves finding differences. Comparison and contrast writing tasks can involve, then, three activities: emphasizing similarities, emphasizing differences, or emphasizing both.

Like every writing task, comparison and contrast is done to achieve a particular purpose. In practical situations you use it to help make a decision. You compare cassette players or professors in order to make an intelligent choice. In academic situations comparison and contrast allows you to compare carefully and thoroughly, on a point-by-point basis, two or more subjects.

How Do You Choose a Subject?

Many times, especially on examinations in other academic courses, the subject for comparison and contrast is already chosen for you. On an economics examination you are asked, "What are the main differences between the public and private sectors?" In political science you are to "compare the political platforms of the Republican and Democratic parties in the last presidential election." Other times, however, you must choose the subject for comparison and contrast.

The choice of subject is crucial. It is best to limit your paragraph or essay to subjects that have obvious similarities or differences. William Zinsser compares his writing process to Dr. Brock's; John McPhee contrasts Florida and California oranges; Bruce Catton pairs Grant and Lee, the two Civil War generals. Two other cautions are also important. First, make sure that there is reason for making the comparison or contrast, that it will reveal something new or interesting or important. Second, limit your paper to important points; do not try to cover everything. You could not expect, for instance, to compare and contrast Arabs and Americans in every aspect of their cultures. Like Edward Hall, you might focus on one significant difference: their attitudes toward public space.

Do You Always Find Both Similarities and Differences?

Comparison and contrast makes sense only if there is some basic similarity between the two subjects. There is no point in comparing two totally unrelated subjects. The mind could be compared to a computer since both process information, but there would be no reason to compare a computer to an orange. Remember, too, that some of the similarities which exist will be obvious and hence not worth writing about. In a paragraph from *Oranges*, John McPhee concentrates on the differences between Florida and California oranges—the similarities (both are oranges) are obvious and are omitted. This does not mean that similarities are not important or should not be mentioned. Bruce Catton, after spending most of his essay pointing out the differences between Grant and Lee, ends with the similarities these two men shared.

Once you have chosen your subject, make a list of the possible points of comparison and contrast. Be sure that those points are shared. William Zinsser, for example, organizes his comparison and contrast around six questions. To each of the six, Zinsser gives first Dr. Brock's response and then his own. The contrast depends upon the two responses to each of the six questions. If Dr. Brock had answered one group of three and Zinsser a different group of three, the contrast would not have worked.

How Do You Use Analogy, Metaphor, and Simile?

Writing a comparison often involves constructing an analogy, an extended comparison in which something complex or unfamiliar is likened to something simple or familiar. The reason for making the analogy is to help your reader understand or visualize the more complex or unfamiliar more easily. For example, if you are trying to explain how the hard disk on your computer is organized, you might use the analogy of a file cabinet. The hard disk, you write, is the file cabinet which is partitioned off into directories (the file drawers) each of which contains subdirectories (the hanging folders) which in turn contain the individual files (the manila folders in which documents are stored).

Analogies are also used to provide a new way of seeing something. J. Anthony Lukas, for example, explains his attraction to the game of pinball by an analogy:

> Pinball is a metaphor for life, pitting man's skill, nerve, persistence, and luck against the perverse machinery of human existence. The playfield is rich with rewards: targets that bring huge scores, bright lights, chiming bells, free balls, and extra games. But is it replete with perils, too: culs-de-sac, traps, gutters, and gobble holes down which the ball may disappear forever.*

Lukas's analogy does not seek to explain the unfamiliar. Probably every reader has seen a pinball game. Rather, the analogy invites the reader to see the game in a fresh way. The suggested

* J. Anthony Lukas, "The Inner Game of Pinball," *The Atlantic*, December 1979, p. 87.

similarity might help the reader understand why arcade games—such as pinball—have a particular significance or attraction.

Two common forms of analogy used in writing are metaphor and simile. A metaphor directly identifies one thing with another. A rocky rapids on a river is, to Gretel Ehrlich, a "stepladder of sequined riffles." To Gail Sheehy, adults moving toward maturity are lobsters who periodically shed their shells in order to grow. A simile, as its name suggests, is also a comparison based on a point or points of similarity. A simile differs from a metaphor by using the words "like" or "as" to link the two things being compared. In this sense, a simile suggests, rather than directly establishes, the comparison. On that February morning when his father died, Scott Russell Sanders saw that the ice "coated the windows like cataracts." Seventeenth-century poet Robert Herrick found a witty similarity: "Fain would I kiss my Julia's dainty leg, / Which is as white and hairless as an egg."

Be careful when you create analogies, similes, and metaphors; do not try, for example, to be too clever. On the other hand, do not avoid such devices altogether. Even though these compressed comparisons are used sparingly in most expository prose, they can be particularly effective tools when you want to construct a comparison.

How Do You Structure a Comparison and Contrast?

Comparison and contrast is not only an intellectual process but also a structural pattern that can be used to organize paragraphs and essays. In comparing and contrasting two subjects, three organizational models are available.

1. *Subject by Subject:* you can treat all of subject A and then all of subject B (A123, B123)
2. *Point by Point:* you can organize by the points of comparison— point 1 in A then point 1 in B (A1/B1, A2/B2, A3/B3)
3. *Mixed Sequence:* you can mix the two patterns together

The three alternatives can be seen in the essays included in this chapter.

Subject by Subject

Bruce Catton's comparison of Robert E. Lee and Ulysses S. Grant uses the subject-by-subject pattern. Paragraphs 5 and 6 of that essay are devoted to Lee; paragraphs 7, 8, and 9 to Grant; paragraph 10 to Lee; paragraph 11 to Grant. As Catton's example suggests, the subject-by-subject pattern for comparison and contrast works in paragraph units. If your comparison paper is fairly short, you could treat all of subject A in a paragraph or group of paragraphs and then all of subject B in a paragraph or group of paragraphs. If your paper is fairly long and the comparisons are fairly complicated, you might want to use either the point-by-point or mixed pattern.

Point by Point

William Zinsser's comparison of his writing process with that of Dr. Brock uses a point-by-point pattern of contrast. The two authors take turns responding to a series of six questions asked by students. The essay then follows a pattern that can be described as A1B1, A2B2, A3B3, A4B4, A5B5, A6B6. In replying to the fourth question, for example, about whether or not feeling "depressed or unhappy" will affect their writing, Brock and Zinsser reply:

> [A4] "Probably it will," Dr. Brock replied. "Go fishing. Take a walk."
>
> [B4] "Probably it won't," I said. "If your job is to write every day, you learn to do it like any other job."

The point-by-point, or alternating, pattern emphasizes the individual points of comparison or contrast rather than the subject as a whole. In college writing, this pattern most frequently devotes a sentence, a group of sentences, or a paragraph to each point, alternating between subject A and subject B. If you use the alternating pattern, you must decide how to order your points—for instance, by beginning or by ending with the strongest or most significant.

Mixed Sequence

In longer pieces of writing, writers typically mix the subject-by-subject and point-by-point patterns. Such an arrangement provides variety for the reader. Suzanne Britt Jordan in her comparison of thin and fat people uses a mixed pattern, so mixed, in fact, that at times it is not easy to see the underlying structure. The essay begins with a subject-by-subject pattern. It is not until the end of her second paragraph, for example, that she even mentions fat people. At other points, such as in paragraph 5, she will start with an explicit point-by-point contrast: "Thin people believe in logic. Fat people see all sides."

Sample Student Essay

COMPARISON AND CONTRAST

John Straumanis is a hurdler on the university's track team. For a comparison and contrast paragraph, John chose a familiar subject, and the first draft of his paragraph, which follows, began with a reference to his own experiences.

EARLIER DRAFT

The 120 and 440 Yard Hurdles

Many people have asked me why there are two hurdle races in track and field. Of course they are referring to the 120 yard and the 440 yard hurdles. Sure, both have ten barriers, but it's because they have almost nothing else in common is my usual reply. The 120 yard hurdle race, being the shorter of the two, is an all-out sprint where speed is of the essence. It is also a fairly simple race. Once the hurdling skill is perfected, most hurdlers run the race without even looking at the hurdles. There are always eight steps to the first hurdle, three steps in between each, then an all-out dash to the finish line. On the other hand, the 440 yard race is one of the most demanding and grueling races invented. It matches the speed of the quartermiler with the skill of a hurdler and the stamina to combine the two. The number of steps in this race varies especially towards the end, so the runner must constantly pay attention to and reanalyze the race. The 440 yard race is also more exciting. More strategy is involved, and every runner's strategy is a little bit different. The race can break open at any minute. These races are so different that many hurdlers do not compete in both, but decide to specialize.

After John had written his first draft, he stopped by the university's Writing Center to talk with a staff member. The first question his tutor asked was, "Why introduce yourself in the first three sentences?" John replied that he was a hurdler and that was why people asked him the question. After a discussion John and his tutor decided that he had two obvious options: either explain his credentials to the reader or drop the personal reference altogether. John felt that since the information he provided was factual and not open to dispute, it was not necessary for him to establish his authority. In the conference John and his tutor also talked about how he had structured his comparison/contrast. The draft paragraph first lists a similarity (each race has ten barriers) and then moves to a subject-by-subject pattern, treating first the 120 yard race and then the 440 yard race. The spacing of the hurdles in the 120 yard race is defined by the number of steps the racer takes, but not as much information is given about the spacing in the 440 yard race. John and his tutor agreed that the reader would probably wonder about that difference. In his revision, John changed his opening sentences, added some new information, and tightened his prose.

REVISED DRAFT

The Highs and Lows of Hurdling

Track and field competition includes two hurdle races: the 120 yard and the 440 yard. Although both races have ten barriers or hurdles, they have almost nothing else in common. The greater distance in the 440 yard race means that the hurdles must be spaced farther apart. In the 120 yard race it is 15 yards to the first hurdle and then 10 yards between each subsequent one. In the 440 yard race it is 49 ¼ yards to the first hurdle and 38 ¼ yards between each. The height of the hurdles is also different: 36 inches in the 440 yard race and 42 inches in the 120 yard race. Because of the distance, the 120 yard race is an all-out sprint where speed is crucial. It is also a fairly simple race. Once the hurdling skill is perfected, most hurdlers run the race without ever looking at the barriers. The number

of steps in the 120 yard race is, therefore, constant—
eight steps to the first hurdle, three in between, and
then a dash to the finish line. On the other hand, the
440 yard race is one of the most demanding and
grueling. It requires the speed of a quartermiler and
the skill of a hurdler. The number of steps in this
race varies, especially near the end, so the runner
must constantly pay attention to and reanalyze the
race. The 440 yard race is also more exciting since
strategy is involved and every runner's strategy is
slightly different. The race can break open at any
second. The two races are so different, in fact, that
many hurdlers choose to specialize in one rather than
try to compete in both.

Some Things to Remember

1. Limit your comparison and contrast to subjects that can be adequately developed in a paragraph or an essay.

2. Make sure that the subjects you are comparing and contrasting have some basic similarities. Make a list of similarities and differences before you begin to write.

3. Decide why the comparison or contrast is important. What does it reveal? Remember to make the reason clear to the reader.

4. Decide what points of comparison or contrast are the most important or the most revealing. In general, omit any points of comparison that would be obvious to anybody.

5. Decide which of the three patterns of comparison and contrast best fits your purpose: subject-by-subject, point-by-point, or mixed.

6. Remember to make clear to your reader when you are switching from one subject to another or from one point of comparison to another.

The Transaction:
Two Writing Processes

WILLIAM ZINSSER

*William Zinsser was born in New York in 1922 and received a B.A.
from Princeton in 1944. For thirteen years he was an editor, critic,
and editorial writer with the New York* Herald Tribune. *He left in
1959 to become a free lance writer and has since written regularly
for leading magazines, including* The New Yorker *and* The Atlantic. *From 1968 to 1972 he was a columnist for* Life. *During the 1970s
he taught nonfiction writing and humor writing and was master of
Branford College at Yale University. He was recently general editor
of the Book-of-the-Month Club. Zinsser is a consultant on writing to
schools, colleges, newspapers, and corporations. He is the author of
eleven books, including* On Writing Well: An Informal Guide to
Writing Nonfiction *(4th ed., 1990), a textbook classic of which* The
New York Times *wrote: ''It belongs on any shelf of serious reference
works for writers.'' In this selection from that book, Zinsser dramatizes two completely different attitudes toward writing.*

1   ABOUT TEN YEARS AGO a school in Connecticut held "a day devoted
to the arts," and I was asked if I would come and talk about
writing as a vocation. When I arrived I found that a second
speaker had been invited—Dr. Brock (as I'll call him), a surgeon
who had recently begun to write and had sold some stories to
national magazines. He was going to talk about writing as an
avocation. That made us a panel, and we sat down to face a
crowd of student newspaper editors, English teachers and parents, all eager to learn the secrets of our glamorous work.

2   Dr. Brock was dressed in a bright red jacket, looking vaguely
bohemian, as authors are supposed to look, and the first question went to him. What was it like to be a writer?

3   He said it was tremendous fun. Coming home from an arduous day at the hospital, he would go straight to his yellow
pad and write his tensions away. The words just flowed. It was
easy.

I then said that writing wasn't easy and it wasn't fun. It *4*
was hard and lonely, and the words seldom just flowed.

Next Dr. Brock was asked if it was important to rewrite. *5*
Absolutely not, he said. "Let it all hang out," and whatever
form the sentences take will reflect the writer at his most natural.

I then said that rewriting is the essence of writing. I pointed *6*
out that professional writers rewrite their sentences repeatedly
and then rewrite what they have rewritten. I mentioned that
E. B. White and James Thurber rewrote their pieces eight or
nine times.

"What do you do on days when it isn't going well?" Dr. *7*
Brock was asked. He said he just stopped writing and put the
work aside for a day when it would go better.

I then said that the professional writer must establish a daily *8*
schedule and stick to it. I said that writing is a craft, not an art,
and that the man who runs away from his craft because he
lacks inspiration is fooling himself. He is also going broke.

"What if you're feeling depressed or unhappy?" a student *9*
asked. "Won't that affect your writing?"

Probably it will, Dr. Brock replied. Go fishing. Take a walk. *10*

Probably it won't, I said. If your job is to write every day, *11*
you learn to do it like any other job.

A student asked if we found it useful to circulate in the *12*
literary world. Dr. Brock said that he was greatly enjoying his
new life as a man of letters, and he told several stories of being
taken to lunch by his publisher and his agent at chic Manhattan
restaurants where writers and editors gather. I said that professional writers are solitary drudges who seldom see other writers.

"Do you put symbolism in your writing?" a student asked *13*
me.

"Not if I can help it," I replied. I have an unbroken record *14*
of missing the deeper meaning in any story, play or movie, and
as for dance and mime, I have never had even a remote notion
of what is being conveyed.

"I *love* symbols!" Dr. Brock exclaimed, and he described *15*
with gusto the joys of weaving them through his work.

So the morning went, and it was a revelation to all of us. *16*
At the end Dr. Brock told me he was enormously interested in

my answers—it had never occurred to him that writing could be hard. I told him I was just as interested in *his* answers—it had never occurred to me that writing could be easy. (Maybe I should take up surgery on the side.)

17   As for the students, anyone might think we left them bewildered. But in fact we probably gave them a broader glimpse of the writing process than if only one of us had talked. For of course there isn't any "right" way to do such intensely personal work. There are all kinds of writers and all kinds of methods, and any method that helps people to say what they want to say is the right method for them. . . .

QUESTIONS ON SUBJECT AND PURPOSE

1. Zinsser uses contrast to make a point about how people write. What is that point?
2. How effective is the beginning? Would the effect have been lost if Zinsser had opened with a statement similar to his final sentence?
3. What process do you use when you write? Does it help in any way to know what other people do? Why? Why not?

QUESTIONS ON STRATEGY AND AUDIENCE

1. Which method of development does Zinsser use for his example? How many points of contrast does he make?
2. Would it have made any difference if he had used another pattern of development? Why?
3. How effective are the short paragraphs? Should they be longer?

QUESTIONS ON VOCABULARY AND STYLE

1. What makes Zinsser's story humorous? Try to isolate several aspects of humor.
2. Zinsser uses a number of parallel structures in his narrative. Make a list of them and be prepared to show how they contribute to the narrative's effectiveness.
3. Be able to explain or define the following: *avocation* (paragraph 1), *bohemian* (2), *arduous* (3), *drone* (12), *mime* (14), *gusto* (15).

WRITING SUGGESTIONS

1. Using the details provided by Zinsser, rewrite the narrative using the subject-by-subject pattern. (Put Dr. Brock's process in one paragraph, Zinsser's advice in another.)

2. Let's be honest—writing instructors and textbooks offer one view of the writing process, but the practice of most writers can differ sharply. Prewriting and revising get squeezed out when a paper is due and only one night is available. In an essay compare and contrast your typical behavior as a writer with the process outlined in this text. Do not be afraid to be truthful.

Prewriting:

a. For 15 minutes freewrite on the topic. Do not stop to edit or check spelling. Just write without stopping about how you write your papers—or how you wrote them before you took this course. Take a short break and then write for another 15 minutes.

b. Based on what you have learned so far in the course, make a list of some steps involved in the writing process. Be sure to include some details or examples under each step.

c. On a separate sheet of paper, divided into halves, list the stages of the ideal writing process on the left-hand side and the stages of your typical (or former) writing process on the right-hand side.

d. Before you begin, weigh the three possible structures for your paper—point-by-point, subject-by-subject, or the mixed sequence. Consider all the alternatives.

Rewriting:

a. Look carefully at the points of comparison or contrast that you have chosen. Are they the most important? The most revealing?

b. Have you adequately developed each point? Have you included appropriate details and examples? Check to make sure that your body paragraphs are more than two or three sentences in length.

c. Copy your introduction onto a separate sheet of paper. Show it to some friends and ask them to be honest—do they want to keep reading? Or is this just another boring English essay?

3. Compare the creative processes of two or more artists. Your library will have a number of books that feature artists (writers, musicians, painters) talking about how they work. Use those interviews or statements as a source of examples. Be sure to document your sources.

Oranges:
Florida and California

JOHN McPHEE

John McPhee was born in Princeton, New Jersey, in 1931, was educated at Princeton University, and studied at Cambridge University in England. He began his career as a writer for television in the mid-1950's and later worked as a journalist and served as an assistant editor for Time *magazine. In 1964, he was hired as a staff writer for* The New Yorker *magazine. Since 1965, McPhee has published numerous books, including* A Sense of Where You Are *(1965),* Oranges *(1967),* The Pine Barrens *(1968),* The Crofter and the Laird *(1969),* Levels of the Game *(1970),* The Deltoid Pumpkin Seed *(1973), and* The Survival of the Bark Canoe *(1975). Two of his books—*Encounters with the Archdruid *(1972) and* The Curve of Binding Energy *(1974)—were nominated for National Book Awards in science. In 1977, McPhee received an award from the American Academy and Institute of Arts and Letters. His most recent books include two geological studies,* Basin and Range *(1981) and* In Suspect Terrain *(1983);* Table of Contents *(1985), a collection of essays about travel and people;* La Place de la Concorde Suisse *(1985), a profile of the Swiss army;* Rising from the Plains *(1986), a geology/travel book;* Outcroppings *(1988), a collection of photographs and essays about the terrain of the west;* The Control of Nature *(1989), a study of human influence on the environment; and* Looking For a Ship *(1990), about the Merchant Marine. In this paragraph from his book* Oranges, *McPhee contrasts Florida and California oranges. On your next trip to the supermarket, compare the two varieties for yourself.*

AN ORANGE grown in Florida usually has a thin and tightly fitting skin, and it is also heavy with juice. Californians say that if you want to eat a Florida orange you have to get into a bathtub first. California oranges are light in weight and have thick skins that break easily and come off in hunks. The flesh inside is marvelously sweet, and the segments almost separate themselves. In Florida, it is said that you can run over a California orange with a ten-ton truck and not even wet the pavement. The differences from which these hyperboles arise will prevail in the two states even if the type of orange is the same. In arid climates, like California's, oranges develop a thick albedo, which is the white part of the skin. Florida is one of the two or three most rained-upon states in the United States. California uses the Colorado River and similarly impressive sources to irrigate its oranges, but of course irrigation can only do so much. The annual difference in rainfall between the Florida and California orange-growing areas is one million one hundred and forty thousand gallons per acre. For years, California was the leading orange state, but Florida surpassed California in 1942, and grows three times as many oranges now. California oranges, for their part, can safely be called three times as beautiful.

QUESTIONS ON SUBJECT AND PURPOSE

1. What are the differences between Florida and California oranges?
2. How does McPhee keep his reader's attention in the paragraph? After all, a paragraph on the differences between Florida and California oranges could be very dull.
3. How does humor work in the paragraph? Why would McPhee use it?

QUESTIONS ON STRATEGY AND AUDIENCE

1. Which method of development does McPhee use for his paragraph? How many points of contrast does he use?
2. Would it have made any difference if he had used another pattern of development? Why? Why not?
3. How as a reader do you react to McPhee's paragraph? Do you want to know more? Does he catch your interest?

QUESTIONS ON VOCABULARY AND STYLE

1. How many examples of parallel structure can you find in the paragraph? How do they help the reader?

2. Why does McPhee quantify the difference in the rainfall? Why does he do it in gallons per acre?

3. What is a hyperbole? Where is it used in this selection?

WRITING SUGGESTIONS

1. Take any two subjects that belong to the same class and in a paragraph contrast them. You might consider possibilities such as:

   a. Two varieties of apples

   b. Two types of soft drinks

   c. Two kinds of running shoes

   d. Two types of potato chips

   Remember to keep your choice fairly simple—you are only writing a paragraph. Do not try to compare them on every point. Select maybe two or three major differences.

2. For a longer essay, take two more complicated subjects and compare and contrast them. Try to select four or five major points. You might choose two subjects, philosophies or ideas that are central to another academic course you are taking or you might consider possibilities such as:

   a. Writing with a pen or typewriter/writing on a word processor

   b. Graded courses/pass-fail courses

   c. Drafted army/volunteer army

   d. Fraternity or sorority life/dorm life

   Remember that there are no bad subjects, just bad approaches to subjects. Be certain that you have a thesis and try to say something interesting and insightful about both subjects.

Prewriting:

   a. Try brainstorming for two possible subjects. Remember that the subjects must have some basic similarities. On a sheet of paper, jot down possible pairs of subjects. Try to work on your idea sheet over a two-day period.

   b. Once you have a promising pair, divide another sheet of paper in half. Make lists of possible points of comparison/contrast. Remember that your points must be parallel.

   c. In the margins, number the points in order of significance. Omit any that are too obvious or irrelevant.

   d. Answer the following question: "What does my comparison/contrast reveal?"

Rewriting:

   a. Which pattern of organization did you use? Make a copy of your paper, cut it apart (or move blocks of text on your word processor), and try another pattern of order.

   b. Look closely at the transitions you have used. Highlight those transitions with a colored pen. Are they adequate?

   c. Concluding is never a simple matter. How did you end? Did you just stop? Did you just reword your introduction? Try another strategy.

3. Extend your comparison/contrast of two subjects by doing some research; do not rely just on personal experience or general knowledge. Remember to document your sources.

That Lean and Hungry Look

SUZANNE BRITT JORDAN

Suzanne Britt Jordan was born in Winston-Salem, North Carolina, and attended Salem College and Washington University. She has been a columnist for the Raleigh News and Observer *and* Stars and Stripes, *European edition. She has also written for the Des Moines* Register and Tribune, *the Baltimore* Sun, Newsday, The New York Times, *and* Newsweek. *She is currently teaching at Meredith College in Raleigh, North Carolina. Jordan's books include a collection of essays,* Show and Tell *(1982);* Skinny People Are Dull and Crunchy Like Carrots *(1982), an expansion of her essay "That Lean and Hungry Look"; and* A Writer's Rhetoric *(1988), a college textbook. This essay originally appeared in the "My Turn" column of* Newsweek *magazine. "Thin people need watching," she asserts, and after years of watching, she has reached a conclusion: "I don't like what I see."*

CAESAR WAS RIGHT. Thin people need watching. I've been watching them for most of my adult life, and I don't like what I see. When these narrow fellows spring at me, I quiver to my toes. Thin people come in all personalities, most of them menacing. You've got your "together" thin person, your mechanical thin person, your condescending thin person, your tsk-tsk thin person, your efficiency-expert thin person. All of them are dangerous.

In the first place, thin people aren't fun. They don't know how to goof off, at least in the best, fat sense of the word. They've always got to be adoing. Give them a coffee break, and they'll jog around the block. Supply them with a quiet evening at home, and they'll fix the screen door and lick S&H green stamps. They say things like "there aren't enough hours in the day." Fat people never say that. Fat people think the day is too damn long already.

Thin people make me tired. They've got speedy little metabolisms that cause them to bustle briskly. They're forever rub-

271

bing their bony hands together and eyeing new problems to "tackle." I like to surround myself with sluggish, inert, easy-going fat people, the kind who believe that if you clean it up today, it'll just get dirty again tomorrow.

4   Some people say the business about the jolly fat person is a myth, that all of us chubbies are neurotic, sick, sad people. I disagree. Fat people may not be chortling all day long, but they're a hell of a lot *nicer* than the wizened and shriveled. Thin people turn surly, mean, and hard at a young age because they never learn the value of a hot-fudge sundae for easing tension. Thin people don't like gooey soft things because they themselves are neither gooey nor soft. They are crunchy and dull, like carrots. They go straight to the heart of the matter while fat people let things stay all blurry and hazy and vague, the way things actually are. Thin people want to face the truth. Fat people know there is no truth. One of my thin friends is always staring at complex, unsolvable problems and saying, "The key thing is . . . ." Fat people never say that. They know there isn't any such thing as the key thing about anything.

5   Thin people believe in logic. Fat people see all sides. The sides fat people see are rounded blobs, usually gray, always nebulous and truly not worth worrying about. But the thin person persists. "If you consume more calories than you burn," says one of my thin friends, "you will gain weight. It's that simple." Fat people always grin when they hear statements like that. They know better.

6   Fat people realize that life is illogical and unfair. They know very well that God is not in his heaven and all is not right with the world. If God was up there, fat people could have two doughnuts and a big orange drink anytime they wanted it.

7   Thin people have a long list of logical things they are always spouting off to me. They hold up one finger at a time as they reel off these things, so I won't lose track. They speak slowly as if to a young child. The list is long and full of holes. It contains tidbits like "get a grip on yourself," "cigarettes kill," "cholesterol clogs," "fit as a fiddle," "ducks in a row," "organize," and "sound fiscal management." Phrases like that.

8   They think these 2,000-point plans lead to happiness. Fat people know happiness is elusive at best and even if they could

get the kind thin people talk about, they wouldn't want it. Wisely, fat people see that such programs are too dull, too hard, too off the mark. They are never better than a whole cheesecake.

Fat people know all about the mystery of life. They are the ones acquainted with the night, with luck, with fate, with playing it by ear. One thin person I know once suggested that we arrange all the parts of a jigsaw puzzle into groups according to size, shape, and color. He figured this would cut the time needed to complete the puzzle by at least 50 percent. I said I wouldn't do it. One, I like to muddle through. Two, what good would it do to finish early? Three, the jigsaw puzzle isn't the important thing. The important thing is the fun of four people (one thin person included) sitting around a card table, working a jigsaw puzzle. My thin friend had no use for my list. Instead of joining us, he went outside and mulched the boxwoods. The three remaining fat people finished the puzzle and made chocolate, double-fudged brownies to celebrate. *9*

The main problem with thin people is they oppress. Their good intentions, bony torsos, tight ships, neat corners, cerebral machinations, and pat solutions loom like dark clouds over the loose, comfortable, spread-out, soft world of the fat. Long after fat people have removed their coats and shoes and put their feet up on the coffee table, thin people are still sitting on the edge of the sofa, looking neat as a pin, discussing rutabagas. Fat people are heavily into fits of laughter, slapping their thighs and whooping it up, while thin people are still politely waiting for the punch line. *10*

Thin people are downers. They like math and morality and reasoned evaluation of the limitations of human beings. They have their skinny little acts together. They expound, prognose, probe, and prick. *11*

Fat people are convivial. They will like you even if you're irregular and have acne. They will come up with a good reason why you never wrote the great American novel. They will cry in your beer with you. They will put your name in the pot. They will let you off the hook. Fat people will gab, giggle, guffaw, gallumph, gyrate, and gossip. They are generous, giving, and gallant. They are gluttonous and goodly and great. What you want when you're down is soft and jiggly, not muscled *12* and stable. Fat people know this. Fat people have plenty of room. Fat people will take you in.

QUESTIONS ON SUBJECT AND PURPOSE

1. What is the subject of Jordan's essay? What expectations does she think that her audience might have about that subject?
2. What major points of contrast between thin and fat people does Jordan isolate?
3. Is there anything serious about Jordan's essay, or is she just trying to make us laugh?

QUESTIONS ON STRATEGY AND AUDIENCE

1. Does Jordan use the point-by-point or the subject-by-subject pattern for her essay?
2. Would it make any difference if Jordan's essay were written from the other point of view—that is, a thin person making fun of fat people? Why or why not?
3. The essay originally appeared in the "My Turn" column of *Newsweek* magazine. In identifying the author, presumably quoting from something that Jordan wrote about herself, *Newsweek* offered this descriptive sentence: "Stately, plump Jordan teaches English at North Carolina State University." Why?

QUESTIONS ON VOCABULARY AND STYLE

1. Characterize the tone of Jordan's essay. What types of sentence structure does she use most frequently? Does she ever write sentence fragments? What types of words does she use?
2. Why might Jordan use so much alliteration in the final paragraph?
3. Be prepared to define the following words: *condescending* (paragraph 1), *inert* (3), *chortling* (4), *wizened* (4), *surly* (4), *nebulous* (5), *machinations* (10), and *rutabagas* (10).

WRITING SUGGESTIONS

1. Using a tone similar to Jordan's, write a paragraph in which you take one side of a traditional pairing such as:

a. short people/tall people

b. early risers/late sleepers

c. tidy people/sloppy people

d. savers/spenders

2. Society has many stereotypes, often even conflicting ones. In a serious essay, contrast a pairing such as the ones listed below. Be sure to explore the cultural stereotype(s) that we have constructed.

    a. smokers/nonsmokers

    b. drinkers/nondrinkers

    c. suntanned people/untanned people

    d. tall people/short people

Prewriting:

a. Jot down some possible subjects on a sheet of paper. For each one, describe the stereotype that society has created. What associations immediately come to mind?

b. Look for public manifestations of that stereotype. For example, how is such a person portrayed on television, in commercials or advertisements? Are there clichés associated with the stereotype?

c. Free associate with a group of friends. "When I say . . . , what do you think of?" Take notes on their reactions.

Rewriting:

a. Look again at how you have arranged your points of contrast. Have you used a subject-by-subject approach or a point-by-point one? Justify in a sentence or two your choice of strategy.

b. Check each body paragraph. Does each have a single focus point? Does each contain enough detail? Remember that paragraphs should contain more than a couple of sentences but should not go on for a page or more.

c. Ask two friends or classmates to read your essay and then describe to you what they liked best and least. Listen to them. Do not let them just say that it is good—you want constructive criticism.

3. Select a stereotype that has changed in recent decades. For example, attitudes toward cigarette smokers have changed

sharply in the past few years. Research those changing stereotypes. You might consult old issues of popular magazines in your school's library for visual examples of that stereotype. Check as well in both general and specialized periodical indexes for shifting public or scientific attitudes toward your subject.

Grant and Lee:
A Study in Contrasts

BRUCE CATTON

Born in Petoskey, Michigan, the son of a Congregationalist minister, Bruce Catton (1899–1978) attended Oberlin College in 1916 but left to serve in World War I. After the war, Catton became a journalist, writing for the Cleveland News, *the* Cleveland Plain Dealer, *and the* Boston American, *as well as editing* American Heritage. *Catton won the Pulitzer Prize and the National Book Award for* A Stillness at Appomattox *(1953). This, along with such works as* Mr. Lincoln's Army *(1951),* This Hallowed Ground *(1956), and* Never Call Retreat *(1965), rank him as one of the major Civil War historians. As this essay demonstrates, Catton's approach to history emphasized the personalities of those who made it. Catton's classic essay was first a radio address in a series of broadcasts made by American historians and then later revised for printed publication.*

WHEN ULYSSES S. GRANT and Robert E. Lee met in the parlor of a modest house at Appomattox Court House, Virginia, on April 9, 1865, to work out the terms for the surrender of Lee's Army of Northern Virginia, a great chapter in American life came to a close, and a great new chapter began. 1

These men were bringing the Civil War to its virtual finish. To be sure, other armies had yet to surrender, and for a few days the fugitive Confederate government would struggle desperately and vainly, trying to find some way to go on living now that its chief support was gone. But in effect it was all over when Grant and Lee signed the papers. And the little room where they wrote out the terms was the scene of one of the poignant, dramatic contrasts in American history. 2

They were two strong men, these oddly different generals, and they represented the strengths of two conflicting currents that, through them, had come into final collision. 3

Back of Robert E. Lee was the notion that the old aristocratic 4

277

concept might somehow survive and be dominant in American life.

5   Lee was tidewater Virginia, and in his background were family, culture, and tradition ... the age of chivalry transplanted to a New World which was making its own legends and its own myths. He embodied a way of life that had come down through the age of knighthood and the English country squire. America was a land that was beginning all over again, dedicated to nothing much more complicated than the rather hazy belief that all men had equal rights, and should have an equal chance in the world. In such a land Lee stood for the feeling that it was somehow of advantage to human society to have a pronounced inequality in the social structure. There should be a leisure class, backed by ownership of land; in turn, society itself should be keyed to the land as the chief source of wealth and influence. It would bring forth (according to this ideal) a class of men with a strong sense of obligation to the community; men who lived not to gain advantage for themselves, but to meet the solemn obligations which had been laid on them by the very fact that they were privileged. From them the country would get its leadership; to them it could look for the higher values—of thought, of conduct, of personal deportment—to give it strength and virtue.

6   Lee embodied the noblest elements of this aristocratic ideal. Through him, the landed nobility justified itself. For four years, the Southern states had fought a desperate war to uphold the ideals for which Lee stood. In the end, it almost seemed as if the Confederacy fought for Lee; as if he himself was the Confederacy ... the best thing that the way of life for which the Confederacy stood could ever have to offer. He had passed into legend before Appomattox. Thousands of tired, underfed, poorly clothed Confederate soldiers, long-since past the simple enthusiasm of the early days of the struggle, somehow considered Lee the symbol of everything for which they had been willing to die. But they could not quite put this feeling into words. If the Lost Cause, sanctified by so much heroism and so many deaths, had a living justification, its justification was General Lee.

7   Grant, the son of a tanner on the Western frontier, was

everything Lee was not. He had come up the hard way, and embodied nothing in particular except the eternal toughness and sinewy fiber of the men who grew up beyond the mountains. He was one of a body of men who owed reverence and obeisance to no one, who were self-reliant to a fault, who cared hardly anything for the past but who had a sharp eye for the future.

These frontier men were the precise opposites of the tidewater aristocrats. Back of them, in the great surge that had taken people over the Alleghenies and into the opening Western country, there was a deep implicit dissatisfaction with a past that had settled into grooves. They stood for democracy, not from any reasoned conclusion about the proper ordering of human society, but simply because they had grown up in the middle of democracy and knew how it worked. Their society might have privileges, but they would be privileges each man had won for himself. Forms and patterns meant nothing. No man was born to anything, except perhaps to a chance to show how far he could rise. Life was competition. 8

Yet along with this feeling had come a deep sense of belonging to a national community. The Westerner who developed a farm, opened a shop or set up in business as a trader, could hope to prosper only as his own community prospered— and his community ran from the Atlantic to the Pacific and from Canada down to Mexico. If the land was settled, with towns and highways and accessible markets, he could better himself. He saw his fate in terms of the nation's own destiny. As its horizons expanded, so did his. He had, in other words, an acute dollars-and-cents stake in the continued growth and development of his country. 9

And that, perhaps, is where the contrast between Grant and Lee becomes most striking. The Virginia aristocrat, inevitably, saw himself in relation to his own region. He lived in a static society which could endure almost anything except change. Instinctively, his first loyalty would go to the locality in which that society existed. He would fight to the limit of endurance to defend it, because in defending it he was defending everything that gave his own life its deepest meaning. 10

The Westerner, on the other hand, would fight with an 11

279

equal tenacity for the broader concept of society. He fought so because everything he lived by was tied to growth, expansion, and a constantly widening horizon. What he lived by would survive or fall with the nation itself. He could not possibly stand by unmoved in the face of an attempt to destroy the Union. He would combat it with everything he had, because he could only see it as an effort to cut the ground out from under his feet.

12   So Grant and Lee were in complete contrast, representing two diametrically opposed elements in American life. Grant was the modern man emerging; beyond him, ready to come on the stage, was the great age of steel and machinery, of crowded cities and a restless, burgeoning vitality. Lee might have ridden down from the old age of chivalry, lance in hand, silken banner fluttering over his head. Each man was the perfect champion of his cause, drawing both his strengths and his weaknesses from the people he led.

13   Yet it was not all contrast, after all. Different as they were— in background, in personality, in underlying aspiration—these two great soldiers had much in common. Under everything else, they were marvelous fighters. Furthermore, their fighting qualities were really very much alike.

14   Each man had, to begin with, the great virtue of utter tenacity and fidelity. Grant fought his way down the Mississippi Valley in spite of acute personal discouragement and profound military handicaps. Lee hung on in the trenches at Petersburg after hope itself had died. In each man there was an indomitable quality . . . the born fighter's refusal to give up as long as he can still remain on his feet and lift his two fists.

15   Daring and resourcefulness they had, too; the ability to think faster and move faster than the enemy. These were the qualities which gave Lee the dazzling campaigns of Second Manassas and Chancellorsville and won Vicksburg for Grant.

16   Lastly, and perhaps greatest of all, there was the ability, at the end, to turn quickly from war to peace once the fighting was over. Out of the way these two men behaved at Appomattox came the possibility of a peace of reconciliation. It was a possibility not wholly realized, in the years to come, but which did, in the end, help the two sections to become one nation again . . . after a war whose bitterness might have seemed to

make such a reunion wholly impossible. No part of either man's life became him more than the part he played in their brief meeting in the McLean house at Appomattox. Their behavior there put all succeeding generations of Americans in their debt. Two great Americans, Grant and Lee—very different, yet under everything very much alike. Their encounter at Appomattox was one of the great moments of American history.

QUESTIONS ON SUBJECT AND PURPOSE

1. According to Catton what were the differences between Grant and Lee? What were the similarities?
2. How were both men representative of America?
3. Why does Catton use contrast in order to make his main point? What is that point?

QUESTIONS ON STRATEGY AND AUDIENCE

1. How does Catton structure his essay? Does he use the subject-by-subject pattern or the point-by-point pattern?
2. How does the structure of the last four paragraphs differ from that of the first part of the essay?
3. Catton devotes most of the essay to contrasting Grant and Lee. How then does he manage to emphasize finally the similarities between the two? Why does he do so?
4. Catton was a very popular historian of the American Civil War. What would be the range of audiences to whom Catton's essay might appeal? What does Catton expect of his audience?

QUESTIONS ON VOCABULARY AND STYLE

1. How does Catton use paragraphing in his essay to make his argument clearer?
2. Does Catton show any bias in his comparison? Is there any point in the essay when it appears that he favors one man over the other?
3. Be able to define the following words: *poignant* (paragraph 2), *sinewy* (7), *obeisance* (7), *tenacity* (11), *diametrically* (12), *burgeoning* (12), *indomitable* (14).

WRITING SUGGESTIONS

1. You did something wrong. It does not matter what it was; it was just wrong. Pick two people you know—parents, friends, relatives—and compare/contrast how they would react to your bad news.

2. In an essay compare two people you know. Remember that there must be some basis for comparison, that is, some basic similarities as well as differences between your subjects. You should also try to make some interesting main point or points based on your comparison. Assume that your reader does not know either person.

Prewriting:

a. Review the advice about describing people given in Chapter 3. Your paper will be more successful if your comparison involves more than physical qualities.

b. With that advice in mind, jot down a list of possible pairs of subjects. Fold sheets of paper into quarters and write one subject's name in the left margin and one in the right margin. In the top two quarters list differences; in the bottom, similarities. You ought to have three or four points of comparison as a minimum.

c. Number those points in order of significance. Omit any that seem too obvious. You will need to decide whether you want to begin with similarities or with differences and whether you will begin or end with the most significant point.

Rewriting:

a. Look carefully at the structural decisions you made in item c above. Remember that any order is possible; it is just a question of what seems to work most effectively. Try changing the order of your body paragraphs. Make a copy of the paper, cut it into pieces, and paste up a new version. Does it work better?

b. Find two peer readers. Once they have finished reading your draft, ask them to answer each of the following questions: First, what is the paper's thesis, or why is this comparison being made? Second, which points of similarity or difference seem the least important? Compare their answers. Do they agree with your answers to those questions?

c. Be honest—how good is your conclusion? Did you have trouble ending? Try freewriting a new ending. Force it to be different from your original conclusion.

3. Choose two figures from history or two current people of some notoriety (for example, politicians, entertainers, artists, scientists, public figures). Research your subjects. Then write an essay in which you compare the two. Remember that there must be some basis or reason for making the comparison.

The Arab World

EDWARD T. HALL

Edward T. Hall—scholar, author, teacher, and lecturer—was born in Webster Groves, Missouri, in 1914. He studied at the University of Denver, earned his master's degree at the University of Arkansas, and received a Ph.D. in anthropology at Columbia University. He has been professor of anthropology at the Illinois Institute of Technology (1963–1967) and at Northwestern University (1967–1977). He is the author of a number of books including The Silent Language *(1959), a study of nonverbal communication;* The Hidden Dimension *(1966), a study of social and personal space;* The Dance of Life *(1983), a study of time in other cultures;* Hidden Differences: Doing Business with the Japanese *(1987), coauthored with Mildred Hall; and* Understanding Cultural Differences: Germans, French and Americans *(1990), a study of the differences in underlying cultural patterns of behavior. In this selection from* The Hidden Dimension, *Hall contrasts American and Arab concepts of public and private space. "Arabs look each other in the eye when talking," Hall writes, "with an intensity that makes most Americans highly uncomfortable."*

1   IN SPITE OF OVER two thousand years of contact, Westerners and Arabs still do not understand each other. Proxemic research reveals some insights into this difficulty. Americans in the Middle East are immediately struck by two conflicting sensations. In public they are compressed and overwhelmed by smells, crowding, and high noise levels; in Arab homes Americans are apt to rattle around, feeling exposed and often somewhat inadequate because of too much space! (The Arab houses and apartments of the middle and upper classes which Americans stationed abroad commonly occupy are much larger than the dwellings such Americans usually inhabit.) Both the high sensory stimulation which is experienced in public places and the basic insecurity which comes from being in a dwelling that is too large provide Americans with an introduction to the sensory world of the Arab.

284

Behavior in Public

Pushing and shoving in public places is characteristic of Middle   2
Eastern culture. Yet it is not entirely what Americans think it
is (being pushy and rude) but stems from a different set of assumptions concerning not only the relations between people
but how one experiences the body as well. Paradoxically, Arabs
consider northern Europeans and Americans pushy, too. This
was very puzzling to me when I started investigating these two
views. How could Americans who stand aside and avoid touching be considered pushy? I used to ask Arabs to explain this
paradox. None of my subjects was able to tell me specifically
what particulars of American behavior were responsible, yet
they all agreed that the impression was widespread among
Arabs. After repeated unsuccessful attempts to gain insight into
the cognitive world of the Arab on this particular point, I filed
it away as a question that only time would answer. When the
answer came, it was because of a seemingly inconsequential
annoyance.

While waiting for a friend in a Washington, D.C., hotel   3
lobby and wanting to be both visible and alone, I had seated
myself in a solitary chair outside the normal stream of traffic.
In such a setting most Americans follow a rule, which is all the
more binding because we seldom think about it, that can be
stated as follows: as soon as a person stops or is seated in a
public place, there balloons around him a small sphere of privacy which is considered inviolate. The size of the sphere varies
with the degree of crowding, the age, sex, and the importance
of the person, as well as the general surroundings. Anyone who
enters this zone and stays there is intruding. In fact, a stranger
who intrudes, even for a specific purpose, acknowledges the
fact that he has intruded by beginning his request with "Pardon
me, but can you tell me . . . ?"

To continue, as I waited in the deserted lobby, a stranger   4
walked up to where I was sitting and stood close enough so
that not only could I easily touch him but I could even hear
him breathing. In addition, the dark mass of his body filled the
peripheral field of vision on my left side. If the lobby had been
crowded with people, I would have understood his behavior,

but in an empty lobby his presence made me exceedingly uncomfortable. Feeling annoyed by this intrusion, I moved my body in such a way as to communicate annoyance. Strangely enough, instead of moving away, my actions seemed only to encourage him, because he moved even closer. In spite of the temptation to escape the annoyance, I put aside thoughts of abandoning my post, thinking, "To hell with it. Why should I move? I was here first and I'm not going to let this fellow drive me out even if he is a boor." Fortunately, a group of people soon arrived whom my tormentor immediately joined. Their mannerisms explained his behavior, for I knew from both speech and gestures that they were Arabs. I had not been able to make this crucial identification by looking at my subject when he was alone because he wasn't talking and he was wearing American clothes.

5   In describing the scene later to an Arab colleague, two contrasting patterns emerged. My concept and my feelings about my own circle of privacy in a "public" place immediately struck my Arab friend as strange and puzzling. He said, "After all, it's a public place, isn't it?" Pursuing this line of inquiry, I found that in Arab thought I had no rights whatsoever by virtue of occupying a given spot; neither my place nor my body was inviolate! For the Arab, there is no such thing as an intrusion in public. Public means public. With this insight, a great range of Arab behavior that had been puzzling, annoying, and sometimes even frightening began to make sense. I learned, for example, that if *A* is standing on a street corner and *B* wants his spot, *B* is within his rights if he does what he can to make *A* uncomfortable enough to move. In Beirut only the hardy sit in the last row in a movie theater, because there are usually standees who want seats and who push and shove and make such a nuisance that most people give up and leave. Seen in this light, the Arab who "intruded" on my space in the hotel lobby had apparently selected it for the very reason I had: it was a good place to watch two doors and the elevator. My show of annoyance, instead of driving him away, had only encouraged him. He thought he was about to get me to move.

6   Another silent source of friction between Americans and Arabs is in an area that Americans treat very informally—the

manners and rights of the road. In general, in the United States we tend to defer to the vehicle that is bigger, more powerful, faster, and heavily laden. While a pedestrian walking along a road may feel annoyed he will not think it unusual to step aside for a fast-moving automobile. He knows that because he is moving he does not have the right to the space around him that he has when he is standing still (as I was in the hotel lobby). It appears that the reverse is true with the Arabs who apparently *take on rights to space as they move.* For someone else to move into a space an Arab is also moving into is a violation of his rights. It is infuriating to an Arab to have someone else cut in front of him on the highway. It is the American's cavalier treatment of moving space that makes the Arab call him aggressive and pushy.

Concepts of Privacy

The experience described above and many others suggested to me that Arabs might actually have a wholly contrasting set of assumptions concerning the body and the rights associated with it. Certainly the Arab tendency to shove and push each other in public and to feel and pinch women in public conveyances would not be tolerated by Westerners. It appeared to me that they must not have any concept of a private zone outside the body. This proved to be precisely the case. 7

In the Western world, the person is synonymous with an individual inside a skin. And in northern Europe generally, the skin and even the clothes may be inviolate. You need permission to touch either if you are a stranger. This rule applies in some parts of France, where the mere touching of another person during an argument used to be legally defined as assault. For the Arab the location of the person in relation to the body is quite different. The person exists somewhere down inside the body. The ego is not completely hidden, however, because it can be reached very easily with an insult. It is protected from touch but not from words. The dissociation of the body and the ego may explain why the public amputation of a thief's hand is tolerated as standard punishment in Saudi Arabia. It also sheds light on why an Arab employer living in a modern apart- 8 ment can provide his servant with a room that is a boxlike cubicle approximately 5 by 10 by 4 feet in size that is not only hung from the ceiling to conserve floor space but has an opening so that the servant can be spied on.

9   As one might suspect, deep orientations toward the self such as the one just described are also reflected in the language. This was brought to my attention one afternoon when an Arab colleague who is the author of an Arab-English dictionary arrived in my office and threw himself into a chair in a state of obvious exhaustion. When I asked him what had been going on, he said: "I have spent the entire afternoon trying to find the Arab equivalent of the English word 'rape.' There is no such word in Arabic. All my sources, both written and spoken, can come up with no more than an approximation, such as 'He took her against her will.' There is nothing in Arabic approaching your meaning as it is expressed in that one word."

10   Differing concepts of the placement of the ego in relation to the body are not easily grasped. Once an idea like this is accepted, however, it is possible to understand many other facets of Arab life that would otherwise be difficult to explain. One of these is the high population density of Arab cities like Cairo, Beirut, and Damascus. According to the animal studies described in the earlier chapters,* the Arabs should be living in a perpetual behavioral sink. While it is probable that Arabs are suffering from population pressures, it is also just as possible that continued pressure from the desert has resulted in a cultural adaptation to high density which takes the form described above. Tucking the ego down inside the body shell not only would permit higher population densities but would explain why it is that Arab communications are stepped up as much as they are when compared to northern European communication patterns. Not only is the sheer noise level much higher, but the piercing look of the eyes, the touch of the hands, and the mutual bathing in the warm moist breath during conversation represent stepped-up sensory inputs to a level which many Europeans find unbearably intense.

11   The Arab dream is for lots of space in the home, which

* Of Hall's *The Hidden Dimension.*

unfortunately many Arabs cannot afford. Yet when he has space, it is very different from what one finds in most American homes. Arab spaces inside their upper middle-class homes are tremendous by our standards. They avoid partitions because Arabs *do not like to be alone.* The form of the home is such as to hold the family together inside a single protective shell, because Arabs are deeply involved with each other. Their personalities are intermingled and take nourishment from each other like the roots and soil. If one is not with people and actively involved in some way, one is deprived of life. An old Arab saying reflects this value: "Paradise without people should not be entered because it is Hell." Therefore, Arabs in the United States often feel socially and sensorially deprived and long to be back where there is human warmth and contact.

Since there is no physical privacy as we know it in the Arab   12
family, not even a word for privacy, one could expect that the Arabs might use some other means to be alone. Their way to be alone is to stop talking. Like the English, an Arab who shuts himself off in this way is not indicating that anything is wrong or that he is withdrawing, only that he wants to be alone with his own thoughts or does not want to be intruded upon. One subject said that her father would come and go for days at a time without saying a word, and no one in the family thought anything of it. Yet for this very reason, an Arab exchange student visiting a Kansas farm failed to pick up the cue that his American hosts were mad at him when they gave him the "silent treatment." He only discovered something was wrong when they took him to town and tried forcibly to put him on a bus to Washington, D.C., the headquarters of the exchange program responsible for his presence in the U.S.

Arab Personal Distances

Like everyone else in the world, Arabs are unable to formulate   13
specific rules for their informal behavior patterns. In fact, they often deny that there are any rules, and they are made anxious by suggestions that such is the case. Therefore, in order to determine how the Arab sets distances, I investigated the use of each sense separately. Gradually, definite and distinctive behavioral patterns began to emerge.

14   Olfaction occupies a prominent place in the Arab life. Not only is it one of the distance-setting mechanisms, but it is a vital part of a complex system of behavior. Arabs consistently breathe on people when they talk. However, this habit is more than a matter of different manners. To the Arab good smells are pleasing and a way of being involved with each other. To smell one's friend is not only nice but desirable, for to deny him your breath is to act ashamed. Americans, on the other hand, trained as they are not to breathe in people's faces, automatically communicate shame in trying to be polite. Who would expect that when our highest diplomats are putting on their best manners they are also communicating shame? Yet this is what occurs constantly, because diplomacy is not only "eyeball to eyeball" but breath to breath.

15   By stressing olfaction, Arabs do not try to eliminate all the body's odors, only to enhance them and use them in building human relationships. Nor are they self-conscious about telling others when they don't like the way they smell. A man leaving his house in the morning may be told by his uncle, "Habib, your stomach is sour and your breath doesn't smell too good. Better not talk too close to people today." Smell is even considered in the choice of a mate. When couples are being matched for marriage, the man's go-between will sometimes ask to smell the girl, who may be turned down if she doesn't "smell nice." Arabs recognize that smell and disposition may be linked.

16   In a word, the olfactory boundary performs two roles in Arab life. It enfolds those who want to relate and separates those who don't. The Arab finds it essential to stay inside the olfactory zone as a means of keeping tab on changes in emotion. What is more, he may feel crowded as soon as he smells something unpleasant. While not much is known about "olfactory crowding," this may prove to be as significant as any other variable in the crowding complex because it is tied directly to the body chemistry and hence to the state of health and emotions. . . . It is not surprising, therefore, that the olfactory boundary constitutes for the Arabs an informal distance-setting mechanism in contrast to the visual mechanisms of the Westerner.

Facing and Not Facing

One of my earliest discoveries in the field of intercultural com-   17
munication was that the position of the bodies of people in
conversation varies with the culture. Even so, it used to puzzle
me that a special Arab friend seemed unable to walk and talk
at the same time. After years in the United States, he could not
bring himself to stroll along, facing forward while talking. Our
progress would be arrested while he edged ahead, cutting
slightly in front of me and turning sideways so we could see
each other. Once in this position, he would stop. His behavior
was explained when I learned that for the Arabs to view the
other person peripherally is regarded as impolite, and to sit or
stand back-to-back is considered very rude. You must be involved when interacting with Arabs who are friends.

One mistaken American notion is that Arabs conduct all   18
conversations at close distances. This is not the case at all. On
social occasions, they may sit on opposite sides of the room and
talk across the room to each other. They are, however, apt to
take offense when Americans use what are to them ambiguous
distances, such as the four- to seven-foot social-consultative
distance. They frequently complain that Americans are cold or
aloof or "don't care." This was what an elderly Arab diplomat
in an American hospital thought when the American nurses
used "professional" distance. He had the feeling that he
was being ignored, that they might not take good care of him.
Another Arab subject remarked, referring to American behavior, "What's the matter? Do I smell bad? Or are they afraid
of me?"

Arabs who interact with Americans report experiencing a   19
certain flatness traceable in part to a very different use of the
eyes in private and in public as well as between friends and
strangers. Even though it is rude for a guest to walk around the
Arab home eying things, Arabs look at each other in ways which
seem hostile or challenging to the American. One Arab informant said that he was in constant hot water with Americans
because of the way he looked at them without the slightest
intention of offending. In fact, he had on several occasions

barely avoided fights with American men who apparently thought their masculinity was being challenged because of the way he was looking at them. As noted earlier, Arabs look each other in the eye when talking with an intensity that makes most Americans highly uncomfortable.

Involvement

20   As the reader must gather by now, Arabs are involved with each other on many different levels simultaneously. Privacy in a public place is foreign to them. Business transactions in the bazaar, for example, are not just between buyer and seller, but are participated in by everyone. Anyone who is standing around may join in. If a grownup sees a boy breaking a window, he must stop him even if he doesn't know him. Involvement and participation are expressed in other ways as well. If two men are fighting, the crowd must intervene. On the political level, *to fail to intervene* when trouble is brewing is to take sides, which is what our State Department always seems to be doing. Given the fact that few people in the world today are even remotely aware of the cultural mold that forms their thoughts, it is normal for Arabs to view *our* behavior as though it stemmed from *their* own hidden set of assumptions.

Feelings about Enclosed Spaces

21   In the course of my interviews with Arabs the term "tomb" kept cropping up in conjunction with enclosed space. In a word, Arabs don't mind being crowded by people but hate to be hemmed in by walls. They show a much greater overt sensitivity to architectural crowding than we do. Enclosed space must meet at least three requirements that I know of if it is to satisfy the Arabs: there must be plenty of unobstructed space in which to move around (possibly as much as a thousand square feet); very high ceilings—so high in fact that they do not normally impinge on the visual field; and, in addition, there must be an unobstructed view. It was spaces such as these in which the Americans referred to earlier felt so uncomfortable. One sees the Arab's need for a view expressed in many ways, even neg-

atively, for to cut off a neighbor's view is one of the most effective ways of spiting him. In Beirut one can see what is known locally as the "spite house." It is nothing more than a thick, four-story wall, built at the end of a long fight between neighbors, on a narrow strip of land for the express purpose of denying a view of the Mediterranean to any house built on the land behind. According to one of my informants, there is also a house on a small plot of land between Beirut and Damascus which is completely surrounded by a neighbor's wall built high enough to cut off the view from all windows!

Boundaries

Proxemic patterns tell us other things about Arab culture. For example, the whole concept of the boundary as an abstraction is almost impossible to pin down. In one sense, there are no boundaries. "Edges" of towns, yes, but permanent boundaries out in the country (hidden lines), no. In the course of my work with Arab subjects I had a difficult time translating our concept of a boundary into terms which could be equated with theirs. In order to clarify the distinctions between the two very different definitions, I thought it might be helpful to pinpoint acts which constituted trespass. To date, I have been unable to discover anything even remotely resembling our own legal concept of trespass. 22

Arab behavior in regard to their own real estate is apparently an extension of, and therefore consistent with, their approach to the body. My subjects simply failed to respond whenever trespass was mentioned. They didn't seem to understand what I meant by this term. This may be explained by the fact that they organize relationships with each other according to closed social systems rather than spatially. For thousands of years Moslems, Marinites, Druses, and Jews have lived in their own villages, each with strong kin affiliations. Their hierarchy of loyalties is: first to one's self, then to kinsman, townsman, or tribesman, co-religionist and/or countryman. Anyone not in these categories is a stranger. Strangers and enemies are very closely linked, if not synonymous, in Arab thought. Trespass in 23 this context is a matter of who you are, rather than a piece of land or a space with a boundary that can be denied to anyone and everyone, friend and foe alike.

24   In summary, proxemic patterns differ. By examining them it is possible to reveal hidden cultural frames that determine the structure of a given people's perceptual world. Perceiving the world differently leads to differential definitions of what constitutes crowded living, different interpersonal relations, and a different approach to both local and international politics.

QUESTIONS ON SUBJECT AND PURPOSE

1. "Proxemics" was coined by Hall and so does not appear in many dictionaries. On the basis of what the word looks like and how Hall uses it in the essay, what does the word seem to mean?

2. What are the key differences or contrasts between Arab and American senses of "olfaction"? Why doesn't Hall describe the American reaction to personal smells?

3. Why is the study of "proxemics" important?

QUESTIONS ON STRATEGY AND AUDIENCE

1. Why might Hall narrate at such great length his confrontation with an Arab in a hotel lobby (paragraphs 3 to 5)? Why not just state the conclusion?

2. From where does Hall draw his information and examples? How authoritative does his argument seem?

3. Although Hall is contrasting Arab and American behavior patterns, he basically concentrates on describing only Arab behavior. Why? What might this strategy have to do with his sense of audience?

QUESTIONS ON VOCABULARY AND STYLE

1. What is the advantage of inventing or using a word like "proxemics"?

2. At a number of points in the essay, Hall creates imaginary dialogues or responses to situations. He puts these sentences in quotation marks. Why might he invent such sentences?

3. Be prepared to define the following words: *cognitive* (paragraph 2), *inviolate* (3), *peripheral* (4), *cavalier* (6), *conveyances* (7), *ego* (8), *facets* (10), *olfaction* (14), *overt* (21), *impinge* (21), *express* (21).

WRITING SUGGESTIONS

1. Based on your observations of friends or roommates and your experiences, contrast in a paragraph two people's attitudes toward a specific issue or behavior. You might consider the following possible subjects:

    a. Telephone habits and use

    b. Shared versus private space

    c. Shared versus private objects

    d. Neatness versus sloppiness

    e. Loudness of conversations or music

    f. Patterns of public behavior

2. Differences such as those Hall writes about are not limited to people from different countries or cultures. People of different ages or socioeconomic backgrounds or with different value systems can have substantial conflicts and disagreements. Compare and contrast the behavioral patterns of any two people. Your essay will work best if you can establish a pattern of differences rather than simply saying that your roommate is neat and you are sloppy.

Prewriting:

    a. Think about people whose behaviors or values are different from yours. Have you ever suddenly realized that the two of you see things in completely different ways? Are there times when you made conscious compromises with this person? Create a list of those people and those times.

    b. Once you have a list of such experiences, select those examples in which the contrast was most obvious and significant.

    c. Try beginning with a striking example of a contrast.

Rewriting:

    a. Convert the list of things to remember at the end of this chapter's introduction into a list of questions. Use those questions as a way of checking your draft.

b. Give the list and your draft to a roommate or classmate and ask for honest answers to those questions.

c. Look again at how you arranged the body of your essay. Is there a definite order in which you have presented the contrasts? What is it? Does any other order seem to work better? Play with some other arrangements.

3. As an objective observer, write an essay on cultural differences between two groups. You should have a central thesis (Hall's was people's differing needs for space). The two cultures can be foreign, or one foreign and the other American, or both subcultures within America. In addition to library research, you will probably also want to interview some representative people. Remember to use specific examples; do not over-generalize; be wary of making biased judgments.

Understanding the Difference

PHYLLIS SCHLAFLY

Born in 1924 in St. Louis, Missouri, Phyllis Schlafly received an A.B. from Washington University. She received an M.A. degree from Radcliffe, and later earned a law degree from Washington University. Schlafly is a well-known and highly vocal opponent of the Equal Rights Amendment and is also active in defending the conservative point of view on other issues. In 1957 she began publication of her monthly newsletter The Phyllis Schlafly Report. *In addition, she is the author of* The Power of the Positive Woman *(1977),* The Power of the Christian Woman *(1981),* Child Abuse in the Classroom *(1984), and* Pornography Victims *(1987). Involved not only in women's issues, Schlafly has written editorials and essays on timely topics, such as the AIDS epidemic and censorship in the schools. In "Understanding the Difference," an excerpt from* The Power of the Positive Woman, *Schlafly classifies men as logical and women as emotional. She also raises a number of issues and questions that were significant in the battle over the ERA.*

THE FIRST REQUIREMENT for the acquisition of power by the Positive Woman is to understand the differences between men and women. Your outlook on life, your faith, your behavior, your potential for fulfillment, all are determined by the parameters of your original premise. The Positive Woman starts with the assumption that the world is her oyster. She rejoices in the creative capability within her body and the power potential of her mind and spirit. She understand that men and women are different, and that those very differences provide the key to her success as a person and fulfillment as a women.

The women's liberationist, on the other hand, is imprisoned by her own negative view of herself and of her place in the world around her. This view of women was most succinctly expressed in an advertisement designed by the principal women's liberationist organization, the National Organization for Women (NOW), and run in many magazines and newspapers and as spot announcements on many television stations. The advertisement showed a darling curlyheaded girl with the caption: "This healthy, normal baby has a handicap. She was born female."

3   This is the self-articulated dog-in-the-manger, chip-on-the-shoulder, fundamental dogma of women's liberation movement. Someone—it is not clear who, perhaps God, perhaps the "Establishment," perhaps a conspiracy of male chauvinist pigs—dealt women a foul blow by making them female. It becomes necessary, therefore, for women to agitate and demonstrate and hurl demands on society in order to wrest from an oppressive male-dominated social structure the status that has been wrongfully denied to women through the centuries.

4   By its very nature, therefore, the women's liberation movement precipitates a series of conflict situations—in the legislatures, in the courts, in the schools, in industry—with man targeted as the enemy. Confrontation replaces cooperation as the watchword of all relationships. Women and men become adversaries instead of partners.

5   The second dogma of the women's liberationists is that, of all the injustices perpetrated upon women through the centuries, the most oppressive is the cruel fact that women have babies and men do not. Within the confines of the women's liberationist ideology, therefore, the abolition of this overriding inequality of women becomes the primary goal. This goal must be achieved at any and all costs—to the woman herself, to the baby, to the family, and to society. Women must be made equal to men in their ability *not* to become pregnant and *not* to be expected to care for babies they may bring into the world.

6   This is why women's liberationists are compulsively involved in the drive to make abortion and child-care centers for all women, regardless of religion or income, both socially acceptable and government-financed. Former Congresswoman Bella Abzug has defined the goal: "to enforce the constitutional right of females to terminate pregnancies that they do not wish to continue."

7   If man is targeted as the enemy, and the ultimate goal of women's liberation is independence from men and the avoidance of pregnancy and its consequences, then lesbianism is

logically the highest form in the ritual of women's liberation. Many, such as Kate Millett, come to this conclusion, although many others do not.

The Positive Woman will never travel that dead-end road. *8* It is self-evident to the Positive Woman that the female body with its baby-producing organs was not designed by a conspiracy of men but by the Divine Architect of the human race. Those who think it is unfair that women have babies, whereas men cannot, will have to take up their complaint with God because no other power is capable of changing that fundamental fact. On some college campuses, I have been assured that other methods of reproduction will be developed. But most of us must deal with the real world rather than with the imagination of dreamers.

Another feature of the woman's natural role is the obvious *9* fact that women can breast-feed babies and men cannot. This functional role was not imposed by conspiratorial males seeking to burden women with confining chores, but must be recognized as part of the plan of the Divine Architect for the survival of the human race through the centuries and in the countries that know no pasteurization of milk or sterilization of bottles.

The Positive Woman looks upon her femaleness and her *10* fertility as part of her purpose, her potential, and her power. She rejoices that she has a capability for creativity that men can never have.

The third basic dogma of the women's liberation movement *11* is that there is no difference between male and female except the sex organs, and that all those physical, cognitive, and emotional differences you *think* are there, are merely the result of centuries of restraints imposed by a male-dominated society and sex-stereotyped schooling. The role imposed on women is, by definition, inferior, according to the women's liberationists.

The Positive Woman knows that, while there are some *12* physical competitions in which women are better (and can command more money) than men, including those that put a premium on grace and beauty, such as figure skating, the superior physical strength of males over females in competitions of strength, speed, and short-term endurance is beyond rational dispute.

13   In the Olympic Games, women not only cannot win any medals in competition with men, the gulf between them is so great that they cannot even qualify for the contests with men. No amount of training from infancy can enable women to throw the discus as far as men, or to match men in push-ups or in lifting weights. In track and field events, individual male records surpass those of women by 10 to 20 percent.

14   Female swimmers today are beating Johnny Weissmuller's records, but today's male swimmers are better still. Chris Evert can never win a tennis match against Jimmy Connors. If we removed lady's tees from golf courses, women would be out of the game. Putting women in football or wrestling matches can only be an exercise in laughs.

15   The Olympic Games, whose rules require strict verification to ascertain that no male enters a female contest and, with his masculine advantage, unfairly captures a woman's medal, formerly insisted on a visual inspection of the contestants' bodies. Science, however, has discovered that men and women are so innately different physically that their maleness/femaleness can be conclusively established by means of a simple skin test of fully clothed persons.

16   If there is *anyone* who should oppose enforced sex-equality, it is the women athletes. Babe Didrikson, who played and defeated some of the great male athletes of her time, is unique in the history of sports.

17   If sex equality were enforced in professional sports, it would mean that men could enter the women's tournaments and win most of the money. Bobby Riggs has already threatened: "I think that men 55 years and over should be allowed to play women's tournaments—like the Virginia Slims. Everybody ought to know there's no sex after 55 anyway."

18   The Positive Woman remembers the essential validity of the old prayer: "Lord, give me the strength to change what I can change, the serenity to accept what I cannot change, and the wisdom to discern the difference." The women's liberationists are expending their time and energies erecting a make-believe world in which they hypothesize that *if* schooling were gender-free, and *if* the same money were spent on male and female sports programs, and *if* women were permitted to compete on

equal terms, *then* they would prove themselves to be physically equal. Meanwhile, the Positive Woman has put the ineradicable physical differences into her mental computer, programmed her plan of action, and is already on the way to personal achievement.

Thus, while some militant women spend their time de- 19 manding more money for professional sports, ice skater Janet Lynn, a truly Positive Woman, quietly signed the most profitable financial contract in the history of women's athletics. It was not the strident demands of the women's liberationists that brought high prizes to women's tennis but the discovery by sports promoters that beautiful female legs gracefully moving around the court made women's tennis a highly marketable television production to delight male audiences.

Many people thought that the remarkable filly named Ruf- 20 fian would prove that a female race horse could compete equally with a male. Even with the handicap of extra weights placed on the male horse, the race was a disaster for the female. The gallant Ruffian gave her all in a noble effort to compete, but broke a leg in the race and, despite the immediate attention of top veterinarians, had to be put away.

Despite the claims of the women's liberation movement, 21 there are countless physical differences between men and women. The female body is 50 to 60 percent water, the male 60 to 70 percent water, which explains why males can dilute alcohol better than women and delay its effect. The average woman is about 25 percent fatty tissue, while the male is 15 percent, making women more buoyant in water and able to swim with less effort. Males have a tendency to color blindness. Only 5 percent of persons who get gout are female. Boys are born bigger. Women live longer in most countries of the world, not only in the United States where we have a hard-driving competitive pace. Women excel in manual dexterity, verbal skills, and memory recall.

Arianna Stassinopoulos in her book *The Female Woman* has 22 done a good job of spelling out the many specific physical differences that are so innate and so all-pervasive that

even if Women's Lib was given a hundred, a thousand, ten

thousand years in which to eradicate *all* the differences between the sexes, it would still be an impossible undertaking
. . .

23   It is inconceivable that millions of years of evolutionary
selection during a period of marked sexual division of labor
have not left pronounced traces on the innate character of men
and women. Aggressiveness, and mechanical and spatial skills,
a sense of direction, and physical strength—all masculine
characteristics—are the qualities essential for a hunter; even
food gatherers need these same qualities for defense and exploration. The prolonged period of dependence of human children, the difficulty of carrying the peculiarly heavy and inert
human baby—a much heavier, clumsier burden than the
monkey infant and much less able to cling on for safety—
meant that women could not both look after their children
and be hunters and explorers. Early humans learned to take
advantage of this period of dependence to transmit rules,
knowledge and skills to their offspring—women needed to
develop verbal skills, a talent for personal relationships, and
a predilection for nurturing going even beyond the maternal
instinct.*

24   Does the physical advantage of men doom women to a life
of servility and subservience? The Positive Woman knows that
she has a complementary advantage which is at least as great—
and, in the hands of a skillful woman, far greater. The Divine
Architect who gave men a superior strength to lift weights also
gave women a different kind of superior strength.

25   The women's liberationists and their dupes who try to tell
each other that the sexual drive of men and women is really
the same, and that it is only societal restraints that inhibit
women from an equal desire, an equal enjoyment, and an equal
freedom from the consequences, are doomed to frustration forever. It just isn't so, and pretending cannot make it so. The
differences are not a woman's weakness but her strength.

26   Dr. Robert Collins, who has had ten years's experience in
listening to and advising young women at a large eastern university, put his finger on the reason why casual "sexual activity"
is such a cheat on women:

* Arianna Stassinopoulos, *The Female Woman* (New York: Random House, 1973)
pp. 30–31.

A basic flaw in this new morality is the assumption that 27
males and females are the same sexually. The simplicity of the
male anatomy and its operation suggest that to a man, sex can
be an activity apart from his whole being, a drive related to
the organs themselves.

In a woman, the complex internal organization, correlated 28
with her other hormonal systems, indicates her sexuality must
involve her total self. On the other hand, the man is orgasm-
oriented with a drive that ignores most other aspects of the
relationship. The woman is almost totally different. She is engulfed in romanticism and tries to find and express her total
feelings for her partner.

A study at a midwestern school shows that 80 percent of 29
the women who had intercourse hoped to marry their partner.
Only 12 percent of the men expected the same.

Women say that soft, warm promises and tender touches 30
are delightful, but that the act itself usually leads to a "Is that
all there is to it?" reaction . . .

[A typical reaction is]: "It sure wasn't worth it. It was no 31
fun at the time. I've been worried every since. . . ."

The new morality is a fad. It ignores history, it denies the 32
physical and mental compositions of human beings, it is in-
tolerant, exploitative, and is oriented toward intercourse, not
love.*

The new generation can brag all it wants about the new 33
liberation of the new morality, but it is still the woman who is
hurt most. The new morality isn't just a "fad"—it is a cheat
and a thief. It robs the woman of her virtue, her youth, her
beauty, and her love—for nothing, just nothing. It has produced
a generation of young women searching for their identity, bored
with sexual freedom, and despondent from the loneliness of
living a life without commitment. They have abandoned the
old commandments, but they can't find any new rules that
work.

The Positive Woman recognizes the fact that, when it comes 34
to sex, women are simply not the equal of men. The sexual
drive of men is much stronger than that of women. That is how
the human race was designed in order that it might perpetuate

* *Chicago Tribune*, August 17, 1975.

itself. The other side of the coin is that it is easier for women to control their sexual appetites. A Positive Woman cannot defeat a man in a wrestling or boxing match, but she can motivate him, inspire him, encourage him, teach him, restrain him, reward him, and have power over him that he can never achieve over her with all his muscle. How or whether a Positive Woman uses her power is determined solely by the way she alone defines her goals and develops her skills.

35   The differences between men and women are also emotional and psychological. Without woman's innate maternal instinct, the human race would have died out centuries ago. There is nothing so helpless in all earthly life as the newborn infant. It will die within hours if not cared for. Even in the most primitive, uneducated societies, women have always cared for their newborn babies. They didn't need any schooling to teach them how. They didn't need any welfare workers to tell them it is their social obligation. Even in societies to whom such concepts as ''ought,'' ''social responsibility,'' and ''compassion for the helpless'' were unknown, mothers cared for their new babies.

36   Why? Because caring for a baby serves the natural maternal need of a woman. Although not nearly so total as the baby's need, the woman's need is nonetheless real.

37   The overriding psychological need of a woman is to love something alive. A baby fulfills this need in the lives of most women. If a baby is not available to fill that need, women search for a baby-substitute. This is the reason why women have traditionally gone into teaching and nursing careers. They are doing what comes naturally to the female psyche. The schoolchild or the patient of any age provides an outlet for woman to express her natural maternal need.

38   This maternal need in women is the reason why mothers whose children have grown up and flown from the nest are sometimes cut loose from their psychological moorings. The maternal need in women can show itself in love for grandchildren, nieces, nephews, or even neighbors' children. The maternal need in some women has even manifested itself in an extraordinary affection lavished on a dog, a cat or a parakeet.

39   This is not to say that every woman must have a baby in

order to be fulfilled. But it is to say that fulfillment for most women involves expressing their natural maternal urge by loving and caring for someone.

The women's liberation movement complains that traditional stereotyped roles assume that women are "passive" and that men are "aggressive." The anomaly is that a women's most fundamental emotional need is not passive at all, but active. A woman naturally seeks to love affirmatively and to show that love in an active way by caring for the object of her affections. [40]

The Positive Woman finds somebody on whom she can lavish her maternal love so that it doesn't well up inside her and cause psychological frustrations. Surely no woman is so isolated by geography or insulated by spirit that she cannot find someone worthy of her maternal love. All persons, men and women, gain by sharing something of themselves with their fellow humans, but women profit most of all because it is part of their very nature. [41]

One of the strangest quirks of women's liberationists is their complaint that societal restraints prevent men from crying in public or showing their emotions, but permit women to do so, and that therefore we should "liberate" men to enable them, too, to cry in public. The public display of fear, sorrow, anger, and irritation reveals a lack of self-discipline that should be avoided by the Positive Woman just as much as by the Positive Man. Maternal love, however, is not a weakness but a manifestation of strength and service, and it should be nurtured by the Positive Woman. [42]

Most women's organizations, recognizing the preference of most women to avoid hard-driving competition, handle the matter of succession of officers by the device of a nominating committee. This eliminates the unpleasantness and the tension of a competitive confrontation every year or two. Many women's organizations customarily use a prayer attributed to Mary, Queen of Scots, which is an excellent analysis by a woman of women's faults: [43]

> Keep us, O God, from pettiness; let us be large in thought, in word, in deed. Let us be done with fault-finding and leave off self-seeking . . . Grant that we may realize it is the little [44]

things that create differences, that in the big things of life we are at one.

45   Another silliness of the women's liberationists is their frenetic desire to force all women to accept the title *Ms* in place of *Miss* or *Mrs.* If Gloria Steinem and Betty Friedan want to call themselves *Ms* in order to conceal their marital status, their wishes should be respected.

46   But that doesn't satisfy the women's liberationists. They want all women to be compelled to use *Ms* whether they like it or not. The women's liberation movement has been waging a consistent campaign to browbeat the media into using *Ms* as the standard title for all women. The women's liberationists have already succeeded in getting the Department of Health, Education and Welfare to forbid schools and colleges from identifying women students as *Miss* or *Mrs.**

47   All polls show that the majority of women do not care to be called *Ms.* A Roper poll indicated that 81 percent of the women questioned said they prefer *Miss* or *Mrs.* to *Ms.* Most married women feel they worked hard for the *r* in their names, and they don't care to be gratuitously deprived of it. Most single women don't care to have their name changed to an unfamiliar title that at best conveys overtones of feminist ideology and is polemical in meaning, and at worst connotes misery instead of joy. Thus, Kate Smith, a very Positive Woman, proudly proclaimed on television that she is "Miss Kate Smith, not Ms." Like other Positive Women, she has been succeeding while negative women have been complaining.

48   Finally, women are different from men in dealing with the fundamentals of life itself. Men are philosophers, women are practical, and 'twas ever thus. Men may philosophize about how life began and where we are heading; women are concerned about feeding the kids today. No woman would ever, as Karl Marx did, spend years reading political philosophy in the British Museum while her child starved to death. Women don't take naturally to a search for the intangible and the abstract. The Positive Woman knows who she is and where she

* HEW—Regulation on Sex Discrimination in Schools and Colleges, effective July 18, 1975, #86.21(c)(4).

is going, and she will reach her goal because the longest journey starts with a very practical first step.

Amaury de Riencourt, in his book *Sex and Power in History*, shows that a successful society depends on a delicate balancing of male and female factors, and that the women's liberation movement, which promotes unisexual values and androgyny, contains within it "a social and cultural death wish and the end of the civilization that endorses it." 49

One of the few scholarly works dealing with woman's role, *Sex and Power in History* synthesizes research from a variety of disciplines—sociology, biology, history, anthropology, religion, philosophy, and psychology. De Riencourt traces distinguishable types of women in different periods in history, from prehistoric to modern times. The "liberated" Roman matron, who is most similar to the present-day feminist, helped bring about the fall of Rome through her unnatural emulation of masculine qualities, which resulted in a large-scale breakdown of the family and ultimately of the empire. 50

De Riencourt examines the fundamental, inherent differences between men and women. He argues that man is the more aggressive, rational, mentally creative, analytical-minded sex because of his early biological role as hunter and provider. Woman, on the other hand, represents stability, flexibility, reliance on intuition, and harmony with nature, stemming from her procreative function. 51

Where man is discursive, logical, abstract, or philosophical, woman tends to be emotional, personal, practical, or mystical. Each set of qualities is vital and complements the other. Among the many differences explained in de Riencourt's book are the following: 52

> Women tend more toward conformity than men—which is why they often excel in such disciplines as spelling and punctuation where there is only one correct answer, determined by social authority. Higher intellectual activities, however, require a mental independence and power of abstraction that they usually lack, not to mention a certain form of aggressive boldness of the imagination which can only exist in a sex that is basically aggressive for biological reasons. 53
>
> To sum up: The masculine proclivity in problem solving 54

307

is analytical and categorical; the feminine, synthetic and contextual . . . Deep down, man tends to focus on the object, on external results and achievements; woman focuses on subjective motives and feelings. If life can be compared to a play, man focuses on the theme and structure of the play, woman on the innermost feelings displayed by the actors.*

55 De Riencourt provides impressive refutation of two of the basic errors of the women's liberation movement: (1) that there are no emotional or cognitive differences between the sexes, and (2) that women should strive to be like men.

56 A more colloquial way of expressing the de Riencourt conclusion that men are more analytical and women more personal and practical is in the different answers that one is likely to get to the question, "Where did you get that steak?" A man will reply, "At the corner market," or wherever he bought it. A woman will usually answer, "Why? What's the matter with it?"

57 An effort to eliminate the differences by social engineering or legislative or constitutional tinkering cannot succeed, which is fortunate, but social relationships and spiritual values can be ruptured in the attempt. Thus the role reversals being forced upon high school students, under which guidance counselors urge reluctant girls to take "shop" and boys to take "home economics," further confuse a generation already unsure about its identity. They are as wrong as efforts to make a left-handed child right-handed.

QUESTIONS ON SUBJECT AND PURPOSE

1. What is Schlafly comparing and contrasting in this selection?
2. Using just the material included here, define the "Positive Woman." With whom is the "Positive Woman" contrasted?
3. According to Schlafly, what are the differences between men and women?
4. What is Schlafly's purpose in this essay? Is it specific (for example, to denounce women's liberationists), or is it more general?

* Amaury de Riencourt, *Sex and Power in History* (New York: David McKay Co., Inc. 1974), p. 56.

308

QUESTIONS ON STRATEGY AND AUDIENCE

1. How does Schlafly structure her argument? Make a brief outline of the selection.
2. What do each of the following add to Schlafly's argument? Why might she include each?
   a. The example of Ruffian (paragraph 20)
   b. The quotations from Stassinopoulos (following paragraph 22), Collins (after 26), and De Riencourt (after 52)
   c. The example of the use of Ms. rather than Mrs. or Miss
3. Reread the opening sentence of the selection. Would anyone disagree with this statement? What is the implication behind this sentence?

QUESTIONS ON VOCABULARY AND STYLE

1. At several points, Schlafly uses clichés. Make a list of those that you recognize. Why does she use them?
2. How would you characterize Schlafly's tone in the selection? How is that tone achieved?
3. Be able to define the following words: *parameters* (paragraph 1), *succinctly* (2), *dogma* (3), *cognitive* (11), *ineradicable* (18), *innate* (22), *anomaly* (40), *quirks* (42), *frenetic* (45), *gratuitously* (47), *polemical* (47), *androgyny* (49), *emulation* (50), *discursive* (52), *proclivity* (54).

WRITING SUGGESTIONS

1. Schlafly sees a number of significant differences between men and women. On the basis of your personal experience, write a paragraph in which you contrast men and women on a single point. Concentrate on a specific attitude or type of behavior. Be sure to use examples to substantiate your contrast.
2. Schlafly uses contrast to define. The "positive woman" is defined through contrasting her both with the "woman's liberationist" and with men. In an essay, use contrast to define something. You might consider the following possibilities:
   a. The ideal mate/relationship/marriage
   b. The ideal career
   c. The ideal college education

d. The greatest good

Do not hesitate to substitute a topic of your choice.

Prewriting:

a. Make a list of at least six possible topics. Do not rush into making a decision on a single one. Instead, jot down ideas over a two-day period. For each topic, note several ways to develop the contrast.

b. Look carefully at Schlafly's writing strategy. Whether you agree with her points or not does not matter; you are examining her strategy as a writer. Try to sketch out a working outline for your essay.

c. Once you have a promising topic and a possible organizational scheme, try freewriting each body paragraph. Write for 15 minutes without stopping. That will allow you to play with ideas and organization without committing yourself to a final, fixed form.

Rewriting:

a. Read each paragraph with a critical eye. Is every sentence relevant? Do you have a clear, controlling focus for each paragraph? If not, do some editing.

b. Are your transitions clearly signaled for the reader? Use a colored pen to mark the transitional devices.

c. Once you have a complete draft, jot down on a separate sheet of paper what troubles you the most about the paper. What could be better? What are you most uneasy about? Allow a day to pass and then try to solve just that particular problem. If your college has a writing center or a peer tutoring program, take your specific problem there.

3. Compare and contrast the modern woman of the 1990s with the turn-of-the-century woman. Select four to six points of comparison/contrast, and, using secondary sources, document the changes that have occurred or have not occurred. How have the role, position, status, and self-definition of women changed during the twentieth century? You might prepare your paper either as a traditional college research paper or as a feature article for a popular magazine. If you are writing a research paper, be sure to document your sources.

A Writer's Revision Process: Why We Need to Learn

WILLIAM OUCHI

William George Ouchi was born in Hawaii in 1943 and received his B.A. from Williams College in 1965. He completed an M.B.A. at Stanford in 1967 and a Ph.D. at the University of Chicago in 1972. A specialist in organizational behavior, he is now a professor of management in the graduate school at the University of California, Los Angeles. His most recent book, co-authored with Jay B. Barney, is Organizational Economics *(1987).*

Reprinted here are two versions of the opening chapter of his best-selling Theory Z: How American Business Can Meet the Japanese Challenge *(1981). On his writing and revising, Ouchi has observed: "My writing almost always represents the expression of several years of data gathering, data analysis, field interviews, and other original work. The great majority of* Theory Z *is a description of that work. The introduction you reproduce represents my attempt to capture the essence of my research, couched in terms which will directly communicate to a large number of readers. My practice is to type my first draft, usually at the rate of approximately 20 pages per day, writing in roughly 12-hour days. My draft went to my editor at Addison-Wesley, who read it through several times, attempting to grasp the underlying structure of my argument. She then suggested to me ways that I might delete, add, and reorganize material. The revision you reproduce is a consequence of my attempt to respond to her suggestions. In my books, my editor has never rewritten a word, but has passed along suggestions and criticisms to me, leaving it to me to incorporate as much advice as I can."*

Theory Z gets its name as a contrast to Theories X and Y advanced by Douglas McGregor in The Human Side of Enterprise *(1960). Those theories represent two different assumptions about what motivates people to work. Theory X assumes that people dislike work and must be coerced and directed to do it; Theory Y assumes that people want to work, derive satisfaction from it, and are self-directed. Ouchi's subject in* Theory Z *is the art of Japanese management and how it can be adapted to American business. "While many Japanese admire the American automobile,'' he observes, ''they would never accept the low quality with which they are put together.''*

REVISED DRAFT★

1   NOT LONG AGO, I arranged a luncheon for two of my Ph.D. students with the vice-president of one of the most respected and largest firms in the United States—a company that regularly appears on lists of the "ten best-managed companies." The luncheon provided an opportunity for these educators of the future to ask our guest questions for which his position and experience had given him a unique perspective. After a discussion ranging over many issues, the students summarized their interests in a single question: "What, in your opinion, is the key issue facing American business over the next decade?" His answer: "The key issue will not be technology or investment, not regulation or inflation. The key issue will be the way in which we respond to one fact—the Japanese know how to manage better than we do."

2   A case in point: A team of engineers and managers from the Buick Division of General Motors Corporation recently visited their dealer in Tokyo, who imports Buick automobiles and sells them to the Japanese. The operation appeared to be a massive repair facility, so they asked how he had built up such a large service business. He explained with some embarrassment that this was *not* a repair facility at all but rather a re-assembly operation where newly delivered cars were disassembled and rebuilt to Japanese standards. While many Japanese admire the American automobile, he noted, they would never accept the low quality with which they are put together.

3   Stories like this one abound. We know that productivity in Japan has increased at 400 percent the rate in the United States over the postwar years. More seriously, we know that productivity in the United States is now improving more slowly than

---

★ Bar indicates areas of major revision.

in any European nation, including the much-maligned United Kingdom. While many observers have marvelled at the success of the Japanese, they have concluded that Japan is one country from which we cannot learn much. They feel Japanese techniques simply are not applicable to our situation.

But our story has a different sequel. The engineers and managers at Buick didn't assume that the Japanese success would work in Flint, Michigan, and they set out to invent their own version of it. They took the Buick Final Assembly Plant, which had dropped to one of the lowest levels of efficiency and quality in the whole corporation, and with the cooperation of workers and their union redesigned the management of that plant in ways that resemble the Japanese approach to management. Within two years, Buick Final Assembly had risen to rank number one among all General Motors assembly plants in quality and efficiency. The ideas that shaped the remaking of General Motors' troubled Buick plant are the basis of what I call the Theory Z approach to management. Quite simply, it suggests that involved workers are the key to increased productivity.

As a nation, we have developed a sense of the value of technology and of a scientific approach to it, but we have meanwhile taken people for granted. Our government appropriates hundreds of millions of dollars for research on new techniques in electrical engineering, physics, and astronomy. It supports the development of complex economic ideas. But almost no funds go to develop our understanding of how to manage and organize people at work, and that is what we have to learn by studying the Japanese. The problem of productivity in the United States will not be solved with monetary policy nor through more investment in research and development. It will only be remedied when we learn how to manage people in such a way that they can work together more effectively. Theory Z offers several such ways. American workers perform just as hard as their Japanese counterparts. American managers want high performance just as much as the Japanese. Increased productivity will not come through harder work. Most employees work as hard as they can, and many work too hard for their own good in trying to catch up. Productivity, I believe, is a problem of social organization or, in business terms, managerial organization. Productivity is a problem that can be worked out through coordinating individual efforts in a productive manner and giving employees the incentives to do so by taking a co-operative, long-range view.

6   The first lesson of Theory Z is trust. Productivity and trust go hand in hand, strange as it may seem. To understand that assertion, observe the development of the British economy during this century. It is a history of mutual distrust between union, government, and management, a distrust that has paralyzed the economy and lowered the English standard of living to a dismal level. Karl Marx foresaw this distrust as the inevitable product of capitalism and the force that, in his view, would bring about the ultimate failure of capitalism.

7   But capitalism and trust need not be mutually exclusive. Thomas Lifson, a young scholar at the Harvard Business School, has studied in detail the Japanese general trading firms, those firms like Mitsui, Mitsubishi, and Sumitomo that maintain offices worldwide and have traditionally served as the sales force for Japanese-produced goods. Undoubtedly these trading companies have played a central role in the successful export strategy of Japanese industry. They have the capacity to move quickly into new markets, to strike deals where no American company can, and to coordinate far-flung operations. According to Lifson, the central feature of the trading firm is an extensive management system that maintains a sense of trust between employees in the trading company. Japanese employees, just like their American counterparts, want to get ahead. They want to make deals beneficial to both their departments and themselves. They work in an environment of tremendous uncertainty, buying and selling copper ore, crude oil, wheat, and televisions. On a typical day, the central office of one of the major trading firms will receive 35,000 telex messages, each one with an offer to buy or sell. Often, the firm's overall profitability will be maximized if an office takes a loss, which will be more than made up in another office so that the company benefits overall. The success of the trading company depends critically upon the willingness of individual offices and employees to make these sacrifices. That willingness exists because the Japanese trading firm uses managerial practices that foster

trust through the knowledge that such sacrifices will always be repaid in the future. Equity will, in the end, be restored.

DISCUSSION QUESTIONS

1. What is the Theory Z approach to management? Why do the Japanese know how to manage better than Americans?

2. How does Ouchi use examples to develop his argument?

3. What is the effect of Ouchi's almost casual beginning—the story about the Buick dealer in Tokyo, the first-person pronoun ("I")? Why not begin with a more formal statement of thesis introduction?

4. What assumptions does Ouchi seem to make about his audience? Is there anything in his word choice or writing style that offers clues to those assumptions?

5. Be able to define the following words: *maligned* (paragraph 3), *sequel* (4), *monetary policy* (5), *telex message* (7), *equity* (7).

EARLIER DRAFT

A TEAM OF ENGINEERS and managers from the Buick Division of   1
General Motors Corporation recently visited their dealer in Tokyo, who imports Buick automobiles and sells them to the Japanese. As they toured his operation, they saw what appeared to be a massive repair facility and asked how he had built up such a large service business. He replied, with some embarrassment, that this was not a repair facility at all but rather a re-assembly operation in which he tore down newly delivered cars and rebuilt them to Japanese standards. While many Japanese admire the American automobile, they would never accept the low quality with which they are put together, he explained.

Stories like this one abound. We know that productivity in   2
Japan has increased at 400% the rate in the U.S. over the postwar years. More seriously, we know that productivity in the U.S. is improving now more slowly than in any European nation, including the often-maligned U.K. While many observers have marvelled at the success of the Japanese, they have sadly concluded that it is one from which we cannot learn much. The

success of the Japanese, it is often said, stems from Japan's relatively recent industrialization, so that they still draw upon a large stock of hard-working farm boys and farm girls who will put in long hours at low pay. It is due to the fact that Japan is still technologically behind the U.S. and thus can make great gains at low cost by borrowing technology, whereas we must invent our own. It is also due, we hear, to the fact that the Japanese have somehow managed to maintain a work ethic, whereas the U.S. has become soft and lazy. The conclusion: the Japanese success is intriguing but not applicable to us.

3   But our story has a different sequel. The engineers and managers at Buick didn't know that the Japanese success wouldn't work in Flint, Michigan, and they set out to invent their version of it. They took the Buick Final Assembly Plant, which had dropped to one of the lowest levels of efficiency and quality in the whole corporation and, with the cooperation of workers and their union, redesigned the management of that plant in ways that resemble the Japanese approach to management. Within two years, Buick Final Assembly has risen to rank number one among all General Motors assembly plants in quality and efficiency.

4   It seems that we, as a nation, have developed a fine sense of the value of technology and of a scientific approach to technology, but we have meanwhile taken people for granted. Our government readily appropriates hundreds of millions of dollars for research on new techniques in electrical engineering, it supports the development of complex economic ideas, but almost nothing goes to develop our understanding of how to manage and organize people at work, and that is what we have to learn from the Japanese. The problem of productivity in the U.S. will not be solved with monetary policy, it will not be solved through more investment in research and development, it will only be solved when we learn how to manage people in such a way that they can work together more effectively.

5   There is a second issue: trust. Productivity and trust go hand in hand, strange as it may seem. To understand that assertion, we need only observe the development of the British economy over the past thirty years. It is a history of mutual distrust between union, government, and management, a distrust that has

paralyzed the economy and lowered the standard of living of all Englishmen to a dismal level. It is the kind of distrust that Karl Marx foresaw as the inevitable product of capitalism and the force that, in this view, will bring about the ultimate failure of capitalism. But capitalism and trust need not be mutually exclusive. Thomas Lifson, a young scholar at the Harvard Business School, has studied in detail the Japanese General Trading Firm, those firms like Mitsui, Mitsubishi, and Sumitomo that maintain offices world-wide and serve as the sales force for Japanese-produced goods. There is no question that these trading companies have played a central role in the successful export strategy of Japanese industry. They have the capacity to move quickly into new markets, to strike deals where no American company can, and to coordinate far-flung operations. According to Lifson, the central feature of the trading firm is an extensive management system that maintains a sense of trust between employees in the trading company. A Japanese employee, just like his American counterpart, is interested in getting ahead. He is interested in making deals that will benefit his department and make him look good. He works in an environment of tremendous uncertainty, buying and selling copper ore, crude oil, wheat, and televisions. On a typical day, the central office of one of the major trading firms will receive 35,000 telex messages, each one with an offer to buy or to sell. Often, the overall profitability of the firm will be maximized if an office takes a loss—that loss will be more than made up in a different office by such an amount that the company benefits overall. In fact, the success of the trading company depends critically upon the willingness of individual offices and employees to make these sacrifices. That willingness exists because the Japanese trading firm has in place a large number of managerial practices that foster trust through the knowledge that such sacrifices will always be repaid in the future. Equity will, in the end, be restored.

QUESTIONS ON THE REVISED DRAFT

1. The most obvious change is the added opening paragraph. How does that introduce or prepare the reader for what follows? Does the change seem to be effective?

2. In the third paragraph Ouchi had originally included three sentences citing often-quoted reasons why the Japanese were successful. In the final draft he omitted those sentences. Why?

3. At the end of the fourth paragraph and again in the fifth, Ouchi added sentences dealing with Theory Z. Why might he have done that? Do these additions seem necessary? Are they helpful?

4. Can you find a single strategy that seems to account for most of the large-scale revisions?

5. Ouchi made a number of minor changes in word choice and in sentence structure. Find an example of each, and be ready to comment on the effect of these changes.

WRITING SUGGESTIONS

1. After you have analyzed the two versions, formulate a thesis about one strategy Ouchi used in revising his work. In a paragraph support your thesis by citing appropriate evidence from the two versions.

2. If Theory Z can be used to build better automobiles, could it also be used to produce better educated students? Using just Ouchi's essay and no outside sources, in an essay show how Theory Z might be applied to high school or college education.

Prewriting:

a. Start with a definition of Theory Z. What is the Theory Z approach to management?

b. Brainstorm some possible applications of that theory to American education.

c. Anticipate your audience's reactions. Make a list of objections that your readers might raise about your proposals. How can each be countered?

Rewriting:

a. Have you defined Theory Z for your reader? Remember that your reader will not necessarily be familiar with Ouchi's argument.

b. Have you made explicit proposals for improving education? Look back through your argument. Do not rely just on generalizations. Be specific.

c. Every essay benefits from an interesting, lively introduction. Make a copy of your introduction, and ask a friend to read it. Does your reader want to keep reading?

3. The comparison between Japanese and American industries, products, and workers is a common one. Research one aspect of the problem, and present your conclusions. You might consider the following topics:

   a. A comparison of worker efficiency

   b. A comparison of product quality

   c. An analysis of why Japanese manufactured goods are so popular with Americans

   d. An argument for "buying American"

   e. An analysis of the effects of Japanese imports upon the American economy

SIX

Process

What do a recipe in a cookbook, a discussion of how the body converts food into energy and fat, a description of how igneous rocks are formed, and three sentences from your college's registration office on how to drop or add a course have in common? Each is a process analysis—either a set of directions for how to do something (make lasagna or drop a course) or a description of how something happens or is done (food is converted or rocks are formed). These two different types of process writing have two different purposes. The function of a set of directions is to allow the reader to duplicate the process; the function of process description is to tell the reader how something happens. The selection from *The Amy Vanderbilt Complete Book of Etiquette* outlines how a young executive woman should deal with the business lunch or dinner. Peter Elbow explains how to do a quick revision of your prose. Joan Didion in "On Keeping a Notebook" and Judith Viorst in "How Books Helped Shape My Life" describe processes not meant to be done or imitated by the reader. Even Didion's purpose, for example, is not to offer the reader advice on how to keep a notebook but rather to describe how and why *she* keeps a notebook.

How Do You Choose a Subject to Write About?

Choosing a subject is not a problem if you have been given a specific assignment—to describe how a congressional bill becomes a law, how a chemistry experiment was performed, how to write an A paper for your English course. Often, however, you have to choose your own subject. Several considerations are crucial in making that decision.

First, choose a subject that can be adequately described or analyzed in the space you have available. When Judith Viorst in "How Books Helped Shape My Life" catalogs the heroines with whom she identified on her "journey into young womanhood," she isolates six examples, one from each stage of her own development. She does not try to identify every influential heroine or every possible influence; she confines her analysis to these six examples.

Second, in a process analysis, as in any other writing assignment, identify the audience to whom you are writing. What does that audience already know about your subject? Are you writing to a general audience, an audience of your fellow classmates, or a specialized audience? You do not want to bore your reader with the obvious, nor do you want to lose your reader in a tangle of unfamiliar terms and concepts. Your choice of subject and certainly your approach to it should be determined by your audience. Peter Elbow's advice on "quick revising" appeared in a writing textbook; he knew or could assume that his audience would be interested in the fine points of such a process. Judith Viorst's essay originally appeared in *Redbook*, a magazine that targets its audience as "women 18–34 years old," obviously a group of readers who would identify with Viorst's experience. Identifying your audience—what they might be interested in, what they already know—will help in both selecting a subject and deciding on how or what to write about it. Subjects can generally be approached from a number of different points of view. A process essay on how to apply eye makeup reaches a large but still limited audience (women who wear eye makeup), but an essay explaining why women wear eye makeup would have, potentially, a much broader audience.

How Do You Structure a Process Paper?

If you have ever tried to assemble something from a set of directions, you know how important it is that each step or stage in the process be clearly defined and properly placed in the sequence. Because process always involves a series of events or steps that must be done or must occur in proper order, the fundamental structure for a process paragraph or essay will be chronological.

Since proper order is essential, begin your planning by making a list of the various steps in the process. Once your list seems complete, arrange the items in the order in which they are performed or in which they occur. Check to make sure that nothing has been omitted or misplaced. If your process is a description of how to do or make something, you should check your arranged list by performing the process according to the directions you have assembled so far. This ordered list will serve as the outline for your process paper.

Converting your list or outline into a paragraph or essay is the next step. Be sure that all of the phrases on your outline have been turned into complete sentences and that any technical terms have been carefully explained for your reader. You will need some way of signaling to your reader each step or stage in the process. On your list, you simply numbered the steps, but in your paragraph or essay you generally cannot use such a device. More commonly, process papers employ various types of step or time markers to indicate order. Step markers like "first," "second," and "third" can be added to the beginnings of either sentences or paragraphs devoted to each individual stage. Time markers like "begin," "next," "in three minutes," or "while this is being done" remind the reader of the proper chronological sequence. Peter Elbow in "Quick Revising" carefully uses time markers to direct his reader ("First," "next," "now," "if after all this").

Sample Student Essay

PROCESS

Like many college students, Lyndsey Curtis had had considerable experience waiting on customers. Lyndsey decided to use that experience as the basis for some simple but relevant advice to any salesperson:

EARLIER DRAFT

Pleasing the Customer

After 2½ years working in an ice cream store and countless times being annoyed by salespeople, I have devised a surefire three-point plan to please your customers.

(1) Always greet the customer with a smile and a friendly ''May I help you?'' Not only does this make him or her feel good, but it has an added bonus for you: if you are friendly to the customer, he or she will be more friendly to you and less likely to give you a hard time. Sometimes this is difficult to do if you have had a hard day, but just remember that there is nothing more aggravating than an unfriendly salesperson. If you absolutely cannot stand to smile at one more person, ask another employee to cover for you and go to the back of the store and scream. You'll feel much better and will be able to face the shoppers pleasantly.

(2) Give the customer your undivided attention. If another employee or your boss needs to know something or to have you do something immediately, then take care of it. Customers will usually understand if you interrupt them to take care of something related to business. Just don't talk about your plans for the weekend or what happened on ''General Hospital'' yesterday.

(3) When the customer leaves, smile and tell him or her to have a nice day or to come back soon. Let him or her know that you appreciate his or her business, and

make him or her want to continue doing business with you.

    The most important thing to remember is that if it weren't for the customer, you wouldn't be getting paid. If you keep this in mind, you shouldn't have any trouble following the guidelines described above.

After Lyndsey had finished a draft of her essay, she went to see her instructor for a conference. Together they discussed what she had written. The obvious strength of her essay was that its central portion—the three-step process—was logically arranged from greeting the customer to concluding the sale. Some other areas of her paper, however, needed attention. Specifically, her instructor suggested that she look again at her opening and closing paragraphs. In the introductory sentence Lyndsey tries to establish her experience both as a salesperson and as a customer, but linking the two together is confusing. In the final paragraph she could reorder the last two sentences so that the climactic statement ("you wouldn't be getting paid") comes at the end of the paper. After this discussion of rhetorical choices (choices made for reasons of effectiveness rather than correctness), Lyndsey asked about her third paragraph. She noticed that she began with a statement—"Give the customer your undivided attention"—only to qualify it in the sentence that follows. One final trouble spot was the fourth paragraph where, in attempting to be nonsexist in her use of pronouns, she was forced into the awkward "him or her." Lyndsey and her instructor arrived at the obvious way to avoid the situation— make the reference plural ("customers"). When Lyndsey revised her paper, she tried to address each of the problems that had been discussed in the conference.

REVISED DRAFT

How to Wait on a Customer

    I've been on both sides of the sales counter, so I can sympathize with both parties. I've worked in an ice cream store for 2½ years, and I know that some customers are obnoxious or rude. On the other hand, however, I've been annoyed by ignorant salespeople who seemed to think that helping me was a great chore. As a result of my experiences, I have devised a surefire three-point plan to please your customers.

(1) Always greet your customers with a smile and a friendly ''May I help you?'' Not only does this make them feel good, but it has an added bonus for you: if you are friendly to them, they will be more friendly to you and less likely to give you a hard time. Sometimes this is difficult to do if you have had a bad day, but just remember that there is nothing more aggravating than an unfriendly salesperson. If you absolutely cannot stand to smile at one more person, ask another employee to cover for you and go to the back of the store and scream! It always worked for me.

(2) Give the customers your undivided attention. They will understand an interruption due to store business, as long as you apologize for it and assure them that you will return to help them as soon as possible. Just don't talk about your plans for the weekend or what happened on ''General Hospital'' yesterday!

(3) When customers leave, smile and tell them to have a nice day or to come back soon. Let them know that you appreciate their business, and make them want to continue doing business with you.

If you have any trouble following the guidelines described above, just keep this in mind: if it weren't for the customers, you wouldn't be getting paid.

Some Things to Remember

1. Choose a subject that can be analyzed and described within the space you have available.
2. Remember that process takes two forms reflecting its two possible purposes: first, to tell the reader how to do something; second, to tell the reader how something happens. Make sure that you have a purpose clearly in mind before you start your paper.

3. Identify your audience and write to that audience. Ask yourself, "Will my audience be interested in what I am writing about?" and "How much does my audience know about this subject?"

4. Make a list of the various steps or stages in the process.

5. Order or arrange a list, checking to make sure nothing is omitted or misplaced.

6. Convert the list into paragraphs using complete sentences. Remember to define any unfamiliar terms or concepts.

7. Use step or time markers to indicate the proper sequence in the process.

8. Check your process one final time to make sure that nothing has been omitted. If you are describing how to do something, use your paper as a guide to the process. If you are describing how something happens, ask a friend to read your process analysis to see whether it is clear.

A Woman Picks Up the Tab

AMY VANDERBILT
and
LETITIA BALDRIGE

Born into a prominent New York family, Amy Vanderbilt (1908–1974) attended New York University from 1926 to 1928. She then worked in a variety of capacities—as an advertising executive, a columnist, the vice-president and president of Publicity Associates, a dress designer, and a wine consultant. With the publication of Amy Vanderbilt's Complete Book of Etiquette *(1932), she came to be considered by many as America's foremost authority on taste and manners. Her other books include* Amy Vanderbilt's Everyday Etiquette *(1952) and* Amy Vanderbilt's Complete Cookbook *(1961). In addition, she wrote the long-running column "Amy Vanderbilt's Etiquette."*

Letitia Baldrige was born in Miami Beach, Florida, received a B.A. from Vassar, and did graduate work at the University of Geneva. She has served as social secretary to Ambassador Clare Booth Luce and First Lady Jacqueline Kennedy, and has been an intelligence officer, public relations director for Tiffany & Company, president of her own public relations firm, and director of consumer affairs for Burlington Industries. In 1978, she revised and expanded Amy Vanderbilt's Complete Book of Etiquette and Amy Vanderbilt's Everyday Etiquette. *Her own books include the autobiographic* Of Diamonds and Diplomats *(1968); a novel,* Public Affairs, Private Relations *(1990); and several guides to social behavior including* Letitia Baldrige's Complete Guide to Executive Manners *(1985),* Complete Guide to a Great Social Life *(1987), and* Complete Guide to the New Manners for the Nineties *(1990). Here the authors discuss a common problem faced by young executive women: how to pick up the tab when dining with a male business companion.*

ONE OF THE THINGS women who are reaching for the executive   *1*
suite are going to have to accept is the financial responsibilities

327

of their new status. They must learn how to do things gracefully that heretofore they may have regarded as a man's duty—such as paying the bill for meals, taxis, or rented limousines. When a woman lunches or dines with a man on business, they are not on a date. If he begins to act as though they were, she should quickly discourage such attempts. (It is up to her to set the mood of business for such meals.) It is perfectly proper for a man to pick up the check for the first business lunch they have together, but she should pick it up the second time, and they should continue alternating, as men properly do. Sometimes these lunch meetings occur twice a year only, so one should keep a record of who took whom to lunch the last time.

2   Some jobs necessitate the transaction of regular business over the lunch table. It makes the situation easier for a woman if that lunch table is situated in her company's executive dining room or at a club, where, as a member, she can sign the bill without a fuss. She should not, however, invite her male colleague to a women's club for a business lunch if that club is used almost exclusively by women at lunchtime. A woman does not mind being overpowered by the number of men in *his* club (in fact she usually quite enjoys it), but a man minds being overpowered by the number of women in *her* club.

3   No one likes a man who is known never to pick up a check. In today's world, people are going to feel the same about a woman who is known never to pick up a tab. The woman executive is going to have to learn how to pay gracefully when it's her turn.

4   In order to save embarrassment all around, who will pay for the next business lunch should be decided without question in advance. If it's a woman's turn, she should make it very clear over the telephone or face to face when the appointment is made that she will be paying. She has only to say with a smile that it really *is* her turn. She should name the time and the place, call the restaurant, and make the reservation in her name.

5   At the end of lunch she should unobtrusively ask for the bill, add the waiter's tip to the total without an agonizing exercise in mathematics, and then use her credit card or sign her name and her company's address on the back of the check (if

she has a charge account there). If she does this quietly, no one around them need be aware of her actions.

If the man she has invited to lunch is really uncomfortable about her paying (and a woman should sense this immediately when she is making arrangements with him beforehand), then it is better to settle the bill with the head waiter away from the table. She should excuse herself at dessert time on the pretext of going to the powder room and make the bill arrangements then. 6

If a head waiter has performed a lot of service at the table, a woman who is paying the bill at an expensive restaurant should tip him just as a man would (from one to three dollars, according to the restaurant and the service). She can include his tip along with the waiter's by writing it on the bill, if she wishes. The woman who is hosting the meal should also tip the hat check person for the coats of her guests, although any guest leaving separately should pay for his or her coat upon leaving. 7

A dilemma confronting men who are the guests of women at business meals is one that has worried women since men began taking them out to restaurants. Many women were taught by their families when they were young (and especially by older brothers) that a girl on a date must always order the least expensive thing on the menu, if she was to be invited out again. I think we should all be careful in our business lives, too, to watch the right-hand column where the prices are. A man who is a guest of a woman should follow his hostess' lead in respect to suggestions she makes from the menu. Particularly if you are the guest of a self-employed person, you should order carefully, because paying for the meal will affect that person financially much more than it would a large corporation. However, corporate expense account or not, it is always better to order moderate-priced items when you are another's guest, keeping a firm check on overly expensive preferences. 8

QUESTIONS ON SUBJECT AND PURPOSE

1. In what way is this selection a process narrative?

2. Why would an etiquette book treat such a topic? Why would it be important?

3. Where did you learn about proper social behavior? Have you ever consulted an etiquette book? Would you in the future? Why or why not?

QUESTIONS ON STRATEGY AND AUDIENCE

1. How is the selection structured? Is the process always clear?

2. On six occasions, the authors enclose additional information or comments within parentheses. Why use this particular device? Is the information enclosed in this way similar in each instance?

3. What assumptions do the writers make about their audience? Characterize their assumed audience.

QUESTIONS ON VOCABULARY AND STYLE

1. How would you describe the tone used in the selection? How is it achieved? How appropriate is it for the audience or the context?

2. What is the effect of the following sentence: "A woman does not mind being overpowered by the number of men in *his* club (in fact, she usually quite enjoys it), but a man minds being overpowered by the number of women in *her* club" (paragraph 2)?

3. Be able to define the following words: *unobtrusively* (paragraph 5), *pretext* (6).

WRITING SUGGESTIONS

1. The traditional rituals of behavior between men and women have changed in recent years. For example, today a woman can ask a man out on a date, but twenty years ago such an action would have been rare or even unthinkable. Select a single area of etiquette in male/female relationships and in a paragraph write an etiquette guide for that particular situation. You might consider writing for several different possible audiences such as:

   a. young adults

   b. middle-aged parents

c. a mature, senior audience

2. Expand what you did in Suggestion 1. Write an essay guide to proper etiquette in several related, common situations.

   Prewriting:

   a. One way to gather ideas is to consult some etiquette books available in the reference section of your college library. Spend some time thumbing through at least two different guides. Make a list of possible topics.

   b. Ask some friends for other possibilities. Did their parents or grandparents provide any etiquette instruction? Did yours? Add these ideas to your list.

   c. Look back over your list. Place an asterisk next to those topics/situations that are fairly common. Remember that for your essay you will need probably three to six developed examples.

   Rewriting:

   a. Jot down a brief list of the examples you used on a separate sheet of paper. Is there a logical principle behind the order you have used? Is there any other way in which the examples might be organized? Try renumbering them.

   b. Have you made clear transitions from one paragraph to another? Use a colored pen to mark those transitions on a copy of your paper.

   c. Before you began writing, you identified an audience. Now that you have finished, answer this question: "Will my audience be interested in my subject?" Remember, there are no bad or boring subjects, just bad and boring approaches to subjects.

3. Etiquette books and columns in newspapers have always been popular in America. Check the best seller list in a Sunday newspaper. Probably half of the books listed offer advice—on widely differing subjects. Study the list and visit a bookstore or library to examine copies. Then analyze the popularity of such books. Why do Americans buy them in such numbers? What do they say about us as a people?

A Manual:
Training for Landlords

FRAN LEBOWITZ

Fran Lebowitz was born in Morristown, New Jersey, in 1950 and now lives in New York City. Prior to becoming a writer, she worked at a number of what she calls "colorful and picturesque" jobs, such as driving taxis and cleaning apartments. She eventually found a job on the advertising staff of Changes *and convinced the editors to publish her book and film reviews. She later became a columnist for Andy Warhol's* Interview *and for* Mademoiselle. *She is best known for her two best-selling collections of satirical essays,* Metropolitan Life *(1978) and* Social Studies *(1981). One reviewer observed, "The quick-witted, quick-tempered Lebowitz may be the funniest chronic complainer on the scene." In this essay from* Metropolitan Life, *Lebowitz uses process analysis to provide a satiric look at the relationship between landlords and tenants. She writes that a landlord should not be "a slave to convention" and has the option of providing such extras as heat, hot water, and walls.*

1   EVERY PROFESSION requires of its members certain skills, talents, or training. Dancers must be light on their feet. Brain surgeons must attend medical school. Candlestick makers must have an affinity for wax. These occupations, though, are only the tip of the iceberg. How do others learn their trades? We shall see.

How to Be a Landlord: An Introduction

2   In order to be a landlord, it is first necessary to acquire a building or buildings. This can be accomplished in either of two ways. By far the most pleasant is by means of inheritance—a method favored not only because it is easy on the pocketbook but also because it eliminates the tedious chore of selecting the property. This manual, however, is not really intended for landlords of that stripe, since such an inheritance invariably includes a ge-

netic composition that makes formal instruction quite superfluous.

Less attractive but somewhat more common (how often   3
those traits go hand in hand) is the method of actual purchase.
And it is here that our work really begins.

Lesson One: Buying

Buildings can be divided into two main groups: cheap and ex-   4
pensive. It should be remembered, however, that these terms
are for professional use only and never to be employed in the
presence of tenants, who, almost without exception, prefer the
words *very* and *reasonable*. If the price of a building strikes you
as excessive, you would do well to consider that wise old slogan
"It's not the initial cost—it's the upkeep," for as landlord you
are in the enviable position of having entered a profession in
which the upkeep is taken care of by the customer. This concept
may be somewhat easier to grasp by simply thinking of yourself
as a kind of telephone company. You will be further encouraged
when you realize that while there may indeed be a wide disparity in building prices, this terrible inequity need not be passed
on to the tenant in the degrading form of lower rent. It should
now be clear to the attentive student that choosing a building
is basically a matter of personal taste and, since it is the rare
landlord who is troubled by such a quality, we shall proceed
to the next lesson.

Lesson Two: Rooms

The most important factor here is that you understand that a   5
room is a matter of opinion. It is, after all, your building, and
if you choose to designate a given amount of space as a room,
then indeed it *is* a room. Specifying the function of the room
is also your responsibility, and tenants need frequently to be
reminded of this as they will all too often display a tendency
to call one of your rooms a closet. This is, of course, a laughable
pretension, since few tenants have ever seen a closet.

Lesson Three: Walls

A certain numbers of walls are one of the necessary evils of the   6
business. And while some of you will understandably bridle at

the expense, the observant student is aware that walls offer a good return on investment by way of providing one of the basic components of rooms. That is not to say that you, as landlord, must be a slave to convention. Plaster and similarly substantial materials are embarrassingly passé to the progressive student. If you are a father, you know that walls can enjoyably be made by children at home or camp with a simple paste of flour and water and some of Daddy's old newspapers. The childless landlord might well be interested in Wallies—a valuable new product that comes on a roll. Wallies tear off easily and *can* be painted, should such a procedure ever be enforced by law.

Lesson Four: Heat

7   The arrival of winter seems invariably to infect the tenant with an almost fanatical lust for warmth. Sweaters and socks he may have galore; yet he refuses to perceive their usefulness and stubbornly and selfishly insists upon obtaining *his* warmth through *your* heat. There are any number of ploys available to the resourceful landlord, but the most effective requires an actual cash outlay. No mind, it's well worth it—fun, too. Purchase a tape recorder. Bring the tape recorder to your suburban home and place it in the vicinity of your heater. Here its sensitive mechanism will pick up the sounds of impending warmth. This recording played at high volume in the basement of the building has been known to stymie tenants for days on end.

Lesson Five: Water

8   It is, of course, difficult for the landlord to understand the tenant's craving for water when the modern supermarket is fairly bursting with juices and soft drinks of every description. The burden is made no easier by the fact that at least some of the time this water must be hot. The difficult situation is only partially alleviated by the knowledge that *hot*, like *room*, is a matter of opinion.

Lesson Six: Roaches

9   It is the solemn duty of every landlord to maintain an adequate supply of roaches. The minimum acceptable roach to tenant

ratio is four thousand to one. Should this arrangement prompt an expression of displeasure on the part of the tenant, ignore him absolutely. The tenant is a notorious complainer. Just why this is so is not certain, though a number of theories abound. The most plausible of these ascribes the tenant's chronic irritability to his widely suspected habit of drinking enormous quantities of heat and hot water—a practice well known to result in the tragically premature demise of hallway light bulbs.

QUESTIONS ON SUBJECT AND PURPOSE

1. According to Lebowitz, what is the major goal of a landlord? A tenant?
2. Probably no reader thinks that Lebowitz is being serious. At what point in the essay do you know that she is not writing a serious analysis of the subject?
3. What possible purpose might Lebowitz have in writing such an essay?

QUESTIONS ON STRATEGY AND AUDIENCE

1. How does Lebowitz structure her essay? Does that structure seem effective?
2. What strategy does Lebowitz use to end the essay? Why not write a conventional ending?
3. What expectations does Lebowitz have about her audience? How do you know?

QUESTIONS ON VOCABULARY AND STYLE

1. How would you describe the tone of the essay? How is that tone achieved and maintained?
2. In what ways are the style and tone of the essay appropriate for both the essay's subject and purpose?
3. Be able to define the following words: *stripe* (paragraph 2), *disparity* (4), *pretension* (5), *bridle* (6), *passé* (6), *ploys* (7), *stymie* (7), *demise* (9).

WRITING SUGGESTIONS

1. In a substantial paragraph, write a training guide for a position such as older or younger brother/sister, roommate, parent, child, spouse. Try to capture a tone similar to Lebowitz's.

2. Your college's office of residence life has asked for an article that offers advice on being a good roommate. The article will appear in a guide sent to incoming freshmen and should be written with a serious, helpful tone. Sarcasm such as Lebowitz uses is inappropriate.

   Prewriting:
   a. Make a list of qualities that you would like to see in a potential roommate. You can draw from your own personal experience, or you can just theorize about those qualities that seem ideal to you.

   b. Poll your friends on the subject. Try for a range of contributors who have had differing experiences with roommates.

   c. Once you have a list of qualities, decide on an order or arrangement. Is there anything inherent in the material that suggests which one should come first or last?

   Rewriting:
   a. Reexamine the tone of your paper. Is it serious? Helpful? Ask a peer reader to evaluate that aspect of your essay.

   b. Look back at the assignment. Remember the type of audience you are writing for. Does your essay appeal to that audience? Does it address that audience in an appropriate style and language?

   c. Check your introduction and conclusion. Remember that the college office wants students to read this. Do you make the subject seem interesting and valuable to your reader? Ask a peer reader to evaluate just your introduction.

3. Assume that you live in an apartment owned by a landlord who certainly appears to have read and believed Lebowitz's essay. What rights do you have as a tenant? How can you redress the wrongs being done to you? Research the rights of a tenant in your community. In a process essay describe how a tenant can go about obtaining satisfaction from a landlord. Be sure to include specific information in your essay. You might assume that your essay will appear in a Sunday newspaper.

Don't Just Stand There

DIANE COLE

Diane Cole was born in Baltimore, Maryland, in 1952. Educated at Radcliffe College (B.A.) and Johns Hopkins University (M.A.), she is a freelance journalist well versed in psychological issues, such as the "fear of finishing," and women's career issues, such as networking and professional ladder climbing. Cole was a contributing editor to Psychology Today *and has also published articles in* The Wall Street Journal, The New York Times, The Washington Post, Newsweek, Ms., *and* Glamour. *She is the author of* Hunting the Headhunters: A Woman's Guide *(1988) and* After Great Pain: A New Life Emerges *(1992). "Don't Just Stand There" originally appeared as part of a national campaign against bigotry in a special supplement to* The New York Times *entitled "A World of Difference" (April 16, 1989), sponsored by the Anti-Defamation League of B'nai B'rith. Here, Cole suggests some courses of action when we are accosted with distasteful, sexual, or racial comments by our peers, bosses, or family members. "Shocked paralysis is often the first response," writes Cole, but she tells us we have more options than we think.*

IT WAS MY office farewell party, and colleagues at the job I was about to leave were wishing me well. My mood was one of ebullience tinged with regret, and it was in this spirit that I spoke to the office neighbor to whom I had waved hello every morning for the past two years. He smiled broadly as he launched into a long, rambling story, pausing only after he delivered the punch line. It was a very long pause because, although he laughed, I did not: This joke was unmistakably anti-Semitic.

I froze. Everyone in the office knew I was Jewish; what could he have possibly meant? Shaken and hurt, not knowing what else to do, I turned in stunned silence to the next well-wisher. Later, still angry, I wondered, what else should I—could I—have done?

Prejudice can make its presence felt in any setting, but hearing its nasty voice in this way can be particularly unnerving.

We do not know what to do and often we feel another form of paralysis as well: We think, "Nothing I say or do will change this person's attitude, so why bother?"

4   But left unchecked, racial slurs and offensive ethnic jokes "can poison the atmosphere," says Michael McQuillan, adviser for racial/ethnic affairs for the Brooklyn borough president's office. "Hearing these remarks conditions us to accept them; and if we accept these, we can become accepting of other acts."

5   Speaking up may not magically change a biased attitude, but it can change a person's behavior by putting a strong message across. And the more messages there are, the more likely a person is to change that behavior, says Arnold Kahn, professor of psychology at James Madison University, Harrisonburg, Va., who makes this analogy: "You can't keep people from smoking in *their* house, but you can ask them not to smoke in *your* house."

6   At the same time, "Even if the other party ignores or discounts what you say, people always reflect on how others perceive them. Speaking up always counts," says LeNorman Strong, director of campus life at George Washington University, Washington, D.C.

7   Finally, learning to respond effectively also helps people feel better about themselves, asserts Cherie Brown, executive director of the National Coalition Building Institute, a Boston-based training organization. "We've found that, when people felt they could at least in this small way make a difference, that made them more eager to take on other activities on a larger scale," she says. Although there is no "cookbook approach" to confronting such remarks—every situation is different, experts stress—these are some effective strategies.

8   *When the "joke" turns on who you are—as a member of an ethnic or religious group, a person of color, a woman, a gay or lesbian, an elderly person, or someone with a physical handicap—shocked paralysis is often the first response. Then, wounded and vulnerable, on some level you want to strike back.*

9   Lashing out or responding in kind is seldom the most effective response, however. "That can give you momentary sat-

isfaction, but you also feel as if you've lowered yourself to that other person's level," Mr. McQuillan explains. Such a response may further label you in the speaker's mind as thin-skinned, someone not to be taken seriously. Or it may up the ante, making the speaker, and then you, reach for new insults—or physical blows.

"If you don't laugh at the joke, or fight, or respond in kind   10
to the slur," says Mr. McQuillan, "that will take the person by surprise, and that can give you more control over the situation." Therefore, in situations like the one in which I found myself— a private conversation in which I knew the person making the remark—he suggests voicing your anger calmly but pointedly: "I don't know if you realize what that sounded like to me. If that's what you meant, it really hurt me."

State how *you* feel, rather than making an abstract statement   11
like, "Not everyone who hears that joke might find it funny." Counsels Mr. Strong: "Personalize the sense of 'this is how I feel when you say this.' That makes it very concrete"—and harder to dismiss.

Make sure you heard the words and their intent correctly   12
by repeating or rephrasing the statement: "This is what I heard you say. Is that what you meant?" It's important to give the other person the benefit of the doubt because, in fact, he may *not* have realized that the comment was offensive and, if you had not spoken up, would have had no idea of its impact on you.

For instance, Professor Kahn relates that he used to include   13
in his exams multiple-choice questions that occasionally contained "incorrect funny answers." After one exam, a student came up to him in private and said, "I don't think you intended this, but I found a number of those jokes offensive to me as a woman." She explained why. "What she said made immediate sense to me," he says. "I apologized at the next class, and I never did it again."

But what if the speaker dismisses your objection, saying,   14
"Oh, you're just being sensitive. Can't you take a joke?" In that case, you might say, "I'm not so sure about that, let's talk about that a little more." The key, Mr. Strong says, is to continue the dialogue, hear the other person's concerns, and point out your

own. "There are times when you're just going to have to admit defeat and end it," he adds, "but I have to feel that I did the best I could."

15   When the offending remark is made in the presence of others—at a staff meeting, for example—it can be even more distressing than an insult made privately.

16   "You have two options," says William Newlin, director of field services for the Community Relations division of the New York City Commission on Human Rights. "You can respond immediately at the meeting, or you can delay your response until afterward in private. But a response has to come."

17   Some remarks or actions may be so outragcous that they cannot go unnoted at the moment, regardless of the speaker or the setting. But in general, psychologists say, shaming a person in public may have the opposite effect of the one you want: The speaker will deny his offense all the more strongly in order to save face. Further, few people enjoy being put on the spot, and if the remark really was not intended to be offensive, publicly embarrassing the person who made it may cause an unnecessary rift or further misunderstanding. Finally, most people just don't react as well or thoughtfully under a public spotlight as they would in private.

18   Keeping that in mind, an excellent alternative is to take the offender aside afterward: "Could we talk for a minute in private?" Then use the strategies suggested above for calmly stating how you feel, giving the speaker the benefit of the doubt, and proceeding from there.

19   At a large meeting or public talk, you might consider passing the speaker a note, says David Wertheimer, executive director of the New York City Gay and Lesbian Anti-Violence Project: You could write, "You may not realize it, but your remarks were offensive because. . . ."

20   "Think of your role as that of an educator," suggests James M. Jones, Ph.D., executive director for public interest at the American Psychological Association. "You have to be controlled."

21   Regardless of the setting or situation, speaking up always raises the risk of rocking the boat. If the person who made the offending remark is your boss, there may be an even bigger risk

to consider: How will this affect my job? Several things can help minimize the risk, however. First, know what other resources you may have at work, suggests Caryl Stern, director of the A World of Difference—New York City campaign: Does your personnel office handle discrimination complaints? Are other grievance procedures in place?

You won't necessarily need to use any of these procedures,   22 Ms. Stern stresses. In fact, she advises, "It's usually better to try a one-on-one approach first." But simply knowing a formal system exists can make you feel secure enough to set up that meeting.

You can also raise the issue with other colleagues who heard   23 the remark: Did they feel the same way you did? The more support you have, the less alone you will feel. Your point will also carry more validity and be more difficult to shrug off. Finally, give your boss credit—and the benefit of the doubt: "I know you've worked hard for the company's affirmative action programs, so I'm sure you didn't realize what those remarks sounded like to me as well as the others at the meeting last week. . . ."

If, even after this discussion, the problem persists, go back   24 for another meeting, Ms. Stern advises. And if that, too, fails, you'll know what other options are available to you.

It's a spirited dinner party, and everyone's having a good time, until   25 *one guest starts reciting a racist joke. Everyone at the table is white, including you. The others are still laughing, as you wonder what to say or do.*

No one likes being seen as a party-pooper, but before de-   26 ciding that you'd prefer not to take on this role, you might remember that the person who told the offensive joke has already ruined your good time.

If it's a group that you feel comfortable in—a family gath-   27 ering, for instance—you will feel freer to speak up. Still, shaming the person by shouting 'You're wrong!' or "That's not funny!" probably won't get your point across as effectively as other strategies. "If you interrupt people to condemn them, it just makes it harder," says Cherie Brown. She suggests trying instead to get at the resentments that lie beneath the joke by asking open-ended questions: "Grandpa, I know you always treat everyone with such respect. Why do people in our family talk that way about black people?" The key, Ms. Brown says, "is to listen to them first, so they will be more likely to listen to you."

28   If you don't know your fellow guests well, before speaking up you could turn discreetly to your neighbors (or excuse yourself to help the host or hostess in the kitchen) to get a reading on how they felt, and whether or not you'll find support for speaking up. The less alone you feel, the more comfortable you'll be speaking up: "I know you probably didn't mean anything by that joke, Jim, but it really offended me. . . ." It's important to say that *you* were offended—not state how the group that is the butt of the joke would feel. "Otherwise," LeNorman Strong says, "you risk coming off as a goody two-shoes."

29   If you yourself are the host, you can exercise more control; you are, after all, the one who sets the rules and the tone of behavior in your home. Once, when Professor Kahn's party guests began singing offensive, racist songs, for instance, he kicked them all out, saying, "You don't sing songs like that in my house!" And, he adds, "they never did again."

30   *At school one day, a friend comes over and says, "Who do you think you are, hanging out with Joe? If you can be friends with those people, I'm through with you!"*

31   Peer pressure can weigh heavily on kids. They feel vulnerable and, because they are kids, they aren't as able to control the urge to fight. "But if you learn to handle these situations as kids, you'll be better able to handle them as an adult," William Newlin points out.

32   Begin by redefining to yourself what a friend is and examining what friendship means, advises Amy Lee, a human relations specialist at Panel of Americans, an intergroup-relations training and educational organization. If that person from a different group fits your requirement for a friend, ask, "Why shouldn't I be friends with Joe? We have a lot in common."

Try to get more information about whatever stereotypes or resentments lie beneath your friend's statement. Ms. Lee suggests: "What makes you think they're so different from us? Where did you get that information?" She explains: "People are learning these stereotypes from somewhere, and they cannot be blamed for that. So examine where these ideas came from." Then talk about how your own experience rebuts them.

Kids, like adults, should also be aware of other resources   33
to back them up: Does the school offer special programs for fighting prejudice? How supportive will the principal, the teachers, or other students be? If the school atmosphere is volatile, experts warn, make sure that taking a stand at that moment won't put you in physical danger. If that is the case, it's better to look for other alternatives.

These can include programs or organizations that bring kids   34
from different backgrounds together. "When kids work together across race lines, that is how you break down the barriers and see that the stereotypes are not true," says Laurie Meadoff, president of CityKids Foundation, a nonprofit group whose programs attempt to do just that. Such programs can also provide what Cherie Brown calls a "safe place" to express the anger and pain that slurs and other offenses cause, whether the bigotry is directed against you or others.

In learning to speak up, everyone will develop a different   35
style and a slightly different message to get across, experts agree. But it would be hard to do better than these two messages suggested by teenagers at CityKids: "Everyone on the face of the earth has the same intestines," said one. Another added, "Cross over the bridge. There's a lot of love on the streets."

QUESTIONS ON SUBJECT AND PURPOSE

1. According to Cole, why should we object to "racial slurs and offensive ethnic jokes"?

2. The body of Cole's essay (paragraphs 8–34) offers strategies to use when confronting offensive remarks or jokes. How does Cole divide or organize this part of her subject?

3. What purposes might Cole have had in writing the essay?

QUESTIONS ON STRATEGY AND AUDIENCE

1. Why does Cole begin the essay with a personal example (paragraphs 1 and 2)?

2. Cole quotes a number of authorities in her essay. Why? What do the quotations and the authorities contribute to the article?

3. Why might Cole include the final section—the advice to children about handling such situations among friends? What does this section suggest about her intended audience?

QUESTIONS ON VOCABULARY AND STYLE

1. Throughout the essay Cole uses first- or second-person pronouns such as "I," "you," and "we." Why? How would the essay differ if she used "one" or "he or she"?

2. At several points (in paragraph 23, for instance), Cole suggests a possible response to a situation, enclosing that remark within quotation marks. Why might she create these imagined sentences for her reader?

3. Be prepared to define the following words: *ebullience* (paragraph 1), *tinged* (1), *rift* (17), *volatile* (33).

WRITING SUGGESTIONS

1. A friend asks to borrow your research paper from last semester, explaining that he or she wants to submit it as his or her own work this semester. You do not want to allow this to happen. In a paragraph offer your friend a written explanation of why you are going to refuse.

2. Cole's essay describes a process—what to do when you encounter prejudice. Select another occasion when we might need advice on how to handle a similarly awkward situation and write an essay offering advice on what to do.

Prewriting:

a. Brainstorm about possible situations—dealing with roommates or friends, observing a classmate cheating on a test. Jot down as many uncomfortable situations as possible.

b. Ask some friends about similar experiences they might have had. How did they react? Try out your ideas on them.

344

c. Select what seems to be the most promising possibility and try freewriting for 20 minutes. Do not worry about your grammar; concentrate on getting some ideas from which to begin writing. If you are not pleased with the result, switch to another topic and try freewriting on it.

Rewriting:

a. Look carefully at the organizational strategy you have used. Are the steps in the process in a logical order? Could you, for example, construct a flow chart outlining those steps?

b. Try writing imaginary responses to the situation as Cole does. Remember to put these sentences within quotation marks. Does that strategy seem effective?

c. Reread your introduction. Does it recreate the situation for the reader? Does it catch a reader's interest? Compare your introductory strategy with that used by Cole.

3. Many colleges and universities have established policies for dealing with sexual harassment and discrimination. Research your own institution's position on these issues. See if, for example, a policy statement is available. You might also wish to interview members of the administration and faculty. Then, using your research, write an essay in which you explain to students how to handle a case of sexual harassment or discrimination.

Quick Revising

PETER ELBOW

Born in New York in 1935, Peter Elbow received a B.A. from Williams College, a B.A. and an M.A. from Exeter College, Oxford, and a Ph.D. in 1969 from Brandeis University. Elbow has held various teaching positions at the Massachusetts Institute of Technology, Franconia College, and Evergreen State College. Currently, he is professor of English at the University of Massachusetts. An insightful analyst of the writing process, Elbow is author of Thoughts on Writing Essays *(1965),* Writing Without Teachers *(1973),* Oppositions in Chaucer *(1975),* Writing with Power *(1981), and* Embracing Contraries: Explorations in Learning and Teaching *(1986). His most recent books are co-authored with Patricia Belanoff:* A Community of Writers *(1988) and* What is English? *(1990). "It is 10:30 P.M. now and you have only ten pages of helter-skelter thinking on paper [and] you need an excellent, polished, full report by tomorrow morning." What do you do? You use Elbow's method of "quick revising."*

1   THE POINT OF QUICK REVISING is to turn out a clean, clear, professional final draft without taking as much time as you would need for major rethinking and reorganizing. It is a clean-and-polish operation, not a growing-and-transforming one. You specifically refrain from meddling with any deeper problems of organization or reconceptualization.

2   The best time to use quick revising is when the results don't matter too much. Perhaps you are not preparing a final, finished product but rather a draft for friends. It has to be clear, easy to read—if possible even a pleasure to read. But it needn't be your best work or your final thinking. Perhaps it's a draft for discussion or perhaps just a chance for people to learn your thinking about some matter as though you were writing a letter to them. Or perhaps you are just writing for yourself but you want to clean up your draft so that it will be easier and more productive to read when you come back to it.

But there is another situation when you can use quick re-   3
vising and unfortunately it is the one when you are most likely
to use it: an occasion that is *very* important when the writing
has to work for an important audience, but you lack time. You
can't afford to re-see, re-think, and re-write completely your
raw writing in the amount of time you have left. Maybe it was
your fault and now you are kicking yourself; maybe it was
unavoidable. But either way you are stuck. It is 10:30 P.M. now
and you have only ten pages of helter-skelter thinking on paper,
you need an excellent, polished, full report by tomorrow morning, and you care very much how the reader reacts to it. In
such situations you have to contend with anxiety as well as
lack of time. You need the discipline of the quick revising process. I will describe it here as though you are preparing a substantial piece of writing for tomorrow morning for an important
audience because I want to stress the experience of battle conditions with live ammunition. (If it is a small job such as writing
that memo in thirty minutes, you probably won't go through
all the separate steps I describe below. You'll probably just stand
up and stretch now after your fifteen minutes of raw writing,
and use your remaining time to look with fresh eyes through
what you've written, figure out what you really want to say,
and just write out your final draft—perhaps using substantial
portions of your raw writing unchanged.)

Quick revising is simple and minimal. A lot depends on   4
having the right spirit: businesslike and detached. A certain
ruthlessness is best of all. Not desperate-ruthless, "Oh God, this
is *awful*, I've *got* to change *everything*," but breezy-ruthless, "Yes,
this certainly does have some problems. I wish I could start over
and get the whole thing right, but not this time. I guess I'll just
have to put the best face on things." If you are too worried
about what you wrote or too involved with it, you'll have to
work overtime to get the right spirit. You need to stand outside
yourself and be someone else.

First, if this piece is for an audience, think about who that   5
audience is and what your purpose is in writing to it. You had
the luxury of putting aside all thoughts of audience and purpose
during the producing stage (if that helped you think and write
better), but now you must keep them in mind as you make

347

critical decisions in revising. Try to see your audience before you as you revise. It's no good ending up with a piece of writing that's good-in-general—whatever that means. You need something that is good for your purpose with your audience. . . .

6   Next, read through all your raw writing and find the good pieces. When I do it, I just mark them with a line in the margin. Don't worry about the criteria for choosing them. It's fine to be intuitive. If the sentence or passage feels good for this purpose or seems important for this audience, mark it.

7   Next, figure out your single main point and arrange your best bits in the best order. It's easiest if you can figure out your main point first. That gives you leverage for figuring out what order to put things in. But sometimes your main point refuses to reveal itself—the one thing you are really trying to *say* here, the point that sums up everything else. All your writing may be circling around or leading up to a main idea that you can't quite figure out yet. In such a dilemma, move on to the job of working out the best order for your good passages. That ordering process—that search for sequence and priorities—will often flush your main point out of hiding.

8   You can just put numbers in the margin next to the good bits to indicate the right order if your piece is short and comfortable for you. But if it is long or difficult you need to make an outline before you can really work out the best order. It helps most to make an outline consist of complete assertions with verbs—*thoughts,* not just *areas.*

9   And of course as you work out this order or outline you will think of things you left out—ideas or issues that belong in your final draft that weren't in your raw writing. You can now indicate each of them with a sentence.

10   If after all this—after getting, as it were, *all* your points and getting them in the right order—you still lack the most important idea or assertion that ties them all together into a unity; if you have connected all this stuff but you cannot find the single thought that pulls it all together, and of course this sometimes happens, you simply have to move on. You have a deadline. There is a good chance that your main idea or center of gravity will emerge later, and even if it doesn't you have other options.

11   The next step is to write out a clean-but-not-quite-final draft

of the whole piece—excluding the very beginning. That is, don't write your first paragraph or section now unless it comes to you easily. Wait till you have a draft of the main body before deciding how to lead up to it—or whether it *needs* leading up to. How can you clearly or comfortably introduce something before you know precisely what it is you are introducing? So just begin this draft with your first definite point. Out of the blue. Start even with your second or third point if the first one raises confusing clouds of "how-do-I-get-started."

Perhaps you can use the good passages almost as they are— 12 copy them or use scissors—and only write transitional elements to get you from one to another. Or perhaps you need to write out most of it fresh. But you can go fast because you have all your points in mind and in order, and probably you have a clearly stated, single main idea holding it all together.

If you don't yet know your single main point, there is a 13 very good chance that it will come to you as you are writing this draft. The process of writing the real thing to the real audience will often drive you to say, "What I'm really trying to make clear to you is . . ." and *there* is your main point. This is especially likely to happen toward the end of your piece as you are trying to sum things up or say why all this is important or makes sense. When your main point emerges late in this way, you may have to go back and fiddle a bit with your structure. It is very common that the last paragraph you write, when you finally say exactly what you mean in the fewest words, is just what you need (with perhaps a minor adjustment) for your first paragraph.

On rare occasions you still won't be able to find your main 14 point. You know this is a coherent train of thought, and you know you are saying something, but you cannot sum it up in one sentence. You are stuck and you now have to make some choices. You can open or close your piece with a clear admission that you haven't focused it yet. This is usually the most helpful strategy when you are writing for yourself. (Sometimes, in fact, stating your dilemma—as dilemma—as accurately as you can, serves to produce the solution.) Or you can just present your train of thought without any statement at all of a single main idea. Or you can try to trick the reader into a feeling of unity

349

with a vague, waffling pseudo-summary. But this is dangerous. If a reader sees you waffling he is liable to be mad or contemptuous, and even if he is not conscious of what you are doing he is liable to be irritated. If it is important—for this audience and situation—to end up with a piece of writing that is genuinely unified and focused, there is nothing for it but radical surgery. Settle for the best idea you *can* find in your writing and make that your main point. Organize what goes with it and throw away everything else. This usually hurts because it means throwing away some of your best bits.

15   So now you have a draft and a clear statement of your main idea. Finally you can write what you need for an introductory paragraph or section. Almost certainly you need something that gives the reader a clear sense of your main point—where you are going. If you have been writing under the pressure of a tight deadline your final draft will probably have some problems, and so this is no time for tricky strategies or leaving the reader in the dark. Subtlety is for when you can get everything just right.

16   This is also the time to make sure you have a satisfactory conclusion: a final passage that sums up everything you have said with the precision and complexity that is only possible now that the reader has read and understood all the details. For example you have to begin an essay for most readers with a general statement that is easy to understand, such as "I want to explain how atomic bombs work," but at the end you can sum up your point more quickly and precisely: "In short, $E = mc^2$."

17   Now you have a draft of the whole thing that probably comes close to what you'll end up with. The next step is to change from writer-consciousness to reader-consciousness. For in writing that draft you were, obviously enough, functioning as a writer: a person trying to put down on paper what you had finally gotten clear in your own mind. Now you should read through this draft *as a reader*. The best way to do this is to read your draft *out loud*: you won't have to search for places that are unclear or awkward or lacking in life, you will *hear* them. If you are in an office or a library or some other place

unsuitable for declaiming, you can get almost as much benefit by silently mouthing or whispering your draft as though you were speaking. If you put your fingers in your ears at the same time, you will actually hear your words good and loud. It is the *hearing* of your own words that serves to get you out of the writer-consciousness and into the audience-consciousness.

Finally, get rid of mistakes in grammar and usage. . . .   *18*

Certain people on certain occasions can afford to collapse   *19* some of these steps together and type out their final, clean copy after they have settled on their main idea and numbered or outlined their best bits. But this means paying attention to spelling, grammar, and usage while you are engaged in trying to write clear language: focusing simultaneously on the pane of glass and on the scene beyond it. It's not a wise or efficient thing to do unless you are an exceptionally fluent and polished writer. Most people—and that includes myself—save time by waiting to the very end before worrying about mistakes in grammar and usage.

Even if you are writing informally for friends you must take   *20* care to get rid of these mistakes. Your friends may say, "Oh, who cares about trivial details of correctness," but in fact most people are prejudiced, even if unconsciously, against writing flawed in this way. They are more apt to patronize your writing or take it less seriously or hold back from experiencing what you are saying if there are mistakes in mechanics.

In thinking about the whole process of quick revising, you   *21* should realize that the essential act is *cutting*. Learn to leave out everything that isn't already good or easily made good. Learn the pleasures of the knife. Learn to retreat, to cut your losses, to be chicken. Learn to say, "Yes, I *care* more about this passage than about any other, I'm involved in it, but for that very reason, I can't make it work right. Out it goes!" Of course you don't need to be so ruthless about cutting if you are writing something to share informally among friends or to save for yourself. You can retain sections that feel important but don't quite work or don't quite fit. You can let your piece be an interesting muddle organizationally or conceptually—*so long as it's not muddled in wording or sentences.* Friends are willing to ponder your not-quite-digested thinking so long as your sentences and paragraphs are clear and easy to understand.

22   When you have *lots* of time for revising you tend to finish with something longer than you have expected. The thing cooks and grows on its own and you have time to integrate that growth. But quick revising usually produces something shorter than you had expected. The reader should probably finish a bit startled: "Done already? This seems a bit skimpy. Still, everything here is well done. Actually, it's not too bad." Better to give your reader mild disappointment at a certain tight skimpiness than to bog him down in a mess so that he stops paying attention or even stops reading.

23   In the last analysis, the main thing for quick revising is to get into the right spirit. Be your brisk, kindly, British aunt who is also a nurse: "Yes. Not to worry. I know it's a mess. But we'll clean it up and make it presentable in no time. It won't be a work of art, ducks, but it'll do just fine."

QUESTIONS ON SUBJECT AND PURPOSE

1. How does a "quick revision" differ from a "major rethinking and reorganizing" (paragraph 1)?

2. Why does Elbow caution against trying to write an opening paragraph too soon?

3. What is involved in changing from "writer-consciousness" to "reader-consciousness" (paragraph 17)?

QUESTIONS ON STRATEGY AND AUDIENCE

1. How does Elbow organize his process? Does he use any step or sequence markers?

2. What is the effect of using metaphors and images when describing the process of writing and revising? Consider each of the following:

   a. "Clean-and-polish operation, not a growing-and-transforming one" (paragraph 1)

   b. "Raw writing" (3)

   c. "Experience of battle conditions with live ammunition" (3)

d. "Flush your main point out of hiding" (7)

e. "Radical surgery" (14)

f. "Focusing simultaneously on the pane of glass and on the scene beyond it" (19)

g. "The thing cooks and grows on its own" (22)

3. Elbow says: "Try to see your audience before you as you revise." Does Elbow seem to see his audience? Who comprises that audience? How do you know?

QUESTIONS ON VOCABULARY AND STYLE

1. Characterize Elbow's tone in the essay. How does he sound? What techniques does Elbow use to develop that tone?

2. Does Elbow ever use sentence fragments? How many?

3. How appropriate is Elbow's conclusion? Does it coincide with the advice that he gives?

4. Be able to define the following words: *refrain* (paragraph 1), *helter-skelter* (3), *intuitive* (6), *leverage* (7), *waffling* (14), *declaiming* (17), *patronize* (20).

WRITING SUGGESTIONS

1. Go through Elbow's essay and make a list of the steps involved in "quick revising." Then summarize his procedure in a process paragraph. Assume that your summary will be handed out to your classmates as a revision guide.

2. Using the material provided in Elbow's essay and your own writing experience, write an essay about how to revise a paper.

Prewriting:

a. Begin by taking notes on Elbow's essay. Add to this material anything else that works for you.

b. Organize the notes into an outline. Remember, you need to order the notes in an appropriate sequence. For example, are the steps chronological (do this, then that)?

c. Make sure that you have provided adequate transitional step or sequence markers. Underline those that you already have, and, if necessary, add others.

Rewriting:

a. Look back over Elbow's essay, and follow his advice in revising your essay.

b. Elbow's essay is very "reader friendly." He tries to make the process sound easy; he is very reassuring. Is that an effective strategy to use in a process essay? What about your essay? What is its tone? Does it sound helpful? Interesting? Or does it sound boring? Ask a peer reader to characterize the tone of your paper.

3. Interview twenty students, asking them what revision means and how they revise their papers. Try to get a mix of students, not just the students in your English class. Use your interviews to write an essay titled "Revising and the College Writer."

How Books Helped
Shape My Life

JUDITH VIORST

Judith Viorst was born in Newark, New Jersey, and educated at Rutgers University. She is a poet, journalist, and writer of children's books. She has worked as contributing editor and columnist for Redbook *magazine and has published in* The New York Times, New York, Venture *and* Washington *magazines. Her better known works include* It's Hard to Be Hip over Thirty and Other Tragedies of Married Life, *a book of poems (1968);* Yes, Married: A Saga of Love and Complaint, *collected prose (1972);* Free to be . . . You and Me, *children's fiction (1974);* Necessary Losses *(1985);* When Did I Stop Being 20 and Other Injustices: Selected Poems from Single to Mid-Life *(1987); and* Forever Fifty and Other Equivocations *(1989). In 1970, Viorst won an Emmy Award for her poetic monologues written for a television special called* Annie: The Women in the Life of a Man. *"How Books Helped Shape My Life" was first published in* Redbook *magazine, a consideration that obviously influenced her choice of subject and approach. Viorst traces the influence of fictional heroines on her own personality—how they served "as ideals, as models, as possibilities."*

IN BOOKS I'VE READ since I was young I've searched for heroines who could serve as ideals, as models, as possibilities—some reflecting the secret self that dwelled inside me, others pointing to whole new ways that a woman (if only she dared!) might try to be. The person that I am today was shaped by Nancy Drew; by Jo March, Jane Eyre and Heathcliff's soul mate Cathy; and by other fictional females whose attractiveness or character or audacity for a time were the standards by which I measured myself.   1

I return to some of these books to see if I still understand   2
the powerful hold that these heroines once had on me. I still understand.

3   Consider teen-aged Nancy Drew—beautiful, blond-haired, blue-eyed girl detective—who had the most terrific life that I as a ten-year-old could ever imagine. Motherless (in other words, quite free of maternal controls), she lived with her handsome indulgent lawyer father in a large brick house set back from the street with a winding tree-lined driveway on the outside and a faithful, nonintrusive housekeeper Hannah cooking yummy meals on the inside. She also had a boy friend, a convertible, nice clothes and two close girl friends—not as perfect as she, but then it seemed to me that no one could possibly be as perfect as Nancy Drew, who in dozens and dozens of books (*The Hidden Staircase, The Whispering Statue, The Clue in the Diary, The Clue of the Tapping Heels*) was resourceful and brave and intelligent as she went around solving mysteries left and right, while remaining kind to the elderly and invariably polite and absolutely completely delightfully feminine.

4   I mean, what else *was* there?

5   I soon found out what else when I encountered the four March sisters of *Little Women*, a sentimental, old-fashioned book about girls growing up in Civil War time in New England. About spoiled, vain, pretty Amy. And sickly, saintly Beth. And womanly, decent Meg. And about—most important of all—gawky, bookworm Jo. Dear Jo, who wasn't as flawless as the golden Nancy Drew but who showed me that girls like her—like *us*— could be heroines. Even if we weren't much to look at. Even if we were clumsy and socially gauche. And even if the transition into young womanhood often appeared to our dubious eye to be difficult and scary and even unwelcome.

6   Jo got stains on her dress and laughed when she shouldn't and lost her temper and didn't display tact or patience or restraint. Jo brought a touch of irreverence to the cultural constraints of the world she lived in. And yet her instincts were good and her heart was pure and her headstrong ways led always to virtue. And furthermore Jo—as I yearned to be—was a writer!

7   In the book the years go by, Beth dies, Meg and Amy marry and Jo—her fierce heart somewhat tamed—is alone. "An old maid, that's what I'm to be. A literary spinster, with a pen for a spouse, a family of stories for children, and twenty years hence

a morsel of fame, perhaps!" . . . Jo sighed, as if the prospect was not inviting.

This worried young reader concurred—not inviting at all!   8

And so I was happy to read of Jo's nice suitor. Mr. Bhaer,   9
not handsome or rich or young or important or witty, but possessed of kindness and dignity and enough intelligence to understand that even a girl who wasn't especially pretty, who had no dazzling charms and who wanted to write might make a wonderful wife. And a wonderful mother. And live happily ever after.

What a relief!   10

What Jo and Nancy shared was active participation in life—   11
they went out and *did*; they weren't simply done to—and they taught and promised me (at a time when mommies stayed home and there was no Women's Movement) that a girl could go out and do and still get a man. Jo added the notion that brusque, ungainly girls could go out and do and still get a man. And Jane of *Jane Eyre*, whose author once said, "I will show you a heroine as small and as plain as myself," added the further idea that such women were able to "feel just as men feel" and were capable of being just as passionate.

Orphaned Jane, a governess at stately Thornfield Hall, was   12
a no-nonsense lady, cool and self-contained, whose lonely, painful childhood had ingrained in her an impressive firmness of character, an unwillingness to charm or curry favor and a sense of herself as the equal of any man. Said Jane to Mr. Rochester, the brooding, haughty, haunted master of Thornfield: "Do you think I am an automaton?—a machine without feelings? Do you think, because I am poor, obscure, plain, and little, I am soulless and heartless? You think wrong!—I have as much soul as you, and full as much heart!"

I loved it that such hot fires burned inside so plain a Jane.   13
I loved her for her unabashed intensity. And I loved her for being so pure that when she learned of Mr. Rochester's lunatic wife, she sacrificed romance for honor and left him immediately.

For I think it's important to note that Nancy and Jo and   14
Jane, despite their independence, were basically as good as girls can be: honest, generous, kind, sincere, reliable, respectable,

possessed of absolute integrity. They didn't defy convention. They didn't challenge the rules. They did what was right, although it might cause them pain. And their virtue was always rewarded—look at Jane, rich and married at last to her Mr. Rochester. Oh, how I identified with Jane!

15 But then I read *Wuthering Heights*, a novel of soul-consuming love on the Yorkshire moors, and Catherine Earnshaw totally captured me. And she captured me, not in spite of her dangerous, dark and violent spirit, but *because* of it.

16 Cathy was as wild as the moors. She lied and connived and deceived. She was insolent, selfish, manipulative and cruel. And by marrying meek, weak Edgar instead of Heathcliff, her destiny, she betrayed a love she described in throbbing, unforgettable prose as . . . elemental:

17 "My love for Heathcliff resembles the eternal rocks beneath—a source of little visible delight, but necessary. Nelly, I *am* Heathcliff—he's always, always in my mind—not as a pleasure, any more than I am always a pleasure to myself—but as my own being. . . ."

18 Now who, at the age of 16, could resist such quivering intensity? Who would settle for less than elemental? Must we untamed creatures of passion—I'd muse as I lay awake in my red flannel nightie—submit ourselves to conventional morality? Or could I actually choose not to be a good girl?

19 Cathy Earnshaw told me that I could. And so did lost Lady Brett, of *The Sun Also Rises*.

20 Brett Ashley was to me, at 18, free, modern, woman incarnate, and she dangled alluring new concepts before my eyes:

21 The value of style: "She wore a slipover jersey sweater and a tweed skirt, and her hair was brushed back like a boy's. She started all that."

22 The glamour of having a dark and tortured past: "Finally, when he got really bad, he used to tell her he'd kill her. . . . She hasn't had an absolutely happy life."

23 The excitement of nonconformity: "I've always done just what I wanted."

24 The importance of (understated) grace under pressure: "Brett was rather good. She's always rather good."

And the thrill of unrepressed sexuality: "Brett's had affairs 25
with men before. She tells me all about everything."

Brett married lovelessly and drank too much and drifted 26
too much and had an irresponsible fling with a bullfighter. But
she also had class—and her own morality. She set her bullfighter free—"I'd have lived with him if I hadn't seen it was
bad for him." And even though she was broke, she lied and
"told him I had scads of it. . . . I couldn't take his money, you
know."

Brett's wasn't the kind of morality that my mother was 27
teaching me in suburban New Jersey. But maybe I wasn't meant
for suburban life. Maybe—I would muse as I carefully lined my
eyes with blue liner—maybe I'm meant for something more
. . . emancipated.

I carried Brett's image with me when, after college, I lived 28
for a while in Greenwich Village, in New York. But I couldn't
achieve her desperate gallantry. And it struck me that Brett was
too lonely and sad, and that Cathy had died too young (and
that Scarlett O'Hara got Tara but lost her Rhett), and that maybe
I ought to forget about unconventionality if the price was going
to be so painfully high. Although I enjoyed my Village fling, I
had no wish to live anguishedly ever after. I needed a heroine
who, like me, wanted just a small taste of the wild before settling
down into happy domesticity.

I found her in *War and Peace*. Her name was Natasha. 29

Natasha, the leading lady of this epic of Russian society 30
during Napoleon's time, was "poetic . . . charming . . . over-
flowing with life," an enchanting girl whose sweet eagerness
and passionate impulsivity were tempered by historic and private tragedies. Betrothed to the handsome and excellent Prince
Andrew, she fell in love with a heel named Anatole, and when
she was warned that this foolish and dangerous passion would
lead to her ruin, "I'll go to my ruin . . .," she said, "as soon as
possible."

It ended badly with Anatole. Natasha tried suicide. Prince 31
Andrew died. Natasha turned pale, thin, subdued. But unlike
Brett and Cathy, her breach with convention was mended and,
at long last, she married Pierre—a decent, substantial, loving
man, the kind of man all our mothers want us to marry.

359

32   In marriage Natasha grew stouter and "the old fire very rarely kindled in her face now." She became an exemplary mother, an ideal wife. "She felt that her unity with her husband was maintained not by the poetic feelings that had attracted him to her but by something else—indefinite but firm as the bond between her own body and soul."

33   It sounded—if not elemental and doomed—awfully nice.

34   I identified with Natasha when, the following year, I married and left Greenwich Village. I too was ready for domesticity. And yet . . . her husband and children became "the subject which wholly engrossed Natasha's attention." She had lost herself—and I didn't want to lose me. What I needed next was a heroine who could reconcile all the warring wants of my nature—for fire and quiet, independence and oneness, ambition and love, and marriage and family.

35   But such reconciling heroines, in novels and real life, may not yet exist.

36   Nevertheless Natasha and Jane and Jo, Cathy, Nancy and Brett—each spoke to my heart and stirred me powerfully. On my journey to young womanhood I was fortunate to have them as my companions. They were, they will always remain, a part of me.

QUESTIONS ON SUBJECT AND PURPOSE

1. How many heroines does Viorst treat? What does she see in each? How are those qualities related to her own maturation?

2. When you were a child did any hero or heroine seem a particularly attractive model? Was he or she a character in a novel? Has television or film replaced novels as a source of models?

3. Why would any reader be interested in an essay explaining how something shaped your life? Did you find anything of interest here? If so, why? If not, why not?

QUESTIONS ON STRATEGY AND AUDIENCE

1. How does Viorst structure her essay? What progression is there? What controls the arrangement of the heroines?

2. Viorst switches the way she handles her examples when she reaches Lady Brett in *The Sun Also Rises*. Why the change?

3. For whom is Viorst writing? What expectations does she have of her audience? Can you find specific evidence to support your assumptions?

QUESTIONS ON VOCABULARY AND STYLE

1. Viorst frequently uses dashes in her sentences. What is the effect of their use?

2. Viorst seems to delight in breaking the rules we might expect writing to obey. Consider the following categories of examples and be able to show how and why each works in the essay:

    a. Informal, even casual words ("yummy," "a heel")

    b. Clichés ("solving mysteries left and right," "live happily ever after")

    c. Sentence fragments

    d. Extremely short paragraphs

3. Be able to define the following words: *gawky* (paragraph 5), *gauche* (5), *brusque* (11), *curry favor* (12), *unabashed* (13), *incarnate* (20).

WRITING SUGGESTIONS

1. We have all admired someone—either a real person or a fictional one. Select one such model and in a paragraph explain why that particular model was important to you at that particular moment. Remember to keep your paragraph focused on what the model meant or represented to you.

2. "How ——— Helped Shape My Life." Using Viorst's essay as a structural model, write a process analysis showing how a series of events, situations, or people helped you grow up.

Prewriting:

    a. A workable subject must meet two criteria. First, the items in the series must be parallel in form. (Viorst's are all characters from books.) Second, the items must have played a role in your life over a length of time. (Viorst's reflect her reading from age 10 to her mid-20s.) With those criteria in mind, brainstorm a list of possible subjects.

b. Narrow your list to the two best possibilities. Then decide how many time periods you will represent. Viorst includes six. That is probably too many for your essay, but be sure to have at least three. Under each subject, list in outline form the time periods you will include with an example from each.

c. Develop each example clearly. Ask friends who are the same age what they remember about their growing up. Ask them to evaluate the examples you plan to use. That might help add important details.

Rewriting:

a. For each of the examples that you include, complete the following statement: "What this example meant to me was ―――." Write your answers on a separate sheet of paper.

b. Look back at Viorst's essay. Not every reader has read these books, so Viorst is careful to explain exactly what was appealing or influential about each one. Have you made your essay accessible to readers?

c. The appeal of Viorst's essay is its universality. Because we all grow up and because we go through certain common stages in that process, we are interested in her analysis. Can you say the same thing about your essay? Have you made it universal enough? Will the reader want to keep reading? Find a peer reader, and check your essay's appeal. If your reader is bored, ask why.

3. In Viorst's preteenage years, girls read Nancy Drew and boys read the Hardy Boys. What do preteenagers read today? Anything? Research the popularity of books with 10- to 12-year-olds today. You might want to talk with a brother or sister or interview a fifth or sixth grade teacher or an elementary or middle school librarian. What changes have occurred? What do those changes tell us?

On Keeping a Notebook

JOAN DIDION

Joan Didion was born in Sacramento in 1934 and received a B.A. from the University of California at Berkeley in 1956. Didion is as famous for her novels Run River *(1963),* Play It As It Lays *(1970),* A Book of Common Prayer *(1977), and* Democracy *(1984), as for her collections of essays* Slouching Towards Bethlehem *(1968) and* The White Album *(1979). In both genres she vividly portrays the personal chaos of modern American life. She has written of a visit to El Salvador in* Salvador *(1983) and has produced a number of screenplays in collaboration with her husband John Gregory Dunne, including* A Star Is Born *(1976) and* True Confessions *(1981). Her latest book,* Miami *(1987), examines Washington's mistreatment of Miami's Cuban population. She has also adapted Hemingway's short story ''Hills Like White Elephants'' into a screenplay for HBO with her husband.*

Here Didion reveals a vital part of her writing process—keeping a notebook. Didion's essay is not a ''how-to-do-something'' process analysis, but she does use process to describe how and why she keeps a notebook. Along the way, she establishes some crucial distinctions between a notebook and a diary. ''The point of my keeping a notebook,'' she writes, ''has never been, nor is it now, to have an accurate factual record of what I have been doing or thinking.''

" 'That woman Estelle,' " the note reads, " 'is partly the reason   *1* why George Sharp and I are separated today.' *Dirty crepe-de-Chine wrapper, hotel bar, Wilmington RR, 9:45 A.M. August Monday morning.*"

Since the note is in my notebook, it presumably has some   *2* meaning to me. I study it for a long while. At first I have only the most general notion of what I was doing on an August Monday morning in the bar of the hotel across from the Pennsylvania Railroad station in Wilmington, Delaware (waiting for a train? missing one? 1960? 1961? why Wilmington?), but I do remember being there. The woman in the dirty crepe-de-

Chine wrapper had come down from her room for a beer, and the bartender had heard before the reason why George Sharp and she were separated today. "Sure," he said, and went on mopping the floor. "You told me." At the other end of the bar is a girl. She is talking, pointedly, not to the man beside her but to a cat lying in the triangle of sunlight cast through the open door. She is wearing a plaid silk dress from Peck & Peck, and the hem is coming down.

3   Here is what it is: the girl has been on the Eastern Shore, and now she is going back to the city, leaving the man beside her, and all she can see ahead are the viscous summer sidewalks and the 3 A.M. long-distance calls that will make her lie awake and then sleep drugged through all the steaming mornings left in August (1960? 1961?). Because she must go directly from the train to lunch in New York, she wishes that she had a safety pin for the hem of the plaid silk dress, and she also wishes that she could forget about the hem and the lunch and stay in the cool bar that smells of disinfectant and malt and make friends with the woman in the crepe-de-Chine wrapper. She is afflicted by a little self-pity, and she wants to compare Estelles. That is what that was all about.

4   Why did I write it down? In order to remember, of course, but exactly what was it I wanted to remember? How much of it actually happened? Did any of it? Why do I keep a notebook at all? It is easy to deceive oneself on all those scores. The impulse to write things down is a peculiarly compulsive one, inexplicable to those who do not share it, useful only accidentally, only secondarily, in the way that any compulsion tries to justify itself. I suppose that it begins or does not begin in the cradle. Although I have felt compelled to write things down since I was five years old, I doubt that my daughter ever will, for she is a singularly blessed and accepting child, delighted with life exactly as life presents itself to her, unafraid to go to sleep and unafraid to wake up. Keepers of private notebooks are a different breed altogether, lonely and resistant rearrangers of things, anxious malcontents, children afflicted apparently at birth with some presentiment of loss.

5   My first notebook was a Big Five tablet, given to me by my mother with the sensible suggestion that I stop whining and

learn to amuse myself by writing down my thoughts. She returned the tablet to me a few years ago; the first entry is an account of a woman who believed herself to be freezing to death in the Arctic night, only to find, when day broke, that she had stumbled onto the Sahara Desert, where she would die of the heat before lunch. I have no idea what turn of a five-year-old's mind could have prompted so insistently "ironic" and exotic a story, but it does reveal a certain predilection for the extreme which has dogged me into adult life; perhaps if I were analytically inclined I would find it a truer story than any I might have told about Donald Johnson's birthday party or the day my cousin Brenda put Kitty Litter in the aquarium.

So the point of my keeping a notebook has never been, nor   6
is it now, to have an accurate factual record of what I have been doing or thinking. That would be a different impulse entirely, an instinct for reality which I sometimes envy but do not possess. At no point have I ever been able successfully to keep a diary; my approach to daily life ranges from the grossly negligent to the merely absent, and on those few occasions when I have tried dutifully to record a day's events, boredom has so overcome me that the results are mysterious at best. What is this business about "shopping, typing piece, dinner with E, depressed"? Shopping for what? Typing what piece? Who is E? Was this "E" depressed, or was I depressed? Who cares?

In fact I have abandoned altogether that kind of pointless   7
entry; instead I tell what some would call lies. "That's simply not true," the members of my family frequently tell me when they come up against my memory of a shared event. "The party was not for you, the spider was *not* a black widow, *it wasn't that way at all.*" Very likely they are right, for not only have I always had trouble distinguishing between what happened and what merely might have happened, but I remain unconvinced that the distinction, for my purposes, matters. The cracked crab that I recall having for lunch the day my father came home from Detroit in 1945 must certainly be embroidery, worked into the day's pattern to lend verisimilitude; I was ten years old and would not now remember the cracked crab. The day's events did not turn on cracked crab. And yet it is precisely that fictitious

crab that makes me see the afternoon all over again, a home movie run all too often, the father bearing gifts, the child weeping, an exercise in family love and guilt. Or that is what it was to me. Similarly, perhaps it never did snow that August in Vermont; perhaps there never were flurries in the night wind, and maybe no one else felt the ground hardening and summer already dead even as we pretended to bask in it, but that was how it felt to me, and it might as well have snowed, could have snowed, did snow.

8   *How it felt to me*: that is getting closer to the truth about a notebook. I sometimes delude myself about why I keep a notebook, imagine that some thrifty virtue derives from prescrving everything observed. See enough and write it down, I tell myself and then some morning when the world seems drained of wonder, some day when I am only going through the motions of doing what I am supposed to do, which is write—on that bankrupt morning I will simply open my notebook and there it will be, a forgotten account with accumulated interest, paid passage back to the world out there: dialogue overheard in hotels and elevators and at the hatcheck counter in Pavillon (one middle-aged man shows his hat check to another and says, "That's my old football number"); impressions of Bettina Aptheker and Benjamin Sonnenberg and Teddy ("Mr. Acapulco") Stauffer; careful *aperçus* about tennis bums and failed fashion models and Greek shipping heiresses, one of whom taught me a significant lesson (a lesson I could have learned from F. Scott Fitzgerald, but perhaps we all must meet the very rich for ourselves) by asking, when I arrived to interview her in her orchid-filled sitting room on the second day of a paralyzing New York blizzard, whether it was snowing outside.

9   I imagine, in other words, that the notebook is about other people. But of course it is not. I have no real business with what one stranger said to another at the hatcheck counter in Pavillon; in fact I suspect that the line "That's my old football number" touched not my own imagination at all, but merely some memory of something once read, probably "The Eighty-Yard Run." Nor is my concern with a woman in a dirty crepe-de-Chine wrapper in a Wilmington bar. My stake is always, of course,

in the unmentioned girl in the plaid silk dress. *Remember what it was to be me*: that is always the point.

It is a difficult point to admit. We are brought up in the 10
ethic that others, any others, all others, are by definition more interesting than ourselves; taught to be diffident, just this side of self-effacing. ("You're the least important person in the room and don't forget it," Jessica Mitford's governess would hiss in her ear on the advent of any social occasion; I copied that into my notebook because it is only recently that I have been able to enter a room without hearing some such phrase in my inner ear.) Only the very young and the very old may recount their dreams at breakfast, dwell upon self, interrupt with memories of beach picnics and favorite Liberty lawn dresses and the rainbow trout in a creek near Colorado Springs. The rest of us are expected, rightly, to affect absorption in other people's favorite dresses, other people's trout.

And so we do. But our notebooks give us away, for however 11
dutifully we record what we see around us, the common denominator of all we see is always, transparently, shamelessly, the implacable "I". We are not talking here about the kind of notebook that is patently for public consumption, a structural conceit for binding together a series of graceful *pensées*; we are talking about something private, about bits of the mind's string too short to use, an indiscriminate and erratic assemblage with meaning only for its maker.

And sometimes even the maker has difficulty with the 12
meaning. There does not seem to be, for example, any point in my knowing for the rest of my life that, during 1964, 720 tons of soot fell on every square mile of New York City, yet there it is in my notebook, labeled "FACT." Nor do I really need to remember that Ambrose Bierce liked to spell Leland Stanford's name "£eland $tanford" or that "smart women almost always wear black in Cuba," a fashion hint without much potential for practical application. And does not the relevance of these notes seem marginal at best?:

In the basement museum of the Inyo County Courthouse in 13
Independence, California, sign pinned to a mandarin coat:

"This MANDARIN COAT was often worn by Mrs. Minnie S. Brooks when giving lectures on her TEAPOT COLLECTION."

Redhead getting out of car in front of Beverly Wilshire Hotel, chinchilla stole, Vuitton bags with tags reading:

MRS LOU FOX

HOTEL SAHARA

VEGAS

14　Well, perhaps not entirely marginal. As a matter of fact, Mrs. Minnie S. Brooks and her MANDARIN COAT pull me back into my own childhood, for although I never knew Mrs. Brooks and did not visit Inyo County until I was thirty, I grew up in just such a world, in houses cluttered with Indian relics and bits of gold ore and ambergris and the souvenirs my Aunt Mercy Farnsworth brought back from the Orient. It is a long way from that world to Mrs. Lou Fox's world where we all live now, and is it not just as well to remember that? Might not Mrs. Minnie S. Brooks help me to remember what I am? Might not Mrs. Lou Fox help me to remember what I am not?

15　But sometimes the point is harder to discern. What exactly did I have in mind when I noted down that it cost the father of someone I know $650 a month to light the place on the Hudson in which he lived before the Crash? What use was I planning to make of this line by Jimmy Hoffa: "I may have my faults, but being wrong ain't one of them"? And although I think it interesting to know where the girls who travel with the Syndicate have their hair done when they find themselves on the West Coast, will I ever make suitable use of it? Might I not be better off just passing it on to John O'Hara? What is a recipe for sauerkraut doing in my notebook? What kind of magpie keeps this notebook? *"He was born the night the Titanic went down."* That seems a nice enough line, and I even recall who said it, but is it not really a better line in life than it could ever be in fiction?

16　But of course that is exactly it: not that I should ever use the line, but that I should remember the woman who said it and the afternoon I heard it. We were on her terrace by the sea, and we were finishing the wine left from lunch, trying to

368

get what sun there was, a California winter sun. The woman whose husband was born the night the *Titanic* went down wanted to rent her house, wanted to go back to her children in Paris. I remember wishing that I could afford the house, which cost $1,000 a month. "Someday you will," she said lazily. "Someday it all comes." There in the sun on her terrace it seemed easy to believe in someday but later I had a low-grade afternoon hangover and ran over a black snake on the way to the supermarket and was flooded with inexplicable fear when I heard the checkout clerk explaining to the man ahead of me why she was finally divorcing her husband. "He left me no choice," she said over and over as she punched the register. "He has a little seven-month-old baby by her, he left me no choice." I would like to believe that my dread then was for the human condition, but of course it was for me, because I wanted to own the house that cost $1,000 a month to rent and because I had a hangover.

It all comes back. Perhaps it is difficult to see the value in having one's self back in that kind of mood, but I do see it; I think we are well advised to keep on nodding terms with the people we used to be, whether we find them attractive company or not. Otherwise they turn up unannounced and surprise us, come hammering on the mind's door at 4 A.M. of a bad night and demand to know who deserted them, who betrayed them, who is going to make amends. We forget all too soon the things we thought we could never forget. We forget the loves and the betrayals alike, forget what we whispered and what we screamed, forget who we were. I have already lost touch with a couple of people I used to be; one of them, a seventeen-year-old, presents little threat, although it would be of some interest to me to know again what it feels like to sit on a river levee drinking vodka-and-orange-juice and listening to Les Paul and Mary Ford and their echoes sing "How High the Moon" on the car radio. (You see I still have the scenes, but I no longer perceive myself among those present, no longer could even improvise the dialogue.) The other one, a twenty-three-year old, bothers me more. She was always a good deal of trouble, and I suspect she will reappear when I least want to see her, skirts too long, shy to the point of aggravation, always the injured party, full of recriminations and little hurts and stories I do not want to hear again, at once saddening me and angering me with her vulnerability and ignorance, an apparition all the more insistent for being so long banished.

18   It is a good idea, then, to keep in touch and I suppose that keeping in touch is what notebooks are all about. And we are all on our own when it comes to keeping those lines open to ourselves: your notebooks will never help me, nor mine you. *"So what's new in the whiskey business?"* What could that possibly mean to you? To me it means a blonde in a Pucci bathing suit sitting with a couple of fat men by the pool at the Beverly HIlls Hotel. Another man approaches, and they all regard one another in silence for a while. "So what's new in the whiskey business?" one of the fat men finally says by way of welcome, and the blonde stands up, arches one foot and dips it in the pool, looking all the while at the cabana where Baby Pignatari is talking on the telephone. That is all there is to that, except that several years later I saw the blonde coming out of Saks Fifth Avenue in New York with her California complexion and a voluminous mink coat. In the harsh wind that day she looked old and irrevocably tired to me, and even the skins in the mink coat were not worked the way they were doing them that year, not the way she would have wanted them done, and there is the point of the story. For a while after that I did not like to look in the mirror, and my eyes would skim the newspapers and pick out only the deaths, the cancer victims, the premature coronaries, the suicides, and I stopped riding the Lexington Avenue IRT because I noticed for the first time that all the strangers I had seen for years—the man with the seeing-eye dog, the spinster who read the classified pages every day, the fat girl who always got off with me at Grand Central—looked older than they once had.

19   It all comes back. Even that recipe for sauerkraut: even that brings it back. I was on Fire Island when I first made that sauerkraut, and it was raining, and we drank a lot of bourbon and ate the sauerkraut and went to bed at ten, and I listened to the rain and the Atlantic and felt safe. I made the sauerkraut again last night and it did not make me feel any safer, but that is, as they say, another story.

QUESTIONS ON SUBJECT AND PURPOSE

1. Why does Didion keep a notebook? What types of things does she record? How does a notebook differ from a diary?

2. In paragraph 7, Didion acknowledges that what she records did not always happen and that, for her purposes, it does not really matter. What does she mean by this? Why would she record "lies"?

3. If the notebook helps Didion remember "what it was to be me" (paragraph 9), why should anyone be interested in her essay? Is the essay as egocentric as the notebook? Is there any purpose to this other than self-discovery—what all this means to *me*, Joan Didion?

QUESTIONS ON STRATEGY AND AUDIENCE

1. The essay follows a pattern of discovery. Didion seems to discover why she keeps a notebook as she writes the essay. But that might also be a lie. She might have known before she wrote the essay. Either way, what does such a pattern add to the essay? Why might Didion have chosen to explain in such a way?

2. How effective is the introduction? The conclusion?

3. What do the examples in her notebook tell Didion? What common thread links all of the examples she uses?

4. What expectations does Didion have of her audience? Are they realized? Use your own reading as a test.

QUESTIONS ON VOCABULARY AND STYLE

1. Why does Didion use typographical devices in the essay (things like the italics or the parentheses or the indented entries in paragraph 13)?

2. At a number of points in the essay Didion will ask a group of questions about a particular entry and then go on to answer them. What is the effect of this stylistic device? How is it related to the structure of the essay?

3. Be able to define the following: *crepe-de-Chine* (paragraph 1), *malcontent* (4), *presentiment* (4), *predilection* (5), *verisimilitude* (7), *aperçus* (8), *implacable* (11), *pensées* (11), *ambergris* (14), *recriminations* (17).

WRITING SUGGESTIONS

1. Using the advice that Didion provides (sometimes indirectly) write a paragraph telling the reader how to keep a notebook. Think of your paragraph as something that could be handed out in your English class. Make your advice clear.

2. Both Didion and Judith Viorst describe by means of process how influences and experiences have shaped their lives. Look back on what has brought you here to this present moment. Then select several important events or influences that helped shape your life. Using those examples, write a process analysis on how you have come to be where you are now.

Prewriting:

   a. The events/experiences/influences need to be linked only by the extent to which they helped shape your life. They can be different in form; that is, one can be a person, one an experience, one a book. You will probably need three or four at least. Brainstorm a possible list of subjects by starting with this question: "What has made me what I am?" Try to get more examples than you will eventually use. Work on your list for several days.

   b. Use freewriting to develop each of the examples that you plan to use. Write for 15 minutes without stopping on each item. You might not use any of this material in your essay, but freewriting will give you a chance to experiment with what you want to say about each item.

   c. Plan an organizational strategy by making an outline. The primary sequence will probably be chronological, but that is not necessary. Didion's examples are not arranged chronologically. Maybe a pattern of discovery is better. Compare the organizational patterns used by Viorst and Didion. Can you use either pattern as a model for your essay?

Rewriting:

   a. Viorst and Didion use two different techniques to begin their essays; Viorst's introduction is a clear statement of her thesis. Didion's is a journalistic "hook" designed to provoke the reader's curiosity. Both are effective. Look at your introduction. Which strategy do you use? Freewrite an alternative beginning to your paper.

   b. Part of the appeal of Didion's essay—like Viorst's—is its universality. We all feel the need to know who we are and who we were. Does your essay have that same appeal? Ask a peer to read your essay and then respond to the following questions: Are the experiences here common? Do you care about the narrator, or do you feel that the narrator is imposing his or her life story on you? Does the writer explain the significance of these events, experiences, and influences? Use your reader's response in revising your essay.

c. It is always good to rethink your organizational strategy. Make a copy of your essay, cut the body paragraphs apart, and rearrange them in an alternative order. (If you are working on a word processor, you can just move text blocks around.) Force yourself to experiment with this change. Is the new order any better? Even if it isn't, the process will make you look in a new way at the sequence you have used.

3. Didion remarks, "I think we are well advised to keep on nodding terms with the people we used to be" (paragraph 17). Try to remember a person you used to be—maybe you at 7 or 14. A photograph is a good place to start. Who were you then? What were your concerns, your fears, your hopes? What was important? Who were your friends? Use a particular moment, a particular memory, or a photograph to recreate the you you used to be.

A Writer's Revision Process:
Revision and Life:
Take It from the Top—Again

NORA EPHRON

Nora Ephron was born in 1941 in New York City. After she received her B.A. from Wellesley College in 1962, Ephron worked as a journalist and columnist for the New York Post, New York *magazine, and* Esquire. *Her books include* Wallflower at the Orgy *(1970),* Scribble, Scribble: Notes on the Media *(1979), and the novel* Heartburn *(1983), which was made into a film. She also wrote the screenplay for* Silkwood *(1983),* When Harry Met Sally *(1989),* Cookie *(1989), and* My Blue Heaven *(1990).*

"Revision and Life," written in response to an invitation to participate in this textbook, was originally published in The New York Times Book Review. *As the title suggests, for Ephron revision and life are closely linked. When she was a college student, with the limitless potential of youth, her goal was "to get to the end"—to finish the piece, to get on with life. As she has grown older, however, revision has come to mean that more lies ahead. "By the time you reach middle age," she observes, "you want more than anything for things not to come to an end; and as long as you are revising, they don't."*

REVISED DRAFT

1   I HAVE BEEN ASKED to write something for a textbook that is meant to teach college students something about writing and revision. I am happy to do this because I believe in revision. I have also been asked to save the early drafts of whatever I write, presumably to show these students the actual process of revision. This too I am happy to do. On the other hand, I suspect that there is just so much you can teach college students about revision; a gift for revision may be a developmental stage—like a 2-year-old's sudden ability to place one block on top of another—that comes along somewhat later, in one's mid-20s, say;

most people may not be particularly good at it, or even interested in it, until then.

When I was in college, I revised nothing. I wrote out my 2 papers in longhand, typed them up and turned them in. It would never have crossed my mind that what I had produced was only a first draft and that I had more work to do; the idea was to get to the end, and once you had got to the end you were finished. The same thinking, I might add, applied in life: I went pell-mell through my four years in college without a thought about whether I ought to do anything differently; the idea was to get to the end—to get out of school and become a journalist.

Which I became, in fairly short order. I learned as a jour- 3 nalist to revise on deadline. I learned to write an article a paragraph at a time—and I arrived at the kind of writing and revising I do, which is basically a kind of typing and retyping. I am a great believer in this technique for the simple reason that I type faster than the wind. What I generally do is to start an article and get as far as I can—sometimes no farther in than a sentence or two—before running out of steam, ripping the piece of paper from the typewriter and starting all over again. I type over and over until I have got the beginning of the piece to the point where I am happy with it. I then am ready to plunge into the body of the article itself. This plunge usually requires something known as a transition. I approach a transition by completely retyping the opening of the article leading up to it in the hope that the ferocious speed of my typing will somehow catapult me into the next section of the piece. This does not work—what in fact catapults me into the next section is a concrete thought about what the next section ought to be about— but until I have the thought the typing keeps me busy, and keeps me from feeling something known as blocked.

Typing and retyping as if you know where you're going is 4 a version of what therapists tell you to do when they suggest that you try changing from the outside in—that if you can't master the total commitment to whatever change you want to make, you can at least do all the extraneous things connected with it, which make it that much easier to get there. I was 25 years old the first time a therapist suggested that I try changing from the outside in. In those days, I used to spend quite a lot of time lying awake at night wondering what I should have said earlier in the evening and revising my lines. I mention this not just because it's a way of illustrating that a gift for revision is practically instinctive, but also (once again) because it's possible that a genuine ability at it doesn't really come into play until one is older—or at least older than 25, when it seemed to me that all that was required in my life and my work was the chance to change a few lines.

5   In my 30's, I began to write essays, one a month for *Esquire* magazine, and I am not exaggerating when I say that in the course of writing a short essay—1,500 words, that's only six double-spaced typewritten pages—I often used 300 or 400 pieces of typing paper, so often did I type and retype and catapult and recatapult myself, sometimes on each retyping moving not even a sentence farther from the spot I had reached the last time through. At the same time, though, I was polishing what I had already written: as I struggled with the middle of the article, I kept putting the beginning through the typewriter; as I approached the ending, the middle got its turn. (This is a kind of polishing that the word processor all but eliminates, which is why I don't use one. Word processors make it possible for a writer to change the sentences that clearly need changing without having to retype the rest, but I believe that you can't always tell whether a sentence needs work until it rises up in revolt against your fingers as you retype it.) By the time I had produced what you might call a first draft—an entire article with a beginning, middle and end—the beginning was in more like 45th draft, the middle in 20th, and the end was almost newborn. For this reason, the beginnings of my essays are considerably better written than the ends, although I like to think no one ever notices this but me.

6   As I learned the essay form, writing became harder for me. I was finding a personal style, a voice if you will, a way of writing that looked chatty and informal. That wasn't the hard part—the hard part was that having found a voice, I had to work hard month to month not to seem as if I were repeating myself. At this point in this essay it will not surprise you to

learn that the same sort of thing was operating in my life. I don't mean that my life had become harder—but that it was becoming clear that I had many more choices than had occurred to me when I was marching through my 20's. I no longer lost sleep over what I should have said. Not that I didn't care—it was just that I had moved to a new plane of late-night anxiety: I now wondered what I should have done. Whole areas of possible revision opened before me. What should I have done instead? What could I have done? What if I hadn't done it the way I did? What if I had a chance to do it over? What if I had a chance to do it over as a different person? These were the sorts of questions that kept me awake and led me into fiction, which at the very least (the level at which I practice it) is a chance to rework the events of your life so that you give the illusion of being the intelligence at the center of it, simultaneously managing to slip in all the lines that occurred to you later. Fiction, I suppose, is the ultimate shot at revision.

Now I am in my 40's and I write screenplays. Screenplays— if they are made into movies—are essentially collaborations, and movies are not a writer's medium, we all know this, and I don't want to dwell on the craft of screenwriting except insofar as it relates to revision. Because the moment you stop work on a script seems to be determined not by whether you think the draft is good but simply by whether shooting is about to begin: if it is, you get to call your script a final draft; and if it's not, you can always write another revision. This might seem to be a hateful way to live, but the odd thing is that it's somehow comforting; as long as you're revising, the project isn't dead. And by the same token, neither are you. 7

It was, as it happens, while thinking about all this one recent sleepless night that I figured out how to write this particular essay. I say "recent" in order to give a sense of immediacy and energy to the preceding sentence, but the truth is that I am finishing this article four months after the sleepless night in question, and the letter asking me to write it, from George Miller of the University of Delaware, arrived almost two years ago, so for all I know Mr. Miller has managed to assemble his textbook on revision without me. 8

Oh, well. That's how it goes when you start thinking about 9 revision. That's the danger of it, in fact. You can spend so much time thinking about how to switch things around that the main event has passed you by. But it doesn't matter. Because by the time you reach middle age, you want more than anything for things not to come to an end; and as long as you're still revising, they don't.

10   I'm sorry to end so morbidly—dancing as I am around the subject of death—but there are advantages to it. For one thing, I have managed to move fairly effortlessly and logically from the beginning of this piece through the middle and to the end. And for another, I am able to close with an exhortation, something I rarely manage, which is this: Revise now, before it's too late.

QUESTIONS FOR DISCUSSION

1. What links does Ephron see between revision and life?

2. How does Ephron structure her essay? What principle of order does she follow?

3. It would have been a simple matter for Ephron to omit the references to this textbook (paragraphs 1 and 8). The *New York Times* audience, for example, would not be interested in knowing these details. Why might she have chosen to include these references in her essay?

4. Why is fiction the "ultimate shot at revision"?

5. What might Ephron mean by her final sentence ("Revise now, before it's too late")?

6. Be able to define the following words: *pell-mell* (paragraph 2), *extraneous* (4), *exhortation* (10).

EARLIER DRAFT
Corresponds to paragraphs 1 and 2

1   I HAVE BEEN ASKED to write something that will show college students something about writing and revision. I am happy to do this because I believe in revision. I have been asked to write something and save all the early drafts, which I am also happy to do. On the other hand, I believe there is just so much you

can teach college students about revision, that an ability for revision is something (a Piaget stage, like a 2½ year old's sudden ability to put one block on top of another) that is acquired slightly later, and that most people aren't particularly good at it or even interested in it until then.

When I was in college, I revised almost nothing. It seems to me (I know my memory isn't what it used to be but I'm fairly sure about this) I typed papers and pretty much turned them in. The same thing I might add applied in life: I pretty much went pell mell through my four years of higher education without a thought about whether I ought to have done anything differently. The things I wrote were a means to an end—to turn in the assignment, I suppose—and so was the way I lived my life—to get out of school and become a journalist.

2

QUESTIONS ON THE REVISION

1. In the revised draft, Ephron omits the reference to Piaget (paragraph 1). Who was Piaget? Why eliminate the reference?

2. In the revised draft, Ephron suggests when it might be that people acquire an interest in revising ("in one's mid-20's, say"). Why add that detail?

3. What changes occur in the following passage from one draft to another? What is the effect of those changes?

Earlier Draft

When I was in college, I revised almost nothing. It seems to me (I know my memory isn't what it used to be but I'm fairly sure about this) I typed papers and pretty much turned them in.

Revised Draft

When I was in college, I revised nothing. I wrote out my papers in longhand, typed them up and turned them in. It would never have crossed my mind that what I had produced was only a first draft and that I had more work to do; the idea was to get to the end, and once you had got to the end you were finished.

4. What is the effect of changing "four years of higher education" to "four years in college"?

WRITING SUGGESTIONS

1. Study the two versions of the opening of Ephron's essay. Formulate a thesis about her revision strategy. In a paragraph assert your thesis and support it with appropriate evidence.

2. On the basis of your own experience as a writer and as a student in this course, argue for or against *requiring* revision in a college writing course. Should a student be forced to do it? Does revision always produce a better paper?

Prewriting:

   a. Remember that regardless of your stand, your argument should be based on solid, meaningful reasons. For example, you should not argue that revision is too much trouble or that it will please your instructor and get you a higher grade. Make a list of reasons.

   b. Interview classmates and friends for their experiences and opinions. Remember to take notes.

   c. Plan a possible organization for your essay. Does an inductive or a deductive approach seem better? In what order will you arrange your reasons? Will you start or end with the strongest reason?

Rewriting:

   a. Check your tone in the essay. Do you sound convincing? Reasonable? Ask a friend or classmate to read your essay and to characterize its tone.

   b. Have you avoided emotionally charged language? Examine your word choice carefully. Underline any words that might seem distorted, inaccurate, or too emotional.

   c. Titles are an important part of any essay. An effective title should clearly signal the essay's subject and should also arouse the reader's interest. Look carefully at your original title. Does it meet those tests? Try writing some alternative titles.

3. What role does revision play in the writing process of faculty and staff at your college or university? Interview a range of people—faculty (especially professors in disciplines other than English) and other professional staff members who write as a regular part of their job (for example, librarians, information

officers, and admissions officers). Using notes from your interviews, write an essay about the revision practices of these writers. Your essay could be a feature article in the campus newspaper.

SEVEN

Cause
and
Effect

It is a rainy morning and you are late for class. Driving to campus in an automobile with faulty brakes, you have an accident. Considering the circumstances, the accident might be attributable to a variety of causes:

you were driving too fast

the visibility was poor

the roads were slippery

the brakes did not work properly

The accident, in turn, could produce a series of consequences or effects:

you miss class

you get a ticket

your license is suspended

you injure yourself or someone else

As this suggests, cause and effect analyses frequently can go in either direction—an examination of the reasons why something occurred or of the effects or consequences that follow from a particular event or situation.

Causes and effects can be either immediate or remote with reference to time. The two lists above include only immediate causes and effects, those things which are most directly linked in time to the accident. Another pair of lists of more remote causes and effects could be compiled—for example, your brakes were faulty because you did not have the money to fix them, or, because of your accident, your insurance rates will go up.

Causes and effects can be either primary or secondary with reference to their significance or importance. If you had not been in a hurry and driving too fast, it might not have mattered that the visibility was poor, the roads were slippery, or your brakes were faulty. Similarly, if you or someone else had been injured, the other consequences would have seemed insignificant in comparison.

In some instances, causes and effects are linked in a chain: if you were driving too fast and tried to stop on slippery roads with inadequate brakes, then each of those causes is interlinked in the inevitable accident. Likewise, the accident means that you will get a ticket, that ticket carries points against your license, your license could as a result be suspended, and either way your insurance rates will certainly climb.

Why Do You Write a Cause and Effect Analysis?

Cause and effect analyses are intended to explain why something happened or what the consequences are or will be of a particular occurrence. Cullen Murphy in "Going to the Cats" offers an explanation of why there are now more households in America with cats than with dogs. E. M. Forster in "My Wood" examines the effects of owning property. Carll Tucker in "Fear of Dearth" suggests reasons why jogging or running is popular. Joan Jacobs Brumberg in "The Origins of Anorexia Nervosa" explains the causes of anorexia nervosa, tracing the disease back to its origins in middle-class families in the nineteenth century. Marie Winn in "The End of Play" sees a dramatic change in the nature of children's play. She attributes that change to three causes and then goes on to suggest some possible effects of the "end" of traditional children's play. Gloria Steinem in "Why Young Women Are More Conservative" analyzes for herself and her readers why women, as they grow older, are more likely to become active in the feminist movement. Finally, Brent Staples in "Black Men and Public Space" examines the impact that he, a black man who likes to walk at night, has on public space. In addition, Staples comments on the effects that peoples' reactions have had on him.

Cause and effect analyses can also be used to persuade readers to do or believe something. Steinem's explanation for the conservatism of most young women is not a direct plea for an awakening of feminine consciousness, but, after reading her essay, it would be more difficult for any reader simply to ignore the issue.

How Do You Choose a Subject?

In picking a subject to analyze, first remember the limits of your assignment. The larger the subject, the more difficult it will be to do justice to. Trying to analyze the causes of the Vietnam war or the effects of the national budget deficit in 500 words is an invitation to disaster. Second, make sure that the relationships you see between causes and effects are genuine. The fact that a particular event preceded another does not necessarily mean that the first caused the second. In logic this error is labeled *post hoc, ergo propter hoc* ("after this, therefore because of this").

How Do You Isolate and Evaluate Causes and Effects?

Before you begin to write, take time to analyze and, if necessary, research your subject thoroughly. It is important that your analysis consider all of the major factors involved in the relationship. Relatively few things are the result of a single cause, and rarely does a cause have a single effect. Gloria Steinem acknowledges that the answer to why young women are conservative is not a simple one—it involves a complex series of reasons.

Depending on your subject, your analysis could be based upon personal experience, thoughtful reflection and examination, or research. E. M. Forster's analysis of the effects of owning property is derived completely from studying his own reactions. Gloria Steinem's explanation comes from a decade's experience as a feminist speaker and organizer, coupled with her own personal experience as a maturing adult. Carll Tucker's

playful examination of the phenomenon of jogging is a thoughtful reflection upon American values—one that required no special research but rather an application of general knowledge to
a specific subject. Marie Winn's research involved extensive interviews with children and concerned adults. Joan Jacobs
Brumberg's essay is also built upon extensive research, especially in printed sources in history, literature, medicine, and
psychology. As these selections show, sometimes causes and
effects are certain and unquestionable. Other times, the relationships are only probable or even speculative.

Once you have gathered a list of possible causes or effects,
the next step is to evaluate each item. Since any phenomenon
can have many causes or many effects, you will need to select
those explanations which seem most relevant or convincing.
Rarely should you list every cause or every effect you can find.
Generally, you choose those causes or effects which are immediate and primary, although the choice is always determined
by your purpose. Tucker, for example, offers a variety of reasons
why people jog, ranging from those which are immediate and
personal ("to lower blood pressure," "to escape a filthy household") to those which are remote and philosophical ("modern
irreligion," "fear of dearth"). He includes the spectrum because
his subject is not why any particular individual jogs, but why
a substantial portion of an entire nation jogs.

How Do You Structure a Cause and Effect Analysis?

By definition, causes precede effects, so a cause and effect analysis involves a linear or chronological order. Most commonly,
you structure your analysis to reflect that sequence. If you are
analyzing causes, typically you begin by identifying the subject
that you are trying to explain and then move to analyze its
causes. Carll Tucker begins with a phenomenon—jogging—
that he feels is an effect or result of a set of values or concerns
that are shared in our society. The rest of his essay seeks to
explain why that phenomenon occurs, to explain its *causes*. Gloria Steinem begins with an observation that has grown out of
her experience, that women, as they grow older, are more likely
to become involved in the feminist movement. Her essay then

offers an explanation for why that might be. Steinem begins with an effect and then moves to an analysis of its causes.

If you are analyzing effects, typically you begin by identifying the subject that produced the effects and then move to enumerate or explain what those effects were. E. M. Forster begins by describing how he came to purchase his "wood" and then describes four distinct effects that ownership had upon him.

Within these two structural patterns, you face one other choice: If you are listing multiple causes or effects, how do you decide in what order to treat them? That arrangement depends upon whether or not the reasons or consequences are linked in a chain. If they happen in a definite sequence, then you would arrange them in an order to reflect that sequence—normally a chronological order (this happened, then this, finally this). This linear arrangement is very similar to what you do in a process narrative except that your purpose is to answer the question "why" rather than "how." Brent Staples' essay follows a chronological pattern of development. It begins with his first experience as a night walker in Chicago and ends with his most recent experiences in Brooklyn. The essay includes a brief flashback as well, to his childhood days in Chester, Pennsylvania. As he is narrating his experiences, Staples explores the reasons why people react as they do when they encounter him at night on a city street. At the same time, Staples analyzes the impact or effects that their reactions have had on him.

But multiple causes and effects are not always linked. Steinem's causes do not occur in any inevitable chronological order, nor do Forster's effects. If the causes or effects that you have isolated are not linked in a chain, then you must find another way in which to order them. They could be organized from immediate to remote, for example. When there is a varying degree of significance or importance, the most obvious structural choice would be to arrange from the primary to the secondary or from the secondary to the primary. Before you make any arrangement, study your list of causes or effects to see whether any principle of order is evident—chronological, spatial, immediate to remote, primary to secondary. If you see a logical order, follow it.

Sample Student Essay

CAUSE AND EFFECT

For a cause and effect analysis Cathy Ferguson chose to examine the effects that television's depiction of violence has on young children.

EARLIER DRAFT

TV Aggression and Children

Let's face it. Television producers are out to make money. Their main concern is with what sells. What does sell? Sensationalism. People like shocking stories. In the effort to sell, the limit of the outrageous on TV has been pushed far beyond what it was, say, ten years ago. Television aggression is one aspect of sensationalism that has been exploited to please a thrill-seeking audience. Television is not showing a greater number of aggressive scenes, but the scenes portray more violent and hostile acts. Psychologists, prompted by concerned parents, have been studying the effects of children viewing increased aggression, since the average program for kids contains 20 acts of violence per hour, while the overall average is only 7 acts of violence per hour. Research reveals three outstanding consequences of viewing greater TV hostility. First of all, TV aggression numbs children to real world violence. One experiment showed that even a brief exposure to a fairly violent show made kids indifferent to the same aggression in real life. Preschoolers are especially affected by TV violence because they are usually unable to distinguish between reality and fantasy. If they see a hostile act, they are liable to believe that it is reality, and accept it as ''the norm.''

This leads to the second effect of viewing TV aggression: a distorted perception of the world. Most TV shows do not present real world consequences of violence; thus children are getting a false picture of

387

their world. Some kids are led to believe that acts of
hostility are normal, common, expected even, and may
lead a fearfully restricted life. In general, however,
most children learn not how to be afraid of violence,
but how to be violent, which is the third and most
drastic effect of viewing television aggression. Almost
all studies show that kids are more aggressive after
they watch an aggressive show, like ''Batman'' or
''Superman,'' than after watching a pro-social show
like ''Mr. Rogers,'' or a neutral show. So, although
sensationalism, especially violent sensationalism, is
making money for TV producers it is also creating a
generation that is numb to real violence, has a
distorted picture of the environment, and is itself
more hostile. These effects are so palpable, it is now
realized that the single best predictor of how
aggressive an 18 year old will be is how much
aggressive television he watched when he was 8 years
old.

After Cathy handed in her first draft, she had a conference
with her instructor. The instructor commented on her effective
use of examples. Because the essay contains specific evidence,
the cause and effect analysis seems much more convincing.

Her instructor offered some specific advice about revisions
in word choice, sentence structure, and paragraph division. He
noted that the essay repeated the phrase "television aggression"
or a related variant seven times. Since condensed forms can be
confusing, he recommended that she indicate that what she was
writing about was aggression, violence, or hostility depicted on
television shows. Since her first draft begins with five very short
sentences and a single-word sentence fragment, he urged her
to combine the sentences in order to reduce the choppy effect.
Finally, he recommended that she use paragraph divisions to
separate the three effects that she discusses. That division would
make it easier for her reader to see the structure of the paper.

Cathy's revision addressed each of the problems that had
been discussed in conference. In addition, she made a number
of minor changes to tighten the prose and make it clearer.

REVISED DRAFT

The Influence of Televised Violence on Children

Let's face it. Television producers are in business to make money. Their main concern is what sells, and nothing sells better than sensationalism. In an effort to gain a larger share of the audience, television producers now treat subject matter that would never have been acceptable ten years ago. The depiction of violence on television is one aspect of that sensationalism, exploited to please a thrill-seeking audience. The number of aggressive scenes shown on television has not increased, but those scenes now portray more violent and hostile acts. This is especially true on shows aimed at children.

Psychologists, prompted by concerned parents, have begun studying the effects on children of viewing this increased aggression. The average program for children contains 20 acts of violence per hour compared to an overall average of 7 acts of violence per hour. Research reveals three significant consequences of viewing violence on television.

First, aggressive acts on television numb children to real world violence. One study showed that even a brief exposure to a fairly violent show made children indifferent to the same aggression in real life. Preschoolers are especially affected by television because they are usually unable to distinguish between reality and fantasy. If they see an aggressive act, they are likely to believe that it is real and so accept it as normal.

This potential confusion leads to the second effect of watching violence on television: a distorted perception of the world. Some children are led to believe that acts of hostility are normal, common, and even expected. As a result, these children may lead a restricted life, afraid of the violence which they imagine lurks everywhere.

In general, however, most children learn not to be afraid of violence but how to be violent—the third and most drastic effect of viewing aggression on television. Almost all studies show that children are more aggressive after they watch a show that includes violence than after watching a show that excludes it.

All three effects are so palpable that it is now realized the single best predictor of how aggressive an 18 year old will be is how much violence he watched on television when he was 8 years old.

Some Things to Remember

1. Choose a topic that can be analyzed thoroughly within the limits of the assignment.
2. Decide upon a purpose: are you trying to explain or to persuade?
3. Determine an audience. For whom are you writing? What does your audience already know about your subject?
4. Analyze and research your subject. Remember to provide factual support wherever necessary. Not every cause and effect analysis can rely on unsupported opinion.
5. Be certain that the relationships you see between causes and effects are genuine.
6. Concentrate your efforts on immediate and primary causes or effects rather than on remote or secondary ones. Do not try to list every cause or every effect that you can.
7. Begin with the cause and then move to effects or begin with an effect and then move to its causes.
8. Look for a principle of order to organize your list of causes or effects. It might be chronological or spatial for example, or it might move from immediate to remote or from primary to secondary.
9. Remember that you are explaining why something happens or what will happen. You are not just describing how.

Going to the Cats

CULLEN MURPHY

Born in 1952, Cullen Murphy graduated from Amherst College with a B.A. in medieval history. He was senior editor of the Wilson Quarterly *from 1977 to 1985 and since then has served as managing editor of the* Atlantic. *Since the early 1970s, he has also written the comic strip* Prince Valiant. *He has contributed essays and articles to* The Atlantic *and* Harper's. *In "Going to the Cats," which originally appeared in* The Atlantic, *Murphy explores the significance of a "new demographic reality: the number of cats in American households is rapidly overtaking, if it has not already overtaken, the number of dogs." Murphy finds important connections between the change from dogs to cats and other trends in contemporary American life.*

EVERY DECADE OR SO the United States of America crosses some portentous new threshold that symbolizes the nation's evolution from one kind of society into another. It crossed one after the Second World War, when for the first time in history American men bought more belts than they did suspenders. It crossed another in the mid-1950s, when the number of tractors on American farms for the first time exceeded the number of horses. Now, in the 1980s, the country faces a new demographic reality: the number of cats in American households is rapidly overtaking, if it has not already overtaken, the number of dogs. According to the Pet Food Institute, a Washington-based trade association, there were about 18 million more dogs than cats in the United States as recently as a decade ago, but today there are 56 million cats and only 52 million dogs. Actually, because millions of unregistered dogs and cats—the illegal aliens of the animal kingdom—go uncounted, it may be that dogs still maintain a slight edge. But sales of dog food are holding steady, whereas sales of cat food have been increasing in recent years at an annual rate of five to eight percent. The trend is clear.

This is not the place to dredge up all the old arguments on

the relative merits of cats and dogs, friend of the mouse though I am. But it does seem to me that the displacement of *Canis familiaris* by *Felis catus* might tell us something larger about the condition of the republic, much as from a single drop of rain (to cite Sherlock Holmes's famous example) one might infer the existence of oceans. Consider an America congenial to the dog: it was a place of nuclear or extended families, of someone always home, of children (or pet) looked after during the day by a parent (or owner), of open spaces and family farms, of sticks and leftovers, of expansiveness and looking outward and being outside: it was the America of Willa Cather and Lassie and Leon Leonwood Bean. Consider an America conducive to the cat: it is a place of working men and women with not much time, of crowded cities, of apartment buildings with restrictive clauses, of day-care and take-out food, of self-absorption and modest horizons; it is the America of Tama Janowitz and *Blade Runner* and The Sharper Image catalogue.

3   These generalizations may, I suppose, be extreme, but they are prompted in part by the new, 1987 edition of the *Statistical Abstract of the United States*, which I recently received in the mail. This may be the best book the government publishes, and I wish I could earmark my taxes every year to pay the salary of its editor. According to the *Abstract*, here is some of what has happened to the country from the time when dogs were an overwhelming majority of household pets (I've chosen the early to middle 1970s) to the present day: the amount of land claimed by cities increased by 191,795 square miles, or 49 percent; the number of people living in cities increased by 33 million; the number of households consisting of only one person doubled, to 21 million, and as a proportion of all households increased by 41 percent; the number of families headed by only one parent more than doubled, to 7 million, and as a proportion of all families increased by 100 percent; the proportion of childless couples with both partners in the labor force increased by 9.5 percent; the proportion of working couples with children under three increased by 56 percent; the proportion of new houses having no more than two bedrooms doubled, and the average size of new housing units shrank by nineteen square feet; the number of people living in a typical rental unit declined by 13

percent, to 2.0, and the number living in the average occupant-owned unit declined by 16 percent, to 2.5; the number of miles Americans traveled (including going to work) increased by 631 billion; the amount of money spent on fast food increased by 153 percent; membership in the Boy Scouts and the Girl Scouts declined by 25 percent. The *Abstract* carries a lot of other suggestive data. It provides a recipe, so to speak, for cats.

I do not propose that we attempt to redress the balance. To be sure, I can imagine certain developments, such as a dramatic worsening of the many social and physical ills with which dogs so nobly help us cope, that might foster a resurgence of the canine population, but this prospect is not, on the whole, very inviting. By the same token, I can imagine expedient ways of reducing the feline population to rough parity with the canine one, although perhaps not without harm to the country's liberal democratic traditions. In the end, I think, there is no turning back the clock. As one who has shaken hands with Rin Tin Tin, I mourn the loss of what was good about dog America. But I accept the inevitability of cat America, and all that this implies about life-styles and public policy. I will be surprised indeed if, after the electorate has spoken in 1988, the next First Pet enters the White House on anything other than little cat feet.

QUESTIONS ON SUBJECT AND PURPOSE

1. What type of society was "dog America"? What type is "cat America"?

2. According to Murphy, why is America "going to the cats"?

3. How does Murphy feel about the change in our society? Point to specific passages that reveal his attitude.

QUESTIONS ON STRATEGY AND AUDIENCE

1. How is this a cause and effect analysis? What is the effect? What are the causes?

2. Why might Murphy include so many statistics in paragraph 3? Is this an effective strategy?

3. Does the essay seem to address any particular audience? Does Murphy seem to have any expectations about his readers?

QUESTIONS ON VOCABULARY AND STYLE

1. Characterize the tone of the essay. How is that tone achieved? Does it seem appropriate for this subject?

2. Identify each item in the following comparison from paragraph 2. Explain what each group of items reveals about the changes in American society:

   > "Willa Cather and Lassie and Leon Leonwood Bean"
   >   as compared to
   > "Tama Janowitz and *Blade Runner* and The Sharper Image catalogue"

3. Be able to define the following words and phrases: *demographic* (paragraph 1), *congenial* (2), *nuclear or extended family* (2), *conducive* (2), *parity* (4).

WRITING SUGGESTIONS

1. Select an object that has become particularly popular during the last few years. In a paragraph analyze the popularity of this item with reference to the shifting values and concerns in our society. In what ways does this object reflect American life today?

2. To commemorate the start of a new decade, your college has decided to bury a time capsule containing objects or materials that typify American college life. You have been asked to assemble four to six items and then in an essay explain your choices. Your essay will be published as a feature article in the campus newspaper.

Prewriting:

a. Remember that the items reflect college life and that your audience is made up of classmates. Before you begin, spend some time thinking about your audience—their characteristics and their concerns. How will that audience influence both what you say and how you say it?

b. Brainstorm about some possible items to include. The items need to be both popular and indicative of our values and concerns in the last few years. Ask friends for suggestions as well.

c. As your list grows, spend 10 to 15 minutes freewriting about each item. Use these freewriting exercises to help define your subject and to analyze the significance of each item. Keep your freewritings focused on both of these concerns.

Rewriting:

a. On a separate sheet of paper, write a one-sentence explanation of the principle of order you have followed in your essay. Brainstorm for some other possibilities for order. Does any alternative order seem more effective?

b. Check how you made the transitions from one item to another, from one paragraph to another. Have you used transitional devices? Do you provide the reader with a clear set of directions about what comes next?

c. Look again at your introduction and conclusion. Put your essay aside, and, without looking at what you have already written, freewrite a new beginning and a new ending. Do not worry about grammar and spelling; concentrate on a new strategy to get your reader interested.

3. Visit your college's library and examine the *Statistical Abstract of the United States*, found in the reference area. Spend some time analyzing the tables and statistics. Look for evidence of change in American society from one period to another. Pick two dates separated by at least a decade. Look for additional sources if necessary. Using the information you have gathered, write a cause and effect research paper analyzing what these changes signaled about American society and why they occurred.

My Wood

E. M. FORSTER

Edward Morgan Forster (1879–1970) was born in London, England, and graduated from King's College, Cambridge University, with a B.A. in classics (1900) and a B.A. in history (1901). In 1910, he earned an M.A., also from Cambridge. Forster spent several years living in Greece, Italy, Egypt, and India. In addition to teaching at Cambridge, he worked as a journalist and as a civil servant in India. He is best known as a novelist, but he also wrote short stories, literary criticism, biographies, histories, and essays. His novels include Where Angels Fear to Tread *(1905),* The Longest Journey *(1907),* A Room with a View *(1908),* Howards End *(1910), and* A Passage to India *(1924). He also published two collections of essays,* Abinger Harvest *(1936) and* Two Cheers for Democracy *(1951). In this essay from* Abinger Harvest, *Forster explores the consequences of owning property. He writes, ''Property produces men of weight, and it was a man of weight who failed to get into the Kingdom of Heaven.''*

1   A FEW YEARS AGO I wrote a book which dealt in part with the difficulties of the English in India. Feeling that they would have had no difficulties in India themselves, the Americans read the book freely. The more they read it the better it made them feel, and a cheque to the author was the result. I bought a wood with the cheque. It is not a large wood—it contains scarcely any trees, and it is intersected, blast it, by a public footpath. Still, it is the first property that I have owned, so it is right that other people should participate in my shame, and should ask themselves, in accents that will vary in horror, this very important question: What is the effect of property upon the character? Don't let's touch economics; the effect of private ownership upon the community as a whole is another question— a more important question, perhaps, but another one. Let's keep to psychology. If you own things, what's their effect on you? What's the effect on me of my wood?

2   In the first place, it makes me feel heavy. Property does

have this effect. Property produces men of weight, and it was a man of weight who failed to get into the Kingdom of Heaven. He was not wicked, that unfortunate millionaire in the parable, he was only stout; he stuck out in front, not to mention behind, and as he wedged himself this way and that in the crystalline entrance and bruised his well-fed flanks, he saw beneath him a comparatively slim camel passing through the eye of a needle and being woven into the robe of God. The Gospels all through couple stoutness and slowness. They point out what is perfectly obvious, yet seldom realized: that if you have a lot of things you cannot move about a lot, that furniture requires dusting, dusters require servants, servants require insurance stamps, and the whole tangle of them makes you think twice before you accept an invitation to dinner or go for a bathe in the Jordan. Sometimes the Gospels proceed further and say with Tolstoy that property is sinful; they approach the difficult ground of asceticism here, where I cannot follow them. But as to the immediate effects of property on people, they just show straightforward logic. It produces men of weight. Men of weight cannot, by definition, move like the lightning from the East unto the West, and the ascent of a fourteen-stone bishop into a pulpit is thus the exact antithesis of the coming of the Son of Man. My wood makes me feel heavy.

In the second place, it makes me feel it ought to be larger. 3

The other day I heard a twig snap in it. I was annoyed at 4 first, for I thought that someone was blackberrying, and depreciating the value of the undergrowth. On coming nearer, I saw it was not a man who had trodden on the twig and snapped it, but a bird, and I felt pleased. My bird. The bird was not equally pleased. Ignoring the relation between us, it took fright as soon as it saw the shape of my face, and flew straight over the boundary hedge into a field, the property of Mrs. Henessy, where it sat down with a loud squawk. It had become Mrs. Henessy's bird. Something seemed grossly amiss here, something that would not have occurred had the wood been larger. I could not afford to buy Mrs. Henessy out, I dared not murder her, and limitations of this sort beset me on every side. Ahab did not want that vineyard—he only needed it to round off his property, preparatory to plotting a new curve—and all the land around my wood has become necessary to me in order to round off the wood. A boundary protects. But—poor little thing—the boundary ought in its turn to be protected. Noises on the edge of it. Children throw stones. A little more, and then a little more, until we reach the sea. Happy Canute! Happier Alexander! And after all, why should even the world be the limit of possession? A rocket containing a Union Jack, will, it is hoped, be shortly fired at the moon. Mars. Sirius. Beyond which . . . But these immensities ended by saddening me. I could not suppose that my wood was the destined nucleus of universal dominion—it is so very small and contains no mineral wealth beyond the blackberries. Nor was I comforted when Mrs. Henessy's bird took alarm for the second time and flew clean away from us all, under the belief that it belonged to itself.

5   In the third place, property makes its owner feel that he ought to do something to it. Yet he isn't sure what. A restlessness comes over him, a vague sense that he has a personality to express—the same sense which, without any vagueness, leads the artist to an act of creation. Sometimes I think I will cut down such trees as remain in the wood, at other times I want to fill up the gaps between them with new trees. But impulses are pretentious and empty. They are not honest movements towards money-making or beauty. They spring from a foolish desire to express myself and from an inability to enjoy what I have got. Creation, property, enjoyment form a sinister trinity in the human mind. Creation and enjoyment are both very, very good, yet they are often unattainable without a material basis, and at such moments property pushes itself in as a substitute, saying, "Accept me instead—I'm good enough for all three." It is not enough. It is, as Shakespeare said of lust, "the expense of spirit in a waste of shame": it is "Before, a joy proposed; behind, a dream." Yet we don't know how to shun it. It is forced on us by our economic system as the alternative to starvation. It is forced on us by an internal defect in the soul, by the feeling that in property may lie the germs of self-development and of exquisite or heroic deeds. Our life on earth is, and ought to be, material and carnal. But we have not learned to manage our materialism and carnality properly; they are still

entangled with the desire for ownership, where (in the words of Dante) "Possession is one with loss."

And this brings us to our fourth and final point: the black- 6
berries.

Blackberries are not plentiful in the meagre grove, but they 7
are easily seen from the public footpath which traverses it, and
all too easily gathered. Foxgloves, too—people will pull up the
foxgloves, and ladies of an educational tendency even grub for
toadstools to show them on the Monday in class. Other ladies, *stiff*
less educated, roll down the bracken in the arms of their gentle- *fern*
men friends. There is paper, there are tins. Pray, does my wood
belong to me or doesn't it? And, if it does, should I not own it
best by allowing no one else to walk there? There is a wood
near Lyme Regis, also cursed by a public footpath, where the
owner has not hesitated on this point. He has built high stone
walls each side of the path, and has spanned it by bridges, so
that the public circulate like termites while he gorges on the
blackberries unseen. He really does own his wood, this able
chap. Dives in Hell did pretty well, but the gulf dividing him
from Lazarus could be traversed by vision, and nothing traverses
it here. And perhaps I shall come to this in time. I shall wall
in and fence out until I really taste the sweets of property. Enormously stout, endlessly avaricious, pseudocreative, intensely
selfish, I shall weave upon my forehead the quadruple crown
of possession until those nasty Bolshies come and take it off
again and thrust me aside into the outer darkness. → *member of
ext reemist wing
" overthrow things*

QUESTIONS ON SUBJECT AND PURPOSE

1. According to Forster, what are the consequences of owning
   property?
2. Is there any irony in buying property from the royalties earned
   from a book about England's problems in India?
3. What purpose(s) might Forster have had in writing the essay?

QUESTIONS ON STRATEGY AND AUDIENCE

1. In what way is this a cause and effect essay?

2. Look at the conclusion of the essay. Why does Forster end in this way? Why not add a more conventional conclusion?

3. What expectations does Forster seem to have about his audience? How do you know?

QUESTIONS ON VOCABULARY AND STYLE

1. Characterize the tone of Forster's essay. Is it formal? Informal? How is that tone achieved?

2. Forster makes extensive use of allusion in the essay. Some of the names are easily recognizable, others less so. Identify the allusions below (all but c are to Biblical stories). How does each fit into the context of the essay?

    a. The wealthy man in the parable (paragraph 2)

    b. Ahab and the vineyard (4)

    c. Canute and Alexander (4)

    d. Dives and Lazarus (7)

3. Be able to define the following words: *asceticism* (paragraph 2), *fourteen-stone* (measure of weight, 2), *depreciating* (4), *pretentious* (5), *carnal* (5), *foxgloves* (7), *bracken* (7), *avaricious* (7), *Bolshies* (Bolsheviks, 7).

WRITING SUGGESTIONS

1. Select something that you own, and in a paragraph describe the consequences of your owning it. Has it changed your behavior?

2. Extend the topic above into an essay. You might choose something such as a house, a car, an expensive stereo, a summer home, a pet, a boat—whatever seems appropriate given your age and background.

Prewriting:

    a. Make a list of possible subjects. For each item try to list at least four possible effects of owning it. Do not commit to a specific subject until you have considered the range of possibilities.

    b. Once you have selected an item, try freewriting for 15 minutes on each consequence of ownership. You are still gathering ideas for your essay; this material will not necessarily become part of your first draft.

c. The consequences will surely vary in terms of their significance and order of importance. Plan out an organizational strategy. Which effect should come first? Try writing each paragraph on a separate sheet of paper so that you can shuffle their order easily. Consider the alternatives.

Rewriting:

a. Make a brief outline of Forster's essay. It can be used as a model. Try to consider the author's strategy—that is, how did Forster solve the problems that this type of essay poses? Do not just imitate his form.

b. The biggest problem might come in the conclusion. Look at what you have written. Have you avoided an ending that starts, "In conclusion, there are four consequences that result from owning a ———."

c. Do you have an interesting title? Do not title your paper "My ———." Remember that titles figure significantly in arousing a reader's curiosity. Brainstorm for some possibilities. Imagine yourself as a copywriter in an advertising agency trying to sell a product.

3. Property ownership has frequently been used throughout history as a precondition for full participation in the affairs of government (voting, for example). A number of states in this country applied such a restriction until the practice was declared unconstitutional. Using outside sources, write a research essay that explains and analyzes, either the reasons for such practices or the reasons against such practices. Be sure to document your sources.

Fear of Dearth

CARLL TUCKER

Carll Tucker was born in New York City in 1951 and received a B.A. from Yale University in 1973. An editor and writer, Tucker began his career as a columnist for the Patent Trader *newspaper. He was theater critic and book columnist for the* Village Voice *from 1974 to 1977 and editor of the* Saturday Review *from 1978 to 1981, for which he wrote a regular column, ''The Back Door,'' from which this selection is drawn. In 1983, Tucker assumed the editorship of the* Patent Trader. *Tucker's subject in ''Fear of Dearth'' is jogging. In a cause and effect analysis, Tucker sets out to explain why Americans choose to jog. ''From a practically infinite array of opportunities,'' he questions, ''we select one that we don't enjoy and can't wait to have done with. Why?''*

1   I HATE JOGGING. Every dawn, as I thud around New York City's Central Park reservoir, I am reminded of how much I hate it. It's so tedious. Some claim jogging is thought conducive; others insist the scenery relieves the monotony. For me, the pace is wrong for contemplation of either ideas or vistas. While jogging, all I can think about is jogging—or nothing. One advantage of jogging around a reservoir is that there's no dry shortcut home.

2   From the listless looks of some fellow trotters, I gather I am not alone in my unenthusiasm: Bill-paying, it seems, would be about as diverting. Nonetheless, we continue to jog; more, we continue to *choose* to jog. From a practically infinite array of opportunities, we select one that we don't enjoy and can't wait to have done with. Why?

3   For any trend, there are as many reasons as there are participants. This person runs to lower his blood pressure. That person runs to escape the telephone or a cranky spouse or a filthy household. Another person runs to avoid doing anything else, to dodge a decision about how to lead his life or a realization that his life is leading nowhere. Each of us has his carrot and stick. In my case, the stick is my slackening physical con-

dition, which keeps me from beating opponents at tennis whom I overwhelmed two years ago. My carrot is to win.

Beyond these disparate reasons, however, lies a deeper cause. It is no accident that now, in the last third of the twentieth century, personal fitness and health have suddenly become a popular obsession. True, modern man likes to feel good, but that hardly distinguishes him from his predecessors.   *4*

With zany myopia, economists like to claim that the deeper cause of everything is economic. Delightfully, there seems no marketplace explanation for jogging. True, jogging is cheap, but then not jogging is cheaper. And the scant and skimpy equipment which jogging demands must make it a marketer's least favored form of recreation.   *5*

Some scout-masterish philosophers argue that the appeal of jogging and other body-maintenance programs is the discipline they afford. We live in a world in which individuals have fewer and fewer obligations. The work week has shrunk. Weekend worship is less compulsory. Technology gives us more free time. Satisfactorily filling free time requires imagination and effort. Freedom is a wide and risky river; it can drown the person who does not know how to swim across it. The more obligations one takes on, the more time one occupies, the less threat freedom poses. Jogging can become an instant obligation. For a portion of his day, the jogger is not his own man; he is obedient to a regimen he has accepted.   *6*

Theologists may take the argument one step further. It is our modern irreligion, our lack of confidence in any hereafter, that makes us anxious to stretch our mortal stay as long as possible. We run, as the saying goes, for our lives, hounded by the suspicion that these are the only lives we are likely to enjoy.   *7*

All of these theorists seem to me more or less right. As the growth of cults and charismatic religions and the resurgence of enthusiasm for the military draft suggest, we do crave commitment. And who can doubt, watching so many middle-aged and older persons torturing themselves in the name of fitness, that we are unreconciled to death, more so perhaps than any generation in modern memory?   *8*

But I have a hunch there's a further explanation of our obsession with exercise. I suspect that what motivates us even   *9* more than a fear of death is a fear of dearth. Our era is the first to anticipate the eventual depletion of all natural resources. We see wilderness shrinking; rivers losing their capacity to sustain life; the air, even the stratosphere, being loaded with potentially deadly junk. We see the irreplaceable being squandered, and in the depths of our consciousness we are fearful that we are creating an uninhabitable world. We feel more or less helpless and yet, at the same time, desirous to protect what resources we can. We recycle soda bottles and restore old buildings and protect our nearest natural resource—our physical health—in the almost susperstitious hope that such small gestures will help save an earth that we are blighting. Jogging becomes a sort of penance for our sins of gluttony, greed, and waste. Like a hair shirt or a bed of nails, the more one hates it, the more virtuous it makes one feel.

10   That is why *we* jog. Why *I* jog is to win at tennis.

QUESTIONS ON SUBJECT AND PURPOSE

1. If asked why they jog, few people would reply, "Fear of dearth." Tucker's essay does not, in fact, concentrate on the obvious and immediate reasons why people jog. Why not analyze those reasons?

2. Characterize America's ideal body types. Why are these characteristics valued? What do they reveal about our society's values and preoccupations?

3. Is Tucker being serious in his analysis? How can you tell?

QUESTIONS ON STRATEGY AND AUDIENCE

1. Tucker offers a series of reasons why people jog. Is there any principle of order underlying his arrangement of those reasons?

2. How effective is Tucker's final paragraph? Does it undercut his causal analysis in the previous paragraphs?

3. What expectations does Tucker seem to have about his audience (readers of the *Saturday Review*)? How do you know?

QUESTIONS ON VOCABULARY AND STYLE

1. How effective is Tucker's title? Why might he have chosen that particular title?

2. Be prepared to discuss how each of the following contributes to Tucker's essay:

   a. the opening sentence

   b. the "carrot and stick" image (paragraph 3)

   c. the paragraph dealing with economic causes (5)

   d. the first-person references

3. Be able to define the following words and phrases: *carrot and stick* (paragraph 3), *myopia* (5), *charismatic religions* (8), *dearth* (9), *hair shirt* (9)

WRITING SUGGESTIONS

1. If you engage in any regular athletic activity, analyze the reasons why you do so. Why that activity? What appeals to you? Why bother? If you avoid any such activity, analyze why you do so. Write a paragraph analyzing the reasons for your activity or inactivity.

2. Select another popular American preoccupation and in an essay analyze the reasons for its popularity. Try to avoid the most obvious reasons and focus instead on what this thing or activity reveals about our society. You might consider one of the following possible topics:

   a. blue jeans

   b. skateboards

   c. mountain bikes

   d. a particular clothing style

   e. MTV or music videos

   f. athletic shoes

   g. VCRs

   Prewriting:

   a. Whatever you choose, it should reveal something popular, yet not obvious. Avoid a scientific or technological development unless it is something that could be considered a national obsession. Make a list of possible subjects. What types of objects do your fellow students own? What is considered an essential possession? What seems distinctively American?

b. If possible, interview some students from another country. How do they answer the questions posed above?

c. Remember that your essay will examine the causes of a particular effect. What are the causes of the popularity of this item? You should have multiple causes. Select your two most promising subjects and brainstorm a list of causes for each.

Rewriting:

a. Look again at your list of causes. Have you analyzed the reasons for the item's popularity? Have you given reasons that illuminate our society or our values?

b. Convert the list of things to remember at the end of the introduction to this chapter into a series of questions. Then answer each question honestly. Try to look at your paper as if someone else wrote it.

c. Presumably your essay, because it is about something that appeals to many people, should be of interest to your readers. With that in mind, try to write an introduction that stimulates reader interest. Assume your essay will appear in a popular magazine. Work to grab your reader's attention. Test your introduction on several peer readers. How do they respond? Do they want to keep reading?

3. The ideal man or woman today is thin, athletic, and suntanned. But what is regarded as perfect at one point in time will change in another. Research the ideal body type for both men and women at three points in the twentieth century— for example, 1900, 1940, and 1990. What did the ideal man or woman look like? How did those ideals reflect the values and concerns of society? Using your research, write an essay in which you first define those types and then analyze what they revealed about America at each point in time. Be sure to document your sources.

The Origins
of Anorexia Nervosa

JOAN JACOBS BRUMBERG

Born in 1944 in Mount Vernon, New York, Joan Jacobs Brumberg was educated at the University of Rochester, earned her M.A. at Boston College, and her Ph.D. in American history at the University of Virginia. She is currently director of women's studies and professor of human development and family studies at Cornell University. She has contributed many articles to scholarly journals, as well as book reviews to such periodicals as The Nation, Science, Isis, Journal of American History, *and* Industrial Labor Relations Review. *Her first book,* Mission for Life: The Story of the Family of Adoniram Judson *(1980), studies a prominent nineteenth-century protestant family to gain insight into American evangelical religion.* Fasting Girls: The Emergence of Anorexia Nervosa as a Modern Disease *(1988) studies the disease from historical, social, and familial perspectives, attempting to explain why anorexia has become so prominent in recent decades. The following selection is from* Fasting Girls *and was published in the August 1988 issue of* Harper's. *Brumberg describes Victorian era attitudes toward eating and confrontation. She asks, ''Why would a daughter affront her parents by refusing to eat?''*

CONTRARY TO the popular assumption that anorexia nervosa is *1* a peculiarly modern disorder, the malady first emerged in the Victorian era—long before the pervasive cultural imperative for a thin female body. The first clinical descriptions of the disorder appeared in England and France almost simultaneously in 1873. They were written by two well-known physicians: Sir William Withey Gull and Charles Lasègue. Lasègue, more than any other nineteenth-century doctor, captured the rhythm of repeated offerings and refusals that signaled the breakdown of reciprocity between parents and their anorexic daughter. By returning to its origins, we can see anorexia nervosa for what it is: a dysfunction in the bourgeois family system.

407

2   Family meals assumed enormous importance in the bourgeois milieu, in the United States as well as in England and France. Middle-class parents prided themselves on providing ample food for their children. The abundance of food and the care in its preparation became expressions of social status. The ambience of the meal symbolized the values of the family. A popular domestic manual advised, "Simple, healthy food, exquisitely prepared, and served upon shining dishes and brilliant silverware . . . a gentle blessing, and cheerful conversation, embrace the sweetest communions and the happiest moments of life." Among the middle class it seems that eating correctly was emerging as a new morality, one that set its members apart from the working class.

3   At the same time, food was used to express love in the nineteenth-century bourgeois household. Offering attractive and abundant meals was the particular responsibility and pleasure of middle-class wives and mothers. In America the feeding of middle-class children, from infancy on, had become a maternal concern no longer deemed appropriate to delegate to wet nurses, domestics, or governesses. Family meals were expected to be a time of instructive and engaging conversation. Participation was expected on both a verbal and gustatory level. In this context, refusing to eat was an unabashedly antisocial act. Anorexic behavior was antithetical to the ideal of bourgeois eating. One advice book, *Common Sense for Maid, Wife, and Mother*, stated: "Heated discussion and quarrels, fretfulness and sullen taciturnity while eating, are as unwholesome as they are unchristian."

4   Why would a daughter affront her parents by refusing to eat? Lasègue's 1873 description of anorexia nervosa, along with other nineteenth-century medical reports, suggests that pressure to marry may have precipitated the illness.

5   Ambitious parents surely understood that by marrying well, at an appropriate moment, a daughter, even though she did not carry the family name, could help advance a family's social status—particularly in a burgeoning middle-class society. As a result, the issue of marriage loomed large in the life of a dutiful middle-class daughter. Although marriage did not generally

occur until the girl's early twenties, it was an event for which she was continually prepared, and a desirable outcome for all depended on the ability of the parents and the child to work together—that is, to state clearly what each wanted or to read each other's heart and mind. In the context of marital expectations, a daughter's refusal to eat was a provocative rejection of both the family's social aspirations and their goodwill toward her. All of the parents' plans for her future (and their own) could be stymied by her peculiar and unpleasant alimentary nihilism. → Traditional Values Are unfounded + existence is Sensless

Beyond the specific anxieties generated by marital pressure, the Victorian family milieu in America and in Western Europe harbored a mélange of other tensions and problems that provided the emotional preconditions for the emergence of anorexia nervosa. As love replaced authority as the cement of family relations, it began to generate its own set of emotional disorders. 6

Possessiveness, for example, became an acute problem in Victorian family life. Where love between parents and children was the prevailing ethic, there was always the risk of excess. When love became suffocating or manipulative, individuation and separation from the family could become extremely painful, if not impossible. In the context of increased intimacy, adolescent privacy was especially problematic: For parents and their sexually maturing daughters, what constituted an appropriate degree of privacy? Middle-class girls, for example, almost always had their own rooms or shared them with sisters, but they had greater difficulty establishing autonomous psychic space. The well-known penchant of adolescent girls for novel-reading was an expression of their need for imaginative freedom. Some parents, recognizing that their daughters needed channels for expressing emotions, encouraged diary-keeping. But some of the same parents who gave lovely marbled journals as gifts also monitored their content. Since emotional freedom was not an acknowledged prerogative of the Victorian adolescent girl, it seems likely that she would have expressed unhappiness in non-verbal forms of behavior. One such behavior was refusal of food. 7

When an adolescent daughter became sullen and chroni- 8

409

cally refused to eat, her parents felt threatened and confused. The daughter was perceived as willfully manipulating her appetite the way a younger child might. Because parents did not want to encourage this behavior, they often refused at first to indulge the favorite tastes or caprices of their daughter. As emaciation became visible and the girl looked ill, many violated the contemporary canon of prudent child-rearing and put aside their moral objections to pampering the appetite. Eventually they would beg their daughter to eat whatever she liked—and eat she must, ''as a sovereign proof of affection'' for them. From the parents' perspective, a return to eating was a confirmation of filial love.

9   The significance of food refusal as an emotional tactic within the family depended on food's being plentiful, pleasing, and connected to love. Where food was eaten simply to assuage hunger, where it had only minimal aesthetic and symbolic messages, or where the girl had to provide her own nourishment, refusal of food was not particularly noteworthy or defiant. In contrast, the anorexic girl was surrounded by a provident, if not indulgent, family that was bound to be distressed by her rejection of its largess.

10   Anorexia nervosa was an intense form of discourse that honored the emotional guidelines that governed the middle-class Victorian family. Refusing to eat was not as confrontational as yelling, having a tantrum, or throwing things; refusing to eat expressed emotional hostility without being flamboyant. And refusing to eat had the advantage of being ambiguous. If a girl repeatedly claimed lack of appetite she might indeed be ill and therefore entitled to special treatment and favors.

11   In her own way, the anorexic was respectful of what historian Peter Gay called ''the great bourgeois compromise between the need for reserve and the capacity for emotion.'' The rejection of food, while an emotionally charged behavior, was also discreet, quiet, and ladylike. The unhappy adolescent who was in all other ways a dutiful daughter chose food refusal from within the symptom repertoire available to her. Precisely because she was not a lunatic, she selected a behavior that she knew would have some efficacy within her own family.

QUESTIONS ON SUBJECT AND PURPOSE

1. According to Brumberg, when did anorexia nervosa emerge as a definable disease? Why did it emerge in that particular time period?

2. On the basis of what Brumberg writes here, who is the most likely candidate for anorexia nervosa?

3. What purpose might Brumberg have in writing about anorexia nervosa?

QUESTIONS ON STRATEGY AND AUDIENCE

1. Brumberg never bothers to define the disorder. Why not?

2. To what extent does isolating the origins of anorexia nervosa help us to understand the disorder in young people today?

3. Brumberg uses quite a few words that might be unfamiliar to many readers. What do her vocabulary choices imply about her sense of audience?

QUESTIONS ON VOCABULARY AND STYLE

1. In paragraphs 2 and 3, Brumberg quotes from two popular domestic manuals of the nineteenth century. What do the quotations contribute to her essay?

2. In paragraph 5, Brumberg uses the phrase "alimentary nihilism" with reference to anorectics. What does the phrase mean?

3. Be prepared to define the following words: *malady* (paragraph 1), *imperative* (1), *reciprocity* (1), *dysfunction* (1), *bourgeois* (1), *milieu* (2), *ambience* (2), *wet nurses* (3), *gustatory* (3), *unabashedly* (3), *antithetical* (3), *taciturnity* (3), *burgeoning* (5), *stymied* (5), *alimentary* (5), *nihilism* (5), *melange* (6), *individuation* (7), *autonomous* (7), *penchant* (7), *prerogative* (7), *caprices* (8), *emaciation* (8), *assuage* (9), *largess* (9), *flamboyant* (10), *efficacy* (11).

WRITING SUGGESTIONS

1. In a paragraph, define your "ideal" body. Then in a second paragraph speculate on the reasons why that body type or shape seems "ideal."

2. Cultural historians have observed that American society is "obesophobic" (excessively or irrationally fearful of fat and being fat). Certainly weight consciousness permeates American society and the weight-loss industries are multimillion dollar businesses. Why?

Prewriting:

a. For a single day, keep a record of every reference that you encounter to being overweight—advertisements in the media, references made by friends, remarks that you overhear. These examples will provide detail in your essay.

b. Think about the "ideal" body types in your society. What does the ideal male or female body look like? Freewrite about that ideal as it relates to you and your friends.

c. Construct a list of possible causes that have contributed to this "fear of fat." Try to come up with at least six possible causes. Discuss possible reasons with some classmates or friends.

Rewriting:

a. Look again at your list of causes and your essay. Is there any order that seems most appropriate? Which cause ought to come first? Which last? Construct several possible outlines or, if you are writing on a word processor, construct several different bodies for your essay. Which arrangement seems to work best?

b. Have you provided enough examples and details to support your analysis and to make your essay interesting to read? Look back over that one-day record. Have you used your best examples?

c. Think about how an article in *Time* or *Newsweek* might introduce such an essay. Does your introduction grab your reader's attention?

3. Anorexia nervosa is only one of a number of diseases that are common today but were previously unknown or undiagnosed. Other examples include Alzheimer's disease, osteoporosis, and premenstrual syndrome. Select a "new" disease or disorder and research its history. When was it first defined? What might account for its emergence during the past decade or two?

The End of Play

MARIE WINN

Marie Winn was born in Czechoslovakia in 1936 and emigrated to the United States with her family in 1939. She attended Radcliffe College and Columbia University. Author and compiler of numerous books, her works include anthologies of children's songs and games, books intended for children, and three critical studies: Children Without Childhood *(1983);* The Plug-In Drug: Television, Children, and the Family *(1977; revised edition, 1985); and* Unplugging the Plug-In Drug *(1987), which offers advice on how to plan a family television turnoff and discusses the possible effects of such an action. In this selection, the fourth chapter in* Children Without Childhood, *Winn laments the disappearance of childhood play. "Whereas a decade or two ago children were easily distinguished from the adult world by the very nature of their play," Winn writes, "today children's occupations do not differ greatly from adult diversions."*

OF ALL THE CHANGES that have altered the topography of childhood, the most dramatic has been the disappearance of childhood play. Whereas a decade or two ago children were easily distinguished from the adult world by the very nature of their play, today children's occupations do not differ greatly from adult diversions. [1]

Infants and toddlers, to be sure, continue to follow certain timeless patterns of manipulation and exploration; adolescents, too, have not changed their free-time habits so very much, turning as they ever have towards adult pastimes and amusements in their drive for autonomy, self-mastery, and sexual discovery. It is among the ranks of school-age children, those six-to-twelve-year-olds who once avidly filled their free moments with childhood play, that the greatest change is evident. In the place of traditional, sometimes ancient childhood games that were still popular a generation ago, in the place of fantasy and make-believe play—"You be the mommy and I'll be the daddy"— [2]

doll play or toy-soldier play, jump-rope play, ball-bouncing play, today's children have substituted television viewing and, most recently, video games.

3   Many parents have misgivings about the influence of television. They sense that a steady and time-consuming exposure to passive entertainment might damage the ability to play imaginatively and resourcefully, or prevent this ability from developing in the first place. A mother of two school-age children recalls: "When I was growing up, we used to go out into the vacant lots and make up week-long dramas and sagas. This was during third, fourth, fifth grades. But my own kids have never done that sort of thing, and somehow it bothers me. I wish we had cut down on the TV years ago, and maybe the kids would have learned how to play."

4   The testimony of parents who eliminate television for periods of time strengthens the connection between children's television watching and changed play patterns. Many parents discover that when their children don't have television to fill their free time, they resort to the old kinds of imaginative, traditional "children's play." Moreover, these parents often observe that under such circumstances "they begin to seem more like children" or "they act more childlike." Clearly, a part of the definition of childhood, in adults' minds, resides in the nature of children's play.

5   Children themselves sometimes recognize the link between play and their own special definition as children. In an interview about children's books with four ten-year-old girls, one of them said: "I read this story about a girl my age growing up twenty years ago—you know, in 1960 or so—and she seemed so much younger than me in her behavior. Like she might be playing with dolls, or playing all sorts of children's games, or jump-roping or something." The other girls all agreed that they had noticed a similar discrepancy between themselves and fictional children in books of the past: those children seemed more like children. "So what do *you* do in your spare time, if you don't play with dolls or play make-believe games or jump rope or do things kids did twenty years ago?" they were asked. They laughed and answered, "We watch TV."

6   But perhaps other societal factors have caused children to

give up play. Children's greater exposure to adult realities, their knowledge of adult sexuality, for instance, might make them more sophisticated, less likely to play like children. Evidence from the counterculture communes of the sixties and seventies adds weight to the argument that it is television above all that has eliminated children's play. Studies of children raised in a variety of such communes, all television-free, showed the little communards continuing to fill their time with those forms of play that have all but vanished from the lives of conventionally reared American children. And yet these counterculture kids were casually exposed to all sorts of adult matters—drug taking, sexual intercourse. Indeed, they sometimes incorporated these matters into their play: "We're mating," a pair of six-year-olds told a reporter to explain their curious bumps and grinds. Nevertheless, to all observers the commune children preserved a distinctly childlike and even innocent demeanor, an impression that was produced mainly by the fact that they spent most of their time playing. Their play defined them as belonging to a special world of childhood.

Not all children have lost the desire to engage in the old-style childhood play. But so long as the most popular, most dominant members of the peer group, who are often the most socially precocious, are "beyond" playing, then a common desire to conform makes it harder for those children who still have the drive to play to go ahead and do so. Parents often report that their children seem ashamed of previously common forms of play and hide their involvement with such play from their peers. "My fifth-grader still plays with dolls," a mother tells, "but she keeps them hidden in the basement where nobody will see them." This social check on the play instinct serves to hasten the end of childhood for even the least advanced children. 7

What seems to have replaced play in the lives of great numbers of preadolescents these days, starting as early as fourth grade, is a burgeoning interest in boy-girl interactions—"going out" or "going together." These activities do not necessarily involve going anywhere or doing anything sexual, but nevertheless are the first stage of a sexual process that used to commence at puberty or even later. Those more sophisticated chil- 8 dren who are already involved in such manifestly unchildlike interests make plain their low opinion of their peers who still *play.* "Some of the kids in the class are real weird," a fifth-grade boy states. "They're not interested in going out, just in trucks and stuff, or games pretending they're monsters. Some of them don't even *try* to be cool."

Video Games Versus Marbles

9   Is there really any great difference, one might ask, between that gang of kids playing video games by the hour at their local candy store these days and those small fry who used to hang around together spending equal amounts of time playing marbles? It is easy to see a similarity between the two activities: each requires a certain amount of manual dexterity, each is almost as much fun to watch as to play, each is simple and yet challenging enough for that middle-childhood age group for whom time can be so oppressive if unfilled.

10   One significant difference between the modern pre-teen fad of video games and the once popular but now almost extinct pastime of marbles is economic: playing video games costs twenty-five cents for approximately three minutes of play; playing marbles, after a small initial investment, is free. The children who frequent video-game machines require a considerable outlay of quarters to subsidize their fun; two, three, or four dollars is not an unusual expenditure for an eight- or nine-year-old spending an hour or two with his friends playing Asteroids or Pac-Man or Space Invaders. For most of the children the money comes from their weekly allowance. Some augment this amount by enterprising commercial ventures—trading and selling comic books, or doing chores around the house for extra money.

11   But what difference does it make *where* the money comes from? Why should that make video games any less satisfactory as an amusement for children? In fact, having to pay for the entertainment, whatever the source of the money, and having its duration limited by one's financial resources changes the nature of the game, in a subtle way diminishing the satisfactions it offers. Money and time become intertwined, as they so often

416

are in the adult world and as, in the past, they almost never were in the child's world. For the child playing marbles, meanwhile, time has a far more carefree quality, bounded only by the requirements to be home by suppertime or by dark.

But the video-game-playing child has an additional burden—a burden of choice, of knowing that the money used for playing Pac-Man could have been saved for Christmas, could have been used to buy something tangible, perhaps something "worthwhile," as his parents might say, rather than being "wasted" on video games. There is a certain sense of adultness that spending money imparts, a feeling of being a consumer, which distinguishes a game with a price from its counterparts among the traditional childhood games children once played at no cost. *12*

There are other differences as well. Unlike child-initiated and child-organized games such as marbles, video games are adult-created mechanisms not entirely within the child's control, and thus less likely to impart a sense of mastery and fulfillment: the coin may get jammed, the machine may go haywire, the little blobs may stop eating the funny little dots. Then the child must go to the storekeeper to complain, to get his money back. He may be "ripped off" and simply lose his quarter, much as his parents are when they buy a faulty appliance. This possibility of disaster gives the child's play a certain weight that marbles never imposed on its light-hearted players. *13*

Even if a child has a video game at home requiring no coin outlay, the play it provides is less than optimal. The noise level of the machine is high—too high, usually, for the child to conduct a conversation easily with another child. And yet, according to its enthusiasts, this very noisiness is a part of the game's attraction. The loud whizzes, crashes, and whirrs of the video-game machine "blow the mind" and create an excitement that is quite apart from the excitement generated simply by trying to win a game. A traditional childhood game such as marbles, on the other hand, has little built-in stimulation; the excitement of playing is generated entirely by the players' own actions. And while the pace of a game of marbles is close to the child's natural physiological rhythms, the frenzied activities of video games serve to "rev up" the child in an artificial way, *14*

417

almost in the way a stimulant or an amphetamine might. Meanwhile the perceptual impact of a video game is similar to that of watching television—the action, after all, takes place on a television screen—causing the eye to defocus slightly and creating a certain alteration in the child's natural state of consciousness.

15   Parents' instinctive reaction to their children's involvement with video games provides another clue to the difference between this contemporary form of play and the more traditional pastimes such as marbles. While parents, indeed most adults, derive open pleasure from watching children at play, most parents today are not delighted to watch their kids flicking away at the Pac-Man machine. This does not seem to them to be real play. As a mother of two school-age children anxiously explains, "We used to do real childhood sorts of things when I was a kid. We'd build forts and put on crazy plays and make up new languages, and just generally we *played.* But today my kids don't play that way at all. They like video games and of course they still go in for sports outdoors. They go roller skating and ice skating and skiing and all. But they don't seem to really *play.*"

16   Some of this feeling may represent a certain nostalgia for the past and the old generation's resistance to the different ways of the new. But it is more likely that most adults have an instinctive understanding of the importance of play in their own childhood. This feeling stokes their fears that their children are being deprived of something irreplaceable when they flip the levers on the video machines to manipulate the electronic images rather than flick their fingers to send a marble shooting towards another marble.

Play Deprivation

17 In addition to television's influence, some parents and teachers ascribe children's diminished drive to play to recent changes in the school curriculum, especially in the early grades.

18   "Kindergarten, traditionally a playful port of entry into formal school, is becoming more academic, with children being taught specific skills, taking tests, and occasionally even having

homework," begins a report on new directions in early child-hood education. Since 1970, according to the United States census, the proportion of three- and four-year-olds enrolled in school has risen dramatically, from 20.5 percent to 36.7 percent in 1980, and these nursery schools have largely joined the push towards academic acceleration in the early grades. Moreover, middle-class nursery schools in recent years have introduced substantial doses of academic material into their daily programs, often using those particular devices originally intended to help culturally deprived preschoolers in compensatory programs such as Headstart to catch up with their middle-class peers. Indeed, some of the increased focus on academic skills in nurs-ery schools and kindergartens is related to the widespread pop-ularity among young children and their parents of *Sesame Street,* a program originally intended to help deprived children attain academic skills, but universally watched by middle-class tod-dlers as well.

Parents of the *Sesame Street* generation often demand a "se-rious," skill-centered program for their preschoolers in school, afraid that the old-fashioned, play-centered curriculum will bore their alphabet-spouting, number-chanting four- and five-year-olds. A few parents, especially those whose children have not attended television classes or nursery school, complain of the high-powered pace of kindergarten these days. A father whose five-year-old daughter attends a public kindergarten de-clares: "There's a lot more pressure put on little kids these days than when we were kids, that's for sure. My daughter never went to nursery school and never watched *Sesame,* and she had a lot of trouble when she entered kindergarten this fall. By October, just a month and a half into the program, she was already flunking. The teacher told us our daughter couldn't keep up with the other kids. And believe me, she's a bright kid! All the other kids were getting gold stars and smiley faces for their work, and every day Emily would come home in tears because she didn't get a gold star. Remember when we were in kindergarten? We were *children* then. We were allowed just to play!" 19

A kindergarten teacher confirms the trend towards early academic pressure. "We're expected by the dictates of the school 20

419

system to push a lot of curriculum," she explains. "Kids in our kindergarten can't sit around playing with blocks anymore. We've just managed to squeeze in one hour of free play a week, on Fridays."

21   The diminished emphasis on fantasy and play and imaginative activities in early childhood education and the increased focus on early academic-skill acquisition have helped to change childhood from a play-centered time of life to one more closely resembling the style of adulthood: purposeful, success-centered, competitive. The likelihood is that these preschool "workers" will not metamorphose back into players when they move on to grade school. This decline in play is surely one of the reasons why so many teachers today comment that their third- or fourth-graders act like tired businessmen instead of like children.

22   What might be the consequences of this change in children's play? Children's propensity to engage in that extraordinary series of behaviors characterized as "play" is perhaps the single great dividing line between childhood and adulthood, and has probably been so throughout history. The make-believe games anthropologists have recorded of children in primitive societies around the world attest to the universality of play and to the uniqueness of this activity to the immature members of each society. But in those societies, and probably in Western society before the middle or late eighteenth century, there was always a certain similarity between children's play and adult work. The child's imaginative play took the form of imitation of various aspects of adult life, culminating in the gradual transformation of the child's play from make-believe work to *real* work. At this point, in primitive societies or in our own society of the past, the child took her or his place in the adult work world and the distinctions between adulthood and childhood virtually vanished. But in today's technologically advanced society there is no place for the child in the adult work world. There are not enough jobs, even of the most menial kind, to go around for adults, much less for children. The child must continue to be dependent on adults for many years while gaining the knowledge and skills necessary to become a working member of society.

This is not a new situation for children. For centuries chil-   23
dren have endured a prolonged period of dependence long after
the helplessness of early childhood is over. But until recent years
children remained childlike and playful far longer than they do
today. Kept isolated from the adult world as a result of deliberate
secrecy and protectiveness, they continued to find pleasure in
socially sanctioned childish activities until the imperatives of
adolescence led them to strike out for independence and self-
sufficiency.

Today, however, with children's inclusion in the adult   24
world both through the instrument of television and as a result
of a deliberately preparatory, integrative style of child rearing,
the old forms of play no longer seem to provide children with
enough excitement and stimulation. What then are these so-
called children to do for fulfillment if their desire to play has
been vitiated and yet their entry into the working world of
adulthood must be delayed for many years? The answer is precisely to get involved in those areas that cause contemporary
parents so much distress: addictive television viewing during
the school years followed, in adolescence or even before, by a
search for similar oblivion via alcohol and drugs; exploration
of the world of sensuality and sexuality before achieving the
emotional maturity necessary for altruistic relationships.

Psychiatrists have observed among children in recent years   25
a marked increase in the occurrence of depression, a state long
considered antithetical to the nature of childhood. Perhaps this
phenomenon is at least somewhat connected with the current
sense of uselessness and alienation that children feel, a sense
that play may once upon a time have kept in abeyance.

QUESTIONS ON SUBJECT AND PURPOSE

1. What reasons does Winn offer in explanation of "the decline
    of play?"
2. According to Winn, what are the consequences of not engag-
    ing in "childish play?"
3. What purpose might Winn have in writing about this subject?
    For example, does she expect to persuade her audience to do
    anything?

QUESTIONS ON STRATEGY AND AUDIENCE

1. What is Winn's primary source of information for the essay?
2. In arranging the three causes, why might Winn begin with the influence of television?
3. On the basis of her strategies and style, what expectations might Winn have about her audience?

QUESTIONS ON VOCABULARY AND STYLE

1. Does Winn seem to approach the subject in a detached, unbiased way, or does she reveal her prejudices? Locate two examples, perhaps in her choice of words, that support your answer.
2. How would you characterize the vocabulary that Winn uses in her essay? For example, does the essay sound as if it might appear in a psychology textbook?
3. Be prepared to define the following words: *topography* (paragraph 1), *diversions* (1), *autonomy* (2), *counterculture communes* (6), *communards* (6), *demeanor* (6), *precocious* (7), *burgeoning* (8), *manifestly* (8), *dexterity* (9), *augment* (10), *optimal* (14), *amphetamine* (14), *compensatory* (18), *propensity* (22), *sanctioned* (23), *imperatives* (23), *integrative* (24), *vitiated* (24), *altruistic* (24), *abeyance* (25).

WRITING SUGGESTIONS

1. Select one type of "play" that you engaged in as a child. In a substantial paragraph explore the impact that type of play had on you as an adult today. What "effect" did it produce?
2. Assuming (even if you do not) that Winn is right when she characterizes children today as feeling a "sense of uselessness and alienation" (paragraph 25), in an essay suggest another series of possible causes for those feelings.

Prewriting:

a. Work on compiling a list of possible causes. Keep thinking about the topic over a several-day period, and jot down ideas several times a day. Try to come up with a list of at least six possible causes.
b. Think about your own childhood or that of your children.

Do your ideas seem to fit those experiences? Try freewriting about four of the most logical possible causes.

c. Decide whether or not to put a persuasive slant on the essay. If you choose to do so, read the introduction to Chapter 9 before you write the first draft.

Rewriting:

a. Look at how you organized the body of your essay. What principle of order did you follow? For example, did you move from the most significant reason to the least? Consider rearranging the middle of your essay. Remember that you need to have a rationale for ordering the causes in the body of your paper.

b. Look again at your analysis. Remember that each cause should help explain where that sense of "uselessness and alienation" comes from. Ask about each body paragraph, "Does this explain why?"

c. If you have put a persuasive slant on your paper, convert the list of things to remember at the end of the introduction to Chapter 9 into a series of questions. Answer those questions. Consider the cautions as well.

3. Do children today feel a greater sense of "uselessness and alienation" than children did earlier in this century? What do modern psychologists say about this? Does the research literature support this conclusion about today's children?

Why Young Women
Are More Conservative

GLORIA STEINEM

*Gloria Steinem was born in 1934 in Toledo, Ohio. She earned her
B.A. degree in government from Smith College in 1956. In 1968,
Steinem helped to found* New York *magazine, for which she is now
a contributing editor. She cofounded* Ms. *magazine in 1971 and
served as its editor until 1987. Steinem has earned recognition as one
of the preeminent leaders of the women's liberation movement and
has been active in civil rights organizations, political campaigning,
and peace movements. She has contributed to such publications as*
Vogue, Cosmopolitan, Time, *and* Esquire. *Her books include* Outrageous Acts and Everyday Rebellions *(1983), a collection of essays, and* Marilyn *(1986), an analysis of Marilyn Monroe's career
in Hollywood.*

*Steinem starts with what appears to be a reasonable assumption—
college-age youth are more likely to be activists and open to change
than their parents. But after a decade of traveling to college campuses,
she realized that her assumption was wrong—the active feminists are
more likely to be middle-aged. In the essay she explores the reason
why women, as they grow older, are more interested in the feminist
movement.*

1 IF YOU HAD ASKED ME a decade or more ago, I certainly would
have said the campus was the first place to look for the feminist
or any other revolution. I also would have assumed that student-age women, like student-age men, were much more likely
to be activist and open to change than their parents. After all,
campus revolts have a long and well-publicized tradition, from
the students of medieval France, whose "heresy" was suggesting that the university be separate from the church, through
the anticolonial student riots of British India; from students who
led the cultural revolution of the People's Republic of China,
to campus demonstrations against the Shah of Iran. Even in

this country, with far less tradition of student activism, the populist movement to end the war in Vietnam was symbolized by campus protests and mistrust of anyone over thirty.

It has taken me many years of traveling as a feminist speaker and organizer to understand that I was wrong about women; at least, about women acting on their own behalf. In activism, as in so many other things, I had been educated to assume that men's cultural pattern was the natural or the only one. If student years were the peak time of rebellion and openness to change for men, then the same must be true for women. In fact, a decade of listening to every kind of women's group—from brown-bag lunchtime lectures organized by office workers to all-night rap sessions at campus women's centers, from housewives' self-help groups to campus rallies—has convinced me that the reverse is more often true. Women may be the one group that grows more radical with age. Though some students are big exceptions to this rule, women in general don't begin to challenge the politics of our own lives until later.

Looking back, I realize that this pattern has been true for my life, too. My college years were full of uncertainties and the personal conservatism that comes from trying to win approval and fit into the proper grown-up and womanly role, whether that means finding a well-to-do man to be supported by or a male radical to support. Nonetheless, I went right on assuming that brave exploring youth and cowardly conservative old age were the norms for everybody, and that I must be just an isolated and guilty accident. Though every generalization based on female culture has many exceptions, and should never be used as a crutch or excuse, I think we might be less hard on ourselves and each other as students, feel better about our potential for change as we grow older—and educate reporters who announce feminism's demise because its red-hot center is not on campus—if we figured out that for most of us as women, the traditional college period is an unrealistic and cautious time. Consider a few of the reasons.

As students, women are probably treated with more equality than we ever will be again. For one thing, we're consumers. The school is only too glad to get the tuitions we pay, or that our families or government grants pay on our behalf. With population rates declining because of women's increased power over childbearing, that money is even more vital to a school's existence. Yet more than most consumers, we're too transient to have much power as a group. If our families are paying our tuition, we may have even less power.

5   As young women, whether students or not, we're still in the stage most valued by male-dominant cultures: we have our full potential as workers, wives, sex partners, and childbearers.

6   That means we haven't yet experienced the life events that are most radicalizing for women: entering the paid-labor force and discovering how women are treated there; marrying and finding out that it is not yet an equal partnership having children and discovering who is responsible for them and who is not; and aging, still a greater penalty for women than for men.

7   Furthermore, new ambitions nourished by the rebirth of feminism may make young women feel and behave a little like a classical immigrant group. We are determined to prove ourselves, to achieve academic excellence, and to prepare for interesting and successful careers. More noses are kept to more grindstones in an effort to demonstrate newfound abilities, and perhaps to allay suspicions that women still have to have more and better credentials than men. This doesn't leave much time for activism. Indeed, we may not yet know that it is necessary.

8   In addition, the very progress into previously all-male careers that may be revolutionary for women is seen as conservative and conformist by outside critics. Assuming male radicalism to be the measure of change, they interpret any concern with careers as evidence of "campus conservatism." In fact, "dropping out" may be a departure for men, but "dropping in" is a new thing for women. Progress lies in the direction we have not been.

9   Like most groups of the newly arrived or awakened, our faith in education and paper degrees also has yet to be shaken. For instance, the percentage of women enrolled in colleges and universities has been increasing at the same time that the percentage of men has been decreasing. Among students entering college in 1978, women *outnumbered* men for the first time. This hope of excelling at the existing game is probably reinforced by

the greater cultural pressure on females to be "good girls" and observe somebody else's rules.

Though we may know intellectually that we need to have   *10* new games with new rules, we probably haven't quite absorbed such facts as the high unemployment rate among female Ph.D.s; the lower average salary among women college graduates of all races than among counterpart males who graduated from high school or less; the middle-management ceiling against which even those eagerly hired new business-school graduates seem to bump their heads after five or ten years; and the barrier-breaking women in nontraditional fields who become the first fired when recession hits. Sadly enough, we may have to personally experience some of these reality checks before we accept the idea that lawsuits, activism, and group pressure will have to accompany our individual excellence and crisp new degrees.

Then there is the female guilt trip, student edition. If we're   *11* not sailing along as planned, it must be our fault. If our mothers didn't "do anything" with their educations, it must have been *their* fault. If we can't study as hard as we think we must (because women still have to be better prepared than men), and have a substantial personal and sexual life at the same time (because women are supposed to care more about relationships than men do), then we feel inadequate, as if each of us were individually at fault for a problem that is actually culture-wide.

I've yet to be on a campus where most women weren't   *12* worrying about some aspect of combining marriage, children, and a career. I've yet to find one where many men were worrying about the same thing. Yet women will go right on suffering from the double-role problem and terminal guilt until men are encouraged, pressured, or otherwise forced, individually and collectively, to integrate themselves into the "women's work" of raising children and homemaking. Until then, and until there are changed job patterns to allow equal parenthood, children will go right on growing up with the belief that only women can be loving and nurturing, and only men can be intellectual or active outside the home. Each half of the world will go on limiting the full range of its human talent.

Finally, there is the intimate political training that hits   *13* women in the teens and early twenties: the countless ways we are still brainwashed into assuming that women are dependent on men for our basic identities, both in our work and our personal lives, much more than vice versa. After all, if we're going to enter a marriage system that's still legally designed for a person and a half, submit to an economy in which women still average about fifty-nine cents on the dollar earned by men, and work mainly as support staff and assistants, or *co*-directors and *vice*-presidents at best, then we have to be convinced that we are not whole people on our own.

14   In order to make sure that we will see ourselves as half-people, and thus be addicted to getting our identity from serving others, society tries hard to convert us as young women into "man junkies"; that is, into people who are addicted to regular shots of male-approval and presence, both professionally and personally. We need a man standing next to us, actually and figuratively, whether it's at work, on Saturday night, or throughout life. (If only men realized how little it matters *which* man is standing there, they would understand that this addiction depersonalizes them, too.) Given the danger to a male-dominant system if young women stop internalizing this political message of derived identity, it's no wonder that those who try to kick the addiction—and, worse yet, to help other women do the same—are likely to be regarded as odd or dangerous by everyone from parents to peers.

15   With all that pressure combined with little experience, it's no wonder that younger women are often less able to support each other. Even young women who espouse feminist goals as individuals may refrain from identifying themselves as "feminist": It's okay to want equal pay for yourself (just one small reform) but it's not okay to want equal pay for women as a group (an economic revolution). Some retreat into individualized career obsessions as a way of avoiding this dangerous discovery of shared experience with women as a group. Others retreat into the safe middle ground of "I'm not a feminist but. . . ." Still others become politically active, but only on issues that are taken seriously by their male counterparts.

16   The same lesson about the personal conservatism of younger women is taught by the history of feminism. If I hadn't

been conned into believing the masculine stereotype of youth as the "natural" time for freedom and rebellion, a time of "sowing wild oats" that actually is made possible by the assurance of power and security later on, I could have figured out the female pattern of activism by looking at women's movements of the past.

In this country, for instance, the nineteenth-century wave   17
of feminism was started by older women who had been through the radicalizing experience of getting married and becoming the legal chattel of their husbands (or the equally radicalizing experience of not getting married and being treated as spinsters). Most of them had also worked in the antislavery movement and learned from the political parallels between race and sex. In other countries, that wave was also led by women who were past the point of maximum pressure toward marriageability and conservatism.

Looking at the first decade of this second wave, it's clear   18
that the early feminist activist and consciousness-raising groups of the 1960s were organized by women who had experienced the civil rights movement, or homemakers who had discovered that raising kids and cooking didn't occupy all their talents. While most campuses of the late sixties were still circulating the names of illegal abortionists privately (after all, abortion could damage our marriage value), slightly older women were holding press conferences and speak-outs about the reality of abortions (including their own, even though that often meant confessing to an illegal act) and demanding reform or repeal of antichoice laws. Though rape had been a quiet epidemic on campus for generations, younger women victims were still understandably fearful of speaking up, and campuses encouraged silence in order to retain their reputation for safety with tuition-paying parents. It took many off-campus speak-outs, demonstrations against laws of evidence and police procedures, and testimonies in state legislatures before most student groups began to make demands on campus and local cops for greater rape protection. In fact, "date rape"—the common campus phenomenon of a young woman being raped by someone she knows, perhaps even by several students in a fraternity house—is just now being exposed. Marital rape, a more difficult legal

issue, was taken up several years ago. As for battered women and the attendant exposé of husbands and lovers as more statistically dangerous than unknown muggers in the street, that issue still seems to be thought of as a largely noncampus concern, yet at many of the colleges and universities where I've spoken, there has been at least one case within current student memory of a young woman beaten or murdered by a jealous lover.

19   This cultural pattern of youthful conservatism makes the growing number of older women going back to school very important. They are life examples and pragmatic activists who radicalize women young enough to be their daughters. Now that the median female undergraduate age in this country is twenty-seven because so many older women have returned, the campus is becoming a major place for cross-generational connections.

20   None of this should denigrate the courageous efforts of young women, especially women on campus, and the many changes they've pioneered. On the contrary, they should be seen as even more remarkable for surviving the conservative pressures, recognizing societal problems they haven't yet fully experienced, and organizing successfully in the midst of a transient student population. Every women's history course, rape hot line, or campus newspaper that is finally covering *all* the news; every feminist professor whose job has been created or tenure saved by student pressure, or male administrator whose consciousness has been permanently changed; every counselor who's stopped guiding women one way and men another; every lawsuit that's been fueled by student energies against unequal athletic funds or graduate school requirements: all those accomplishments are even more impressive when seen against the back-drop of the female pattern of activism.

21   Finally, it would help to remember that a feminist revolution rarely resembles a masculine-style one—just as a young woman's most radical act toward her mother (that is, connecting as women in order to help each other get some power) doesn't look much like a young man's most radical act toward his father (that is, breaking the father-son connection in order to separate identities or take over existing power).

It's those father-son conflicts at a generational, national   22
level that have often provided the conventional definition of
revolution; yet they've gone on for centuries without basically
changing the role of the female half of the world. They have
also failed to reduce the level of violence in society, since both
fathers and sons have included some degree of aggressiveness
and superiority to women in their definition of masculinity, thus
preserving the anthropological model of dominance.

Furthermore, what current leaders and theoreticians define   23
as revolution is usually little more than taking over the army
and the radio stations. Women have much more in mind than
that. We have to uproot the sexual caste system that is the most
pervasive power structure in society, and that means trans-
forming the patriarchal values of those who run the institutions,
whether they are politically the "right" or the "left," the fathers
or the sons. This cultural part of the change goes very deep,
and is often seen as too intimate, and perhaps too threatening,
to be considered as either serious or possible. Only conflicts
among men are "serious." Only a takeover of existing institutions is "possible."

That's why the definition of "political," on campus as else-   24
where, tends to be limited to who's running for president, who's
demonstrating against corporate investments in South Africa,
or which is the "moral" side of some conventional revolution,
preferably one that is thousands of miles away.

As important as such activities are, they are also the most   25
comfortable ones when we're young. They provide a sense of
virtue without much disruption in the power structure of our
daily lives. Even when the most consistent energies on campus
are actually concentrated around feminist issues, they may be
treated as apolitical and invisible. Asked "What's happening on
campus?" a student may reply, "The antinuke movement,"
even though that resulted in one demonstration of two hours,
while student antirape squads have been patrolling the campus
every night for two years and women's studies have begun to
transform the very textbooks we read.

No wonder reporters and sociologists looking for revolution   26
on campus often miss the depth of feminist change and activity
that is really there. Women students themselves may dismiss it

as not political and not serious. Certainly, it rarely comes in the masculine sixties style of bombing buildings or burning draft cards. In fact, it goes much deeper than protesting a temporary symptom—say, the draft—and challenges the right of one group to dominate another, which is the disease itself.

27　　Young women have a big task of resisting pressures and challenging definitions. Their increasing success is a miracle of foresight and courage that should make us all proud. But they should know that they, too, may grow more radical with age.

28　　One day, an army of gray-haired women may quietly take over the earth.

QUESTIONS ON SUBJECT AND PURPOSE

1. What does Steinem mean by the word *conservative?* In what ways are young women conservative?
2. According to Steinem, what are the causes of this conservatism?
3. In what ways do women's cultural patterns differ from men's?

QUESTIONS ON STRATEGY AND AUDIENCE

1. How does Steinem structure her cause and effect analysis? Is there a particular order to her list of causes?
2. How effective is Steinem's conclusion? Does it seem appropriate? Why or why not?
3. What assumptions does Steinem make about her audience? How are those assumptions revealed in the essay?

QUESTIONS ON VOCABULARY AND STYLE

1. Why does Steinem write in the first person ("I")? How would the essay be different if she had avoided all first-person references? If she had not interwoven her experiences with the social commentary?
2. How would you describe Steinem's tone in the essay? What does that tone come from? How formal or informal is her language? Her sentence structure?
3. Be able to define the following words: *demise* (paragraph 3), *transient* (4), *espouse* (15), *chattel* (17), *denigrate* (20).

WRITING SUGGESTIONS

1. In a paragraph summarize Steinem's analysis. Do not quote her exactly. Focus instead on summarizing her reasons for this phenomenon.

2. The 1990s have been a relatively quiet time on college campuses, with few protests about anything. Why should this be? What accounts for the quiet atmosphere on campuses? In a cause and effect essay aimed at your college classmates, explore this situation. As a variation, you might write for an audience of parents of the average college freshman today.

Prewriting:

a. If you accept the premise that college students today are not active in social and political issues, you will need to isolate some possible reasons or causes for that apathy. Start by asking yourself what is particularly important to *you;* what are *you* concerned about? As you list the topics, try to record a reason for each concern. (For example, "I am concerned about getting a high-paying job because by the time I graduate, I will have borrowed $15,000 to finance my education.")

b. Extend your information-gathering by polling friends and classmates. Develop both a list of concerns and a list of possible explanations for those concerns. Ideally you should interview ten people, trying for a wide range of ages and backgrounds.

c. Look over the list that you have gathered. Some reasons for student concerns will be more common and more significant than others. Since you are trying to explain the generalized behavior of a large group of people, concentrate on reasons which seem primary and immediate. Place an asterisk next to those items on your lists that seem most important. Then plan an order for those items. You will need to cite at least three possible causes for the apathy of students.

Rewriting:

a. How have you defined your audience? On a separate sheet of paper, analyze the characteristics of that audience. Now look back at the draft of your essay. Have you written to that audience? List the specific ways in which your essay—

in its introduction, its style, its examples—acknowledges that audience.

b. Find at least one peer reader. Ask the reader if your essay seems like an adequate (or insightful) explanation. Does the essay analyze your generation? Is it fair? Does it distort?

c. Although Steinem's essay is long and sophisticated, it can serve as a good structural model. Study it again as a writer looking to see how another writer handled a similar subject. You are not imitating form; you are observing technique.

3. On the average, women today still do not earn as much money as men, although the "fifty-nine cents on the dollar" cited by Steinem has increased slightly. Research the problem. Why do women earn less? Present your evidence in a cause and effect analysis. Remember to document your sources carefully.

A Writer's Revision Process:
Black Men and Public Space

BRENT STAPLES

Born in Chester, Pennsylvania, Brent Staples graduated from Widener University in 1973 and earned a Ph.D. in psychology from the University of Chicago in 1982. He worked for the Chicago Sun-Times *as a reporter before coming to* The New York Times *in 1985. At the* Times, *he was an editor on the* Book Review, *then first assistant metropolitan editor, and recently he was appointed to the editorial board to write on politics and culture. He has contributed articles to the* Times, Essence, *and* Harper's *about such topics as race relations, Yale sweatshirts, accountants, and sports fans. "Black Men and Public Space" was originally published in the "Can Men Have It All?" section of the September 1986 issue of* Ms. *magazine as, "Just Walk on By: A Black Man Ponders His Power to Alter Public Space." In revised and edited form, it was reprinted in the December 1986 issue of* Harper's *under the new title "Black Men and Public Space."*

REVISED DRAFT

MY FIRST VICTIM was a woman—white, well dressed, probably   *1*
in her early twenties. I came upon her late one evening on a
deserted street in Hyde Park, a relatively affluent neighborhood
in an otherwise mean, impoverished section of Chicago. As I
swung onto the avenue behind her, there seemed to be a discreet, uninflammatory distance between us. Not so. She cast
back a worried glance. To her, the youngish black man—a
broad six feet two inches with a beard and billowing hair, both
hands shoved into the pockets of a bulky military jacket—
seemed menacingly close. After a few more quick glimpses, she
picked up her pace and was soon running in earnest. Within
seconds she disappeared into a cross street.

That was more than a decade ago. I was twenty-two years   *2*
old, a graduate student newly arrived at the University of Chi-

435

cago. It was in the echo of that terrified woman's footfalls that I first began to know the unwieldy inheritance I'd come into—the ability to alter public space in ugly ways. It was clear that she thought herself the quarry of a mugger, a rapist, or worse. Suffering a bout of insomnia, however, I was stalking sleep, not defenseless wayfarers. As a softy who is scarcely able to take a knife to a raw chicken—let alone hold one to a person's throat—I was surprised, embarrassed, and dismayed all at once. Her flight made me feel like an accomplice in tyranny. It also made it clear that I was indistinguishable from the muggers who occasionally seeped into the area from the surrounding ghetto. That first encounter, and those that followed, signified that a vast, unnerving gulf lay between nighttime pedestrians—particularly women—and me. And I soon gathered that being perceived as dangerous is a hazard in itself. I only needed to turn a corner into a dicey situation, or crowd some frightened, armed person in a foyer somewhere, or make an errant move after being pulled over by a policeman. Where fear and weapons meet—and they often do in urban America—there is always the possibility of death.

3   In that first year, my first away from my hometown, I was to become thoroughly familiar with the language of fear. At dark, shadowy intersections, I could cross in front of a car stopped at a traffic light and elicit the *thunk, thunk, thunk, thunk* of the driver—black, white, male, or female—hammering down the door locks. On less traveled streets after dark, I grew accustomed to but never comfortable with people crossing to the other side of the street rather than pass me. Then there were the standard unpleasantries with policemen, doormen, bouncers, cabdrivers, and others whose business it is to screen out troublesome individuals *before* there is any nastiness.

4   I moved to New York nearly two years ago and I have remained an avid night walker. In central Manhattan, the near-constant crowd cover minimizes tense one-on-one street encounters. Elsewhere—in SoHo, for example, where sidewalks are narrow and tightly spaced buildings shut out the sky—things can get very taut indeed.

5   After dark, on the warrenlike streets of Brooklyn where I live, I often see women who fear the worst from me. They seem

to have set their faces on neutral, and with their purse straps strung across their chests bandolier-style, they forge ahead as though bracing themselves against being tackled. I understand, of course, that the danger they perceive is not a hallucination. Women are particularly vulnerable to street violence, and young black males are drastically overrepresented among the perpetrators of that violence. Yet these truths are no solace against the kind of alienation that comes of being ever the suspect, a fearsome entity with whom pedestrians avoid making eye contact.

It is not altogether clear to me how I reached the ripe old   6
age of twenty-two without being conscious of the lethality nighttime pedestrians attributed to me. Perhaps it was because in Chester, Pennsylvania, the small, angry industrial town where I came of age in the 1960s, I was scarcely noticeable against a backdrop of gang warfare, street knifings, and murders. I grew up one of the good boys, had perhaps a half-dozen fistfights. In retrospect, my shyness of combat has clear sources.

As a boy, I saw countless tough guys locked away; I have   7
since buried several, too. They were babies, really—a teenage cousin, a brother of twenty-two, a childhood friend in his mid-twenties—all gone down in episodes of bravado played out in the streets. I came to doubt the virtues of intimidation early on. I chose, perhaps unconsciously, to remain a shadow—timid, but a survivor.

The fearsomeness mistakenly attributed to me in public   8
places often has a perilous flavor. The most frightening of these confusions occurred in the late 1970s and early 1980s, when I worked as a journalist in Chicago. One day, rushing into the office of a magazine I was writing for with a deadline story in hand, I was mistaken for a burglar. The office manager called security and, with an ad hoc posse, pursued me through the labyrinthine halls, nearly to my editor's door. I had no way of proving who I was. I could only move briskly toward the company of someone who knew me.

Another time I was on assignment for a local paper and   9
killing time before an interview. I entered a jewelry store on the city's affluent Near North Side. The proprietor excused herself and returned with an enormous red Doberman pinscher

straining at the end of a leash. She stood, the dog extended toward me, silent to my questions, her eyes bulging nearly out of her head. I took a cursory look around, nodded, and bade her good night.

10   Relatively speaking, however, I never fared as badly as another black male journalist. He went to nearby Waukegan, Illinois, a couple of summers ago to work on a story about a murderer who was born there. Mistaking the reporter for the killer, police officers hauled him from his car at gunpoint and but for his press credentials would probably have tried to book him. Such episodes are not uncommon. Black men trade tales like this all the time.

11   Over the years, I learned to smother the rage I felt at so often being taken for a criminal. Not to do so would surely have led to madness. I now take precautions to make myself less threatening. I move about with care, particularly late in the evening. I give a wide berth to nervous people on subway platforms during the wee hours, particularly when I have exchanged business clothes for jeans. If I happen to be entering a building behind some people who appear skittish, I may walk by, letting them clear the lobby before I return, so as not to seem to be following them. I have been calm and extremely congenial on those rare occasions when I've been pulled over by the police.

12   And on late-evening constitutionals I employ what has proved to be an excellent tension-reducing measure: I whistle melodies from Beethoven and Vivaldi and the more popular classical composers. Even steely New Yorkers hunching toward nighttime destinations seem to relax, and occasionally they even join in the tune. Virtually everybody seems to sense that a mugger wouldn't be warbling bright, sunny selections from Vivaldi's *Four Seasons*. It is my equivalent of the cowbell that hikers wear when they know they are in bear country.

QUESTIONS FOR DISCUSSION

1. What does Staples mean by the phrase "public space?" In what way is he capable of altering it?
2. What is the effect of Staples's opening sentences in the essay?

3. What type of evidence does Staples provide to illustrate his point—that black men alter public space?

4. What purpose might Staples have had in writing the essay?

5. Staples's essay originally appeared in *Ms.* magazine. What assumptions could Staples have made about his audience?

6. Be prepared to define the following words: *discreet* (paragraph 1), *dicey* (2), *errant* (2), *taut* (4), *warrenlike* (5), *bandolier* (5), *solace* (5), *entity* (5), *bravado* (7), *ad hoc* (8), *cursory* (9), *skittish* (11), *congenial* (11), *constitutionals* (12).

EARLIER DRAFT

Paragraph A (originally appeared between paragraphs 4 and 5 of the *Harper's* version)

Black men have a firm place in New York mugging literature. Norman Podhoretz in his famed (or infamous) 1963 essay, "My Negro Problem—And Ours," recalls growing up in the terror of black males; they "were tougher than we were, more ruthless," he writes—and as an adult on the Upper West Side of Manhattan, he continues, he cannot constrain his nervousness when he meets black men on certain streets. Similarly, a decade later, the essayist and novelist Edward Hoagland extols a New York where once "Negro bitterness bore down mainly on other Negroes." Where some see mere panhandlers, Hoagland sees "a mugger who is clearly screwing up his nerve to do more than just *ask* for money." But Hoagland has "the New Yorker's quick-hunch posture for broken-field maneuvering" and the bad guy swerves away.

Paragraph B (originally appeared between paragraphs 6 and 7 of the *Harper's* version)

Many things go into the making of a young thug. One of those things is the consummation of the male romance with the power to intimidate. An infant discovers that random flailings send the baby bottle flying out of the crib and crashing to the floor. Delighted, the joyful babe repeats those motions again and again, seeking to duplicate the feat. Just so, I recall the point at which some of my boyhood friends were finally seduced by the perception of themselves as tough guys. When a mark cowered and surrendered his money without resistance, myth and reality merged—and paid off. It is, after all, only manly to embrace the power to frighten and intimidate. We, as men, are not supposed to give an inch of our lane on the highway; we are to seize the fighter's edge in work and in play and even in love; we are to be valiant in the face of hostile forces.

Unfortunately, poor and powerless young men seem to take all of this nonsense literally. . . .

QUESTIONS ON THE REVISED DRAFT

1. When the earlier draft was first published in *Ms.*, it was titled "Just Walk on By." When it appeared in *Harper's* (revised draft), it was retitled "Black Men and Public Space." Why might the title have been changed?

2. The whole of paragraph A (reproduced above) in the earlier draft was deleted when the essay appeared in *Harper's*. Why? What does Staples do in that paragraph that he does not do elsewhere?

3. The whole of paragraph B (reproduced above) in the earlier draft was also deleted when the essay appeared in *Harper's*. Why?

WRITING SUGGESTIONS

1. Select a time when you were scared while in a public space. Narrate your experience in a paragraph, trying at the same time to explain why you reacted as you did. Was your fear justified? In what way? You can also turn the topic around by describing a time when you scared someone else while in a public space. Narrate your experience in a paragraph, focusing as well on your reaction to that experience.

2. Regardless of our age or sex or color, we all provoke reactions from people who do not know us. Sometimes, in fact, we go out of our way to elicit that reaction—dressing in a certain way, driving a particular type of car, engaging in an unusual

activity, wearing our hair in a peculiar style. Describe the behavior by which you have elicited reactions and analyze how and why people react as they do.

Prewriting:

a. Think about the image that you either consciously or unconsciously project. Try to define that image in a couple of sentences. How do you create that image?

b. Make a list of people's reactions to you. What have you noticed about their responses? What is typical? Make a list of those reactions and then jot down next to each item a possible explanation for that reaction.

c. Ask some friends, or even some casual acquaintances, how they respond to you and why. Be sure to explain to them why you want to know—that might encourage them to respond in a helpful manner. Be prepared to be surprised.

Rewriting:

a. Try to find an effective incident with which to begin. Do not try to imitate Staples's introduction, especially his suspenseful example.

b. Be sure that you have offered explanations for why people react to you as they do.

c. Remember that your analysis of reactions needs to be organized in a logical manner. Why have you chosen the order you have? Is there any other way in which those reactions could be organized?

3. Who mugs whom? Research the problem of assault or mugging either in the country as a whole or in your own community. What are your chances of being mugged? Who is likely to do it to you? Where is it most likely to happen? If you decide to focus on your own community or college campus, remember to interview the local police.

EIGHT

Definition

On the mid-term examination in your introductory economics class only the essay question remains to be answered: "What is capitalism?" You are tempted to write the one-sentence definition you memorized from the glossary of your textbook and dash from the room. On the other hand, it is unlikely that your professor will react positively or even charitably to such a skimpy (and memorized) response. Instead, you realize that what is needed is an extended definition—one that explains what factors were necessary before capitalism could emerge, what elements are most characteristic of a capitalistic economy, how capitalism differs from other economic systems, how a capitalistic economy works, how capitalism is linked to technology and politics. What you need is a narrative, a division, a comparison and contrast, a process, and a cause and effect analysis all working together to give you a full definition of what is finally a very complex term.

When you are asked to define a word, you generally do two things: first, you provide a dictionary-like definition, normally a single sentence; and second, if the occasion demands, you provide a longer, extended definition, analyzing the subject, giving examples or details. If you use technical or specialized words that may be unfamiliar to your reader, you include a parenthetical definition: "Macro-economics, the portion of economics concerned with large-scale movements such as inflation and deflation, is particularly interested in changes in the GNP, or gross national product."

442

Most writing situations, especially those you encounter in college, require extended definitions. The selections in this chapter define a variety of subjects, and they suggest how differently definitions can be handled. Theodore M. Bernstein defines and illustrates what a *cliché* is; Gordon Allport tackles the complex term *prejudice*; Marie Winn explains what it means to be a "TV addict"; Judy Syfers tries to define the term *wife* and the associations that many people have with that word; Susan Brownmiller explores the meaning of the word *femininity* in our society; Gloria Naylor explains how the meaning of a word depends upon who uses it when she confronts the label *nigger*; and Susan Orlean defines, through illustration, the significance that we attach to the phrase *Saturday night*.

Definitions can be denotative or connotative or a mixture of the two. Dictionary definitions are denotative; that is, they offer a literal and explicit definition of a word. Theodore M. Bernstein provides a denotative definition of a cliché: "an overworked, commonplace expression." But words do not always just have literal meanings; they often carry either positive or negative connotations, and these connotations can vary depending on the situation. The term *democracy*, especially when used during wartime, suggests not just a form of government, but a whole way of life. *Saturday night* refers to a specific time of the week, but the phrase also suggests something more: it is, as Susan Orlean writes, the one night of the week "worth living for." To illustrate that significance, Orlean records the results of her several-year-long search for how Americans spend their Saturday nights.

How Much Do You Include in a Definition?

Every word, whether it refers to a specific physical object or to the most theoretical concept, has a dictionary definition. Whether that one-sentence definition is sufficient depends upon why you are defining the word. Complex words, words with many nuances and connotations, generally require more of a definition than a single sentence can possibly provide. Moreover, one-sentence definitions often contain other words and phrases that need to be defined as well. Gordon Allport in "The Nature of Prejudice" starts with a dictionary definition of the word *prejudice*: "thinking ill of others without sufficient warrant." What, though, is "sufficient warrant"? Allport must then define the phrase "sufficient warrant" by offering a series of examples. Allport shows that a complex word such as *prejudice* needs an extended definition.

Similarly, if you were asked, "What is a wife?" you could reply, "A woman married to a man." While that definition is accurate, it does not convey any sense of what such a relationship might involve. Judy Syfers's "I Want a Wife" defines the word by showing what men (or some men) expect in a wife. Her essay divides and lists a wife's many responsibilities— things expected of her by an actual or potential husband. Syfers's essay, comically overstated as it is, offers a far more meaningful definition of the term *wife* than any one-sentence dictionary entry. Her intention surely was to reveal inequality in marriage, and she makes her point by listing a stereotypical set of male expectations.

Writing a definition is a fairly common activity in college work. In your literature course you are asked to define the romantic movement; in art history, the baroque period; in psychology, abnormal behavior. Since a single-sentence definition can never do justice to such complicated terms, an extended definition is necessary. In each case, the breadth and depth of your knowledge is being tested; your professor expects you to formulate a definition that accounts for the major subdivisions and characteristics of the subject. Your purpose is to convince your professor that you have read and mastered the assigned materials and can select and organize them, often adding some special insight of your own, into a logical and coherent response.

How Do You Structure a Definition?

Sentence definitions are relatively easy to write. You first place the word in a general class ("A wife is a woman") and then add any distinguishing features that set it apart from other members of the class ("married to a man"). The types of definitions you are asked to write are generally more detailed than dictionary entries. How then do you get from a single sentence to a paragraph or an essay?

Extended definitions do not have a structure peculiar to themselves. That is, when you write a definition you do not have a predetermined structural pattern as you do with comparison and contrast, division and classification, process, or cause and effect. Instead, definitions are constructed by using all of the various strategies discussed in this book. Theodore M. Bernstein uses examples to define the term *cliché*. As the selections progress from this fairly short and simple definition to the more complex ones, the types of strategies that the writers employ, in addition to example, increase. Marie Winn uses analogy to liken addiction to television viewing to addiction to alcohol or drugs and through a pattern of cause and effect shows why television experiences do not provide "true nourishment" for a viewer. Judy Syfers's definition of a wife uses division to organize the many types of responsibilities demanded of a wife. Susan Brownmiller begins with a narrative of her own experiences with femininity as she moved from childhood into adulthood and then employs a cause and effect analysis to show how cultural biases help define and condition "feminine" behavior.

Once you have chosen a subject for definition, think first about its essential characteristics, steps, or parts. What examples would best define it? Then plan your organization by seeing how those details can be presented most effectively to your reader. If your definition involves breaking a subject into its parts, use division or possibly even process. If you are defining by comparing your subject to another, use a comparison and contrast structure. If your subject is defined as the result of some causal connection, use a cause and effect structure. Definitions can also involve narration, description, and even persuasion. The longer the extended definition, the greater is the likelihood that your paper will involve a series of structures.

Sample Student Essay

DEFINITION

Like many people, Lyndsey Curtis is a cat lover, and that determined her choice of subject. Lyndsey, probably influenced by having read Judy Syfers's essay, decided to define the *essence* of a cat:

EARLIER DRAFT

Felis Catus

Webster's New Collegiate Dictionary defines *cat* as ''a carnivorous mammal (*Felis catus*) long domesticated and kept by man as a pet or for catching rats and mice.'' That is fine if you are interested in a scientific definition. In my opinion, however, it doesn't even begin to tap into the essence of that phenomenon known as ''cat.''

Cats perform many practical services. On cold winter nights, they keep your feet as warm as an electric blanket but without using electricity. They act as alarm clocks in the morning; it's time for you to get up when they want to be fed. Wouldn't you rather wake up to the gentle but insistent tap of a soft furry paw on your forehead than to a loud, obnoxious buzzing noise anyway? Cats are very entertaining. They are excellent subjects for photographs, as you can easily determine by setting foot inside any true cat lover's home; the walls are inevitably adorned with pictures of his or her favorite feline. They provide ''musical enjoyment'' for you and your neighbors when they ''sing'' to each other on warm summer nights. They can supply topics for hours of conversation between mutual cat lovers, who always enjoy recounting their favorite cat story. More important, however, is the emotional completeness a cat brings to your life.

When you've lived with cats your whole life as I have, you begin to realize that they are really just like people and that they become members of your family

very quickly. Cats are very reliable; you can always
depend on them to know when it is time to go out, when
it is time to play, when it is time to eat, and when it
is time to sleep (most of the day). They teach children
about responsibility, love, and the importance of
caring for another living being. In addition, they
provide companionship for many lonely people. They
sense when you are feeling upset or depressed and will
always try to make you feel better by climbing up onto
your lap with a great purr. A cat's love is
unconditional as long as you care for him or her
properly. They'll love you despite all your faults;
they'll love you when it seems that no one else in the
world will. They'll greet you at the door when you come
home after a rough day at the office and will listen to
your problems and complaints without interrupting. Cats
are always there when you need a friend. B. Kliban, in
his 1975 book *Cat*, put it very aptly when he defined a
cat as ''one Hell of a nice animal, frequently mistaken
for a meatloaf.''

On the peer editing checksheet for definition essays, one of
the questions concerned opening sentences: "Does the essay
avoid the standard 'according to Webster. . . '?" When Lyndsey's essay was read in class during a peer editing session, several students asked about the wisdom of beginning in this way.
The class agreed, however, that even though it is generally not
a good idea to begin a definition with a quotation from a dictionary, the device works fairly well here since Lyndsey is trying
to show how inadequate that denotative definition is. The
strong point of the essay, everyone felt, was its division into
"practical services" and "emotional completeness." The transition between the two halves comes smoothly and naturally.
The other area that troubled the peer readers was Lyndsey's
ending. As one student observed, "Your final quotation from
Kliban's book seems inappropriate. You have been making
some light-hearted but still serious points, and to end suddenly
on such a cynical quotation introduces an abrupt change in
tone." When Lyndsey came to revise her essay, she tried to
address the problems that the peer editors had raised.

REVISED DRAFT

The Essence of Cat

The dictionary defines *cat* as ''a carnivorous mammal (*Felis catus*) long domesticated and kept by man as a pet or for catching rats and mice.'' That is fine if you are interested in a scientific definition. In my opinion, however, it does not even begin to tap into the essence of that phenomenon known as ''cat.''

Cats perform many practical services. On cold winter nights, they keep your feet as warm as an electric blanket would, but they do it without using electricity. They act as alarm clocks in the morning; it is time to get up when they want to be fed. Wouldn't you rather wake up to the gentle but insistent tap of a soft paw on your forehead than to a loud, obnoxious buzzing noise? Cats are very entertaining. They are excellent subjects for photographs, as you can easily see from the pictures of felines that cover the walls of any true cat lover's home. They provide ''musical enjoyment'' for you and your neighbors, ''singing'' to each other on warm summer nights. They can supply topics for hours of conversation between cat lovers, who always enjoy recounting their favorite cat stories. More important, however, is the emotional completeness a cat brings to your life.

When you have lived with cats your whole life as I have, you begin to realize that they are really just like people and that they become members of your family very quickly. Cats are very reliable; you can always depend on them to know when it is time to eat, and when it is time to sleep (most of the day). They teach children about responsibility, love, and the importance of caring for another living being. In addition, they provide companionship for many lonely people. They sense when you are feeling upset or depressed and will always try to make you feel better by climbing onto your lap with a great purr. A cat's love is unconditional as long as you care for him or her properly. Cats will love you despite all your faults; they will love you when it seems that no one else in the world will. They will greet you at the door when

```
you come home after a rough day at the office and will
listen to your problems and complaints without
interrupting. Cats are always there when you need a
friend.
```

Some Things to Remember

1. Choose a subject that can be reasonably and fully defined within the limits of your paper. That is, make sure it is neither too limited nor too large.

2. Determine a purpose for your definition.

3. Spend time analyzing your subject to see what its essential characteristics, steps, or parts are.

4. Write a dictionary definition for your subject. Do this even if you are writing an extended definition. The features that set your subject apart from others in its general class reveal what must be included in your definition.

5. Choose examples that are clear and appropriate.

6. Decide which of the organizational patterns will best convey the information you have gathered.

7. Be careful about beginning, "According to Webster. . . ." There are usually more effective and interesting ways to announce your subject.

Clichés

THEODORE M. BERNSTEIN

Theodore M. Bernstein (1904–1979) was born in New York City and educated at Columbia University, receiving a B.A. in 1924 and a B.Litt. in 1925. Immediately after graduation, he joined The New York Times *as a copy editor. Within the Times organization, he held a variety of positions, including assistant managing editor and editor, from 1951 to 1978, of "Winners and Sinners," an in-house bulletin that critiqued the writing and usage of the* Times *staff. His position,* Newsweek *magazine observed, was that of "linguistic policeman." Bernstein was an authority on English usage and served as a consultant to the* Random House Dictionary *and the* American Heritage Dictionary. *Beginning in 1972 he wrote a syndicated column, "Bernstein on Words." His many books include* Headlines and Deadlines: A Manual for Copy Editors *(3rd ed., 1961),* Watch Your Language *(1958),* More Language That Needs Watching *(1962),* The Careful Writer: A Modern Guide to English Usage *(1965), and* Miss Thistlebottom's Hobgoblins: The Careful Writer's Guide to Taboos, Bugbears, and Outmoded Rules of English Usage *(1971). In this selection from* The Careful Writer, *Bernstein displays his usual wit and ingenuity in defining cliché.*

1   WHEN ARCHIMEDES' BATH ran over and he discovered something about specific gravity, he was perhaps justified in sprinting into the street without his clothes and exulting. But that does not mean that every kid who sees his Saturday night bath overflow is justified in dashing outdoors naked shouting, "Eureka!" The distinction here is somewhat akin to that between the coiner of a bright phrase and the mere echoer of that phrase. It is the echoing that turns the phrase into a cliché—that is, an overworked, commonplace expression—and the echoer should realize that he has no claim to originality.

2   This is not to say that all clichés should be avoided like, shall we say, the plague. It is no more possible—or desirable— to do that than it is to abolish gravity. Many of today's clichés

are likely to be tomorrow's standard English, just as many of today's standard words were yesterday's metaphors: *thunderstruck, astonish, cuckold, conclave, sanguine,* and thousands of others that form a substantial part of any dictionary. Moreover, the cliché is sometimes the most direct way of expressing a thought. Think of the circumlocution that is avoided by saying that someone has a *dog-in-the-manger attitude.* To attempt to write around a cliché will often lead to pompous obscurity. And for a writer to decide to banish all clichés indiscriminately would be to hamstring—yes, *hamstring*—his efforts.

There are many varieties of clichés. Some are foreign 3
phrases (*coup de grâce; et tu, Brute*). Some are homely sayings or are based on proverbs ("You can't make an omelet without breaking eggs," *blissful ignorance*). Some are quotations ("To be or not to be"; "Unwept, unhonored, and unsung"). Some are allusions to myth or history (*Gordian knot, Achilles' heel*). Some are alliterative or rhyming phrases (*first and foremost, high and dry*). Some are paradoxes (*in less than no time, conspicuous by its absence*). Some are legalisms (*null and void, each and every*). Some are playful euphemisms (*A fate worse than death, better half*). Some are figurative phrases (*leave no stone unturned, hit the nail on the head*). And some are almost meaningless small change (*in the last analysis, by the same token*).

QUESTIONS ON SUBJECT AND PURPOSE

1. What is a cliché? Why are clichés so common?
2. If clichés are "overworked" and "commonplace" (paragraph 1), why not "banish" them (paragraph 2)? How would a writer know when to avoid clichés and when to use them?
3. For class discussion, list at least six additional clichés that are a part of your everyday speech. Can they be classified using the categories Bernstein mentions in the third paragraph?

QUESTIONS ON STRATEGY AND AUDIENCE

1. Why does Bernstein begin with the reference to Archimedes? Why not just begin with the definition?
2. What structural devices does Bernstein use to order his paragraphs? How are they a part of his attempt at definition?

451

3. What expectations does Bernstein have of his audience? Find specific evidence to support your conclusion.

QUESTIONS ON VOCABULARY AND STYLE

1. In the second paragraph, Bernstein cites some examples of "yesterday's metaphors" that are "today's standard words." Check each word in a dictionary. How were these words metaphoric?
2. Why does Bernstein use clichés in his second paragraph? How many does he use?
3. Be able to define the following words: *specific gravity* (paragraph 1), *Eureka (1), akin (1), circumlocution (2), pompous (2), hamstring (2), euphemisms (3).*

WRITING SUGGESTIONS

1. Select one of the following words (or a similar word) and define it in a paragraph. Consult a dictionary before beginning. Remember to use examples to make your definition clear and interesting.

   a. euphemism

   b. spoonerism

   c. malapropism

   d. cant

   e. jargon

2. Select a concept central to another academic subject you are studying this semester. Using your textbook and whatever other sources might be available, define that word or idea for a general audience. Remember to make your definition interesting through the use of appropriate examples.

   Prewriting:

   a. Remember that you will need to choose a subject that is complex enough to require an extended definition. On the other hand, you will probably want to avoid a technical subject that is of little interest to a general reader. With these two cautions in mind, use the textbooks from your other courses as guides, and make a list of possible subjects.

   b. List several possibilities down the left-hand side of a sheet of paper. In the space to the right, analyze each subject from the point of view of your potential audience. What might a general audience know about this subject? Is that audience likely to be interested in or to have opinions about the subject? Answer these questions for each topic.

c. Visit the current periodicals section of your library and spend some time looking at magazines such as *Time* and *Newsweek*. If either magazine contained an article on the same subject as yours, how would it be handled? How do they write for a general audience? Study appropriate articles in either magazine. Pay attention to the strategy and style of the articles.

Rewriting:

a. Make a copy of your essay, and ask a peer reader to respond to it. Tell that reader to mark any section or any word in the essay that seems too technical or inadequately explained. Try to get a reader who is relatively unfamiliar with the subject.

b. Return to some sample issues of magazines such as *Time* or *Newsweek*. Study the introductions to articles with related topics. Have you used a similar strategy to begin your essay? If you have not, pretend that your essay will appear in a magazine, and try to write an introduction that your editor would like.

c. Also study the conclusions of some magazine articles. Do you conclude in a similar way? If you have not, try free-writing a new ending for your essay.

3. The reference room of your college's library will have a number of guides to English usage. Consult at least six different reference books on the subject *cliché*. Write a definition of the term with appropriate examples. You should also comment on whether clichés are ever appropriate in writing. Your essay will be used as a handout in the freshman English program at your college or university, so remember your audience.

The Nature of Prejudice

GORDON ALLPORT

Born in Montezuma, Indiana, Gordon Allport (1897–1967) earned his B.A., M.A., and Ph.D. degrees at Harvard University and did postgraduate work at the Universities of Berlin and Hamburg, Germany, and Cambridge University. He held a number of honorary doctorate degrees from various universities as well. In 1939 he was elected president of the American Psychological Association. As a professor of psychology at Dartmouth College and then at Harvard, he was a pioneer in the psychology of personality. His major book is Pattern and Growth in Personality *(1961), but he wrote widely on a variety of other subjects, including* The Psychology of Radio *(1935),* The Psychology of Rumor *(1947), and* The Individual and His Religion *(1950). The following selection is excerpted from* The Nature of Prejudice *(1954). In attempting to define "prejudice," Allport distinguishes between overcategorization, misconception, prejudgment, and prejudice. "The net effect of prejudice," Allport concludes, "is to place the object of prejudice at some disadvantage not merited by his own misconduct."*

Definition

1 THE WORD *prejudice*, derived from the Latin noun *praejudicium*, has, like most words, undergone a change of meaning since classical times. There are three stages in the transformation.

(1) To the ancients, *praejudicium* meant a *precedent*—a judgment based on previous decisions and experiences.

(2) Later, the term, in English, acquired the meaning of a judgment formed before due examination and consideration of the facts—a premature or hasty judgment.

(3) Finally the term acquired also its present emotional flavor of favorableness or unfavorableness that accompanies such a prior and unsupported judgment.

2 Perhaps the briefest of all definitions of prejudice is: *thinking ill of others without sufficient warrant.* This crisp phrasing contains the two essential ingredients of all definitions—reference to un-

founded judgment and to a feeling-tone. It is, however, too brief for complete clarity.

In the first place, it refers only to *negative* prejudice. People may be prejudiced in favor of others; they may think *well* of them without sufficient warrant. The wording offered by the New English Dictionary recognizes positive as well as negative prejudice:

> A feeling, favorable or unfavorable, toward a person or thing, prior to, or not based on, actual experience.

While it is important to bear in mind that biases may be *pro* as well as *con*, it is none the less true that *ethnic* prejudice is mostly negative. A group of students was asked to describe their attitudes toward ethnic groups. No suggestion was made that might lead them toward negative reports. Even so, they reported eight times as many antagonistic attitudes as favorable attitudes. In this volume, accordingly, we shall be concerned chiefly with prejudice *against*, not with prejudice *in favor of*, ethnic groups.

The phrase "thinking ill of others" is obviously an elliptical expression that must be understood to include feelings of scorn or dislike, of fear and aversion, as well as various forms of antipathetic conduct: such as talking against people, discriminating against them, or attacking them with violence.

Similarly, we need to expand the phrase "without sufficient warrant." A judgment is unwarranted whenever it lacks basis in fact. A wit defined prejudice as "being down on something you're not up on."

It is not easy to say how much fact is required in order to justify a judgment. A prejudiced person will almost certainly claim that he has sufficient warrant for his views. He will tell of bitter experiences he has had with refugees, Catholics, or Orientals. But, in most cases, it is evident that his facts are scanty and strained. He resorts to a selective sorting of his own few memories, mixes them up with hearsay, and overgeneralizes. No one can possibly know *all* refugees, Catholics, or Orientals. Hence any negative judgment of these groups *as a whole* is, strictly speaking, an instance of thinking ill without sufficient warrant.

Sometimes, the ill-thinker has no first-hand experience on

455

which to base his judgment. A few years ago most Americans thought exceedingly ill of Turks—but very few had ever seen a Turk nor did they know any person who had seen one. Their warrant lay exclusively in what they had heard of the Armenian massacres and of the legendary crusades. On such evidence they presumed to condemn all members of a nation.

8   Ordinarily, prejudice manifests itself in dealing with individual members of rejected groups. But in avoiding a Negro neighbor, or in answering "Mr. Greenberg's" application for a room, we frame our action to accord with our categorical generalization of the group as a whole. We pay little or no attention to individual differences, and overlook the important fact that Negro X, our neighbor, is not Negro Y, whom we dislike for good and sufficient reason; that Mr. Greenberg, who may be a fine gentleman, is not Mr. Bloom, whom we have good reason to dislike.

9   So common is this process that we might define prejudice as:

> an avertive or hostile attitude toward a person who belongs to a group, simply because he belongs to that group, and is therefore presumed to have the objectionable qualities ascribed to the group.

This definition stresses the fact that while ethnic prejudice in daily life is ordinarily a matter of dealing with individual people it also entails an unwarranted idea concerning a group as a whole.

10   Returning to the question of "sufficient warrant," we must grant that few if any human judgments are based on absolute certainty. We can be reasonably, but not absolutely, sure that the sun will rise tomorrow, and that death and taxes will finally overtake us. The sufficient warrant for any judgment is always a matter of probabilities. Ordinarily our judgments of natural happenings are based on firmer and higher probabilities than our judgments of people. Only rarely do our categorical judgments of nations or ethnic groups have a foundation in high probability.

11   Take the hostile view of Nazi leaders held by most Americans during World War II. Was it prejudiced? The answer is

No, because there was abundant available evidence regarding the evil policies and practices accepted as the official code of the party. True, there may have been good individuals in the party who at heart rejected the abominable program; but the probability was so high that the Nazi group constituted an actual menace to world peace and to humane values that a realistic and justified conflict resulted. The high probability of danger removes an antagonism from the domain of prejudice into that of realistic social conflict.

In the case of gangsters, our antagonism is not a matter of prejudice, for the evidence of their antisocial conduct is conclusive. But soon the line becomes hard to draw. How about an ex-convict? It is notoriously difficult for an ex-convict to obtain a steady job where he can be self-supporting and self-respecting. Employers naturally are suspicious if they know the man's past record. But often they are more suspicious than the facts warrant. If they looked further they might find evidence that the man who stands before them is genuinely reformed, or even that he was unjustly accused in the first place. To shut the door merely because a man has a criminal record has *some* probability in its favor, for many prisoners are never reformed; but there is also an element of unwarranted prejudgment involved. We have here a true borderline instance.

We can never hope to draw a hard and fast line between "sufficient" and "insufficient" warrant. For this reason we cannot always be sure whether we are dealing with a case of prejudice or nonprejudice. Yet no one will deny that often we form judgments on the basis of scant, even nonexistent, probabilities.

Overcategorization is perhaps the commonest trick of the human mind. Given a thimbleful of facts we rush to make generalizations as large as a tub. One young boy developed the idea that all Norwegians were giants because he was impressed by the gigantic stature of Ymir in the saga, and for years was fearful lest he meet a living Norwegian. A certain man happened to know three Englishmen personally and proceeded to declare that the whole English race had the common attributes that he observed in these three.

There is a natural basis for this tendency. Life is so short, and the demands upon us for practical adjustments so great,

12

13

14

15

457

that we cannot let our ignorance detain us in our daily trans-actions. We have to decide whether objects are good or bad by classes. We cannot weigh each object in the world by itself. Rough and ready rubrics, however coarse and broad, have to suffice.

16   Not every overblown generalization is a prejudice. Some are simply *misconceptions*, wherein we organize wrong infor-mation. One child had the idea that all people living in Min-neapolis were "monopolists." And from his father he had learned that monopolists were evil folk. When in later years he discovered the confusion, his dislike of dwellers in Minneapolis vanished.

17   Here we have the test to help us distinguish between or-dinary errors of prejudgment and prejudice. If a person is ca-pable of rectifying his erroneous judgments in the light of new evidence he is not prejudiced. *Prejudgments become prejudices only if they are not reversible when exposed to new knowledge.* A prej-udice, unlike a simple misconception, is actively resistant to all evidence that would unseat it. We tend to grow emotional when a prejudice is threatened with contradiction. Thus the difference between ordinary prejudgments and prejudice is that one can discuss and rectify a prejudgment without emotional resistance.

18   Taking these various considerations into account, we may now attempt a final definition of negative ethnic prejudice— one that will serve us throughout this book. Each phrase in the definition represents a considerable condensation of the points we have been discussing:

> Ethnic prejudice is an antipathy based upon a faulty and in-flexible generalization. It may be felt or expressed. It may be directed toward a group as a whole, or toward an individual because he is a member of that group.

The net effect of prejudice, thus defined, is to place the object of prejudice at some disadvantage not merited by his own mis-conduct.

QUESTIONS ON SUBJECT AND PURPOSE

1. In understanding prejudice, what roles do the following play?
   a. Overcategorization

458

b. Prejudgments

2. According to Allport, can prejudice ever be justified? Can it become "realistic social conflict"?

3. Will defining the term "prejudice" have any impact on people's behavior?

QUESTIONS ON STRATEGY AND AUDIENCE

1. What does the history of the word "prejudice" show?

2. With what type of prejudice is Allport concerned? Why?

3. For whom does Allport seem to be writing? How does audience seem to connect with purpose in this selection?

QUESTIONS ON VOCABULARY AND STYLE

1. Where might you expect to find such a selection? Could it appear in a popular magazine? In a reference work?

2. Allport uses certain visual devices in his text such as numbering (paragraph 1), italicized words and sentences, and indented sentences. What effect do such devices have on you as a reader?

3. Be prepared to define the following words: *warrant* (paragraph 2), *elliptical* (4), *aversion* (4), *antipathetic* (4), *avertive* (9), *rubrics* (15), *rectifying* (17), *antipathy* (18).

WRITING SUGGESTIONS

1. In a substantial paragraph, define the term "enemy." When are you justified in your prejudice? You might want to read Keen's "Faces of the Enemy" (Chapter 4) before beginning your paper.

2. In an essay write an extended definition of *discrimination* (or a similar term approved by your instructor).

Prewriting:

a. Make a list of several situations in which the word might be used. Think of these situations as possible examples to be used in your essay.

b. Make a list of present-day associations or connotations that the word has.

459

c. Before you begin your draft, write an extended definition of the term such as the one that Allport writes in paragraph 18.

Rewriting:

a. Check your introduction. Have you avoided beginning with a sentence such as "According to the *New English Dictionary*. . ."? Copy your introduction onto a separate sheet of paper. Ask a roommate or classmate to read it. Does your audience want to continue reading?

b. Check each individual paragraph. Is there a unified idea that controls each one? Make a copy of your essay and highlight the topic sentence or key idea of each paragraph with a colored pen.

c. Evaluate your conclusion. Do you conclude or just stop? Did you just repeat in slightly altered words what you wrote in the introduction? Check the advice offered in the Glossary. If your conclusion seems weak, try freewriting several alternative endings.

3. Visit your college's library and research the history of a complex word through the *Oxford English Dictionary* or any other similar dictionary based on historical principles. Pick a word whose dictionary definition is not adequate to cover the complexities conveyed by the word. Then, in an essay based on your research, review the word's history, show how and why it needs an extended definition, and then through examples and qualifications build a more satisfactory definition.

Television Viewing as an Addiction

MARIE WINN

Another example of Marie Winn's work ("The End of Play") can be found in Chapter 7, and biographical information is given there. In this selection from The Plug-In Drug: Television, Children, and the Family *(1977; revised edition, 1985), Winn defines television viewing as potentially addictive since it can have adverse effects on the viewer's personality and lifestyle.*

THE WORD "addiction" is often used loosely and wryly in con- 1
versation. People will refer to themselves as "mystery book addicts" or "cookie addicts." E. B. White writes of his annual
surge of interest in gardening: "We are hooked and are making
an attempt to kick the habit." Yet nobody really believes that
reading mysteries or ordering seeds by catalogue is serious
enough to be compared with addictions to heroin or alcohol.
The word "addiction" is here used jokingly to denote a tendency to overindulge in some pleasurable activity.

People often refer to being "hooked on TV." Does this, too, 2
fall into the lighthearted category of cookie eating and other
pleasures that people pursue with unusual intensity, or is there
a kind of television viewing that falls into the more serious
category of destructive addiction?

When we think about addiction to drugs or alcohol, we 3
frequently focus on negative aspects, ignoring the pleasures that
accompany drinking or drug-taking. And yet the essence of any
serious addiction is a pursuit of pleasure, a search for a "high"
that normal life does not supply. It is only the inability to function without the addictive substance that is dismaying, the dependence of the organism upon a certain experience and an
increasing inability to function normally without it. Thus a person will take two or three drinks at the end of the day not
merely for the pleasure drinking provides, but also because he
"doesn't feel normal" without them.

An addict does not merely pursue a pleasurable experience 4 and need to experience it in order to function normally. He needs to *repeat* it again and again. Something about the particular experience makes life without it less than complete. Other potentially pleasurable experiences are no longer possible, for under the spell of the addictive experience, his life is peculiarly distorted. The addict craves an experience and yet he is never really satisfied. The organism may be temporarily sated, but soon it begins to crave again.

5 Finally a serious addiction is distinguished from a harmless pursuit of pleasure by its distinctly destructive elements. A heroin addict, for instance, leads a damaged life: his increasing need for heroin in increasing doses prevents him from working, from maintaining relationships, from developing in human ways. Similarly an alcoholic's life is narrowed and dehumanized by his dependence on alcohol.

6 Let us consider television viewing in the light of the conditions that define serious addictions.

7 Not unlike drugs or alcohol, the television experience allows the participant to blot out the real world and enter into a pleasurable and passive mental state. The worries and anxieties of reality are as effectively deferred by becoming absorbed in a television program as by going on a "trip" induced by drugs or alcohol. And just as alcoholics are only inchoately aware of their addiction, feeling that they control their drinking more than they ready do ("I can cut it out any time I want—I just like to have three or four drinks before dinner"), people similarly overestimate their control over television watching. Even as they put off other activities to spend hour after hour watching television, they feel they could easily resume living in a different, less passive style. But somehow or other while the television set is present in their homes, the click doesn't sound. With television pleasures available, those other experiences seem less attractive, more difficult somehow.

8 A heavy viewer (a college English instructor) observes: "I find television almost irresistible. When the set is on, I cannot ignore it. I can't turn it off. I feel sapped, will-less, enervated. As I reach out to turn off the set, the strength goes out of my arms. So I sit there for hours and hours."

9 The self-confessed television addict often feels he "ought"

to do other things—but the fact that he doesn't read and doesn't plant his garden or sew or crochet or play games or have conversations means that those activities are no longer as desirable as television viewing. In a way a heavy viewer's life is as imbalanced by his television "habit" as a drug addict's or an alcoholic's. He is living in a holding pattern, as it were, passing up the activities that lead to growth or development or a sense of accomplishment. This is one reason people talk about their television viewing so ruefully, so apologetically. They are aware that it is an unproductive experience, that almost any other endeavor is more worthwhile by any human measure.

Finally it is the adverse effect of television viewing on the   10
lives of so many people that defines it as a serious addiction. The television habit distorts the sense of time. It renders other experiences vague and curiously unreal while taking on a greater reality for itself. It weakens relationships by reducing and sometimes eliminating normal opportunities for talking, for communicating.

And yet television does not satisfy, else why would the   11
viewer continue to watch hour after hour, day after day? "The measure of health," writes Lawrence Kubie, "is flexibility. . . and especially the freedom to cease when sated." But the television viewer can never be sated with his television experiences—they do not provide the true nourishment that satiation requires—and thus he finds that he cannot stop watching.

QUESTIONS ON SUBJECT AND PURPOSE

1. How does Winn define the term *addiction*?
2. How effective is Winn's comparison of a television addict to an alcoholic or a drug abuser?
3. Why, according to Winn, are people apologetic when they talk about their television viewing?

QUESTIONS ON STRATEGY AND AUDIENCE

1. Why might Winn write five paragraphs about addictions in general before introducing her thesis about television addiction?

2. How does the example of the college instructor in paragraph 8 contribute to Winn's argument?

3. What expectations does Winn seem to have of her audience? Point to specific ideas and techniques in the text that support your conclusion.

QUESTIONS ON VOCABULARY AND STYLE

1. What associations are suggested by words such as "sapped," "will-less," and "enervated" in paragraph 8?

2. At a number of points in the essay, Winn encloses words within quotation marks. Why does she do so?

3. Be able to define the following words: *wryly* (paragraph 1), *sated* (2), *inchoately* (7), *enervated* (8), *ruefully* (9).

WRITING SUGGESTIONS

1. Many people get hooked on something—baseball card collecting, exercising, buying clothes, eating a particular food, performing particular daily rituals, washing and waxing their automobiles. In a paragraph define and illustrate your obsession.

2. In paragraph 9 Winn asserts that "almost any other endeavor is more worthwhile [than television viewing] by any human measure." In an essay, define and illustrate the possible meaning(s) of the phrase "a worthwhile human endeavor."

Prewriting:

a. What constitutes, for you, "worthwhile" activity? Brainstorm on the topic to generate a range of possibilities. Specifically what is it about this activity that makes it worthwhile? How would you like to spend your time? What makes you feel good about each activity?

b. Interview a group of classmates or fellow students. Try to get a range of ages and backgrounds. Ask each to list worthwhile human endeavors.

c. Remember that your essay will include both generalizations that reflect important human values and specific examples that illustrate those general categories. Once you have a list of examples, make sure that you classify them into broader categories.

Rewriting:

a. Look back over the advice on classifying contained in the introduction to Chapter 4. Check to make sure that you have clearly grouped your examples. Can any examples be organized differently? Consider a new outline for your essay.

b. Check each body paragraph. Does each have a clearly stated or implied topic statement? Make a photocopy of your essay, and underline in colored ink that key idea. Do all of the examples in the paragraph relate to that statement?

c. Coming up with an effective, interesting title is not always an easy matter. Moreover, it does not always seem important when you are worried about finishing the essay. Look back at your title. Does it provoke reader interest? Is this a title that you might find in a magazine? Brainstorm for some new possibilities.

3. How typical are Winn's views? That is, do other researchers agree that television viewing can be addictive? Research the problem. How would the term *addictive* be defined by the scientific community? Is excessive television viewing really dangerous? Your school's reference librarians can help you locate relevant information. You might also look for reviews of Winn's two books on the subject of television. (See the headnote at the start of the selection.) Document your sources.

I Want a Wife

JUDY SYFERS

Judy Syfers was born in 1937 in San Francisco, California, and received a B.F.A. in painting from the University of Iowa. She was married in 1960 and raised two children. Now divorced, she lives in San Francisco. As a free-lance writer, Syfers has written essays on such topics as union organizing, abortion, and the role of women in society. Syfers's most frequently reprinted essay is "I Want a Wife," which originally appeared in Ms. magazine in 1971. After examining the stereotypical male demands in marriage, Syfers concludes, "Who wouldn't want a wife?"

write topic sentences

1   I BELONG TO THAT classification of people known as wives. I am A Wife. And, not altogether incidentally, I am a mother.

2   Not too long ago a male friend of mine appeared on the scene fresh from a recent divorce. He had one child, who is, of course, with his ex-wife. He is obviously looking for another wife. As I thought about him while I was ironing one evening, it suddenly occurred to me that I, too, would like to have a wife. Why do I want a wife?

3   I would like to go back to school so that I can become economically independent, support myself, and, if need be, support those dependent upon me. I want a wife who will work and send me to school. And while I am going to school I want a wife to take care of my children. I want a wife to keep track of the children's doctor and dentist appointments. And to keep track of mine, too. I want a wife to make sure my children eat properly and are kept clean. I want a wife who will wash the children's clothes and keep them mended. I want a wife who is a good nurturant attendant to my children, who arranges for their schooling, makes sure that they have an adequate social life with their peers, takes them to the park, the zoo, etc. I want a wife who takes care of the children when they are sick, a wife who arranges to be around when the children need special care, because, of course, I cannot miss classes at school. My wife must

arrange to lose time at work, and not lose the job. It may mean a small cut in my wife's income from time to time, but I guess I can tolerate that. Needless to say, my wife will arrange and pay for the care of the children while my wife is working.

I want a wife who will take care of my physical needs. I want a wife who will keep my house clean. A wife who will pick up after me. I want a wife who will keep my clothes clean, ironed, mended, replaced when need be, and who will see to it that my personal things are kept in their proper place so that I can find what I need the minute I need it. I want a wife who cooks the meals, a wife who is a good cook. I want a wife who will plan the meals, do the necessary grocery shopping, prepare the meals, serve them pleasantly, and then do the cleaning up while I do my studying. I want a wife who will care for me when I am sick and sympathize with my pain and loss of time from school. I want a wife to go along when our family takes a vacation so that someone can continue to care for me and my children when I need a rest and change of scene. 4

I want a wife who will not bother me with rambling complaints about a wife's duties. But I want a wife who will listen to me when I feel the need to explain a rather difficult point I have come across in my course of studies. And I want a wife who will type my papers for me when I have written them. 5

I want a wife who will take care of the details of my social life. When my wife and I are invited out by my friends, I want a wife who will take care of the babysitting arrangements. When I meet people at school that I like and want to entertain, I want a wife who will have the house clean, will prepare a special meal, serve it to me and my friends, and not interrupt when I talk about the things that interest me and my friends. I want a wife who will have arranged that the children are fed and ready for bed before my guests arrive so that the children do not bother us. I want a wife who takes care of the needs of my guests so that they feel comfortable, who makes sure that they have an ashtray, that they are passed the hors d'oeuvres, that they are offered a second helping of the food, that their wine glasses are replenished when necessary, that their coffee is served to them as they like it. And I want a wife who knows that sometimes I need a night out by myself. 6

7   I want a wife who is sensitive to my sexual needs, a wife who makes love passionately and eagerly when I feel like it, a wife who makes sure that I am satisfied. And, of course, I want a wife who will not demand sexual attention when I am not in the mood for it. I want a wife who assumes the complete responsibility for birth control, because I do not want more children. I want a wife who will remain sexually faithful to me so that I do not have to clutter up my intellectual life with jealousies. And I want a wife who understands that *my* sexual needs may entail more than strict adherence to monogamy. I must, after all, be able to relate to people as fully as possible.

8   If, by chance, I find another person more suitable as a wife than the wife I already have, I want the liberty to replace my present wife with another one. Naturally I will expect a fresh, new life; my wife will take the children and be solely responsible for them so that I am left free.

9   When I am through with school and have a job, I want my wife to quit working and remain at home so that my wife can more fully and completely take care of a wife's duties.

10   My God, who *wouldn't* want a wife?

QUESTIONS ON SUBJECT AND PURPOSE

1. In what way is this a definition of a wife? Why does Syfers avoid a more conventional definition?

2. Is Syfers being fair? Is there anything that she leaves out of her definition that you would have included?

3. What purpose might Syfers have been trying to achieve?

QUESTIONS ON STRATEGY AND AUDIENCE

1. How does Syfers structure her essay? What is the order of the development? Could the essay have been arranged in any other way?

2. Why does Syfers identify herself by her roles—wife and mother—at the beginning of the essay? Is that information relevant in any way?

3. What assumptions does Syfers have about her audience (the readers of *Ms.* magazine)? How do you know?

QUESTIONS ON VOCABULARY AND STYLE

1. How does Syfers use repetition in the essay? Why? Does it work? What effect does it create?

2. How effective is Syfers's final rhetorical question? Where else in the essay does she use a rhetorical question?

3. Be able to define the following words: *nurturant* (paragraph 3), *hor d'oeuvres* (6), *replenished* (6), *monogamy* (7).

WRITING SUGGESTIONS

1. Using the material provided by Syfers, write a paragraph definition of a wife. Be serious; do not try to paraphrase or to imitate Syfers's style.

2. In an essay define a word such as *husband, lover, friend, mother, father,* or *grandparent.* Define indirectly by showing what such a person does or should do.

Prewriting:

a. Select a word as a possible subject. Then write down a dictionary definition. The inadequacies of such a short definition (for example, *wife*: "a woman married to a man") will be obvious. What expectations do you have about the role or function of the person in this position? Make a list.

b. Try freewriting about the items on the list you have just made. Treat each expectation as the subject for a separate freewriting. You might not use any of the prose that you produce here; you are trying to generate ideas.

c. Plan an organizational strategy. Look carefully at how Syfers puts her essay together. How does she structure the middle of her essay? Can you use a similar structure?

Rewriting:

a. Characterize the tone of what you have written. For example, are you serious or satirical? Is it formal or informal? Does your tone complement your purpose? Look back through your essay, and imagine how it would sound to a reader.

b. Check each paragraph in your essay. Is there a consistent, unified subject for each? That unity might be expressed in an explicit topic sentence, or it might just be implicit.

c. Look again at your introduction and conclusion. Avoid imitating Syfers's strategies—especially her conclusion. Look at the advice on introductions and conclusions in the Glossary. Be honest about what you have written. Could either be stronger, clearer, more interesting?

3. What does it mean to be a wife in another culture? Choose at least two other cultures and research those societies' expectations of a wife. Try to find cultures that show significant differences. Using your research, write an essay offering a comparative definition of *wife*. Assume that your audience is American. Be certain to document your sources.

Femininity

SUSAN BROWNMILLER

*Born in 1935 in Brooklyn, New York, Susan Brownmiller was ed-
ucated at Cornell University and at the Jefferson School of Social
Science. Before beginning her writing and editorial work for publications such as* The Village Voice *and* Newsweek, *Brownmiller
was an actress for four years. She now works as a free-lance writer,
often contributing to* The New York Times, Esquire, *and* Newsweek. *Brownmiller's concern for women and the women's movement
is emphasized in her book* Against Our Will: Men, Women, &
Rape *(1975). Her concern for women also motivated her to found*
Women Against Pornography. *Brownmiller's* Femininity *(1984) explores the origins of femininity using biological, cultural, and sociological evidence. Her latest book,* Waverly *(1989), is a novel based
on a true story of a battered wife and her abused daughter. This
selection, taken from the Prologue to* Femininity, *attempts to define
the term.*

WE HAD A GAME in our house called "setting the table" and I   1
was Mother's helper. Forks to the left of the plate, knives and
spoons to the right. Placing the cutlery neatly, as I recall, was
one of my first duties, and the event was alive with meaning.
When a knife or a fork dropped to the floor, that meant a man
was unexpectedly coming to dinner. A falling spoon announced
the surprise arrival of a female guest. No matter that these visitors never arrived on cue, I had learned a rule of gender identification. Men were straight-edged, sharply pronged and formidable, women were softly curved and held the food in a
rounded well. It made perfect sense, like the division of pink
and blue that I saw in babies, an orderly way of viewing the
world. Daddy, who was gone all day at work and who loved
to putter at home with his pipe, tobacco and tool chest, was
knife and fork. Mommy and Grandma, with their ample proportions and pots and pans, were grownup soup spoons, large
and capacious. And I was teaspoon, small and slender, easy to
hold and just right for pudding, my favorite dessert.

2   Being good at what was expected of me was one of my earliest projects, for not only was I rewarded as most children are, for doing things right, but excellence gave pride and stability to my childhood existence. Girls were different from boys, and the expression of that difference seemed mine to make clear. Did my loving, anxious mother, who dressed me in white organdy pinafores and Mary Janes and who cried hot tears when I got them dirty, give me my first instruction? Of course. Did my doting aunts and uncles with their gifts of pretty dolls and miniature tea sets add to my education? Of course. But even without the appropriate toys and clothes, lessons in the art of being feminine lay all around me and I absorbed them all: the fairy tales that were read to me at night, the brightly colored advertisements I pored over in magazines before I learned to decipher the words, the movies I saw, the comic books I hoarded, the radio soap operas I happily followed whenever I had to stay in bed with a cold. I loved being a little girl, or rather I loved being a fairly princess, for that was who I thought I was.

3   As I passed through a stormy adolescence to a stormy maturity, femininity increasingly became an exasperation, a brilliant, subtle esthetic that was bafflingly inconsistent at the same time that it was minutely, demandingly concrete, a rigid code of appearance and behavior defined by do's and don't-do's that went against my rebellious grain. Femininity was a challenge thrown down to the female sex, a challenge no proud, self-respecting young woman could afford to ignore, particularly one with enormous ambition that she nursed in secret, alternately feeding or starving its inchoate life in tremendous confusion.

4   "Don't lose your femininity" and "Isn't it remarkable how she manages to retain her femininity?" had terrifying implications. They spoke of a bottom-line failure so irreversible that nothing else mattered. The pinball machine had registered "tilt," the game had been called. Disqualification was marked on the forehead of a woman whose femininity was lost. No records would be entered in her name, for she had destroyed her birthright in her wretched, ungainly effort to imitate a man. She walked in limbo, this hapless creature, and it occurred to me that one day I might see her when I looked in the mirror.

If the danger was so palpable that warning notices were freely posted, wasn't it possible that the small bundle of resentments I carried around in secret might spill out and place the mark on my own forehead? Whatever quarrels with femininity I had I kept to myself; whatever handicaps femininity imposed, they were mine to deal with alone, for there was no women's movement to ask the tough questions, or to brazenly disregard the rules.

Femininity, in essence, is a romantic sentiment, a nostalgic   5
tradition of imposed limitations. Even as it hurries forward in the 1980s, putting on lipstick and high heels to appear well dressed, it trips on the ruffled petticoats and hoopskirts of an era gone by. Invariably and necessarily, femininity is something that women had more of in the past, not only in the historic past of prior generations, but in each woman's personal past as well—in the virginal innocence that is replaced by knowledge, in the dewy cheek that is coarsened by age, in the "inherent nature" that a woman seems to misplace so forgetfully whenever she steps out of bounds. Why should this be so? The XX chromosomal message has not been scrambled, the estrogen-dominated hormonal balance is generally as biology intended, the reproductive organs, whatever use one has made of them, are usually in place, the breasts of whatever size are most often where they should be. But clearly, biological femaleness is not enough.

Femininity always demands more. It must constantly re-   6
assure its audience by a willing demonstration of difference, even when one does not exist in nature, or it must seize and embrace a natural variation and compose a rhapsodic symphony upon the notes. Suppose one doesn't care to, has other things on her mind, is clumsy or tone-deaf despite the best instruction and training? To fail at the feminine difference is to appear not to care about men, and to risk the loss of their attention and approval. To be insufficiently feminine is viewed as a failure in core sexual identity, or as a failure to care sufficiently about oneself, for a woman found wanting will be appraised (and will appraise herself) as mannish or neutered or simply unattractive, as men have defined these terms.

We are talking, admittedly, about an exquisite esthetic.   7

473

Enormous pleasure can be extracted from feminine pursuits as a creative outlet or purely as relaxation; indeed, indulgence for the sake of fun, or art, or attention, is among femininity's great joys. But the chief attraction (and the central paradox, as well) is the competitive edge that femininity seems to promise in the unending struggle to survive, and perhaps to triumph. The world smiles favorably on the feminine woman: it extends little courtesies and minor privilege. Yet the nature of this competitive edge is ironic, at best, for one works at femininity by accepting restrictions, by limiting one's sights, by choosing an indirect route, by scattering concentration and not giving one's all as a man would to his own, certifiably masculine, interests. It does not require a great leap of imagination for a woman to understand the feminine principle as a grand collection of compromises, large and small, that she simply must make in order to render herself a successful woman. If she has difficulty in satisfying femininity's demands, if its illusions go against her grain, or if she is criticized for her shortcomings and imperfections, the more she will see femininity as a desperate strategy of appeasement, a strategy she may not have the wish or the courage to abandon, for failure looms in either direction.

8   It is fashionable in some quarters to describe the feminine and masculine principles as polar ends of the human continuum, and to sagely profess that both polarities exist in all people. Sun and moon, yin and yang, soft and hard, active and passive, etcetera, may indeed be opposites, but a linear continuum does not illuminate the problem. (Femininity, in all its contrivances, is a very active endeavor.) What, then, is the basic distinction? The masculine principle is better understood as a driving ethos of superiority designed to inspire straightforward, confident success, while the feminine principle is composed of vulnerability, the need for protection, the formalities of compliance and the avoidance of conflict—in short, an appeal of dependence and good will that gives the masculine principle its romantic validity and its admiring applause.

9   Femininity pleases men because it makes them appear more masculine by contrast; and, in truth, conferring an extra portion of unearned gender distinction on men, and unchallenged space in which to breathe freely and feel stronger, wiser, more com-

petent, is femininity's special gift. One could say that masculinity is often an effort to please women, but masculinity is known to please by displays of mastery and competence while femininity pleases by suggesting that these concerns, except in small matters, are beyond its intent. Whimsy, unpredictability and patterns of thinking and behavior that are dominated by emotion, such as tearful expressions of sentiment and fear, are thought to be feminine precisely because they lie outside the established route to success.

If in the beginnings of history the feminine woman was 10 defined by her physical dependency, her inability for reasons of reproductive biology to triumph over the forces of nature that were the tests of masculine strength and power, today she reflects both an economic and emotional dependency that is still considered "natural," romantic and attractive. After an unsettling fifteen years in which many basic assumptions about the sexes were challenged, the economic disparity did not disappear. Large numbers of women—those with small children, those left high and dry after a mid-life divorce—need financial support. But even those who earn their own living share a universal need for connectedness (call it love, if you wish). As unprecedented numbers of men abandon their sexual interest in women, others, sensing opportunity, choose to demonstrate their interest through variety and a change in partners. A sociological fact of the 1980s is that female competition for two scarce resources—men and jobs—is especially fierce.

So it is not surprising that we are currently witnessing a 11 renewed interest in femininity and an unabashed indulgence in feminine pursuits. Femininity serves to reassure men that women need them and care about them enormously. By incorporating the decorative and the frivolous into its definition of style, femininity functions as an effective antidote to the unrelieved seriousness, the pressure of making one's way in a harsh, difficult world. In its mandate to avoid direct confrontation and to smooth over the fissures of conflict, femininity operates as a value system of niceness, a code of thoughtfulness and sensitivity that in modern society is sadly in short supply.

There is no reason to deny that indulgence in the art of 12 feminine illusion can be reassuring to a woman, if she happens to be good at it. As sexuality undergoes some dizzying revisions, evidence that one is a woman "at heart" (the inquisitor's question) is not without worth. Since an answer of sorts may be furnished by piling on additional documentation, affirmation can arise from such identifiable but trivial feminine activities as buying a new eyeliner, experimenting with the latest shade of nail color, or bursting into tears at the outcome of a popular romance novel. Is there anything destructive in this? Time and cost factors, a deflection of energy and an absorption in fakery spring quickly to mind, and they need to be balanced, as in a ledger book, against the affirming advantage.

QUESTIONS ON SUBJECT AND PURPOSE

1. How does Brownmiller define "femininity"?
2. How does femininity change as a woman grows older? How has it changed throughout this century?
3. On the basis of this selection, how does Brownmiller seem to feel about femininity?

QUESTIONS ON STRATEGY AND AUDIENCE

1. In what way(s) does the table-setting analogy in paragraph 1 serve as an introduction to the distinctions between femininity and masculinity?
2. How does Brownmiller structure the essay? Make a brief outline.
3. Who is Brownmiller's audience? What in the text defines or suggests who that audience is?

QUESTIONS ON VOCABULARY AND STYLE

1. Characterize Brownmiller's tone in the selection. How does she feel about femininity? About the "renewed interest" in femininity?
2. At several points in the essay, Brownmiller encloses material within parentheses. What is the effect of doing that? Why not set it off using commas or dashes?
3. Be able to define the following words: *capacious* (paragraph 1), *esthetic* (3), *inchoate* (3), *appeasement* (7), *ethos* (8).

WRITING SUGGESTIONS

1. What do you think are desirable feminine or masculine traits in the ideal mate? In a paragraph, explore your expectations of an ideal mate by defining either masculinity or femininity.

2. In an essay, define the term "masculinity."

Prewriting:

   a. Part of your definition, like Brownmiller's, has been shaped by expectations learned from family and culture. How, for example, would your grandparents or parents define the term? How does a man act? What does he do? What does he not do? Consider the term from both perspectives. If possible, ask your parents or grandparents to answer these questions.

   b. Ask a series of friends or classmates to answer the questions posed above. Try to get a range of informants of varying ages and backgrounds. How do their answers differ from the answers of your grandparents or parents?

   c. How is masculinity defined in our society? What images are projected by magazines, television, comic book characters, movies? Look around you, take notes, jot down examples to support your generalizations.

Rewriting:

   a. Have you provided enough examples to support your generalizations? Go through a photocopy of your essay and underline generalizations in one color and examples in another. Is there a good balance between the two?

   b. Look carefully at your conclusion. You want to end forcefully; you do not just want to repeat the same ideas and words used in your introduction. Reread your essay several times, and then try freewriting a new conclusion. Aim for a completely different ending than the one you originally wrote.

   c. Once you have a complete draft, jot down on a separate sheet of paper what troubles you the most about the essay. What could be better? Allow a day to pass, then try to solve that problem. If your school has a writing center or peer tutoring program, take your specific problem there.

3. How have society's definitions of masculinity and femininity

changed over time? Choose one of the two terms, and research its shifting definitions over the past two hundred years. What did society expect of a man or a woman in 1800? In 1900? What will society expect in the 1990s? What is considered masculine or feminine? Concentrate on the major changes or similarities. Present your findings in an essay that might appear in a popular magazine.

A Word's Meaning Can Often Depend on Who Says It

GLORIA NAYLOR

Born in 1950 in New York City, Gloria Naylor worked in a variety of positions, including seven years as a missionary for Jehovah's Witnesses, before going to college. She graduated from Brooklyn College of the City University of New York in 1981 and then earned her M.A. in Afro-American Studies at Yale University in 1983. She has contributed many articles to magazines such as Southern Review, Essence, Ms., *and* Life. *Her books have dealt with black, and especially black female, experiences in different social strata of America. Her first book,* The Women of Brewster Place *(1982), which won the American Book Award for best first novel and was made into a television movie, follows the lives of seven black urban women.* Linden Hills *(1985), which loosely follows the structure of Dante's* Inferno, *is about the materialism of a black, middle class suburb.* Mama Day *(1988), which has connections with Shakespeare's* The Tempest, *is about an island settled by American slaves and ruled by a woman with magical powers. ''A Word's Meaning Can Often Depend on Who Says It'' was first published in 1986 in the ''Her's'' column in* The New York Times. *Naylor reflects upon the word ''nigger'' and how its meaning changes depending on who says it. ''There must have been dozen of times that* nigger *was spoken in front of me before I reached the third grade,'' she writes. ''But I didn't 'hear' it until it was said by a small of pair of lips that had already learned it could be a way to humiliate me.''*

LANGUAGE IS the subject. It is the written form with which I've managed to keep the wolf away from the door and, in diaries, to keep my sanity. In spite of this, I consider the written word inferior to the spoken, and much of the frustration experienced by novelists is the awareness that whatever we manage to capture in even the most transcendent passages falls far short of the richness of life. Dialogue achieves its power in the dynamics of a fleeting moment of sight, sound, smell, and touch.

479

2   I'm not going to enter the debate here about whether it is language that shapes reality or vice versa. That battle is doomed to be waged whenever we seek intermittent reprieve from the chicken and egg dispute. I will simply take the position that the spoken word, like the written word, amounts to a nonsensical arrangement of sounds or letters without a consensus that assigns "meaning." And building from the meanings of what we hear, we order reality. Words themselves are innocuous; it is the consensus that gives them true power.

3   I remember the first time I heard the word *nigger*. In my third-grade class, our math tests were being passed down the rows, and as I handed the papers to a little boy in back of me, I remarked that once again he had received a much lower mark than I did. He snatched his test from me and spit out that word. Had he called me a nymphomaniac or a necrophiliac, I couldn't have been more puzzled. I didn't know what a nigger was, but I knew whatever it meant, it was something he shouldn't have called me. This was verified when I raised my hand, and in a loud voice repeated what he had said and watched the teacher scold him for using a "bad" word. I was later to go home and ask the inevitable question that every black parent must face—"Mommy, what does *nigger* mean?"

4   And what exactly did it mean? Thinking back, I realize that this could not have been the first time the word was used in my presence. I was part of a large extended family that had migrated from the rural South after World War II and formed a close-knit network that gravitated around my maternal grandparents. Their ground-floor apartment in one of the buildings they owned in Harlem was a weekend mecca for my immediate family, along with countless aunts, uncles, and cousins who brought along assorted friends. It was a bustling and open house with assorted neighbors and tenants popping in and out to exchange bits of gossip, pick up an old quarrel, or referee the ongoing checkers game in which my grandmother cheated shamelessly. They were all there to let down their hair and put up their feet after a week of labor in the factories, laundries, and shipyards of New York.

5   Amid the clamor, which could reach deafening propor-

tions—two or three conversations going on simultaneously, punctuated by the sound of a baby's crying somewhere in the back rooms or out on the street—there was still a rigid set of rules about what was said and how. Older children were sent out of the living room when it was time to get into the juicy details about "you-know-who" up on the third floor who had gone and gotten herself "p-r-e-g-n-a-n-t!" But my parents, knowing that I could spell well beyond my years, always demanded that I follow the others out to play. Beyond sexual misconduct and death, everything else was considered harmless for our young ears. And so among the anecdotes of the triumphs and disappointments in the various workings of their lives, the word *nigger* was used in my presence, but it was set within contexts and inflections that caused it to register in my mind as something else.

In the singular, the word was always applied to a man who 6
had distinguished himself in some situation that brought their approval for his strength, intelligence, or drive:

"Did Johnny *really* do that?" 7

"I'm telling you, that nigger pulled in $6,000 of overtime 8
last year. Said he got enough for a down payment on a house."

When used with a possessive adjective by a woman—"my 9
nigger"—it became a term of endearment for her husband or boyfriend. But it could be more than just a term applied to a man. In their mouths it became the pure essence of manhood—a disembodied force that channeled their past history of struggle and present survival against the odds into a victorious statement of being: "Yeah, that old foreman found out quick enough—you don't mess with a nigger."

In the plural, it became a description of some group within 10
the community that had overstepped the bounds of decency as my family defined it. Parents who neglected their children, a drunken couple who fought in public, people who simply refused to look for work, those with excessively dirty mouths or unkempt households were all "trifling niggers." This particular circle could forgive hard times, unemployment, the occasional bout of depression—they had gone through all of that themselves—but the unforgivable sin was a lack of self-respect.

A woman could never be a "nigger" in the singular, with 11

its connotation of confirming worth. The noun *girl* was its closest equivalent in that sense, but only when used in direct address and regardless of the gender doing the addressing. *Girl* was a token of respect for a woman. The one-syllable word was drawn out to sound like three in recognition of the extra ounce of wit, nerve, or daring that the woman had shown in the situation under discussion.

12   "G-i-r-l, stop. You mean you said that to his face?"

13   But if the word was used in a third-person reference or shortened so that it almost snapped out of the mouth, it always involved some element of communal disapproval. And age became an important factor in these exchanges. It was only between individuals of the same generation, or from any older person to a younger (but never the other way around), that *girl* would be considered a compliment.

14   I don't agree with the argument that use of the word *nigger* at this social stratum of the black community was an internalization of racism. The dynamics were the exact opposite: the people in my grandmother's living room took a word that whites used to signify worthlessness or degradation and rendered it impotent. Gathering there together, they transformed *nigger* to signify the varied and complex human beings they knew themselves to be. If the word was to disappear totally from the mouths of even the most liberal of white society, no one in that room was naive enough to believe it would disappear from white minds. Meeting the word head-on, they proved it had absolutely nothing to do with the way they were determined to live their lives.

15   So there must have been dozens of times that *nigger* was spoken in front of me before I reached the third grade. But I didn't "hear" it until it was said by a small pair of lips that had already learned it could be a way to humiliate me. That was the word I went home and asked my mother about. And since she knew that I had to grow up in America, she took me in her lap and explained.

QUESTIONS ON SUBJECT AND PURPOSE

1. Are the definitions that Naylor offers denotative or connotative? See the Glossary for definitions of those two terms.

2. In what ways does Naylor's family use the word "nigger"? How does their use differ from the way in which the third-grader uses the word?

3. What purpose or purposes does Naylor appear to have in the essay?

QUESTIONS ON STRATEGY AND AUDIENCE

1. Why does Naylor preface her essay with the two introductory paragraphs? Why not begin with paragraph 3?

2. In paragraphs 11–13, Naylor defines the term "girl." How does that definition fit into the essay? Why include it?

3. Naylor's essay originally appeared in *The New York Times*. What influence might the place of publication have had on the nature of the essay?

QUESTIONS ON VOCABULARY AND STYLE

1. What does Naylor seem to mean when she observes: "words themselves are innocuous; it is the consensus that gives them true power"?

2. What is the effect of the following clichés: "to keep the wolf away from the door" (paragraph 1), "the chicken and egg dispute" (2), "let down their hair" (5), "meeting the word head-on" (14).

3. Be prepared to define the following words: *innocuous* (paragraph 2), *necrophiliac* (3), *mecca* (4), *clamor* (5), *anecdotes* (5), *unkempt* (10), *trifling* (10), *connotation* (11), *stratum* (14).

WRITING SUGGESTIONS

1. Select a common word that has a range of connotations or associations. In a paragraph define that word by including examples of how the word might be used.

2. In an essay write an extended definition of a word that carries

a range of connotations. Remember to get your instructor's approval of your word.

Prewriting:

a. Make a list of at least six possibilities. Choose words that are used frequently and have a variety of meanings. Ask your friends for suggestions as well.

b. Go to the reference room of your school's library and using a range of dictionaries, including dictionaries of slang, see how many different meanings and associations you can find.

c. Look back over the details that you plan to include in your extended definition. What organizational strategy seems appropriate? Are you dividing the subject into parts? Are you defining through comparison? Sketch out a possible framework that organizes the examples and details you plan to use.

Rewriting:

a. Check your introduction. Copy your introduction onto a separate sheet of paper. Does your reader want to continue reading? Does your introduction stimulate interest?

b. Check each individual paragraph. Is there a unified idea that controls each one? Make a copy of your essay, and highlight the topic sentence or key idea of each paragraph with a colored pen.

c. Evaluate the conclusion that you have written. Do you conclude or just stop? Do you just repeat in slightly altered words what you wrote in the introduction? Check the advice about introductions and conclusions offered in the Glossary. If your conclusion seems weak, try freewriting at least one alternative ending.

3. Research the history of one "hate" word. Where did it originate? Why? What connotations does the word have? Have those connotations changed over the years? The many dictionaries in the reference department of your college's library will be a good place in which to start your research.

A Writer's Revision Process: Saturday Night

SUSAN ORLEAN

Susan Orlean, a collector of southern folk art, toothpaste tubes, truck-stop souvenirs, vintage syrup dispensers, and globes, is a free-lance journalist who writes about the oddities of life. Raised in Cleveland, Ohio, and currently living in Manhattan, she wrote for Williamette Week *in Portland, Oregon, and then became arts columnist for the* Boston Phoenix. *The articles she now contributes to magazines such as* The New Yorker, Rolling Stone, Vogue, The New York Times Magazine, GQ, *and* House and Garden *frequently deal with popular culture (idiosyncratic American subcultures, ceremonies, and personalities) and often have been tinted with historical or sociological information. Her first book,* Red Sox and Bluefish *(1987), was a collection of essays originally published in the* Boston Globe Magazine *focusing on what distinguishes New England from other parts of America. Her latest book,* Saturday Night *(1990), is an informal study of people's activities on Saturday night. To research her book, Orlean spent three and half years observing and accompanying ''average'' individuals on Saturday nights. Her conclusion: ''If you add them up, there are many more weekdays in our lives than there are Saturday nights, but Saturday night is the one worth living for.''*

The essay reprinted here was adapted and revised from Saturday Night *and published in the February 11, 1990, issue of* The New York Times Magazine.

MAGAZINE VERSION

SATURDAY NIGHT is different from any other. On Saturday night, 1
people get together, go dancing, bowling, drinking, out to dinner, get drunk, get killed, kill other people, go out on dates, visit friends, go to parties, listen to music, sleep, gamble, watch television, go cruising, and sometimes fall in love—just as they do every other night of the week. But on Saturday night they do all these things more often and with more passion and intent.

485

Even having nothing to do on Saturday night is different from having nothing to do on, say, Thursday afternoon, and being alone on Saturday night is different from being alone on any other night of the week.

2   For most people Saturday is the one night that neither follows nor precedes work, when they expect to have a nice time, when they want to be with their friends and lovers and not with their bosses, employees, teachers, landlords, or relatives—unless those categories happen to include friends or lovers. Saturday night is when you want to do what you want to do and not what you have to do. In the extreme, this leads to what I think of as the Fun Imperative: the sensation that a Saturday night not devoted to having a good time is a major human failure and evidence of a possible character flaw. The particularly acute loneliness you can feel only on Saturday night is the Fun Imperative unrequited. But most of the time Saturday night is a medium of enjoyment.

3   For the last few years, I have traveled around the country and spent Saturday nights with a variety of people in a variety of situations, with the intention not to define Saturday night but to illustrate it. What I wanted to know about Saturday night was not so much what is fun to do with your spare time as what, given some spare time and no directives or obligations, people do.

4   Distinguishing Saturday night from the rest of the week began around 700 B.C. with the introduction in Assyria of once-a-week "evil days," and it has remained constant throughout human history, including but not ending with *Saturday Night Fever*. I don't know of anything else that has social significance spanning ancient Babylonia and Babylon, L.I.

5   The origin of Saturday night's distinctiveness was religious—one day each week set aside as sacred, to contrast with the six others that were profane—and over time became economic (a day of rest versus a day of labor). Before this century, days of rest were permitted mainly so that laborers could restore—"recreate," in Victorian terms—their strength and then return to another six days of hard work.

6   Eventually, as affluence and easy credit spread through the

American middle class after World War II, weekend "recreation" became an end in itself. Fun was viewed as an entitlement of the middle class rather than as exclusive right of the rich and elite. The satisfying life, after the war, included an imperative to have fun, and Saturday night was the center of it.

How is Saturday night different now from the past? There 7 is no doubt that AIDS has quashed some of the abandon that Saturday night both symbolized and contained—not just in gay nightclubs, but in all bars and clubs and parties. There are other ways social behavior and Saturday night have changed in tandem. A sex researcher told me he believed many people used to have sex only on Saturday nights, in some cases because it was their only chance, and in others because an unconscious sense of guilt made them feel it was improper on "regular" nights of the week. He also ventured that having sex on Saturday night was titillating for some people because it was only hours before they would go to church. Sexual liberation, the researcher concluded, has probably changed that. Then there's the effect of indoor plumbing on Saturday night: When baths were once-a-week events at the neighborhood bathhouse, Saturday had the distinction of being bath night for most people.

Saturday night happens to be when most people take part 8 in whatever is the current entertainment trend. They might watch a break-dance contest one month, and a lip-synching contest the next, and a lambada-dance demonstration the one after that. I began to think of this aspect of Saturday night culture as the Palace of Social Meteors. Every city I've ever visited seems to have a bar or nightclub called the Palace, the local showcase for whatever the current public diversion happens to be. I made a practice of avoiding the Palaces and all study of Social Meteors. Bar life is certainly a constant of the American Saturday night, but the ancillary activities that take place in them, I'm convinced, are mostly new ways to get people to spend money on drinks, and their evanescence proves only that people get bored with the ways they keep busy in bars.

It's hard to think about Saturday night without realizing 9 that chronological time itself is something of an anachronism these days. Schedules are less rigid now than in the past. When I was a kid, grocery stores closed at six and were never open on Sundays. I still remember the first time I went to a twenty-four hour grocery at four in the morning, thinking that something fundamental had changed forever. You used to be out of luck for money on the weekend if you didn't get to the bank by three on Friday. Now most people I know don't even know when banks are open because they use twenty-four-hour automatic-teller machines. Most stores are now open every day, since blue laws were repealed.

10　　The way we perceive time changed when the American economy shifted from agriculture to industry. On a farm, the significant unit of time is a season. On an assembly line, though, you're inside all the time and you work all year round and you have no interaction with the natural physical world, so seasons no longer matter. What matters is the week, and you know that if you're annoyed to be back at work, it's probably Monday, and if you just got paid and feel more cheerful, it's Friday, and if you're happy, it's the weekend.

11　　Now, as manufacturing, with its regular hours and rigid schedules, is displaced by a service and high-tech economy that runs incessantly, night and day, the convention of the five-day work week and the two-day weekend is coming apart. Many workers have unusual schedules—swing shifts, night work, three-day weekends. They also have their pay deposited electronically, bank by phone, shop at midnight, and tape *The Tonight Show* and watch it at breakfast. The idea of having to get to a bank by three on Friday or to watch Johnny Carson at midnight seems, in the 1990s, nostalgic.

12　　Murray Melbin, a sociologist at Boston University, recently wrote that we have run out of land to colonize, so we are now colonizing nighttime, operating businesses twenty-four hours a day, and setting up services to obviate the importance of time. Many people work from their homes via computer work stations and modem hookups and don't have work schedules. Soon, the week as we know it won't mean anything. Some people see this as liberation. Other people—I'm inclined to include myself in this camp—think it sounds awful. Maybe it would eliminate the problems of getting to work on time, but that's only because it means you're at work all the time. And the more the structure of the week disappears the less extraordinary and special Saturday night will be.

I am not an enthusiast of the seamless week. I think the *13* Assyrians had it right when they decided it was comforting to divide infinity into comprehensible, repeating units of time with distinct qualities. In particular, I would consider losing the singular nature of Saturday night—one night set aside to be off-limits to obligations—kind of a shame.

Not long ago, I spent an interesting Saturday night in Elk- *14* hart, Ind. I had gone there to write about a local imbroglio that pitted the Mayor, a young man with conservative tastes, against a group of people who liked to spend their Saturday evenings cruising in fancy cars through downtown. The Mayor saw the issue as a traffic problem; the cruisers saw his efforts as an infringement on their inalienable right to have fun on weekends. I saw it as a chance to see how seriously people take Saturday night.

I arranged to meet the cruisers at nine o'clock, so I could *15* ride with them on Main Street. At seven, I went to an Italian restaurant someone had recommended. I hoped the restaurant would be a quiet hole-in-the-wall. It was not. It was the sort of place that attracts every birthday celebration, first date, last date, prom date, anniversary party, engagement celebration, and stag party within a 200-mile radius. I am not unaccustomed to being alone in a crowd, but this was the first time in my life I had dined alone at a restaurant—let alone a restaurant preferred by big, ostentatiously convivial groups of people—on a Saturday night. It was a largely disagreeable sensation.

I noticed that I was being noticed by the people seated near *16* me. I decided that the best defense was to look busy, but reading the label on the aspirin bottle in my purse took only a minute. Next, I read the menu. Then I turned to the place mat, which had only a photograph of a beach—I never thought I would see the day when I would miss place mats with puzzles on them. I wondered whether I could leave without being too obvious, and if I left, whether I could get a more secluded dinner somewhere else.

489

17   My musing was interrupted by my waitress, a tall woman with curly brown hair, a high forehead and a voice that could cut through dry wall. Her name tag said MARIAN. She greeted me and asked if I was meeting someone. I said I wasn't. "Here on vacation?" she asked. When I said I was in town doing work, she gave me a long look full of pity. At that point, all I wanted was to get a quick dinner and get out. Marian, however, dawdled. After she took my order, she tidied my place setting and filled my water glass. She checked my salt and pepper shakers. I began to suspect that in her eyes I was a statistical freak—in the category of customers, a Fourth of July snowstorm. Finally, she grabbed a waitress passing by, turned her so she could look at me, and said in a loud, clear voice, "Just look at her! My God! All by herself and working on Saturday night!"

18   After that dinner, and after I had gone cruising, I set out to see how Americans spend Saturday night. Is it regional? Is it a matter of age and marital status? Relative wealth? Urban versus suburban versus rural? Is there such a thing as a typical Southern Saturday night, or a middle-aged Saturday night, or a working-class Saturday night? Is there some place that has sprung up to replace the vanished town squares and bars and bowling alleys where people used to gather when they wanted to get together and had no particular place to go?

19   This task had a few challenges. For one thing, many people, including me, often spend Saturday night at home. For a reporter, this is a tough world to infiltrate. And judging by many of the Saturday nights I've spent this way, their pleasures are too self-referential to bear description. It is also true that in the era of disaster news, people have come to expect to be written about only when something exceptional takes place in their lives. Quite often, people would ask me to come back when the town was having its jazz festival or mariachi festival or rodeo. That wasn't what I was after. I had this notion that Saturday night itself was a good enough subject. I liked the contrariness of examining leisure in an era that is career-crazy, and average citizens in an era that celebrates celebrity.

20   There were a few things about Saturday night I wanted to figure out. For instance, even though Saturday night is itself a democratic occasion, I wondered if most people choose to spend

it undemocratically—that is, to spend it around people just like themselves. Some Saturday night situations don't appear to have any social parameters. One Saturday night, I hung around the emergency room of a large veterinary hospital in New York City. I'd heard there were certain animal accidents (cats falling out of windows, especially) that seemed to happen mostly on Saturday nights, and I wanted to find out why. I also wondered whether there was any similarity to the people who ended up at such a place on Saturday night when they didn't have an emergency. Some flattened cats did come in (it was a hot night, and a lot of people had probably left their windows open) but there were also a lot of people who just chose that night to have their dogs' teeth cleaned or their sick parakeets put to sleep. Except for sharing a somewhat unconventional notion of pet care, these people apparently had nothing in common. The animal emergency center aside, I saw some white people at a black church social I went to, and some black kids and a few upper-middle-class white kids hanging around the white, blue-collar Elkhart cruising crowd. But generally, it seems that Saturday night acts as a subset intensifier.

The possibility of a dateless, hourless, calendarless future 21 notwithstanding, I was happy to discover that Saturday night still does have a distinct personality and effect on most people. People still act differently on Saturday night for no reason other than it's Saturday night. For instance, there are fewer long-distance calls made Saturday night than any other night of the week. What is it about Saturday night that inhibits the urge to make calls? Is it that so many people are out, or that those who happen to be at home assume that anyone they want to call is out? Or does it just feel weird?

On Saturday night, there are the fewest airplane flights, the 22 most murders, most taped radio shows, fewest television viewers, most visits to the emergency room, fewest suicides, most scheduled showings of *The Rocky Horror Picture Show*, most people breaking their diets, most liquor sold by the glass, the fewest number of calls to businesses offering products on television, and the highest number of reported incidents of cowtoppling in rural Pennsylvania. These might at first seem like weird spe-

491

cifics—information dead ends, like knowing that 75 percent of all Iowans think Scotch tape is the best modern invention—but they really add up to a picture of what Saturday night in America is like.

23   It is a time when people listen to prerecorded radio shows, are too busy to watch television, have accidents, don't feel like killing themselves, go out for the evening and forget to close their windows and own curious cats with bad depth perception, feel like seeing campy movies, are in the mood to eat with abandon, drink in bars, aren't in the mood to order the five-volume set of Slim Whitman's greatest hits or aren't home to fall victim to the ad, see cows sleeping in pastures and are inspired to tip them over just for fun. It's in keeping with what the Assyrians had in mind when they first established the seven-day week.

24   For the last few years, while considering the nature of Saturday night, I have kept a clipping from the *Chicago Tribune* wire service over my desk, headlined: "Leisure Time Shrinks By 32 Percent." The article says: "Since 1973, the median number of hours worked by Americans has increased by 20 percent, while the amount of leisure time available to the average person has dropped by 32 percent. The difference between the rise in working hours and the drop in leisure time has been the time that people spend on work around the house and other responsibilities that do not qualify as work. The trend toward less and less leisure time has been steady and inexorable, according to a Harris Survey."

25   If the law of supply and demand is universally true, the shrinking of leisure time could only serve to make Saturday night more valuable. In a world with 32 percent less leisure time, wouldn't a night imbued with pleasure and abandon remain an important and welcome tonic, no matter how irrelevant the conventional notion of time may come to be?

26   That equation seemed especially evident to me in Elkhart. It is a classic working-class town—more than half of its residents are employed at building, servicing, selling, or outfitting recreational vehicles and customized vans—and the people I met there are probably among those Americans whose leisure

time is shrinking the fastest. Accordingly, they considered Saturday night a matter of enormous consequence. "The week is just something I get through until Saturday night," one man told me.

When Mayor James Perron banned cruising on Main Street, 27 it set off three years of furious public debate. The superficial concern was traffic flow. What really got everyone roiled up was the idea that the city was legislating their leisure time. "I'm a working man and I pay my taxes," the same man said, "but no one's going to tell me how to spend my weekend. That's all mine."

I also have posted over my desk something I found buried 28 in a survey about leisure-time activity. It says: "Fifty-four percent of those surveyed have sex at least once a week but ranked it below gardening and visiting relatives as regular activities."

For a year or so, I didn't really know why I was so taken 29 with this piece of arcane data except for its innate comic value. I went to spend Saturday night in a few dozen different places around the country. Time and time again I saw that Saturday night was indeed something special—a time when people are most at ease with themselves. Surveys and statistics of any sort began to seem less important once I realized that Saturday night is mostly mythic: larger than life, more meaningful the less closely it is examined, romantic in the purest way, more an idea than an event.

At last I figured out why that survey seemed to have a 30 particular connection to my interest in Saturday night. According to the survey, most people have sex less often than they garden or visit their relatives, but I'm positive that they still consider sex the larger, more mystical, more mythic, more important, more noteworthy experience. That is how I finally feel about Saturday night. It is a matter of quality over quantity. If you add them up, there are many more weekdays in our lives than there are Saturday nights, but Saturday night is the one worth living for.

QUESTIONS FOR DISCUSSION

1. In what type of Saturday night activity is Orlean interested?

2. Why might Orlean trace very briefly the origins of Saturday night's "distinctiveness"?

3. In paragraph 18, Orlean describes some of the questions that she sought to answer. Yet in the essay, she does not (and cannot because of space) provide answers to those questions. How does she handle that problem? Isn't the reader left wondering?

4. Toward the end of the essay—in paragraphs 24 and 25—Orlean quotes from two newspaper articles. What does each quotation add to the essay?

5. What expectations might Orlean reasonably have about her audience?

6. Be prepared to define the following words: *unrequited* (paragraph 2), *profane* (5), *affluence* (6), *imperative* (6), *ancillary* (8), *evanescence* (8), *anachronism* (9), *blue laws* (9), *obviate* (12), *imbroglio* (14), *ostentatiously* (15), *convivial* (15), *mariachi* (19), *inexorable* (24), *imbued* (25), *arcane* (29), *innate* (29).

BOOK VERSION

The essay version of "Saturday Night" as it appeared in The New York Times Magazine *was slightly different from the way it appeared as the introduction to the book* Saturday Night. *The essay must stand alone. It cannot depend upon text in subsequent chapters, but it also does not need to introduce the text that follows. Orlean had to revise the material for the essay version. Reproduced below are the first seven paragraphs of the introduction to her book* Saturday Night.

1 NOT LONG AGO, I spent an interesting Saturday night in Elkhart, Indiana. I had gone there to write about a local imbroglio that pitted the mayor, a young man with conservative tastes, against a group of people who liked to spend their Saturday evenings cruising in fancy cars through downtown. The mayor saw the issue as a traffic problem; the cruisers saw his efforts to stop cruising in Elkhart as an infringement on their inalienable right to have fun on weekends. I saw it as a chance to see how seriously people take Saturday night.

I arranged to meet the cruisers at nine o'clock so I could ride with them on Main Street. At seven I got hungry, so I drove to an Italian restaurant someone had recommended to me. I was alone and it was Saturday night and I didn't want to feel out of place, so I hoped the restaurant would be a quiet hole-in-the-wall. It was not. It was the sort of place that attracts every birthday celebration, first date, last date, prom date, anniversary party, engagement celebration, and stag party within a two-hundred-mile radius. All around me were couples, people on dates, groups of friends, and a few family reunions; a big birthday party was under way at the table next to mine. It was a large restaurant, and there were no other single diners. I am not unaccustomed to being alone in a crowd, but this was the first time in my life I had dined alone at a restaurant—let alone a restaurant preferred by big, ostentatiously convivial groups of people—on a Saturday night. It was an uncommon and largely disagreeable sensation. I saw that I was being noticed by the people seated near me. It made me feel as if I had walked out of the house without any pants on. I decided that the best defense was to look busy, but reading the label on the aspirin bottle in my purse took only a minute. Next, I read the menu. Then I turned to the place mat, which had only a photograph of a beach on it—I never thought I would see the day when I would miss those place mats with puzzles on them, but this was it. I wondered whether I could leave without being too obvious, and if I left, whether I could get a more secluded dinner somewhere else.

My musing was interrupted by my waitress, a tall woman with curly brown hair, a high forehead, and a voice that could cut through drywall. Her name tag said MARIAN. She greeted me and asked if I was meeting someone. I said I wasn't. ''Here on vacation?'' she asked. When I said I was in town doing work, she gave me a long look full of pity and proceeded to take my order. At that point, all I wanted was to get a quick dinner and get out. I hoped that Marian would speed me on my way. Marian, however, dawdled. She tidied my place setting and filled my water glass. She eyed me. I looked away. She checked my salt and pepper shakers. I began to suspect that in her eyes I was a statistical freak—a Fourth of July snowstorm of cus-

2

3

tomers. She dawdled some more. Another minute passed. Finally, just as she was walking away, Marian grabbed a waitress passing by, turned her so she could get a good look at me, and said in her loud, clear voice, "Just look at her! My god! All by herself and working on Saturday night!"

4   After that dinner, and after I had gone cruising, I was convinced: Saturday night is different from any other night. On Saturday night, people get together, go dancing, go bowling, go drinking, go out to dinner, get drunk, get killed, kill other people, go out on dates, visit friends, go to parties, listen to music, sleep, gamble, watch television, go cruising, and sometimes fall in love—just as they do every other night of the week, but they do all these things more often and with more passion and intent on Saturday night. Even having nothing to do on a Saturday night is different than having nothing to do on, say, Thursday afternoon, and being alone on a Saturday night is different from being alone on any other night of the week. For most people Saturday is the one night that neither follows nor precedes work, when they expect to have a nice time, when they want to be with their friends and lovers and not with their parents, bosses, employees, teachers, landlords, or relatives—unless those categories happen to include friends or lovers. Saturday night is when you want to do what you want to do and not what you have to do. In the extreme, this leads to what I think of as the Fun Imperative: the sensation that a Saturday night not devoted to having a good time is a major human failure and possible evidence of a character flaw. The particularly acute loneliness you can feel only on Saturday night is the Fun Imperative unrequited. But most of the time Saturday night is a medium of enjoyment. Observing different kinds of people in different parts of America who live in different sorts of circumstances at leisure on Saturday night seemed like a perfect opportunity to observe them in their most natural and self-selected setting—like studying an elephant romping in the Ngorongoro Crater as opposed to studying an elephant carrying an advertising sandwich-board in front of a used-car lot in Miami.

5   After my trip to Elkhart, I decided to travel around the country and spend Saturday nights with a variety of people in

a variety of situations, with the intention not to define Saturday night but to illustrate it. What I wanted to know about Saturday night was not so much what is fun to do with your spare time as what, given some spare time and no directives or obligations, people find themselves doing. I wanted to know what determines how Americans spend Saturday night. Is it mainly regional? Is it a matter of age and marital status? Relative wealth? Urban versus suburban versus rural? Is there such a thing as a typical Southern Saturday night, or a middle-aged Saturday night, or a working-class Saturday night? Is there someplace everyone goes on Saturday night—that is, is there something that has sprung up to replace the vanished town squares and bars and bowling alleys where people used to gather when they wanted to get together and had no particular place to go?

This task had a few challenges. For one thing, many people, including me, often spend Saturday night with friends at home. For a reporter, this is a tough world to infiltrate and an impossible one to write about, and judging by many of the Saturday nights I've spent this way, their pleasures are too self-referential to bear description. So for the record, I will note here that a great many people across America spend a great many Saturday nights at home with their family or their friends. It is also true that in the era of disaster news, people have come to expect to be written about only when something exceptional or shocking takes place in their lives. When I showed interest in a subject people considered terribly ordinary—Saturday night in the life of a suburban baby-sitter, for instance—I had some explaining to do. All I could say was that I was looking for things that were neither exceptional nor shocking, and that would reveal what a typical Saturday night was like for somebody—say, an eighty-two-year-old woman who liked to dance, or an Air Force officer on Saturday-night missile duty, or a Park Avenue hostess with a reputation to maintain. Quite often, people would ask me to come back when the town was having its jazz festival or mariachi festival or rodeo. That wasn't what I was after. I had this notion that Saturday night itself was a good enough subject. I liked the idea of writing about people in a setting that had nothing to do with business or government or concession stands. I liked the contrariness of examining leisure in an era that is obsessed with work, and writing about average citizens in an era that celebrates celebrity.

7   Obviously, there are about two hundred million ways Americans spend their Saturday nights, and quite obviously I could not document any sizable percentage of them. I decided early on to be impressionistic rather than encyclopedic—to take a ride across the country, with stops along the way, rather than to attempt a door-to-door survey. Relieved of the impossible burden of comprehensiveness, I was drawn to certain themes (what it is like to work on Saturday night, for instance, and the too-common experience of Saturday-night murder); types of people (the Park Avenue maven, the recovering drug addict); places (the busiest restaurant in the United States); communities (the Louisiana blacks who have settled in Houston); classic Saturday-night situations (the life of a lounge band). I expected to report on someone on a date and never did (my belief in the Heisenberg Principle of the observer affecting the observed dissuaded me); I expected to spend no time whatsoever in churches and ended up in them three times. There is nothing exhaustive about my final results and I employed no quota system: I would give in to what seemed interesting, informed by a wish to throw as broad and engaging a net as I could.

QUESTIONS ON THE REVISION

1. Perhaps the most obvious change between the book version and the magazine version is that Orlean has rearranged the opening paragraphs. The book version begins with the restaurant incident in Indiana (paragraph 14 to the first line of paragraph 18), then inserts paragraphs 1–3, and finally returns again to paragraphs 18–20. What is the effect of this reorganization?

2. Look closely at the changes that Orlean made in the description of the scene at the restaurant in Indiana (book: paragraphs 2–3; magazine: paragraphs 15–17). What is the nature of those changes?

3. Paragraphs 6 and 7 in the book version are completely changed in the magazine version (paragraph 19). In fact, the whole of paragraph 7 is deleted from the essay. What is the nature of

the changes that Orlean makes in these paragraphs, and why might she have deleted so much?

4. The book version completely omits the material about Elkhart that Orlean places in paragraphs 26 and 27 of the magazine version. Why might Orlean have chosen to include more material on Elkhart in the essay?

WRITING SUGGESTIONS

1. While no other night of the week might mean as much as Saturday, for most of us certain nights have patterns or habits that we associate with them. In a paragraph define and characterize another night of the week.

2. In paragraph 18, Orlean poses a number of questions about Saturday night and whether or not its activities are determined by geography, age, or marital or socioeconomic status. What do you and your relatives and friends (regardless of your age) do on a Saturday night? What would be a typical activity?

Prewriting:

a. Make a list of what you have done for the past four Saturday nights. What is the dominant activity? Ask as many friends as you can what they typically do. Do you see any variations? To what might you attribute those differences?

b. Notice that effective detail combined with generalizations makes Orlean's essay work. Be sure to include some narration in your essay—remember that you are describing what you typically do. You might use one night as an example.

c. Watch that you do not repeat the types of generalizations that Orlean makes. You do not need to trace the history of Saturday night or generalize about how the concept of time is changing. Orlean has already done this. Focus on your Saturday nights.

Rewriting:

a. Look again at how you have structured your draft. Make a brief outline of the essay. Does its arrangement seem to make logical sense? Should the body paragraphs be reordered in any other way?

b. Every paper benefits from a good title. What about yours?

Does it accurately represent your paper? Is it interesting? Catchy? Provocative? Does it arouse your reader's curiosity? If not, try brainstorming a series of alternative titles.

c. What troubles you most about your paper? Take that single problem to your college writing center or to your instructor. Do so at least a day before your final draft is due.

3. The newspaper clipping from which Orlean quotes in paragraph 24 states that Americans are working more hours and have less leisure time. Research that finding. Are Americans still working more? Why? Is that true for workers in all jobs? Just some? Be sure to use both business and sociological periodicals in your search for information about the work week and the American blue- and white-collar worker.

NINE

Argument
and
Persuasion

We live in a world of persuasive messages—billboards, advertisements in newspapers and magazines, commercials on television and radio, signs on stores, bumper stickers, T-shirts with messages, and manufacturers' logos on clothing. Advertisements demonstrate a wide range of persuasive strategies. Sometimes they appeal to logic or reason—they ask you to compare the features available on this automobile and its price with any competitor and judge for yourself. More often they appeal to your emotions or feelings—you will not be stylish unless you wear this particular brand of jeans; you are not a real man unless you drink this brand of beer or smoke this cigarette. Arguments are frequently divided in this way—those that appeal to logic and reason and those that appeal to emotions and prejudices. Legal briefs and scientific proofs are good examples of logical arguments; political and social propaganda, of emotional arguments. Jesse Jackson in "Why Blacks Need Affirmative Action" appeals to reason, citing specific factual evidence to support his claims; Marya Mannes in "Wasteland" appeals to the readers' emotions, describing "the mark of savages, the testament of wasters, the stain of prosperity" that litters our landscape. More typically, argumentation blends the two types of appeal. But no matter what strategy you use, in argumentation your objective is the same: to persuade the reader to believe or act in a certain way.

Whether you realize it or not, you already have had extensive experience in constructing arguments and in persuading an audience. Every time you try to persuade someone to do or to believe something, you have to argue. Consider a hypothetical example: You are concerned about your father's health. He smokes cigarettes, avoids exercise, is overweight, and works long hours in a stressful job. Even though you are worried, he is completely unconcerned and has always resisted your family's efforts to change his ways. Your task is to persuade him to change or modify his life style, and doing so involves making its dangers clear, offering convincing reasons for change, and urging specific action.

Establishing the dangers is the first step, and you have a wide range of medical evidence from which to draw. That evidence involves statistics, testimony or advise from doctors, and case histories of men who have suffered the consequences of years of abusing or ignoring their health. From that body of material, you select those items which are most likely to touch your obstinate father. He might not be moved by cold statistics citing life-expectancy tables for smokers and nonexercisers, but he might be touched by the story of a friend his age who suffered a heart attack or stroke. The evidence you gather and use becomes a part of the convincing reasons for change that you offer in your argument. If your father persists in ignoring his health, he is likely to suffer some consequences. You might at this point include in your argument motivational appeals. If he is not concerned about what will happen to him, what about his family? What will they do if he dies?

Having gotten your father to realize and acknowledge the dangers inherent in his life style and to understand the reasons why he should make changes, it remains to urge specific action. In framing a plan for that action, you again need to consider your audience. If you urge your father to stop smoking immediately, join a daily exercise class at the local YMCA or health club, go on a thousand-calorie-a-day diet, and find a new job, chances are that he will think your proposal too drastic even to try. Instead, you might urge a more moderate plan, phasing in changes over a period of time or offering compromises (for example, that he work fewer hours).

How Do You Analyze Your Audience?

Argumentation or persuasion, unlike the other forms or types of writing included in this text, has a special purpose—to persuade its audience. Because you want your reader to agree with your position or act as you urge, you need to analyze your audience before you start to write. Try to answer each of the following questions:

Who are my readers?

What do they already know about this subject?

How interested are they likely to be?

How impartial or prejudiced are they going to be?

What values do my readers share?

Is my argument going to challenge any of my readers' beliefs or values?

What types of evidence are most likely to be effective?

Is my plan for requested action reasonable?

Your argumentative strategy should always reflect an awareness of your audience. Even in the hypothetical example concerning your father, it is obvious that some types of evidence would be more effective than others and that some solutions or plans for action would be more reasonable and, therefore, more acceptable than others.

The second important consideration in any argument is to anticipate your audience's objections and be ready to answer them. Debaters study both sides of an argument so that they can effectively counter any opposition. In arguing the abortion issue, the Right-to-Life speaker has to be prepared to deal with subjects such as abnormal fetuses or pregnancy caused by rape or incest. The Pro-Choice speaker must face questions about when life begins and when the rights of the unborn might take precedence over the mother's rights.

What Does It Take to Persuade Your Reader?

In some cases nothing will persuade your reader. For example, if you are arguing for legalized abortion, you will never convince a reader who believes that an embryo is a human being from the moment of conception. Abortion to that reader will always be murder. It is extremely difficult to argue any position that is counter to your audience's moral or ethical values. It is also difficult to argue a position that is counter to your audience's normal patterns of behavior. For example, you could reasonably argue that your readers ought to stop at all red lights and to obey the speed limit. However, the likelihood of persuading your audience to do these two things—even though not doing so breaks the law—is slim.

These cautions are not meant to imply that you should argue only "safe" subjects or that winning is everything. Choose a subject about which you feel strongly; present a fair, logical argument; express honest emotion; but avoid distorted evidence or inflammatory language. Even if no one is finally persuaded, at least you have offered a clear, intelligent explanation of your position.

In most arguments you have two possible types of support—you can supply factual evidence, and you can appeal to your reader's values. Suppose, for example, you are arguing that professional boxing should be prohibited because it is dangerous. The reader may or may not accept your premise but at the very least would expect some support for your assertion. Your first task would be to gather evidence. The strongest evidence is factual—statistics dealing with the number of fighters each year who are fatally injured or mentally impaired. You might quote appropriate authorities—physicians, scientists, former fighters—on the risks connected with professional boxing. You might relate several instances or even a single example of a particular fighter who was killed or permanently injured while boxing. You might describe in detail how blows strike the body or head; you might trace the process by which a series of punches can cause brain damage. You might catalog the effects that years of physical punishment can produce in the human body. In your argument you might use some or all of this factual evidence. Your job as a writer is to gather the best—the most accurate and the most effective—evidence and present it in a clear and orderly way for your reader.

You can also appeal to your reader's values. You could

argue that a sport in which a participant can be killed or permanently injured is not a "sport" at all. You could argue that the objective of a boxing match—to render one fighter unconscious or unable to continue—is different in kind from any other sport and not one that we, as human beings, should condone, let alone encourage. Appeals to values can be extremely effective.

One final thing is crucially important in persuading your reader. You must sound (and be) fair, reasonable, and credible in order to win the respect and possibly the approval of your reader. Readers distrust arguments that are loaded with unfair or inflammatory language, faulty logic, and biased or distorted evidence.

Should You Argue Logically or Emotionally?

Effective argumentation generally involves appealing to both reason and emotion. It is often easier to catch your reader's attention by using an emotional appeal. Demonstrators against vivisection, the dissecting of animals for laboratory research, display photographs of the torments suffered by these animals. Organizations that fight famine throughout the world use photographs of starving children. Advertisers use a wide range of persuasive tactics to touch our fears, our anxieties, our desires. But the types of argumentative writing that you are asked to do in college or in your job rarely allow for only emotional evidence.

Since logic or reason is so crucial to effective argumentation, you will want to avoid logical fallacies or errors. When you construct your argument, make sure that you have avoided the following common mistakes:

Ad hominem argument (literally to argue "to the person"): criticizing a person's position by criticizing his or her personal character. If an underworld figure asserts that boxing is the manly art of self-defense, you do not counter his *argument* by claiming that he makes money by betting on the fights.

Ad populum argument (literally to argue "to the people"): appealing to the prejudices of your audience instead of offering facts or reasons. You do not defend boxing by asserting that it is part of the American way of life and that anyone who criticizes it is a Communist who seeks to undermine our society.

Appeal to an unqualified authority: using testimony from someone who is unqualified to give it. In arguing against boxing, your relevant authorities would be physicians, or scientists, or former fighters—people who have had some direct experience. You do not quote a professional football player or your dermatologist.

Begging the question: assuming as true what you are trying to prove. "Boxing is dangerous and because it is dangerous it ought to be outlawed." The first statement ("boxing is dangerous") is the premise you set out to prove, but the second statement uses that unproved premise as a basis for drawing a conclusion.

Either/or: stating or implying that there are only two possibilities. Do not assert that the two choices are either to ban boxing or to allow this legalized murder to continue. Perhaps other changes might make the sport safer and hence less objectionable.

Faulty analogy: using an inappropriate or superficially similar analogy as evidence. "Allowing a fighter to kill another man with his fists is like giving him a gun and permission to shoot to kill." The analogy might be vivid, but the two acts are far more different than they are similar.

Hasty generalization: basing a conclusion on evidence that is atypical or unrepresentative. Do not assert that *every* boxer has suffered brain damage just because you can cite a few well-known cases.

Non sequitur (literally "it does not follow"): arriving at a conclusion not justified by the premises or evidence. "My father has watched many fights on television; therefore, he is an authority on the physical hazards that boxers face."

Oversimplification: suggesting a simple solution to a complex problem. "If professional boxers were made aware of the risks they take, they would stop boxing."

How Do You Structure an Argument?

You construct an argument in either of two ways: you begin with your premise and then provide evidence or support or you begin with your evidence and then move to your conclusion. Jesse Jackson starts with a premise: blacks need affirmative action to achieve "educational and economic equity and parity." He then supports that premise by citing statistics comparing the number of whites in certain professions to the number of blacks. He anticipates and counters the obvious objection to affirmative action —that it is unfair to whites. Lewis Thomas in "On Medicine and the Bomb" structures his essay in the opposite way. He begins by giving examples of what modern medicine can achieve in dealing with patients suffering from lethal radiation injuries, burns, and massive trauma. But these advances, he observes, are achieved at great cost in individual cases. Medicine, given the technology, manpower, and money, can save an individual life, but in the event of a nuclear war, casualties would number in the millions. As a result, Thomas concludes, "modern medicine has nothing whatever to offer, not even a token benefit, in the event of thermonuclear war." Richard Rodriguez in "None of This Is Fair" traces how affirmative action programs have advanced, perhaps unfairly, his own career. That evidence leads him to conclude that such programs often fail to help those who are really the disadvantaged.

If you are constructing an argument based upon a formal, logical progression, you can use either inductive or deductive reasoning. An *inductive* argument begins with specific evidence and then moves to a generalized conclusion to account for that evidence. The detective pieces together the evidence in an investigation and arrives at a conclusion: the butler did it. Lewis Thomas's essay moves basically in an inductive pattern. He starts with particular examples and moves to a general truth: medicine cannot cope with thermonuclear war.

A *deductive* argument moves in the opposite direction: it starts with a general truth and moves to a specific application of that truth. Harry Edwards in "Educating Black Athletes" begins with a general statement: "Student athletes . . . have informally agreed to a contract with the universities they attend: athletic performance in exchange for an education. The athletes have kept their part of the bargain; the universities have not." In the rest of the essay, Edwards provides the evidence that has led him to that conclusion.

The simplest form of a deductive argument is the *syllogism*, a three-step argument involving a major premise, a minor premise, and a conclusion. Few essays—either those you write or those you read—can be reduced to a syllogism. Our thought patterns are rarely so logical, our reasoning rarely so precise. Although few essays state a syllogism explicitly, syllogisms do plan a role in shaping an argument. For example, both Jesse Jackson and Martin Luther King, Jr. begin with the same syllogism, even though it is not directly stated in either selection:

Major premise: All people should have equal opportunities.
Minor premise: Blacks are people.
Conclusion: Blacks should have equal opportunities.

Despite the fact that a syllogism is a precise structural form, you should not assume that a written argument will imitate it; that the first paragraph or group of paragraphs will contain a major premise; the next, a minor premise; and the final, a conclusion. Syllogisms can be basic to an argument without being a framework upon which it is constructed.

No matter how you structure your argument, one final consideration is important. Since the purpose of argumentation is to get a reader to agree with your position or to act in a particular way, it is always essential to end your paper decisively. Endings can be used in a variety of ways. You can end with a call to action. Martin Luther King's speech rises to an eloquent, rhythmical exhortation to his people to continue to fight until they are "free at last." You can end with a serious question. Lewis Thomas concludes by questioning "what has gone wrong in the minds of statesmen in this generation" that has allowed the stockpiling of nuclear weapons. You can end by suggesting what steps are necessary. The final section of Edwards's essay outlines some ways in which America must demonstrate "a greater concern for and commitment to educational quality."

508

Sample Student Essay

ARGUMENT AND PERSUASION

Beth Jaffe decided to tackle a subject on the minds of many career-minded, dollar-conscious college students: why do you have to take so many courses outside of your major? Beth's argument is sure to arouse the attention of every advocate of a liberal arts education, and you might consider exploring the subject for a paper.

EARLIER DRAFT

Reducing College Requirements

With the high costs of college still on the rise, it is not fair to make college students pay for courses labeled ''requirements'' which are not part of their major. Although many students want a well-rounded college education, many cannot afford to pay for one. By eliminating all of the requirements that do not pertain to a student's major, college costs could be cut tremendously. At the University of Delaware, for example, a student in the College of Arts and Science is required to take twelve credits of arts and humanities, twelve of culture and institutions of time, twelve of human beings and their environment, and thirteen of natural phenomena or science which include at least one lab. Although some of their major courses may fit into these categories, many others do not. Frequently students do not like and are not interested in the courses which fit into the four categories and feel they are wasting their money by paying for courses they do not enjoy, do not put much work into, and usually do not get much out of. It should be an option to the student to take these extra courses. Why should a humanities or social studies major have to take biology or chemistry? Many of these students thought their struggle with science was over after high school

```
only to come to college and find yet more
''requirements'' in the sciences. Students are getting
degrees in one area of concentration. They should be
able to take only courses in their field of study and
not have to waste their money on courses they have no
desire to take.
```

Beth's essay, with her permission, was duplicated and discussed in class. Not surprisingly, it provoked a lively reaction. One student asked Beth whether she was serious and exactly what it was that she was proposing. Beth admitted that she did not advocate turning a college education into career training but that she had a number of friends who were deeply in debt because of their four-year education. "Why not just cut some requirements?" Beth asked. Several other students then suggested that since she did not really advocate an extreme position, maybe she could find a compromise proposal. Her instructor added that she might find a way of rewording her remarks about science classes. Few people, after all, are sympathetic to a position that seems to say, "I don't want to do that. It's too hard. It's too boring."

When Beth revised her paper, she tried to follow the advice the class had offered. In addition, she made the problem vivid by using her roommate as an example and by pointing out what specifically might be saved by the Jaffe proposal.

REVISED DRAFT

```
            Lowering the Cost of a College Education
        When my roommate graduates in June, she will be
$10,000 in debt. The debt did not come from spring
breaks in Fort Lauderdale or a new car. It came from
four years of college expenses, expenses that were not
covered by the money she earned as a part-time waitress
or by the small scholarship she was awarded annually.
So now in June at age 21, with her first full-time job
(assuming she gets one), Alison can start repaying her
student loans.
```

Alison's case is certainly not unusual. In fact, because she attends a state-assisted university, her debt is less than it might be. We cannot expect education to get cheaper. We cannot expect government scholarship programs to get larger. We cannot ask that students go deeper and deeper into debt. We need a new way of combating this cost problem. We need the Jaffe proposal.

If colleges would eliminate some of the general education course requirements, college costs could be substantially lowered. At the University of Delaware, for example, a student at the College of Arts and Science is required to take twelve credits of arts and humanities, twelve of culture and the institutions of time, twelve of human beings and their environment, and thirteen of natural phenomena or science, including at least one laboratory course. Approximately half of these requirements are fulfilled by courses which are required for particular majors. The others are not, and these are likely to be courses that students are not interested in and so get little out of.

If some of these requirements were eliminated, a student would need approximately twenty-five credits less for bachelor's degree. If a student took a heavier load or went to summer school, he or she could graduate either one or two semesters earlier. The result would cut college costs by anywhere from one-eighth to one-fourth.

The Jaffe proposal does decrease the likelihood that a college graduate will receive a well-rounded education. On the other hand, it allows students to concentrate their efforts in courses which they feel are relevant. Perhaps most important, it helps reduce the burden that escalating college costs have placed on all of us.

Some Things to Remember

1. Choose a subject that allows for the possibility of persuading your reader. Avoid emotionally charged subjects that resist logical examination.

2. Analyze your audience. Who are your readers? What do they already know about your subject? How are they likely to feel about it? How impartial or prejudiced are they going to be?

3. Make a list of the evidence or reasons you will use in your argument. Analyze each piece of evidence to see how effective it might be in achieving your end.

4. Honest emotion is fair, but avoid anything that is distorted, inaccurate, or inflammatory. Argue with solid, reasonable, fair, and relevant evidence.

5. Avoid the common logical fallacies listed in this introduction.

6. Make a list of all the possible counterarguments or objections your audience might have. Think of ways in which you can respond to those objections.

7. Decide how to structure your essay. You can begin with a position and then provide evidence. You can begin with the evidence and end with a conclusion. Which structure seems to fit your subject and evidence better?

8. End forcibly. Conclusions are what listeners and readers are most likely to remember. Repeat or restate your position. Drive home the importance of your argument.

Why Blacks Need Affirmative Action

JESSE JACKSON

Jesse Jackson was born in Greenville, South Carolina, in 1941. He received a B.A. in sociology in 1964 from the North Carolina Agricultural and Technical State University and later studied at the Chicago Theological Seminary, eventually becoming a Baptist minister in 1968. Jackson has been president of the National Rainbow Coalition since 1984 and a presidential candidate in the elections of 1984 and 1988. A collection of his speeches, sermons, and essays, Straight from the Heart, *was published in 1987 and a collection of his 1988 campaign speeches and memorabilia,* Keep Hope Alive, *appeared in 1988. He has been a syndicated columnist for the Los Angeles* Times Syndicate *since 1989 and has also hosted a talk show, ''Jesse Jackson,'' a forum for contemporary social and political issues, since 1990.*

In this selection from an essay that appeared in Regulation *(September/October 1978), a publication of the American Enterprise Institute for Public Policy, Jackson argues the need for affirmative action programs. Jackson's remarks were prompted in part by the legal testing of such programs, especially in the Bakke case. In 1973 and 1974 Allan Bakke, a white male, was denied admission to the Davis Medical College of the University of California. In both years, other, less qualified applicants were accepted through a special admissions program that reserved 16 places out of a total class of 100 for nonwhite applicants. Claiming that he was denied equal protection of the law and hence was a victim of reverse discrimination, Bakke sued, and his case was eventually heard by the United States Supreme Court. In 1978, the court ruled that Bakke had been discriminated against and had to be admitted to the school. At the same time, the court held that affirmative action programs could legally continue only if they were not based on a rigid quota system.*

ACCORDING TO a recent publication of the Equal Employment   1
Opportunity Commission, at the present rate of "progress" it

will take forty-three years to end job discrimination—hardly a reasonable timetable.

2   If our goal is educational and economic equity and parity—and it is—then we need affirmative action to catch up. We are behind as a result of discrimination and denial of opportunity. There is one white attorney for every 680 whites, but only one black attorney for every 4,000 blacks, one white physician for every 659 whites, but only one black physician for every 5,000 blacks; and one white dentist for every 1,900 whites, but only one black dentist for every 8,400 blacks. Less that 1 percent of all engineers—or of all practicing chemists—is black. Cruel and uncompassionate injustice created gaps like these. We need creative justice and compassion to help us close them.

3   Actually, in the U.S. context, "reverse discrimination" is illogical and a contradiction in terms. Never in the history of mankind has a majority, with power, engaged in programs and written laws that discriminate against itself. The only thing whites are giving up because of affirmative action is unfair advantage—something that was unnecessary in the first place.

4   Blacks are not making progress at the expense of whites, as new accounts make it seem. There are 49 percent more whites in medical school today and 64 percent more whites in law school than there were when affirmative action programs began some eight years ago.

5   In a recent column, William Raspberry raised an interesting questions. Commenting on the *Bakke* case, he asked, "What if, instead of setting aside 16 of 100 slots, we added 16 slots to the 100?" That, he suggested, would allow blacks to make progress and would not interfere with what whites already have. He then went on to point out that this, in fact, is exactly what has happened in law and medical schools. In 1968, the year before affirmative action programs began to get under way, 9,571 whites and 282 members of minority groups entered U.S. medical schools. In 1976, the figures were 14,213 and 1,400 respectively. Thus, under affirmative action, the number of "white places" actually rose by 49 percent: white access to medical training was not diminished, but substantially increased. The trend was even more marked in law schools. In 1969, the first year for which reliable figures are available, 2,933 minority-

group members were enrolled; in 1976, the number was up to 8,484. But during the same period, law school enrollment for whites rose from 65,453 to 107,064—an increase of 64 percent. In short, it is a myth that blacks are making progress at white expense.

Allan Bakke did not really challenge preferential treatment   6 in general, for he made no challenge to the preferential treatment accorded to the children of the rich, the alumni and the faculty, or to athletes or the very talented—only to minorities.

QUESTIONS ON SUBJECT AND PURPOSE

1. What is affirmative action? How does it aid members of minority groups?
2. What is "educational and economic equity and parity"? What would it take to achieve both?
3. What is reverse discrimination? According to Jackson, does it exist?
4. What is Jackson's purpose in this essay? Do you think he achieves that purpose effectively?

QUESTIONS ON STRATEGY AND AUDIENCE

1. How does Jackson's argument differ from Mannes's in "Wasteland" or from Rodriguez's in "None of This Is Fair," two other essays in this chapter?
2. How are Jackson's statistics particularly relevant to the argument he is making? Is there any difference between the kind of statistics used in paragraph 2 and those used in paragraph 5?
3. Would Jackson's argument be equally effective with any audience? Why or why not?

QUESTIONS ON VOCABULARY AND STYLE

1. Characterize the tone of Jackson's argument. How does he sound? How do the language, examples, and sentence structures contribute to achieving that tone?
2. How does Jackson use parallel structures in paragraphs 2 and 5 to make his argument clearer?

3. Be able to define the following words or phrases: *equity* (paragraph 2), *parity* (2), *affirmative action* (2), *reverse discrimination* (3), *Bakke case* (5).

WRITING SUGGESTIONS

1. In a paragraph argue for the justice of affirmative action programs. Do not use statistics. Instead appeal to more basic and general human values.

2. Are minorities and women equally represented on the faculty of your college or university? Check the proportions and then in an essay argue for or against the need to achieve "educational and economic equity and parity." Assume that your essay will be published in the student newspaper.

Prewriting:

a. Before you begin writing you will need accurate information. An Affirmative Action Office can provide those statistics. (Check a telephone directory to locate that office.)

b. Statistics about the undergraduate population of your college will also help. The admissions office or the dean of students should be able to provide a breakdown by sex, race, and nationality. That information will also help you to define your audience.

c. On the basis of this evidence and your own feelings, decide upon a position. Make a list of the evidence and the reasons you will use in your paper.

d. Copy that list onto the left-hand side of a separate sheet of paper. On the right-hand side, try to anticipate the objections that your audience might have.

Rewriting:

a. Find a classmate or roommate to read your essay. Ask that reader to evaluate your position. Does your reader agree? Why or why not? Listen carefully to your reader's reactions.

b. Is your essay structured inductively or deductively? Briefly outline a new strategy. Which of the two arrangements seems more effective? Ask your reader to evaluate both strategies.

c. Look at your conclusion. Arguments—either emotional or logical—need to end forcefully. Freewrite a totally different ending to your essay. Ask your reader to evaluate both.

3. Similar statistical information is available for women, or Hispanics, or Native Americans, or Chinese-Americans, or any other minority in the United States. Choose one such group and research the progress that has been made during the last 10 to 20 years. Have affirmative action programs benefited that minority? Why or why not? Using your research, in an essay argue for the effectiveness (or ineffectiveness) of such programs for this minority. Be sure to document your sources.

Wasteland

MARYA MANNES

Marya Mannes (1904-1990), novelist, essayist, and journalist, was born in New York City. She worked as a feature editor for Vogue *magazine and later, during World War II, acted as an intelligence analyst for the United States government. She held a variety of positions such as staff writer for* The Reporter, *feature editor for* Glamour *magazine, and columnist for* The New York Times. *Her publications include* Message *from a* Stranger, *a novel (1948);* Subverse, *a collection of satirical verse (1959); and* Out of My Time, *an autobiography (1971). She received many awards for her biting and satiric magazine essays on American arts, education, and morals. Many of those essays were published in the collections* But Will It Sell? *(1953),* More in Anger *(1958), and* The New York I Know *(1961). In this selection from* More in Anger, *Mannes offers an emotional indictment of our tendency to pollute the environment.*

1   CANS. BEER CANS. Glinting on the verge of a million miles of roadways, lying in scrub, grass, dirt, leaves, sand, mud, but never hidden. Piels, Rheingold, Ballantine, Schaefer, Schlitz, shining in the sun or picked up by moonlight or the beams of headlights at night; washed by rain or flattened by wheels, but never dulled, never buried, never destroyed. Here is the mark of savages, the testament of wasters, the stain of prosperity.

2   Who are these men who defile the grassy borders of our roads and lanes, who pollute our ponds, who spoil the purity of our ocean beaches with the empty vessels of their thirst? Who are the men who make these vessels in millions and then say, "Drink—and discard"? What society is this that can afford to cast away a million tons of metal and to make of wild and fruitful land a garbage heap?

3   What manner of men and women need thirty feet of steel and two hundred horsepower to take them, singly, to their small destinations? Who demand that what they eat is wrapped so that forests are cut down to make the paper that is thrown away,

518

and what they smoke and chew is sealed so that the sealers can be tossed in gutters and caught in twigs and grass?

What kind of men can afford to make the streets of their   4
towns and cities hideous with neon at night, and their roadways hideous with signs by day, wasting beauty; who leave the carcasses of cars to rot in heaps; who spill their trash into ravines and make smoking mountains of refuse for the town's rats? What manner of men choke off the life in rivers, streams, and lakes with the waste of their produce, making poison of water?

Who is as rich as that? Slowly the wasters and despoilers   5
are impoverishing our land, our nature, and our beauty, so that there will not be one beach, one hill, one lane, one meadow, one forest free from the debris of man and the stigma of his improvidence.

Who is so rich that he can squander forever the wealth of   6
earth and water for the trivial needs of vanity or the compulsive demands of greed; or so prosperous in land that he can sacrifice nature for unnatural desires? The earth we abuse and the living things we kill will, in the end, take their revenge; for in exploiting their presence we are diminishing our future.

And what will we leave behind us when we are long dead?   7
Temples? Amphorae? Sunken treasure?

Or mountains of twisted, rusted steel, canyons of plastic   8
containers, and a million miles of shores garlanded, not with the lovely wrack of the sea, but with the cans and bottles and light bulbs and boxes of a people who conserved their convenience at the expense of their heritage; and whose ephemeral prosperity was built on waste.

QUESTIONS ON SUBJECT AND PURPOSE

1. What is Mannes's thesis? Summarize it in a single sentence.
2. How many examples of waste does Mannes cite? What do they have in common?
3. What purpose does Mannes want to achieve? Does it work? How do you as a reader respond to each paragraph?

QUESTIONS ON STRATEGY AND AUDIENCE

1. In what way is Mannes's essay persuasive? How does it differ

from a formal argument? What would it take to make it into one?

2. In paragraph 5, Mannes writes: "There will not be one beach, one hill, one lane, one meadow, one forest free from the debris of man and the stigma of his improvidence." Does that seem an accurate statement to make? Is it exaggerated? Why would Mannes make it?

3. Who is Mannes's audience? What assumptions does she make of it? How can you tell from the essay?

QUESTIONS ON VOCABULARY AND STYLE

1. How frequently does Mannes use rhetorical questions? What is the effect of such a device? How is it appropriate for her essay?

2. Why does Mannes use such a short paragraph (7)? Why not merge it with the longer paragraph that follows?

3. Be able to define the following words: *verge* (paragraph 1), *defile* (2), *despoiler* (5), *stigma* (5), *improvidence* (5), *squander* (6), *amphorae* (7), *garlanded* (8), *ephemeral* (8).

WRITING SUGGESTIONS

1. Select a place on campus or in town that shows the effect of what Mannes is saying. In a paragraph describe the place with the intention of persuading your readers to do something about pollution.

2. Select one of the other examples of waste that Mannes finds —or an example of your own—and in an essay persuade your reader to *do* something about the problem. Some possible examples from Mannes's essay include:

   a. large cars and trucks
   b. abandoned cars
   c. excessive packaging

Prewriting:

   a. Before you choose a subject, spend a day looking for examples of waste in your environment. As you walk around your campus or your neighborhood, what do you see? Take notes.

520

b. Once you have a subject, brainstorm a possible outline for your essay. Look at your notes. Where can your examples be placed in your proposed structure?

c. Using your outline as a guide, freewrite for 15 minutes about each point that you wish to make.

Rewriting:

a. Make a copy of your essay, and highlight in one color all emotionally charged words and phrases. Highlight in another color all factual examples. Is your argument based on emotion or factual evidence?

b. Look at all of the emotionally charged words and phrases. How will your audience react to these? Do you avoid distorted or inflammatory statements?

c. What exactly do you want your reader to do about this problem? Do you make that call to action clear in your conclusion? If not, try writing another ending.

3. What has the community in which you live (or in which you attend school) done about recycling? Research the local options that are available, and then argue for an extension of those efforts. Make specific, workable recommendations. Remember that while your audience will probably not be hostile, it might be indifferent. Direct your essay toward an audience of local residents.

Women Know How to Fight

RUTH WESTHEIMER

Ruth Westheimer, who is famous for her 4' 7" frame, German accent, and sex advice on television and radio, was born in 1928 in Frankfurt, Germany, to Jewish parents. Sent off to a Swiss school at the age of ten, she became an orphan when her parents presumably were killed in a Nazi concentration camp during World War II. After the war, she immigrated to Palestine and joined the Haganah, a Jewish militant group that fought for an independent Jewish state and unlimited Jewish immigration. In 1950 she moved to Paris, France, and earned a degree in psychology from the Sorbonne—without even a high school education. She moved to New York City in 1956 where she earned an M.A. at the New School for Social Research and a Ed.D. from Columbia University. Before hosting her own radio show ("Sexually Speaking," 1980) and television shows ("Good Sex with Doctor Ruth Westheimer," 1984; "The Doctor Ruth Show," 1985; "Ask Doctor Ruth," 1987), she worked at a Planned Parenthood clinic in Harlem, New York, and established her own family counseling practice, which she continues today. Her books include Dr. Ruth's Guide to Good Sex *(1983);* First Love: A Young People's Guide to Sexual Information *(1985);* Dr. Ruth's Guide for Married Lovers *(1986); and* All in a Lifetime *(1987), her autobiography. She has written a monthly column for* Playgirl, *has lectured around the country, has her own board game, and has acted in a movie,* One Woman or Two *(1986). Currently, she writes a syndicated advice column, "Ask Dr. Ruth," and is a contributing editor to* Redbook Magazine. *"Women Know How to Fight" was originally published in* The New York Times *on February 11, 1990. She writes: "All that is keeping women out of combat is the same discrimination we've faced breaking into every other male-dominated position."*

1   As AMERICANS, we can count ourselves lucky that in this century the wars we have engaged in have barely touched our soil. But in all wars, there is at least one country that has to endure its

ravages, and the women and children of that land face nearly the same hardships as the men who do the actual fighting.

Since women don't escape war, and the nature of combat has changed so that the need for upper body strength is no longer preeminent, all that is keeping women out of combat is the same discrimination we've faced breaking into every other male-dominated position.   2

I come to this conclusion from my own experiences. At the age of sixteen I immigrated to Palestine from Europe, where I became a member of the Haganah, the main underground army of the Jews. I learned to assemble a rifle in the dark and was trained as a sniper so that I could hit the center of the target time after time. As it happened, I never did get into actual combat, but that didn't prevent my being severely wounded. I almost lost both my feet as a result of a bombing attack on Jerusalem.   3

Now were it up to me, I would abolish all warfare. But having lost my family at the hands of the Nazis, I know that we need our armed forces in order to protect our freedoms. And there is no reason why our troops have to be composed only of one sex.   4

My daughter, Miriam, lived in Israel for six years and underwent the same rigorous training as a member of the Israeli Army as the men. Not only was it something she wanted to do for Israel, but she also gained a lot from her experience. She shared in the warmth of the army's esprit de corps and tested herself in ways she never would have done in America.   5

When the first armies were formed, the course of battle took courage, which women share equally with men, and strength, which we do not. But though I am only 4 feet 7 inches tall, with a gun in my hand I am the equal of a soldier who's 6 feet 7—and perhaps even at a slight advantage, as I make a smaller target.   6

This is not to say hand-to-hand fighting is a thing of the past, but it is no longer the predominant method. That a general would want the biggest, strongest men in the front lines goes without question, but it is also true that women could fill many, many other roles—from driving a tank to dropping a bomb to   7 firing a cannon to acting as snipers. A fighting spirit is the most important ingredient in the makeup of a fighter.

8   Of course, there are those men who say women don't belong on the battlefield for the same reasons they said we didn't belong in the corporate board room, the assembly line, the police force, or the executive mansion. They're worried that the battle of the sexes will affect the outcome of the battle. While I'm a romantic who likes it when a man offers me flowers, when I'm wearing my hat as psychologist or interviewer or whatever, I can be as tough as the next guy—and if you don't believe me, just ask anyone I've gone up against.

9   Women are demanding equal rights, and most deservedly are getting them. But with those rights come equal responsibilities. Until these, too, are conferred, I don't believe men will ever consider women their true equals.

QUESTIONS ON SUBJECT AND PURPOSE

1. What does Westheimer want women to be able to do?
2. In what way does Westheimer link women's roles in the military to women's roles in society?
3. Obviously an editorial in a newspaper will not influence the policy of the U.S. government. Why then write such an editorial? What might Westheimer hope to accomplish?

QUESTIONS ON STRATEGY AND AUDIENCE

1. What role does Westheimer's personal experience play in her essay? Why might she refer to those experiences?
2. Is Westheimer's argument structured inductively or deductively?
3. What assumptions could Westheimer make about her audience?

QUESTIONS ON VOCABULARY AND STYLE

1. On the basis of the essay itself, what can the reader tell about Westheimer? What type of personality does she project?
2. What associations do readers have with the word "discrimination?" When she implies that the practice of keeping

women out of combat roles is discriminatory, what reaction can Westheimer expect from her readers?

3. Be prepared to define the following words: *ravages* (paragraph 1), *preeminent* (2), *esprit de corps* (5).

WRITING SUGGESTIONS

1. In a paragraph describe a time when you encountered an obstacle because of your age, sex, race, religion, physical appearance, or socioeconomic status. Describe the experience briefly, and then argue against the unfairness of such discrimination.

2. Your local newspaper, hearing about your distinguished achievements in freshman English, has called, asking you to write an editorial opinion on a timely subject of your choice— either a local or a national issue. Do so.

Prewriting:

a. Go to your library and locate at least six examples of the type of editorial opinion that you have been asked to write. Study each to see how the writers approach the problem.

b. Make a list of subjects about which you feel strongly enough to want to express an opinion. Try freewriting for 10 minutes about each of the subjects.

c. Imagine your audience. What are they like? How are they going to react to what you are writing? Try to anticipate their objections to your argument by making a list of possible reactions.

Rewriting:

a. Did you organize your essay inductively or deductively? In a paragraph, written to yourself, define your choice of structure. Why was this structure the right choice for your essay?

b. Reread your essay. Remember that your audience will be a general one, but one that is likely to have definite opinions about this subject. Have you written to that general audience? Have you chosen your vocabulary and sentence structures with that audience in mind? Have you avoided inflammatory language?

c. An effective title is important to an essay. It should represent the essay but also attract a reader's attention. Write several possible titles for your essay. Ask a friend to comment on each.

3. Since World War I the United States has had women serving in the military, although the roles that those women have occupied have changed greatly. Research the history of women in the U.S. armed forces concentrating on how their roles have been defined over the years. Then formulate a thesis about the subject (for example, "The military has consistently discriminated against women" or "The military has led the way in providing equal opportunity for women") and argue for that thesis using the evidence you have uncovered in your research.

I Have a Dream

MARTIN LUTHER KING, JR.

Martin Luther King, Jr. (1929–1968) was born in Atlanta, the son of a Baptist minister. Ordained in his father's church in 1947, King received a doctorate in theology from Boston University in 1955. In that same year he achieved national prominence by leading the Montgomery, Alabama, bus boycott where he put into practice his ideas of nonviolent resistance derived from Thoreau and Gandhi. King joined the Southern Christian Leadership Conference in 1959 and became a central figure in the civil rights movement, organizing protests and marches, including the August 1963 ''March on Washington.'' King was Time's *1963 Man of the Year and was awarded the Nobel Peace Prize in 1964. He was assassinated in Memphis in 1968. His birthday, January 15, is celebrated as a national holiday.*

King's ''I Have a Dream'' speech was delivered at the Lincoln Memorial to an audience of 250,000 people who assembled in Washington, D.C., on August 28, 1963. That march, commemorating in part the hundredth anniversary of Lincoln's Emancipation Proclamation, was intended as an act of ''creative lobbying'' to win the support of Congress and the president for pending civil rights legislation. It was King's most carefully crafted speech, and he spent days worrying over each paragraph, sentence, and mark of punctuation. The final product is one of the most memorable and moving examples of American oratory.

FIVE SCORE years ago, a great American, in whose symbolic shadow we stand, signed the Emancipation Proclamation. This momentous decree came as a great beacon light of hope to millions of Negro slaves who had been seared in the flames of withering injustice. It came as a joyous daybreak to end the long night of captivity.

But one hundred years later, we must face the tragic fact that the Negro is still not free. One hundred years later, the life of the Negro is still sadly crippled by the manacles of segregation and the chains of discrimination. One hundred years later, the

Negro lives on a lonely island of poverty in the midst of a vast ocean of material prosperity. One hundred years later, the Negro is still languishing in the corners of American society and finds himself an exile in his own land. So we have come here today to dramatize an appalling condition.

3   In a sense we have come to our nation's capital to cash a check. When the architects of our republic wrote the magnificent words of the Constitution and the Declaration of Independence, they were signing a promissory note to which every American was to fall heir. This note was a promise that all men would be guaranteed the unalienable rights of life, liberty, and the pursuit of happiness.

4   It is obvious today that America has defaulted on this promissory note insofar as her citizens of color are concerned. Instead of honoring this sacred obligation, America has given the Negro people a bad check; a check which has come back marked "insufficient funds." But we refuse to believe that the bank of justice is bankrupt. We refuse to believe that there are insufficient funds in the great vaults of opportunity of this nation. So we have come to cash this check—a check that will give us upon demand the riches of freedom and the security of justice. We have also come to this hallowed spot to remind America of the fierce urgency of *now*. This is no time to engage in the luxury of cooling off or to take the tranquilizing drugs of gradualism. *Now* is the time to make real the promises of Democracy. *Now* is the time to rise from the dark and desolate valley of segregation to the sunlit path of racial justice. *Now* is the time to open the doors of opportunity to all of God's children. *Now* is the time to lift our nation from the quicksands of racial injustice to the solid rock of brotherhood.

5   It would be fatal for the nation to overlook the urgency of the moment and to underestimate the determination of the Negro. This sweltering summer of the Negro's legitimate discontent will not pass until there is an invigorating autumn of freedom and equality. 1963 is not an end, but a beginning. Those who hope that the Negro needed to blow off steam and will now be content will have a rude awakening if the nation returns to business as usual. There will be neither rest nor tranquillity in America until the Negro is granted his citizenship

rights. The whirlwinds of revolt will continue to shake the foundations of our nation until the bright day of justice emerges.

But there is something that I must say to my people who   6
stand on the warm threshold which leads into the palace of justice. In the process of gaining our rightful place we must not be guilty of wrongful deeds. Let us not seek to satisfy our thirst for freedom by drinking from the cup of bitterness and hatred. We must forever conduct our struggle on the high plane of dignity and discipline. We must not allow our creative protest to degenerate into physical violence. Again and again we must rise to the majestic heights of meeting physical force with soul force. The marvelous new militancy which has engulfed the Negro community must not lead us to a distrust of all white people, for many of our white brothers, as evidenced by their presence here today, have come to realize that their destiny is tied up with our destiny and their freedom is inextricably bound to our freedom. We cannot walk alone.

And as we walk, we must make the pledge that we shall   7
march ahead. We cannot turn back. There are those who are asking the devotees of civil rights, "When will you be satisfied?" We can never be satisfied as long as the Negro is the victim of the unspeakable horrors of police brutality. We can never be satisfied as long as our bodies, heavy with the fatigue of travel, cannot gain lodging in the motels of the highways and the hotels of the cities. We cannot be satisfied as long as the Negro's basic mobility is from a smaller ghetto to a larger one. We can never be satisfied as long as a Negro in Mississippi cannot vote and a Negro in New York believes he has nothing for which to vote. No, no, we are not satisfied, and we will not be satisfied until justice rolls down like waters and righteousness like a mighty stream.

I am not unmindful that some of you have come here out   8
of great trials and tribulations. Some of you have come fresh from narrow jail cells. Some of you have come from areas where your quest for freedom left you battered by the storms of persecution and staggered by the winds of police brutality. You have been the veterans of creative suffering. Continue to work with the faith that unearned suffering is redemptive.

Go back to Mississippi, go back to Alabama, go back to   9

South Carolina, go back to Georgia, go back to Louisiana, go back to the slums and ghettos of our northern cities, knowing that somehow this situation can and will be changed. Let us not wallow in the valley of despair.

10   I say to you today, my friends, that in spite of the difficulties and frustrations of the moment I still have a dream. It is a dream deeply rooted in the American dream.

11   I have a dream that one day this nation will rise up and live out the true meaning of its creed: ''We hold these truths to be self-evident: that all men are created equal.''

12   I have a dream that one day on the red hills of Georgia the sons of former slaves and the sons of former slave owners will be able to sit down together at the table of brotherhood.

13   I have a dream that one day even the state of Mississippi, a desert state sweltering with the heat of injustice and oppression, will be transformed into an oasis of freedom and justice.

14   I have a dream that my four little children will one day live in a nation where they will not be judged by the color of their skin but by the content of their character.

15   I have a dream today.

16   I have a dream that one day the state of Alabama, whose governor's lips are presently dripping with the words of interposition and nullification, will be transformed into a situation where little black boys and black girls will be able to join hands with little white boys and white girls and walk together as sisters and brothers.

17   I have a dream today.

18   I have a dream that one day every valley shall be exalted, every hill and mountain shall be made low, the rough places will be made plain, and the crooked places will be made straight, and the glory of the Lord shall be revealed, and all flesh shall see it together.

19   This is our hope. This is the faith with which I return to the South. With this faith we will be able to hew out of the mountain of despair a stone of hope. With this faith we will be able to transform the jangling discords of our nation into a beautiful symphony of brotherhood. With this faith we will be able to work together, to pray together, to struggle together, to go to

jail together, to stand up for freedom together, knowing that
we will be free one day.

This will be the day when all of God's children will be able   20
to sing with new meaning

> My country, 'tis of thee,
> Sweet land of liberty,
>   Of thee I sing:
> Land where my fathers died,
> Land of the pilgrims' pride,
> From every mountain-side
>   Let freedom ring.

And if America is to be a great nation this must become   21
true. So let freedom ring from the prodigious hilltops of New
Hampshire. Let freedom ring from the mighty mountains of
New York. Let freedom ring from the heightening Alleghenies
of Pennsylvania!

Let freedom ring from the snowcapped Rockies of Colo-   22
rado!

Let freedom ring from the curvaceous peaks of California!   23

But not only that; let freedom ring from Stone Mountain   24
of Georgia!

Let freedom ring from Lookout Mountain of Tennessee!   25

Let freedom ring from every hill and molehill of Mississippi.   26
From every mountainside, let freedom ring.

When we let freedom ring, when we let it ring from every   27
village and every hamlet, from every state and every city, we
will be able to speed up that day when all of God's children,
black men and white men, Jews and Gentiles, Protestants and
Catholics, will be able to join hands and sing in the words of
the old Negro spiritual, "Free at last! free at last! thank God
almighty, we are free at last!"

QUESTIONS ON SUBJECT AND PURPOSE

1. What is King's dream?
2. King's essay was a speech—delivered orally before thousands
   of marchers and millions of television viewers. How are its
   oral origins revealed in the written version?

3. In what way is King's speech an attempt at persuasion? Whom was he trying to persuade to do what?

QUESTIONS ON STRATEGY AND AUDIENCE

1. Why does King begin with the words "Five score years ago"? Why does he say at the end of paragraph 6, "We cannot walk alone"? What do such words have to do with the context of King's speech?
2. How does King structure his speech? Is there an inevitable order or movement? How effective is his conclusion?
3. What expectations does King have of his audience? How do you know that?

QUESTIONS ON VOCABULARY AND STYLE

1. How many examples of figurative speech (images, metaphors, similes) can you find in the speech? What effect does such figurative language have?
2. The speech is full of parallel structures. See how many you can find. Why does King use so many?
3. Be able to define the following words: *seared* (paragraph 1), *manacles* (2), *languishing* (2), *promissory note* (3), *unalienable* (3), *invigorating* (5), *inextricably* (6), *tribulations* (8), *nullification* (16), *prodigious* (21).

WRITING SUGGESTIONS

1. In a paragraph argue for equality for a minority on your campus—it should be a serious concern (the handicapped, a sexual, racial, or religious minority, returning adults, commuters).
2. Expand your subject begun in suggestion 1 above to essay length.

   Prewriting:

   a. To write convincingly about such a problem you will need specific information drawn from your own experience and/ or the experiences of others. Interview several members of the minority group about whom you are writing. Take notes on index cards.

   b. Organize your cards by sorting them into groups according to topic. Make a list of those topics, and then convert the list into a working outline.

c. What objections or reservations might your audience have? Try to imagine a critic's objections to your essay.

Rewriting:

a. Highlight all the specific evidence in your essay. Remember that details make an argument effective. Have you included enough? Each body paragraph needs details and examples.

b. Check each paragraph for a unified idea. Is there a single focused idea controlling the paragraph? Jot down a key word or phrase for each paragraph.

c. Find someone to read your essay. Does your reader find your argument fair? Convincing? If the reader disagrees, ask for specific reasons why.

3. In order to comply with federal guidelines, colleges have had to make extensive structural modifications to grant handicapped people equal access to all facilities. Research the problem on your campus. What has been done? What remains to be done? Argue for the importance of such changes.

On Medicine and the Bomb

LEWIS THOMAS

Lewis Thomas was born in Flushing, New York, in 1913 and after graduating from Princeton and Harvard Medical School worked as a pathologist and medical administrator at Tulane University, Bellevue Hospital, the University of Minnesota, and Yale University School of Medicine. From 1973 to 1983 he held key administrative positions at Memorial Sloan-Kettering Cancer Center. Thomas's essays have appeared frequently in scientific journals, and in 1971 he began the column "Notes of a Biology Watcher" for the New England Journal of Medicine. *His first collection of these columns,* The Lives of a Cell *(1974), won the National Book Award and was a best seller. Later books are* The Medusa and the Snail *(1979);* The Youngest Science *(1983), a memoir of his medical career; and* Late Night Thoughts on Listening to Mahler's Ninth Symphony *(1983). Recently, he has published* Et Cetera, Et Cetera: Notes of a Word-Watcher *(1990), a collection of essays about the genealogies of certain words and how language traces our social history. In "On Medicine and the Bomb," from Thomas's collection* Late Night Thoughts on Listening to Mahler's Ninth Symphony, *he explains that medical advances made in treating cancer, burn, and trauma victims have "nothing whatever to offer, not even a token benefit, in the event of thermonuclear war."*

1   IN THE COMPLICATED but steadily illuminating and linked fields of immunology, genetics, and cancer research, it has become a routine technical maneuver to transplant the bone-marrow cells of one mouse to a mouse of a different line. This can be accomplished by irradiating the recipient mouse with a lethal dose of X rays, enough to destroy all the immune cells and their progenitors, and replacing them with the donor's marrow cells. If the new cells are close enough in their genetic labels to the recipient's own body cells, the marrow will flourish and the mouse will live out a normal life span. Of course, if the donor cells are not closely matched, they will recognize the difference

between themselves and the recipient's tissues, and the result, the so-called graft-versus-host reaction, will kill the recipient in the same way that a skin graft from a foreign mouse is destroyed by the lymphocytes of a recipient.

It is a neat biological trick, made possible by detailed knowledge of the genetics involved in graft rejection. Any new bone-marrow cells can survive and repopulate the recipient's defense apparatus provided the markers on the cell surfaces are the same as those of the donor, and precise techniques are now available for identifying these markers in advance. 2

Something like this can be done in human beings, and the technique of bone-marrow transplantation is now becoming available for patients whose marrows are deficient for one reason or another. It is especially useful in the treatment of leukemia, where the elimination of leukemic cells by X ray and chemotherapy sometimes causes the simultaneous destruction of the patient's own immune cells, which must then be replaced if the patient is to survive. It is a formidable procedure, requiring the availability of tissue-match donors (usually members of the patient's family), and involving extremely expensive and highly specialized physical facilities—rooms equipped for absolute sterility to prevent infection while the new cells are beginning to propagate. Not many hospitals are outfitted with units for this kind of work, perhaps twenty or twenty-five in the United States, and each of them can take on only a few patients at a time. The doctors and nurses who work in such units are among the most specialized of clinical professionals, and there are not many of them. All in all, it is an enormously costly venture, feasible in only a few places but justifiable by the real prospect of new knowledge from the associated research going on in each unit, and of course by the lifesaving nature of the procedure when it works. 3

This, then, is the scale on which contemporary medicine possesses a technology for the treatment of lethal X-irradiation. 4

The therapy of burns has improved considerably in recent years. Patients with extensively burned skin who would have died ten years ago are now, from time to time, being saved from death. The hospital facilities needed for this accomplishment are comparable, in their technical complexity and cost, to the 5 units used for bone-marrow transplantation. Isolation rooms with special atmospheric controls to eliminate all microbes from the air are needed, plus teams of trained professionals to oversee all the countless details of management. It is still a discouraging undertaking, requiring doctors and nurses of high spirit and determination, but it works often enough to warrant the installation of such units in a limited number of medical centers. Some of these places can handle as many as thirty or forty patients at a time, but no more than that number.

6   The surgical treatment of overwhelming trauma underwent a technological transformation during the Korean and Vietnam wars, and it is now possible to do all sorts of things to save the lives of injured people—arteries and nerves can be successfully reconnected, severed limbs sewn back in place, blood substitutes infused, shock prevented, massive damage to internal organs repaired. Here also, special units with highly trained people are essential, elaborate facilities for rapid transport to the hospital are crucial, and the number of patients that can be handled by a unit is minimal.

7   These are genuine advances in medical science. The medical profession can be proud of them, and the public can be confident that work of this kind will steadily improve in the future. The prospects for surviving various kinds of injury that used to be uniformly fatal are better now than at any other time in history.

8   If there were enough money, these things could be scaled up to meet the country's normal everyday needs with tailor-made centers for the treatment of radiation injury, burns, and massive trauma spotted here and there in all major urban centers, linked to outlying areas by helicopter ambulances. It would cost large sums to build and maintain, but the scores, maybe hundreds, of lives saved would warrant the cost.

9   The Department of Defense ought to have a vested interest in enhancing this array of technologies, and I suppose it does. I take it for granted that substantial sums are being spent from the R & D funds of that agency to improve matters still further. In any conventional war, the capacity to rescue injured personnel from death on the battlefield does more than simply

restore manpower to the lines: its effect on troop morale has traditionally been incalculable.

But I wonder if the hearts of the long-range planners in DOD can really be in it. *10*

Military budgets have to be put together with the same *11* analytic scrutiny of potential costs versus benefits that underlies the construction of civilian budgets, allowing for the necessarily different meanings assigned by the military to the terms "cost" and "benefit." It is at least agreed that money should not be spent on things that will turn out to be of no use at all. The people in the Pentagon offices and their counterparts in the Kremlin where the questions of coping with war injuries are dealt with must be having a hard time of it these days, looking ahead as they must look to the possibility of thermonuclear war. Any sensible analyst in such an office would be tempted to scratch off all the expense items related to surgical care of the irradiated, burned, and blasted, the men, women, and children with empty bone marrows and vaporized skin. What conceivable benefit can come from sinking money in hospitals subject to instant combustion, only capable of salvaging, at their intact best, a few hundred of the victims who will be lying out there in the hundreds of thousands? There exists no medical technology that can cope with the certain outcome of just one small, neat, so-called tactical bomb exploded over a battlefield. As for the problem raised by a single large bomb, say a twenty-megaton missile (equivalent to approximately two thousand Hiroshimas) dropped on New York City or Moscow, with the dead and dying in the millions, what would medical technology be good for? As the saying goes, forget it. Think of something else. Get a computer running somewhere in a cave, to estimate the likely numbers of the lucky dead.

The doctors of the world know about this, of course. They *12* have known about it since the 1945 Hiroshima and Nagasaki "episodes," but it has dawned on them only in the last few years that the public at large may not understand. Some of the physicians in this country and abroad are forming new organizations for the declared purpose of making it plain to everyone that modern medicine has nothing whatever to offer, not even a token benefit, in the event of thermonuclear war. Unlike their response to other conceivable disasters, they do not talk of the need for more research or ask for more money to expand existing facilities. What they say is, in effect, count us out.

13   It is not a problem that has any real connection to politics. Doctors are not necessarily pacifists, and they come in all sorts of ideological stripes. What they have on their minds and should be trying to tell the world, in the hope that their collective professional opinion will gain public attention and perhaps catch the ears of political and military leaders everywhere, is simply this: if you go ahead with this business, the casualties you will instantly produce are beyond the reach of any health-care system. Since such systems here and abroad are based in urban centers, they will vanish in the first artificial suns, but even if they were miraculously to survive they could make no difference, not even a marginal difference.

14   I wish the psychiatrists and social scientists were further along in their fields than they seem to be. We need, in a hurry, some professionals who can tell us what has gone wrong in the minds of statesmen in this generation. How is it possible for so many people with the outward appearance of steadiness and authority, intelligent and convincing enough to have reached the highest positions in the governments of the world, to have lost so completely their sense of responsibility for the human beings to whom they are accountable? Their obsession with stockpiling nuclear armaments and their urgency in laying out detailed plans for using them have, at the core, aspects of what we would be calling craziness in other people, under other circumstances. Just before they let fly everything at their disposal, and this uniquely intelligent species begins to go down, it would be a small comfort to understand how it happened to happen. Our descendants, if there are any, will surely want to know.

QUESTIONS ON SUBJECT AND PURPOSE

1. What is the link between medicine and the bomb? Can medicine cope with the bomb? Why or why not?

2. How does the problem of "cost" and "benefit" apply in this situation?

3. What is the purpose of Thomas's final paragraph? How is this an appropriate conclusion to his essay?

QUESTIONS ON STRATEGY AND AUDIENCE

1. Why does Thomas begin his essay with three examples of medical progress? How does each relate to the larger issue Thomas is discussing?

2. In what way can this be seen as an argument? Does Thomas intend it to be one? How can you tell?

3. What is the effect of paragraph 10? Why is it so short?

4. What assumptions does Thomas make about his audience? How do those assumptions influence or shape his essay?

QUESTIONS ON VOCABULARY AND STYLE

1. Characterize Thomas's tone in the essay. Is he objective, militant, resigned, angry? Can you find specific evidence to support your characterization?

2. What is the effect of short, informal sentences such as those used at the end of paragraphs 11 and 12? Why are such sentences appropriate at these points in the essay?

3. Be able to define the following words: *immunology* (paragraph 1), *progenitor* (1), *lymphocytes* (1), *trauma* (6), *R & D funds* (9), *tactical bomb* (11).

WRITING SUGGESTIONS

1. To a certain extent this is an argument based on fact: medicine cannot cope with thermonuclear war. But what can be done? Write a persuasive paragraph or paragraphs in which you argue for the need for nuclear weapons or for the need to abolish nuclear weapons.

2. As thermonuclear devices proliferate in nations around the world, the threat of an accident or of intentional use of such weapons increases. Write a persuasive essay about the dangers of any nation's maintaining thermonuclear weapons—either offensive or defensive. Remember that your audience always assumes that such a large issue is out of its hands anyway.

539

Prewriting:

a. Visit your college's library since you will need some background information at the very least about the number of countries that currently have thermonuclear devices.

b. What action or reaction do you want to elicit in your audience? Write a specific statement.

c. Will you use an inductive or a deductive argument? Make a list of the advantages or disadvantages of both arrangements.

Rewriting:

a. Check each paragraph in your essay to see if it has an explicit or implicit topic sentence. Underline that sentence or write the implicit topic sentence alongside the paragraph.

b. Ask a peer reader to evaluate your essay. Is it persuasive? What does it ask the reader to do?

c. What one problem or part of your essay seems the most troubling? Take that specific problem to your instructor or to your college's writing center.

3. With the Gulf War in 1991, scientists have increasingly been worried about the dangers of biological warfare. Research the types of biological weapons that can be used in warfare and the effects that each produces. Then, on the basis of that background research, argue for some form of international control over biological agents. Remember to document your sources.

None of This Is Fair

RICHARD RODRIGUEZ

Born in 1944 in San Francisco, Richard Rodriguez, the son of Span-
ish-speaking Mexican-American parents, first learned English in
grade school. He received a B.A. in English from Stanford University
in 1967, an M.A. from Columbia University, and a Ph.D. from the
University of California at Berkeley. He also studied at the Warburg
Institute in London. His autobiographic Hunger of Memory: The
Education of Richard Rodriguez *(1982) is an important study of*
the Mexican-American experience, with special attention given to bi-
lingualism. He writes of his regret at losing his Spanish heritage by
being assimilated into the English-speaking world; but he disapproves
of bilingual education and of the reverse discrimination occasioned
by affirmative action programs. Rodriguez's essays have appeared in
magazines such as American Scholar, Saturday Review *and* College English. *He is presently associate editor at Pacific News Service*
in San Francisco. In ''None of This Is Fair'' Rodriguez uses his
personal experience to argue the ineffectiveness of affirmative action
programs in reaching those people who are seriously disadvantaged.

MY PLAN TO BECOME a professor of English—my ambition during
long years in college at Stanford, then in graduate school at
Columbia and Berkeley—was complicated by feelings of embarrassment and guilt. So many times I would see other Mexican-Americans and know we were alike only in race. And yet,
simply because our race was the same, I was, during the last
years of my schooling, the beneficiary of their situation. Affirmative Action programs had made it all possible. The disadvantages of others permitted my promotion; the absence of
many Mexican-Americans from academic life allowed my des-
ignation as a "minority student."

For me opportunities had been extravagant. There were
fellowships, summer research grants, and teaching assistant-
ships. After only two years in graduate school, I was offered
teaching jobs by several colleges. Invitations to Washington

1

2

conferences arrived and I had the chance to travel abroad as a "Mexican-American representative." The benefits were often, however, too gaudy to please. In three published essays, in conversations with teachers, in letters to politicians and at conferences, I worried the issue of Affirmative Action. Often I proposed contradictory opinions. Though consistent was the admission that—because of an early, excellent education—I was no longer a principal victim of racism or any other social oppression. I said that but still I continued to indicate on applications for financial aid that I was a Hispanic-American. It didn't really occur to me to say anything else, or to leave the question unanswered.

3   Thus I complied with and encouraged the odd bureaucratic logic of Affirmative Action. I let government officials treat the disadvantaged condition of many Mexican-Americans with my advancement. Each fall my presence was noted by Health, Education, and Welfare department statisticians. As I pursued advanced literary studies and learned the skill of reading Spenser and Wordsworth and Empson, I would hear myself numbered among the culturally disadvantaged. Still, silent, I didn't object.

4   But the irony cut deep. And guilt would not be evaded by averting my glance when I confronted a face like my own in a crowd. By late 1975, nearing the completion of my graduate studies at Berkeley, I was so wary of the benefits of Affirmative Action that I feared my inevitable success as an applicant for a teaching position. The months of fall—traditionally that time of academic job-searching—passed without my applying to a single school. When one of my professors chanced to learn this in late November, he was astonished, then furious. He yelled at me: Did I think that because I was a minority student jobs would just come looking for me? What was I thinking? Did I realize that he and several other faculty members had already written letters on my behalf? Was I going to start acting like some other minority students he had known? They struggled for success and then when it was almost within reach, grew strangely afraid and let it pass. Was that it? Was I determined to fail?

5   I did not respond to his questions. I didn't want to admit to him, and thus to myself, the reason I delayed.

I merely agreed to write to several schools. (In my letter I 6
wrote: "I cannot claim to represent disadvantaged Mexican-
Americans. The very fact that I am in a position to apply for
this job should make that clear.") After two or three days, there
were telegrams and phone calls, invitations to interviews, then
airplane trips. A blur of faces and the murmur of their soft
questions. And, over someone's shoulder, the sight of campus
buildings shadowing pictures I had seen years before when I
leafed through Ivy League catalogues with great expectations.
At the end of each visit, interviewers would smile and wonder
if I had any questions. A few times I quietly wondered what
advantage my race had given me over other applicants. But that
was an impossible question for them to answer without embarrassing me. Quickly, several persons insisted that my ethnic
identity had given me no more than a "foot inside the door;"
at most, I had a "slight edge" over other applicants. "We just
looked at your dossier with extra care and we liked what we
saw. There was never any question of having to alter our standards. You can be certain of that."

In the early part of January, offers arrived on stiffly elegant 7
stationery. Most schools promised terms appropriate for any
new assistant professor. A few made matters worse—and almost more tempting—by offering more: the use of university
housing; an unusually large starting salary; a reduced teaching
schedule. As the stack of letters mounted, my hesitation increased. I started calling department chairmen to ask for another
week, then 10 more days—"more time to reach a decision"—
to avoid the decision I would need to make.

At school, meantime, some students hadn't received a single 8
job offer. One man, probably the best student in the department,
did not even get a request for his dossier. He and I met outside
a classroom one day and he asked about my opportunities. He
seemed happy for me. Faculty members beamed. They said they
had expected it. "After all, not many schools are going to pass
up getting a Chicano with a Ph.D. in Renaissance literature,"
somebody said, laughing. Friends wanted to know which of the
offers I was going to accept. But I couldn't make up my mind.
February came and I was running out of time and excuses. (One
chairman guessed my delay was a bargaining ploy and increased

his offer with each of my calls.) I had to promise a decision by the 10th; the12th at the very latest.

9   On the 18th of February, late in the afternoon, I was in the office I shared with several other teaching assistants. Another graduate student was sitting across the room at his desk. When I got up to leave, he looked over to say in an uneventful voice that he had some big news. He had finally decided to accept a position at a faraway university. It was not a job he especially wanted, he admitted. But he had to take it because there hadn't been any other offers. He felt trapped, and depressed, since his job would separate him from his young daughter.

10   I tried to encourage him by remarking that he was lucky at least to have found a job. So many others hadn't been able to get anything. But before I finished speaking I realized that I had said the wrong thing. And I anticipated his next question.

11   "What are your plans?" he wanted to know. "Is it true you've gotten an offer from Yale?"

12   I said that it was. "Only, I still haven't made up my mind."

13   He stared at me as I put on my jacket. And smiling, then unsmiling, he asked if I knew that he too had written to Yale. In his case, however, no one had bothered to acknowledge his letter with even a postcard. What did I think of that?

14   He gave me no time to answer.

15   "Damn!" he said sharply and his chair rasped the floor as he pushed himself back. Suddenly, it was to *me* that he was complaining. "It's just not right, Richard. None of this is fair. You've done some good work, but so have I. I'll bet our records are just about equal. But when we look for jobs this year, it's a different story. You get all of the breaks."

16   To evade his criticism, I wanted to side with him. I was about to admit the injustice of Affirmative Action. But he went on, his voice hard with accusation. "It's all very simple this year. You're a Chicano. And I am a Jew. That's the only real difference between us."

17   His words stung me: there was nothing he was telling me that I didn't know. I had admitted everything already. But to hear someone else say these things, and in such an accusing tone, was suddenly hard to take. In a deceptively calm voice, I responded that he had simplified the whole issue. The phrases

544

came like bubbles to the tip of my tongue: "new blood"; "the importance of cultural diversity"; "the goal of racial integration." These were all the arguments I had proposed several years ago—and had long since abandoned. Of course the offers were unjustifiable. I knew that. All I was saying amounted to a frantic self-defense. I tried to find an end to a sentence. My voice faltered to a stop.

"Yeah, sure," he said. "I've heard all that before. Nothing you say really changes the fact that Affirmative Action is unfair. You see that, don't you? There isn't any way for me to compete with you. Once there were quotas to keep my parents out of certain schools; now there are quotas to get you in and the effect on me is the same as it was for them." 18

I listened to every word he spoke. But my mind was really on something else. I knew at that moment that I would reject all of the offers. I stood there silently surprised by what an easy conclusion it was. Having prepared for so many years to teach, having trained myself to do nothing else, I had hesitated out of practical fear. But now that it was made, the decision came with relief. I immediately knew I had made the right choice. 19

My colleague continued talking and I realized that he was simply right. Affirmative Action programs *are* unfair to white students. But as I listened to him assert his rights, I thought of the seriously disadvantaged. How different they were from white, middle-class students who come armed with the testimony of their grades and aptitude scores and self-confidence to complain about the unequal treatment they now receive. I listen to them. I do not want to be careless about what they say. Their rights are important to protect. But inevitably when I hear them or their lawyers, I think about the most seriously disadvantaged, not simply Mexican-Americans, but of all those who do not ever imagine themselves going to college or becoming doctors: white, black, brown. Always poor. Silent. They are not plaintiffs before the court or against the misdirection of Affirmative Action. They lack the confidence (my confidence!) to assume their right to a good education. They lack the confidence and skills a good primary and secondary education provides and which are prerequisites for informed public life. They remain silent. 20

21   The debate drones on and surrounds them in stillness. They are distant, faraway figures like the boys I have seen peering down from freeway overpasses in some other part of town.

QUESTIONS ON SUBJECT AND PURPOSE

1. In paragraph 4, Rodriguez makes reference to the "irony" of the situation. In what ways was it ironic?
2. Why does Rodriguez decide to reject all of the offers?
3. Is Rodriguez criticizing affirmative action policies? How could such policies reach or change the lives of those who are really seriously disadvantaged?

QUESTIONS ON STRATEGY AND AUDIENCE

1. To what extent does Rodriguez present a formal argument based on an appeal to reason? To what extent does he attempt to persuade through an appeal to emotion? Which element is stronger in the piece?
2. What is the difference between objectively stating an opinion and narrating a personal experience? Do we as readers react any differently to Rodriguez's story as a result?
3. What expectations does Rodriguez have of his audience? How do you know that?

QUESTIONS ON VOCABULARY AND STYLE

1. In paragraphs 11 through 18, Rodriguez dramatizes a scene with a fellow student. He could have just summarized what was said without using dialogue. What advantage is gained by developing the scene?
2. Be prepared to discuss the significance of the following sentences:
   a. "For me opportunities had been extravagant" (paragraph 2).
   b. "The benefits were often, however, too gaudy to please" (paragraph 2).
   c. "The phrases came like bubbles to the tip of my tongue" (paragraph 17).
   d. "Always poor. Silent" (paragraph 20).

3. What is the effect of the simile ("like the boys I have seen . . .) Rodriguez uses in the final line?

WRITING SUGGESTIONS

1. Rodriguez proposes no solutions to the problem of education for disadvantaged minorities. What, though, might be suggested? How could the seriously disadvantaged be reached? In a paragraph argue for a particular change in affirmative action policies.

2. Expand your subject begun in suggestion 1 to essay length.

   Prewriting:

   a. One possible starting point would be to gather some information about education in America. For example, how many Americans are illiterate? What exactly do those statistics indicate? Ask a reference librarian for help.

   b. Realistically, what might be done to help the seriously disadvantaged? Try to list at least ten realistic possibilities.

   c. Investigate local agencies trying to address these problems. The blue pages of your telephone book contain a variety of sources. Contact three such agencies for information.

   Rewriting:

   a. Convert the list of things to remember at the end of the introduction to this chapter into a checklist. Reread your essay, and check to see if you followed the list.

   b. Ask a peer reader to critique your essay using that same checklist. Pay attention to the reader's criticisms as well as praise.

   c. What gave you the most trouble in this paper? List two things. Then, go back and tackle just those two problems.

3. How successful have affirmative action programs been? Research their history and their success. Have those most seriously disadvantaged really been helped? Using your evidence, take some aspect of these programs, and write an essay persuading your readers that it should be continued, expanded, changed, or dropped. Be sure to document your sources.

Educating Black Athletes

HARRY EDWARDS

Born in 1942 in St. Louis, Harry Edwards earned a B.A. at San Jose State University. Despite offers to play professional football, he chose instead to accept a Woodrow Wilson Fellowship to Cornell University, from which he earned an M.A. and Ph.D. in sociology. Currently on the faculty of the University of California at Berkeley, he is the author of The Revolt of the Black Athlete *(1969);* Sociology of Sport *(1973);* The Struggle that Must Be *(1981), his autobiography; and* Playing to Win: A Short Guide to Sensible Black Sports Participation *(1982). In "Educating Black Athletes," which appeared in* The Atlantic, *Edwards defends the NCAA's controversial Rule 48, which stipulates that athletes at Division I and II colleges must achieve a minimum SAT score of 700 (or a score of 15 on the ACT) and a C average in eleven designated high school courses in order to participate in college athletics during their freshman year. Edwards also raises many doubts about the adequacy of American education.*

1   FOR DECADES, student athletes, usually seventeen-to-nineteen-year-old freshmen, have informally agreed to a contract with the universities they attend: athletic performance in exchange for an education. The athletes have kept their part of the bargain; the universities have not. Universities and athletic departments have gained huge gate receipts, television revenues, national visibility, donors to university programs, and more, as a result of the performances of gifted basketball and football players, of whom a disproportionate number of the most gifted and most exploited have been black.

2   While blacks are not the only student athletes exploited, the abuses usually happen to them first and worst. To understand why, we must understand sports' impact upon black society; how popular beliefs that blacks are innately superior athletes, and that sports are "inherently" beneficial, combine with the life circumstances of young blacks, and with the aspirations

of black student athletes, to make those students especially vulnerable to victimization.

Sports at all levels are widely believed to have achieved   *3*
extraordinary, if not exemplary, advances in the realm of interracial relations since the time when Jackie Robinson became the first black to play major-league baseball. To some extent, this reputation has been deliberately fostered by skilled sports propagandists eager to project "patriotic" views consistent with America's professed ideals of racial justice and equality of opportunity. To a much greater extent, however, this view of sports has been encouraged by observers of the sporting scene who have simply been naive about the dynamics of sports as an institution, about their relationship to society generally, and about the race-related realities of American sports in particular.

Many misconceptions about race and sports can be traced   *4*
to developments in sports that would appear on the surface to represent significant racial progress. For instance, though blacks constitute only 11.7 percent of the U.S. population, in 1982 more than 55 percent of the players in the National Football League were black, and, in 1981, twenty-four of the twenty-eight first-round NFL draft choices were black. As for the two other major professional team sports, 70 percent of the players making National Basketball Association rosters during the 1982–1983 season, and 80 percent of the starters that same season, were black, while 19 percent of America's major-league baseball players at the beginning of the 1982 season were black.

Black representation on sports honor rolls has been even   *5*
more disproportionate. For example, the past nine Heisman trophies, awarded each year to the "best" collegiate football player in the land, have gone to blacks. In the final rushing statistics of the 1982 NFL season, thirty-six of the top forty running backs were blacks. In 1982, not a single white athlete was named to the first team of a major Division I All-American basketball roster. Similarly, twenty-one of the twenty-four athletes selected for the 1982 NBA All-Star game were black. Since 1955, whites have won the NBA's "most valuable player" award only five times as opposed to twenty-three times for blacks. And, of course, boxing championships in the heavier weight divisions have been dominated by black athletes since

the 1960s. But a judicious interpretation of these and related figures points toward conclusions quite different from what one might expect.

6   Patterns of opportunity for blacks in American sports, like those in the society at large, are shaped by racial discrimination, a phenomenon that explains the disproportionately high number of talented black athletes in certain sports and the utter exclusion of blacks from most other American sports, as well as from decision-making and authority positions in virtually all sports.

7   Most educated people today accept the idea that the level of black representation and the quality of black performance in sports have no demonstrable relationship to race-linked genetic characteristics. Every study purporting to demonstrate such a relationship has exhibited critical deficiencies in the methodological, theoretical, or conceptual design. Moreover, the factors determining the caliber of sports performances are so complex and disparate as to render ludicrous any attempt to trace athletic excellence to a single biological feature.

8   Thus, despite a popular view that blacks are "natural" athletes, physically superior to athletes from other groups, the evidence tends to support cultural and social—rather than biological—explanations of their athletic success.

9   Briefly:

—Thanks to the mass media and to long-standing traditions of racial discrimination limiting blacks' access to many high-prestige occupational opportunities, the black athlete is much more visible to black youths, than, say, black doctors or black lawyers. Therefore, unlike white children, who see many different potential role models in the media, black children tend to model themselves after, or to admire as symbolically masculine, the black athlete—the one prevalent and positive black success figure they are exposed to regularly, year in and year out, in America's white-dominated mass media.

—The black family and the black community tend to reward athletic achievement much more and earlier than any other activity. This also lures more young blacks into sports-career aspirations than the actual opportunities for sports success would warrant.

—Because most American sports activities are still devoid of any significant black presence, the overwhelming majority of aspiring black athletes emulate established black role models and seek careers in four or five sports—basketball, football, baseball, boxing, and track. The brutally competitive selection process that ensues eliminates all but the most skilled black athletes by the time they reach the collegiate and advanced-amateur ranks. The competition is made all the more intense because even in these sports, some positions (such as quarterback, center, and middle linebacker in football, and catcher in baseball) are relatively closed to blacks.

—Finally, sports are seen by many black male youths as a means of proving their manhood. This tends to be extraordinarily important to blacks, because the black male in American society has been systematically cut off from mainstream routes of masculine expression, such as economic success, authority positions, and so forth.

Despite the great pool of athletic talent generated in black society, black athletes still get fewer than one in ten of the athletic scholarships given out in the United States. And, at least partially as a result of the emphasis placed upon developing their athletic talents from early childhood, an estimated 25 to 35 percent of male black high school athletes qualifying for athletic scholarships cannot accept those scholarships because of accumulated academic deficiencies. Many of these young men eventually end up in what is called, appropriately enough, the "slave trade"—a nationwide phenomenon involving independent scouts who, for a fee (usually paid by a four-year college), search out talented but academically "high-risk" black athletes and place them in accommodating junior colleges, where their athletic skills are further honed while they earn the grades they need to transfer to the sponsoring four-year schools. 10

Of those who are eventually awarded collegiate athletic scholarships, studies indicate, as many as 65 to 75 percent may never graduate from college. Of the 25 to 35 percent who do eventually graduate from the schools they play for, an estimated 75 percent graduate either with physical-education degrees or in majors created specifically for athletes and generally held in low repute. The problem with these "jock majors," and in- 11 creasingly with the physical-education major as well, is that they make poor credentials in the job market. One might assume that ample occupational opportunities would be available to outstanding black former athletes, at least within the sports world. But the reality is quite different. To begin with, the overwhelming majority of black athletes, whether scholarship-holders or professional, have *no* post-career, occupational plans or former preparation for any type of post-career employment either inside or outside sports. These blacks are unemployed more often, and earn less when they do have jobs, than their non-athletic college peers; they are also likely to switch jobs more often, to hold a wider variety of jobs, and to be less satisfied with the jobs they hold—primarily because the jobs tend to be dull, dead-end, or minimally rewarding.

12   Few Americans appreciate the extent to which the overwhelming majority of young males seeking affluence and stardom through sports are foredoomed to fail. The three major team sports provide approximately 2,663 jobs for professional athletes, regardless of color, in a nation of 226 million people, roughly half of whom are male. This means that only one American male in about 42,000 is a professional football, basketball, or baseball player.

13   While the proportion of blacks in professional basketball is 70 percent, in professional football 55 percent, and in professional baseball 19 percent, only about 1,400 black people (up from about 1,100 since the establishment of the United States Football League) are making a living as professional athletes in these three major sports today. And if one adds to this number all the black professional athletes in all other American sports, all the blacks in minor and semiprofessional sports leagues, and all the black trainers, coaches, and doctors in professional sports, one sees that fewer than 2,400 black Americans can be said to be making a living in professional athletics today.

14   This situation, considered in combination with the black athlete's educational underdevelopment, helps explain why so many black athletes not only fail to achieve their expectations of life-long affluence but also frequently fall far short of the levels achieved by the non-athletic peers.

15   Despite the fact, then, that American basketball, boxing,

football, and baseball competitions have come more and more to look like Ghana playing Nigeria, sport continues to loom like a fog-shrouded minefield for the overwhelming majority of black athletes. It has been a treadmill to oblivion rather than the escalator to wealth and glory it was believed to be. The black athlete who blindly sets out today to fill the shoes of Dr. J., Reggie J., Magic J., Kareem Abdul-J., or O.J. may well end up with "No J."—no job that he is qualified to do in our modern, technologically sophisticated society. At the end of his sports career, the black athlete is not likely to be running or flying through airports like O.J. He is much more likely to be sweeping up airports—if he has the good fortune to land even that job.

These are the tragic circumstances that prompted Joe Paterno, 1982 Division I football "Coach of the Year" of the New York Football Writers' Association, to exclaim in January from the floor of the 1983 NCAA convention in San Diego: "For fifteen years we have had a race problem. We have raped a generation and a half of young black athletes. We have taken kids and sold them on bouncing a ball and running with a football and that being able to do certain things athletically was going to be an end in itself. We cannot afford to do that to another generation." With that statement, Coach Paterno gave impetus to the passage of the NCAA's "Rule 48," which set off what is probably the most heated race-related controversy within the NCAA since the onset of widespread racial integration in major-college sports programs during the 1950s and 1960s.   16

Put most simply, Rule 48 stipulates that, beginning in 1986, freshman athletes who want to participate in sports in any of the nation's 277 Division I colleges and universities must have attained a minimum score of 700 (out of a possible 1,600) on the Scholastic Aptitude Test (SAT) or a score of 15 (out of a possible 36) on the American College Test (ACT), and must have achieved a C average in eleven designated high school courses, including English, mathematics, social sciences, and physical sciences. Further, *The N.C.A.A. News* reported, Rule 48   17

does not interfere with the admissions policies of any Division

I institution. Nonqualifiers under this legislation may be admitted and attend class. Such a student could compete as a sophomore if he or she satisfies the satisfactory-progress rules and would have four varsity seasons starting as a sophomore if he or she continues to make satisfactory progress.

Further, under related Proposal No. 49-B, any student who achieves at least 2.0 in all high school courses but does not meet the new terms of No. 48 can receive athletically related financial aid in his or her first year, but cannot practice or compete in intercollegiate athletics. This student would have three varsity years of participation remaining.

18   The outcry in response to the passage of Rule 48 was immediate. Ironically, the most heated opposition to the rule came from black civil-rights leaders and black college presidents and educators—the very group one might have expected to be most supportive of the action. Their concern was over those provisions of Rule 48 specifying minimum test scores as a condition for sports participation, particularly the 700 score on the S.A.T. Leading the black criticism of the NCAA's new academic standards were the National Association For Equal Opportunity in Higher Education (NAFEO), representing 114 traditionally black colleges and universities; the National Alliance of Black School Educators (NABSE); Rev. Jesse Jackson, president of People United To Serve Humanity (Operation PUSH); Rev. Benjamin Hooks, executive director of the National Association for the Advancement of Colored People (NAACP); and Rev. Joseph Lowery, president of the Southern Christian Leadership Conference (SCLC). They argued, first, that blacks were not consulted in the formulation of Rule 48; second, that the minimum SAT score requirement was arbitrary; and finally, that the SAT and ACT are racist diagnostic tests, which reflect a cultural bias favoring whites. They believed that the 700 SAT and 15 ACT score requirements would unfairly penalize black student athletes, given that 55 percent of black students generally score lower than 700 on the SAT and 69 percent score lower than 15 on the ACT. And why would the majority of NCAA Division I institutions vote to support a rule that would reduce participation opportunities for black athletes? For NAFEO and its supporters, the answer was clear. The most outspoken among

the critics of Rule 48 was Dr. Jesse N. Stone, Jr., the president of the Southern University System of Louisiana, who said:

> The end result of all this is that the black athlete has been too good. If it [Rule 48] is followed to its logical conclusion, we say to our youngsters, "Let the white boy win once in a while." This has set the black athlete back twenty-five or thirty years. The message is that white schools no longer want black athletes.

Members of the American Council on Education (ACE) committee charged with developing Rule 48 vehemently denied claims that no blacks were involved in the process. Whatever the truth of the matter, the majority of black NCAA delegates felt that their interests and views had not been represented. 19

I could not agree more with NAFEO, Jackson, Hooks, Lowery, *et al.* on their contention that the minimum SAT and ACT test scores are arbitrary. Neither the ACE nor the NCAA has yet provided any reasoned or logical basis for setting the minimum scores. But whereas NAFEO and others say that the scores are arbitrary and too high, I contend that they are arbitrary and so *low* as to constitute virtually no standards at all. I have other, more fundamental disagreements with the NAFEO position. 20

One need not survey very much literature on the racist abuse of diagnostic testing in this country to appreciate the historical basis of NAFEO's concerns about rigidly applied test standards. But the demand that Rule 48 be repealed on the grounds that its test-score requirements are racist and will unfairly affect blacks is both factually contestable and strategically regrettable. The evidence is overwhelming that the SAT and the ACT discriminate principally on the basis of class, rather than race. The greater discrepancy between black and white scores occurs on the math section of the SAT, where cultural differences between the races logically would have the least impact. Even on the verbal sections of these diagnostic tests, differences in black and white scores are at least partially explained as class-related phenomena. As Dr. Mary Frances Berry, a NAFEO supporter, asserts: 21

> A major differential [among test scores] was *not* between black and white students, but between students from well-off fam-

ilies and students from poor families. The better-off the family, the higher the score—for whites *and* blacks.

22   Dr. Norman C. Francis, president of the traditionally black Xavier University of Louisiana and immediate past chairman of the College Board, agrees:

> The SAT is not merely a measure of potential aptitude, as many believe, but is also an achievement test which accurately measures what students have learned to that point. Most students do poorly on the test simply because they have never been taught the concepts that will help them to understand what testing and test-taking is all about. It is an educational disadvantage, not an inability to learn . . . The plain truth is that students in poorer schools are never taught to deal with word problems and . . . critical analysis. The problem therefore is not with the students, nor with the test, but rather with an educational system which fails to teach youngsters what they need to know.

23   Rule 48, therefore, involves far more than a simple black-white controversy, as 1981 SAT test statistics bear out. While 49 percent of black male students in 1981 failed to achieve at least a 700 on the combined SAT, as compared with 14 percent of the whites and 27 percent of other minorities, far more whites (31,140) and other minorities (27,145) than blacks (15,330) would have been affected under Rule 48.

24   Furthermore, between 1981 and 1982, blacks' verbal scores rose nine points and mathematics scores rose four points, compared with a two-point gain in verbal and a one-point gain in math for the white majority.

25   NAFEO claims that black athletes would have less access to traditionally white Division I institutions in the wake of Rule 48. But even though proportionately more blacks score below Rule 48's minimum-score requirements, it is unlikely that significant numbers of blacks would be deprived of opportunities to attend traditionally white schools on athletic scholarships. Indeed, if the enrollment of black athletes falls off at any Division I schools for this reason, I submit that the schools most likely to suffer will be the traditionally black colleges. NCAA disciplinary records show that traditionally white institutions have led the way in amateur-athletic rules infractions and in

exploiting black athletes. Why? Because they have the largest financial investment in their athletic programs, and because they and their athletic personnel stand to reap the greatest rewards from athletic success. With so much at stake, why would schools that for so long have stretched, bent, and broken rules to enroll black athletes no longer want them?

The loopholes in Rule 48 are sufficient to allow any school   26
to recruit any athlete it really wants. Junior colleges are not covered under the rule, so schools could still secure and develop athletes not eligible for freshman sports participation at four-year Division I colleges. Further, Rule 48 allows Division I schools to recruit freshman athletes who are academically ineligible to participate, and even to provide them with financial support. After several meetings with NAFEO representatives, Rev. Jesse Jackson, and others, I am strongly convinced that for many within the ranks of Rule 48's detractors, fiscal rather than educational issues are the priority concern. The overwhelming majority of athletes recruited by traditionally black Division I schools are black, score below Rule 48 minimum-test-score requirements, and tend to need financial support in order to attend college. However, because they have far more modest athletic budgets than traditionally white schools, traditionally black schools are not nearly so able to provide financial support for both a roster of active athletes and a long roster of newly recruited athletes ineligible for athletic participation under Rule 48. Traditionally black Division I schools, already at a recruiting disadvantage owing to smaller budgets and less access to lucrative TV exposure, would be placed at an even more critical recruiting disadvantage, since they would not be able to afford even those athletes they would ordinarily be able to get.

Thus, the core issue in the Rule 48 controversy is not racist   27
academic standards, or alleged efforts by whites to resegregate major-college sports, so much as parity between black and white institutions in the collegiate athletic arms race.

Strategically, the position of NAFEO, the NABSE, and the   28
black civil-rights leaders vis-à-vis Rule 48 poses two problems. First, they have missed the greatest opportunity since the *Brown* v. *Board of Education of Topeka* case thirty years ago to make an

impressive statement about quality and equality in education. And, since they had the attention of the nation, they also squandered a rare opportunity to direct a national dialogue on restructuring the role and stipulating the rights of athletes in the academy. Second, with no real evidence to support their claims of racist motives on the part of Rule 48's white supporters, or of simple race bias in the rule's stipulations, these black educators and civil-rights leaders left the unfortunate and unintended impression that they were against *all* academic standards because they believed that black students are unable to achieve even the moderate standards established under Rule 48.

29 Notwithstanding the transparent criticisms leveled by Rule 48's detractors, the measure does contain some real flaws relative to its proposed goal of shoring up the academic integrity of Division I athletic programs. First, the standards stipulated in Rule 48 are *too low*. A score of 700 on the SAT, for example, projects less than a fifty-fifty chance of graduating from most Division I schools.

30 Second, Rule 48 does not address in any way the educational problems of students once they have matriculated, which is where the real educational rip-off of collegiate student athletes has occurred. Rather, it establishes standards of high school preparation and scholastic achievement necessary for students who wish to participate in college sports as freshmen.

31 Nonetheless, the NCAA action is worthy of support, not as a satisfactory solution to the educational problems of big-time collegiate sports but as a step—a very small and perhaps even inept step—toward dealing with these problems. Rule 48 communicates to young athletes, beginning with those who are sophomores in high school, that we expect them to develop academically as well as athletically. In California, 320,000 students each year participate in California Interscholastic Federation athletic programs and most undoubtedly aspire to win athletic scholarships to Division I institutions. However, only 5 percent of these students will ever participate in college sports at any level (including junior college), and the overwhelming majority will never even enroll at a four-year school. If Rule 48 does indeed encourage greater academic seriousness among high school athletes, the vast majority of high school student

athletes who are *not* going on to college may benefit most from the NCAA's action—since they face the realities of life after sports immediately upon graduation from high school.

Further, were I not to support Rule 48, I would risk communicating to black youth in particular that I, a nationally known black educator, do not believe that they have the capacity to achieve a 700 score on the SAT, with three years to prepare for the test, when they are given a total of 400 points simply for answering a single question in each of the two sections of the test, and when they have a significant chance of scoring 460 by a purely random marking of the test. Finally, I support the NCAA's action because I believe that black parents, black educators, and the black community must insist that black children be taught and that they learn whatever subject matter is necessary to excel on diagnostic and all other skills tests. 32

Outcries of "racism," and calls for black boycotts of our exemptions from such tests, seem to me neither rational nor constructive long-term responses to the problem of black students' low test scores. Culture can be learned and taught. Class-specific values and perspectives can be learned and taught. And this is what we should be about as black educators—preparing our young people to meet the challenges they face on these tests, and, by extension, in this society. 33

I believe that (1) student athletes and non-athletes alike should be given diagnostic tests on a recurrent basis to assure skills achievement, (2) test-score standards should and must be raised, based upon the skill demands and challenges of our contemporary world, and (3) the test standards set should be established as post-enrollment goals and not pre-enrollment obstacles. 34

In the case of scholarship athletes, every institution should have the right to set its own academic enrollment standards. But those same institutions *must* acknowledge a binding corollary obligation and responsibility to develop and implement support programs sufficiently effective to fulfill their implied contracts with the athletes recruited. 35

For all of its divisive impact, the debate over Rule 48 has illuminated a much larger crisis involving the failure of this nation to educate its young, athletes and non-athletes, properly. 36

In 1967, the national average on the SAT was 958; by 1982, it had dropped to 893. Furthermore, even students who score well on diagnostic tests frequently require remedial work to handle college-level course work. From 1975 to 1980, the number of remedial math courses in public four-year colleges increased by 72 percent; they now constitute a quarter of all math courses offered by those institutions. At two-year colleges, 42 percent of math courses are below the level of college algebra.

37   In high school transcripts, according to a study done for the National Commission on Excellence in Education, credit value for American history has declined by 11 percent over the past fifteen years, for chemistry by 6 percent, for algebra by 7 percent, and for French by 9 percent. In the same period, credit value for remedial English has risen by 39 percent and for driver education by 75 percent. Only 31 percent of recent high school graduates took intermediate algebra, only 16 percent took geography, and only 13 percent took French. High school students have abandoned college-preparatory and vocational-education "tracks" in droves, so that between 1964 and 1979 the number who chose the "general" track rose from 12 to 42 percent. About 25 percent of all credits earned by general-track graduates were in physical and health education, driver education, home management, food and cooking, training for adulthood and marriage, remedial courses, and for work experience outside school.

38   Part of the problem is with our teachers: the way they are recruited, their low status, and their even lower rewards. According to a recent article in *U.S. News & World Report*, "A study conducted for the National Institute of Education, which looked at college graduates who entered teaching in the late '70s, found that those with the highest academic ability were much more likely to leave their jobs than those who were lower achievers. Among high-achieving students, only 26 percent intended to teach at age thirty, as compared with approximately 60 percent of those with the lowest academic ability." In yet another study, one third of the nearly 7,000 prospective teachers who took the California minimum-competency test failed to meet the most basic skills requirements. And in 1982, the average SAT score of students indicating teaching as their intended field of

study ranked twenty-six among average scores achieved by students declaring twenty-nine different fields of interest.

Black colleges are not blameless with respect to inadequate 39 teacher preparation. Currently, at least twenty states require teacher candidates to pass a state qualifying exam. In Florida, 79 percent of white teacher-college graduates achieved a passing rate, compared with 35 percent for black test-takers. The two black schools that produce the largest number of black teacher candidates in that same state had the worst passing rates—37 percent and 16 percent.

That state's Association of Black Psychologists held a press 40 conference and denounced the tests as "instruments of European cultural imperialism," and urged the black community— as a front—to resist the tests. But there is really only one legitimate concern relative to such tests: Do they measure what should be taught in schools of education if teachers are to be competent?

The majority of black students today come from schools in 41 which blacks either predominate or make up the entire student body. And much—if not most—of the failure to educate black youths has occurred under black educators. In the 1960s, from Ocean Hill-Brownsville, in New York, to Watts, in California, blacks quite rightly criticized inner-city schools where white teachers and white superintendents were indifferent to the learning abilities of black students. Many of these school systems now have a majority of black teachers and black superintendents, and many black students still do not learn. Can we afford to be any less critical when white incompetence is replaced by black incompetence? Given what is at stake, the answer must be an emphatic and resounding No. We must let all of our educators know that if they are not competent to do their jobs, they have no business in our schools.

But pointing out teachers' inadequacies is not enough. For 42 all of its modernity, education still advances on "four legs." Though formal instruction takes place in the classroom, education is the result of coordinated effort on the part of parents, the school, the community, and the larger society. Parents who do not participate in school activities, who do not attend parent-teacher conferences to review their children's academic progress, who generally show little or no interest in school-related issues—indeed, who do not know, and have never even asked, the name of the teacher charged with instructing their children—over the years communicate to those children the idea that education doesn't matter. The community that undercuts the solvency of its libraries and schools communicates the idea that education doesn't matter. The school that emphasizes and revels in the glories of sports, while fighting efforts to set academic standards for sports participation, communicates the idea that education doesn't matter.

43 Current national policy, which calls for severe cuts in educational funding, and defense expenditures of $1.6 trillion over the next four years, is both contradictory and shortsighted. Education *is* a national-defense issue. As Jefferson pointed out at this nation's birth, an educated, informed populace is necessary to the operation of a viable democracy. As the world's leading democracy, we simply cannot afford the current burden of 26 million adults who are functionally illiterate and 46 million who are only marginally literate. Since the 1970s, the U.S. military has found that it must print comic-book versions of some of its manuals in order to accommodate the educational deficiencies of troops charged with operating and maintaining some of the most sophisticated weapons in history. Along with greater emphasis upon parental involvement in schools, insistence upon teacher competence, and greater academic expectations of our students, we must put more, not less, money into education.

44 The National Center for Education Statistics estimates that the average 1980-1981 salary for classroom teachers was $17,602—up from $9,269 in 1971. However, in constant 1981 dollars, teachers have lost money, because their 1971 average salary translates to roughly $20,212. The outlook for the future is equally bleak. Education cannot attract and hold the best-trained and most competent people without offering competitive salaries. Particularly in the more technologically applicable disciplines, education is suffering a severe "brain-drain." Thus, in 1981, nationwide, half the teachers hired to teach high school math and science were not certified to teach those subjects, while more than forty states reported shortages of qualified teachers in those areas.

Compared with other national school systems, American   *45*
education comes up short. The American school year is 180
days, and the average student misses roughly eighteen of those,
but Japan, Germany, and most other industrial nations require
at least 220 days a year. In the Soviet Union, students from the
first grade on attend school six days a week. About 35 percent
of their classwork is in science. They take five years of arithmetic, then are introduced to algebra and geometry, followed
by calculus. The national minimum curriculum also calls for
one year each of astronomy and mechanical drawing, four years
of chemistry, five years of physics, and six years of biology.

In sum, education must be put at the very top of the U.S.   *46*
domestic agenda. Clearly, we must demonstrate greater concern
for and commitment to educational quality for all American
youths—athletes as well as non-athletes. I am confident that
with adequate support and proper encouragement, they can
achieve whatever levels of performance are necessitated by the
challenges they face. In today's world, neither they nor we have
any other choice.

QUESTIONS ON SUBJECT AND PURPOSE

1. According to Edwards, in what ways are the "patterns of opportunity for blacks in American sports . . . shaped by racial
   discrimination"?
2. Does Edwards have any objections to Rule 48? If so, what are
   they?
3. What purpose does Edwards seem to have in this essay? To
   what extent is he writing about issues larger than Rule 48?

QUESTIONS ON STRATEGY AND AUDIENCE

1. Edwards develops his points through a detailed use of facts
   and figures. How do these numbers and statistics contribute
   to his argument? How do they contrast with the arguments
   that he quotes from his opponents?
2. At one point (paragraph 32), Edwards identifies himself as a
   "nationally known black educator." What is the effect of such
   identification? Why not make it earlier in the essay?

3. How might Edwards define his audience? To whom is he writing? Is he writing, for example, to young black athletes? Point to specific features in the essay that suggest an awareness of audience.

QUESTIONS ON VOCABULARY AND STYLE

1. Characterize the tone of Edwards's essay. Does he ever use emotionally charged language? Or does he just let the statistics speak for themselves?

2. At several points throughout the essay, Edwards quotes other authorities. What do these quotations contribute to his argument? Why use them at all?

3. Be able to define the following words: *judicious* (paragraph 5), *disparate* (7), *ludicrous* (7), *emulate* (9), *honed* (10), *affluence* (12), *impetus* (16), *lucrative* (26), *vis-à-vis* (28), *inept* (31), *corollary* (35), *divisive* (36), *viable* (43).

WRITING SUGGESTIONS

1. Many high schools have implemented minimum grade point averages for participation in any extracurricular activity (for example, athletics, musical organizations, theater, social or academic clubs). In a paragraph, drawing upon your own experiences or the experiences of others you knew in high school, argue for or against such requirements.

2. Colleges and universities compete for gifted athletes in a variety of sports by offering athletic scholarships. On the other hand, few, if any, colleges offer scholarships for students to work on the campus newspaper or to perform in theatrical productions (or to take part in any other activities that occur on college campuses). In an essay argue for or against offering scholarships to students to perform or participate in non-athletic activities.

Prewriting:

a. It might be wise to establish first the nature of the scholarships that your school already offers. In how many areas other than athletics are scholarships offered? Your school's admissions office can probably provide a convenient breakdown. The information might also be available in a current undergraduate catalog.

   b. Brainstorm a list of activities that might be supported in a way similar to athletics. A listing of campus organizations might provide some suggestions. Choose activities that are currently not supported.

   c. Make a list of the advantages and disadvantages that would arise from such a plan. In what ways are these other activities unlike college athletics and, therefore, not entitled to funding?

Rewriting:

   a. Remember that a successful argument is generally one that is reasonable and fair. Regardless of the side you took, have you avoided distorted or exaggerated language? Reexamine your essay to make sure.

   b. Ask a classmate or roommate to read your essay. Ask your reader if she or he agrees with your position. Ask for specific reasons why or why not. Do not ignore such feedback; a persuasive or argumentative essay works only if it wins the support of its readers.

   c. Look again at your conclusion. Did you end forcefully? Did you make it clear what you want your audience to do or believe? If not, try freewriting a new conclusion to your essay.

3. What has been the effect of Rule 48? Research the impact of the ruling on college and high school athletic programs. Then, using that research, write an essay in support of or in opposition to Rule 48. Be sure to document your sources.

A Writer's Revision Process: Sis Boom Bah Humbug

PATRICIA McLAUGHLIN

Patricia McLaughlin was born in Boston in 1945. She was educated at Rosemont College in Pennsylvania, Boston University, and the Annenberg School of Communications at the University of Pennsylvania. Her writing career began when she won a writing contest for Vogue *magazine while still in college. She worked as a fashion writer for the Philadelphia* Bulletin *and then on the* Pennsylvania Gazette *(the alumni magazine at the University of Pennsylvania) for five years. She has also been a freelance writer and a magazine editor for an insurance company. Since 1983 McLaughlin has written a column called "Lifestyle," which has been syndicated since 1988, for the Philadelphia* Inquirer.

"Sis Boom Bah Humbug" appeared in the September 30, 1990, Sunday magazine section of the Philadelphia Inquirer. *In discussing how the essay evolved through a number of drafts, McLaughlin revealed how advice from a reader and an editor helped shape the final version: "I wasn't happy with the first draft, and asked a friend to read it. She found it infuriating that the task force would tell the bump-and-grinders they couldn't bump and grind, both because of the implication that campus rape was their fault, and because it abridged their freedom. It was just the idea I needed—I agreed with her, and besides, I love being able to disagree with both sides at once. But my editor thought the last two grafs [paragraphs] . . . not only made the column too long, but weakened what sounded to him like the real ending, the indictment of the values the Illinettes [the University of Illinois' "squad of pompom girls"] embody and the advice to transfer to charm school, so he cut it. I wanted the idea back in so, working together over the phone, we came up with a way to put it in the middle in the* Inquirer *version, and let the indictment of Illinette values stand as the ending. But I still wasn't completely happy with it, so I rewrote it a little more before I sent it to the syndicate, giving more weight to the abridgment-of-women's freedom issue, and changing the ending a little."*

REVISED DRAFT

THINGS DON'T get ritualized at random. It's no accident that, when   *1*
you go to a football game, you see testosterone-crazed, bulked-
up young males trying to pound each other into jelly out on
the field while, on the sidelines, lissome young females prance
around with hardly any clothes on, swiveling their pelvises and
hollering in unison about how wonderful and important and
thrilling the efforts of the young males are.

Imagine the reverse: fierce, muscular young women slam-   *2*
ming into each other out on the playing field while pretty, scan-
tily clad young men gyrate on the sidelines, urging the young
women on to victory. Now imagine it happening every fall Saturday afternoon on campuses all over America and, on TV, with
a somewhat older cast, on Sunday afternoons and Monday
nights.

No way. One of the reasons football is so satisfying—to   *3*
those it satisfies, at least—is that it rhymes with the way we
think things should be: men doing things, women looking
pretty, men at the center of attention, women on the sidelines,
men in charge of the violence, women there to provide a sexual
charge.

Of course, by some people's lights, the sex roles football   *4*
reflects are obsolete, which makes some of those people despise
football, and makes others want to change it.

For instance, last winter the University of Illinois Campus   *5*
Task Force on Sexual Assault, Abuse and Violence recommended that the University ban dancing by the Illinettes, its
squad of pompom girls, as one of the campus "activities that
project women as sexual objects." The Task Force had been
convened after a survey of women students found that nearly
one in six had been the victim of a criminal sexual assault.

The Illinettes, naturally, failed to see that the appallingly   *6*
high campus rape rate was their fault. And they were right.
Telling them their line-dancers can't bump and grind at football
games is a totally screwy way to prevent rape. It drags up the
old idea that rape is women's fault—that short skirts or sexy
dancing or practically anything that reminds a man that a
woman is female can drive him so totally gaga that he simply

can't help himself. No reasonable person believes this. Besides, it's just not fair to restrict women's freedom in order to keep men from committing crimes. Carry the Illinois ban on sexy dancing to its extreme, and you have women in purdah, so constrained by fear of men's supposedly ungovernable sexual impulses that they have no lives left.

7   On the other hand, it's not easy to swallow the Illinettes' contention that what they do is "a serious sport."

8   I'm not saying it doesn't take muscles and talent and practice. Indeed, bump-and-grind line dancing is gaining adherents—and causing controversy—at schools across the country; there are even national competitions. But how many serious sports require sparkly Spandex chorus-girl costumes and high-heeled white boots and Dynasty hair? Even more to the point, how many serious sports exist mainly to glorify the accomplishments of people participating in a whole different sport?

9   Withal, the Illinettes contend that they're "role models" for women on campus. God forbid.

10   The trouble with pompom girls—whether they bump and grind or not—is that they reflect a destructively narrow view of what women are good for and what they better be good at. The values they embody are: being thin, being beautiful, being coordinated, having white teeth and lots of hair and lots of energy, smiling, staying in shape, and wearing sexy little costumes. The role they play at football games suggests that a woman's principal role in life should be encouraging men, and supporting them, and making them feel good about themselves, and telling them how great they are, and getting everybody else to say so too.

11   If Illinois' women students can't come up with better role models, they may as well pack up and transfer to charm school.

QUESTIONS FOR DISCUSSION

1. What does McLaughlin mean when she writes, "Things don't get ritualized at random"?

2. Why does McLaughlin object to "pompom" girls?

3. Although she finds such activities offensive, McLaughlin does not support a campus ban on such organizations. Why?

4. What does McLaughlin's title suggest? Is it an effective title for the essay?

5. Be prepared to define the following words: *lissome* (paragraph 1), *gyrate* (2), *gaga* (6), *purdah* (6).

EARLIER DRAFT

The only substantive changes that McLaughlin made in the essay from the first draft to the last occurred in the second half of the essay, from paragraph 6 on. That section of the first draft is reproduced below.

THE ILLINETTES (correctly) failed to see that this was any of their fault and, though they agreed to quit doing the bump-and-grind line dancing that worried the task force, they still don't see why they should have to. "We consider this a serious sport," Illinettes captain Pam Withers told *Time* magazine last winter. Indeed, bump-and-grind line dancing is gaining adherents at schools across the country; there are even national competitions.

I'm not saying it doesn't take muscles and talent and practice. But how many serious sports require sparkly Spandex chorus-girl costumes and high-heeled white boots and Dynasty hair? Even more to the point, how many serious sports exist mainly to glorify the accomplishments of people participating in a whole different sport?

The task force wanted to ban the Illinettes for fear they'd give male college students the idea that women are sex objects. I worry more about the ideas they might give little girls.

Withers, defending the Illinettes, said they're campus role models, and no doubt they are. But what kind of role models are they? What kind of message are they sending about what girls should value about themselves, and what their possibilities are? The values the Illinettes embody are: being thin, being beautiful, being coordinated, having white teeth and lots of hair and lots of energy, smiling, staying in shape, and wearing sexy little costumes. The role they play at football games suggests that a woman's principal role in life should be encouraging men, and supporting them, and making them feel good about themselves, and telling them how great they are, and getting everybody else to say so too.

These values make a lot of sense for a society looking to produce more Vanna Whites and Marla Mapleses. But if we're looking for Marie Curies and Georgia O'Keeffes and Edith Whartons, maybe it's time to change channels.

QUESTIONS ON THE REVISION

1. Why might McLaughlin have eliminated the references to Pam Withers, the captain of the Illinettes?

2. Focus just on paragraph 6 in the first draft and in the final version. Specifically, what was the nature of the changes that McLaughlin introduced?

3. McLaughlin completely rewrote the ending of the essay. Why might she have dropped the first draft ending—with its references to specific women?

4. In a second draft of the essay, McLaughlin substituted still another ending, which was then later worked into an earlier section of the essay. How effective is this second draft version as a conclusion to the essay?

Second Draft Ending

As my friend Paula asked, Why do they figure the only way to keep men from committing crimes is to restrict women's freedom? It's insidious, because it begins to suggest that rape is women's own fault, and that the only way to protect them from men's presumably ungovernable sexual appetites is to restrict their freedom. Carried to its extreme, it leaves women in purdah, so constrained by the presumably ungovernable sexual appetites of men that they have no lives.

WRITING SUGGESTIONS

1. Study the changes that McLaughlin made in the second half of the essay. Formulate a thesis about the reason(s) for one or more of those changes. Then in a paragraph assert your thesis and support it with evidence from the text.

2. In a serious essay, respond to McLaughlin's argument. Your essay might take several possible forms:

a. Disagree with her position and argue in support of such "pompom" squads.

b. Agree with her position, but suggest a compromise alternative to such practices.

c. Agree with her position and write an essay in which you try to dissuade young women from joining such activities.

Prewriting:

a. Regardless of the position you plan to take, make a list of all the reasons you can think of for both sides of the argument. Which reasons seem the most effective?

b. Brainstorm about your audience—how are they likely to feel about the position you are taking? Jot down what you anticipate and then try out your argument on friends. How do they react?

c. Remember that the first section of your essay should have two parts—one that introduces the subject to your reader in an interesting, readable way and one that summarizes McLaughlin's position. Do you have both sections?

Rewriting:

a. Look again at how you structured your essay. Have you started or ended with your strongest point? If you reversed the order, would your paper be more effective? Try it.

b. Check through your essay line by line. Mark any words or phrases that might be ineffective or might detract from your argument. Ask a classmate, friend, your instructor, or a tutor from your writing center to evaluate each marked example.

c. Check your language. Have you used words that are too emotionally charged? Remember that calling people names or distorting the opposition's position might make you feel better, but it will never help you persuade an audience.

3. You have been asked by the dean of students at your college or university to prepare a report making recommendations about campus activities that appear to portray women in sexist roles (for example, cheerleaders, majorettes, homecoming or campus queens). The dean wants you to include research about what other colleges or universities have done with this issue. Research the problem through the various periodicals that deal with feminist issues and higher education (such as

The Chronicle of Higher Education). You might interview your own dean of students as well. Has this ever been an issue on your campus?

Glossary

Abstract words refer to ideas or generalities—words such as "truth," "beauty," and "justice." The opposite of an abstract word is a *concrete* one. In Susan Allen Toth's first description of her Boston adventures in "Up, Up, and Away" (p. 126), she sampled "German cooking," but in the revision the abstract word "cooking" is replaced with the concrete and precise noun "sausages." Gordon Allport's "The Nature of Prejudice" (p. 454) defines an abstract word through a series of examples. See *Concrete*.

Allusion is a reference to an actual or fictional person, object, or event. The assumption is that the reference will be understood or recognized by the reader. For that reason, allusions work best when they draw upon a shared experience or heritage. Allusions to famous literary works or to historically prominent people or events are likely to have meaning for many readers for an extended period of time. Martin Luther King, Jr., in "I Have a Dream" (p. 527) alludes to biblical verses, spirituals, and patriotic songs. If an allusion is no longer recognized by an audience, it loses its effectiveness in conjuring up a series of significant associations.

Analogy is an extended comparison in which an unfamiliar or complex object or event is likened to a familiar or simple one in order to make the former more vivid and more easily understood. Inappropriate or superficially similar analogies should not be used, especially as evidence in an argument. See *Faulty analogy* in the list of logical fallacies on pp. 505–6.

Argumentation or **persuasion** seeks to move a reader, to gain support, to advocate a particular type of action. Traditionally, argumentation appeals to logic and reason, while persuasion appeals to emotion and sometimes prejudice. See the introduction to Chapter 9.

Cause and effect analyses explain why something happened or what the consequences are or will be from a particular occurrence. See the introduction to Chapter 7.

Classification is a form of division, but instead of starting with a single subject as a *division* does, classification starts with many items, and groups or classifies them in categories. See the introduction to Chapter 4.

Cliché is an overused common expression. The term is derived from a French word for a stereotype printing block. Just as many identical copies can be made from such a block, so clichés are typically words and phrases used so frequently that they become stale and ineffective. Everyone uses clichés in speech: "in less than no time" they "spring to mind" but "in the last analysis" a writer ought to "avoid them like the plague," even though they always seem "to hit the nail on the head." Theodore Bernstein offers a good definition and many examples in "Clichés" (p. 450).

Coherence is achieved when all parts of a piece of writing work together as a harmonious whole. If a paper has a well-defined thesis that controls its structure, coherence will follow. In addition, relationships between sentences, paragraphs, and ideas can be made clearer for the reader by using pronoun references, parallel structures (see *Parallelism*), and transitional words and phrases (see *Transitions*).

Colloquial expressions are informal words and phrases used in conversation, but inappropriate for more formal writing situations. Occasionally, professional writers use colloquial expressions in order to create an intentional informality. Adam Smith in "Everyday Drugs" (p. 200) begins with a formal, scientific description of xanthines but shifts in the final two paragraphs to a more informal diction using colloquial expressions such as "stuff," "perkin' in the pot," and "okay and non-okay" drugs.

Comparison involves finding similarities between two or more things, people, or ideas. See the introduction to Chapter 5.

Conclusions should always leave the reader feeling that a paper has come to a logical and inevitable end, that the communication is now complete. As a result, an essay that simply stops, or weakly trails off, or moves into a previously unexplored area, or raises new or distracting problems lacks that necessary sense of closure. Endings often cause problems because they are written last and, therefore, often rushed. With proper planning, you can always write an effective and appropriate ending. Keep the following points and strategies in mind:

1. An effective conclusion grows out of a paper—it needs to be logically related to what has been said. It might restate the thesis, summarize the exposition or argument, apply or reflect upon the subject under discussion, tell a related story, call for a course of action, or state the significance of the subject.

2. The extent to which a conclusion can repeat or summarize is determined in large part by the length of the paper. A short paper should not have a conclusion that repeats, in slightly varied words, the introduction. A long essay, however, often needs a conclusion that conveniently summarizes the significant facts or points discussed in the paper.

3. The appropriateness of a particular type of ending is related to a paper's purpose. An argumentative or persuasive essay—one that asks the reader to do or believe something—can always conclude with a statement of the desired action—vote for, do this, do not support. A narrative essay can end at the climactic moment in the action, such as E. B. White's recognition of mortality in "Once More to the Lake" (p. 116). An expository essay in which points are arranged according to significance can end with the major point.

4. The introduction and conclusion can be used as a related pair to frame the body of an essay. Frequently in a conclusion you can return to or allude to an idea, an expression, or an illustration used at the beginning of the paper and so enclose the body.

Concrete words describe things that exist and can be experienced through the senses. Abstractions are rendered understandable and specific through concrete examples. See *Abstract*.

Connotation and **denotation** refer to two different types of definition of words. A dictionary definition is denotative—it offers a literal and explicit definition of a word. But words often have more than just literal meanings, for they can carry positive or negative associations or connotations. The denotative definition of "wife" is "a woman married to a man," but as Judy Syfers shows in "I Want a Wife" (p. 466), the word *wife* carries a series of connotative associations as well.

Contrast involves finding differences between two or more things, people, or ideas. See the introduction to Chapter 5.

Deduction is the form of argument that starts with a general truth and then moves to a specific application of that truth. See the introduction to Chapter 9.

Definition involves placing a word first in a general class and then adding distinguishing features that set it apart from other members of that class: "A wife is a woman (general class) married to a man (distinguishing feature)." Most college writing assignments in definition require extended definitions in which a subject is analyzed with appropriate examples and details. See the introduction to Chapter 8.

Denotation. See *Connotation and denotation*.

Description is the re-creation of sense impressions in words. See the introduction to Chapter 3.

Dialect. See *Diction*.

Diction is the choice of words used in speaking or writing. It is frequently divided into four levels: formal, informal, colloquial, and slang. Formal diction is found in traditional academic writing, such as books and scholarly articles; informal diction, generally characterized by words common in conversation contexts, by contractions, and by the use of the first person ("I"), is found in articles in popular magazines. James Villas's "E Pluribus Onion" (p. 247) exhibits formal diction; Judith Viorst's "How Books Helped Shape My Life" (p. 355), informal. See *Colloquial expressions* and *Slang*.

Two other commonly used labels are also applied to diction:

Nonstandard. Words or expressions not normally used by educated speakers. An example would be *ain't*.

Dialect. Regional or social differences in a language exhibited in word choice, grammatical usage, and pronunciation. Dialects are primarily spoken rather than written, but are often reproduced or imitated in narratives. William Least Heat-Moon in "Nameless, Tennessee" (p. 156) captures the dialect of his speakers.

Division breaks a subject into parts. It starts with a single subject and then subdivides that whole into smaller units. See the introduction to Chapter 4.

Essay literally means an attempt, and in writing courses the word is used to refer to brief papers, generally between 500 to 1000 words, on restricted subjects. Essays can be formal and academic, like Bernard Berelson's "The Value of Children" (p. 237), or informal and humorous, like Russell Baker's "Computer Fallout" (p. 52).

Example is a specific instance used to illustrate a general idea or statement. Effective writing requires examples to make generalizations clear and vivid to a reader. William Safire's "Words for Nerds" (p. 67) is comprised of dozens of examples of campus slang drawn from student contributors. See the introduction to Chapter 1.

Exposition comes from a Latin word meaning "to expound or explain." It is one of the four modes into which writing is subdivided—the other three being *narration, description*, and *argumentation*. Expository writing is information-conveying; its purpose is to inform its reader. This purpose is achieved through a variety of organizational patterns including *division and classification, comparison and contrast, process analysis, cause and effect*, and *definition*.

Figures of speech are deliberate departures from the ordinary and literal meanings of words in order to provide fresh, insightful perspectives or emphasis. The figures are most commonly used in descriptive passages and include the following:

> **Simile.** A comparison of two dissimilar things generally introduced by the words "as" or "like." Annie Dillard in "On Being Chased" (p. 104) describes the result of automobile

tires passing through snow on a Pittsburgh street by using a simile: "The cars' tires laid behind them on the snowy street a complex trail of beige chunks like crenellated castle walls."

Metaphor. An analogy that directly identifies one thing with another. After Scott Russell Sanders in "The Inheritance of Tools" (p. 170) accidentally strikes his thumb with a hammer, he describes the resulting scar using a metaphor: "A white scar in the shape of a crescent moon began to show above the cuticle, and month by month it rose across the pink sky of my thumbnail."

Personification. An attribution of human qualities to an animal, idea, abstraction, or inanimate object. Gretel Ehrlich in "A River's Route" (p. 164) describes the layers of rock over which the river runs as "brown bellies."

Hyperbole. A deliberate exaggeration, often done to provide emphasis or humor. John McPhee in comparing Florida and California oranges (p. 267) resorts to hyperbole: "Californians say that if you want to eat a Florida orange you have to get into a bathtub first . . . In Florida it is said that you can run over a California orange with a ten-ton truck and not even wet the pavement."

Understatement. The opposite of hyperbole, or a deliberate minimizing done to provide emphasis or humor. In William Least Heat-Moon's "Nameless, Tennessee" (p. 156), Miss Ginny Watts explains how she asked her husband to call the doctor unless he wanted to be "shut of" (rid of) her. Her husband, Thurmond, humorously uses understatement in his reply: "I studied on it."

Rhetorical questions. Questions not meant to be answered, but instead to provoke thought. Marya Mannes in "Wasteland" (p. 518) poses strings of rhetorical questions.

Paradox. A seeming contradiction used to catch a reader's attention. An element of truth or rightness often lurks beneath the contradiction.

Generalizations are assertions or conclusions based upon some specific instances. The value of a generalization is determined by the quality and quantity of examples upon which it is based. Bob Greene in "Cut" (p. 58) formulates a generalization—being cut from an athletic team makes men superachievers later in life—on the basis of five examples. For such a generalization to have validity, however, a proper statistical sample would be essential.

Hyperbole. See *Figures of speech.*

Illustration is providing specific examples for general words or ideas. A writer illustrates by using *examples.*

Induction is the form of argument that begins with specific evidence and then moves to a generalized conclusion that accounts for the evidence. See the introduction to Chapter 9.

Introductions need to do two essential things: first, catch or arouse a reader's interest, and second, state the thesis of the paper. In achieving both objectives, an introduction can occupy a single paragraph or several. The length of an introduction should always be proportional to the length of the essay—short papers should not have long introductions. Because an introduction introduces what follows, it is always easier to write after a draft of the body of the paper has been completed. When writing an introduction, keep the following strategies in mind:

1. Look for an interesting aspect of the subject that might arouse the reader's curiosity. It could be a quotation, an unusual statistic, a narrative, a provocative question or statement. It should be something that will make the reader want to continue reading, and it should be appropriate to the subject at hand.

2. Provide a clear statement of purpose and thesis, explaining what you are writing about and why.

3. Remember that an introduction establishes a tone or point of view for what follows, so be consistent—an informal personal essay can have a casual, anecdotal beginning, but a serious academic essay needs a serious, formal introduction.

4. Suggest to the reader the structure of the essay that follows. Knowing what to expect makes it easier for the audience to read actively.

Irony occurs when a writer says one thing but means another. Fran Lebowitz in "A Manual: Training for Landlords" (p. 332) offers advice to would-be landlords on how to trick and abuse tenants. Lebowitz's suggestions are ironic; she is not advocating such a plan of action, but instead is dramatizing the tenant-landlord relationship from the tenant's point of view.

Metaphor. See *Figures of speech.*

Narration involves telling a story, and all stories—whether they are personal experience essays, imaginative fiction, or historical narratives—have the same essential ingredients: a series of events arranged in an order and told by a narrator for some particular purpose. See the introduction to Chapter 2.

Nonstandard diction. See *Diction.*

Objective writing is an impersonal, factual approach to a particular subject. Bernard Berelson's "The Value of Children" (p. 237) is primarily objective in its approach. Writing frequently blends the objective and subjective together. See *Subjective.*

Paradox. See *Figures of speech.*

Parallelism places words, phrases, clauses, sentences, or even paragraphs equal in importance in equivalent grammatical form. The similar forms make it easier for the reader to see the relationships that exist among the parts; they add force to the expression. Martin Luther King, Jr.'s "I Have a Dream" speech (p. 527) exhibits each level of parallelism: words ("When all God's children, black and white men, Jews and Gentiles, Protestants and Catholics"), phrases ("With this faith, we will be able to work together, to pray together, to struggle together, to go to jail together, to stand up for freedom together"), clauses ("Go back to Mississippi, go back to Alabama, go back to South Carolina, go back to Georgia, go back to Louisiana, go back to the slums and ghettos of our northern cities"), sentences ("the one hundred years later" pattern in paragraph 2), and paragraphs (the "I have a dream" pattern in paragraphs 11 to 18).

Person is a grammatical term used to refer to a speaker, the individual being addressed, or the individual being referred to. English has three persons: first (I or we), second (you), and third (he, she, it, or they).

Personification. See *Figures of speech.*

Persuasion. See *Argumentation and persuasion.*

Point of view is the perspective or angle the writer adopts toward a subject. In narratives, point of view is either first person (I) or third person (he, she, it). First-person narration implies a *subjective* approach to a subject; third-person narration promotes an *objective* approach. Point of view can be limited (revealing only what the narrator knows) or omniscient (revealing what anyone else in the narrative thinks or feels). Sometimes the phrase "point of view" is used simply to describe the writer's attitude toward the subject.

Premise in logic is a proposition—a statement of a truth—that is used to support or help support a conclusion. For an illustration, see p. 508.

Process analysis takes two forms: a set of directions intended to allow a reader to duplicate a particular action, or a description intended to tell a reader how something happens. See the introduction to Chapter 6.

Proofreading is a systematic check of a piece of writing to make sure that it contains no grammatical or mechanical errors. A proofreading is something quite different from a revision. See *Revision*.

Purpose is intention or the reason why a writer writes. Three purposes are fundamental: to entertain, to inform, or to persuade. Purposes are not necessarily separate or discrete; all can be combined together. An effective piece of writing has a well-defined purpose.

Revision means "to see again." A revision involves a careful, active scrutiny of every aspect of a paper—subject, audience, thesis, paragraph structures, sentence constructions, and word choice. Revising a piece of writing involves something more complicated and more wide-ranging than proofreading. See *Proofreading*.

Rhetorical questions. See *Figures of speech*.

Satire pokes fun at human behavior or institutions in order to correct them. Judy Syfers in "I Want a Wife" (p. 466) satirizes the stereotypical male demands of a wife, implying that marriage should be a more understanding partnership. Fran Lebowitz in "A Manual: Training for Landlords" (p. 332) satirizes both the materialism and the indifference of landlords.

Simile. See *Figures of speech.*

Slang is common, casual, conversational language that is inappropriate in formal speaking or writing. Slang is frequently used to make or define social groups—a private, shared language not understood by outsiders. William Safire's "Words for Nerds" (p. 67) lists examples of campus slang. As Safire's essay demonstrates, slang changes constantly and is, therefore, always dated. For that reason alone, it is always best to avoid using slang in writing.

Style is the arrangement of words that a writer uses to express meaning. The study of an author's style would include an examination of diction or word choice, figures of speech, sentence constructions, and paragraph divisions.

Subject is what a piece of writing is about. See also *Thesis.* Bruce Catton's subject in "Grant and Lee" (p. 277) is the two generals; his thesis is that the two represented or symbolized "two diametrically opposed elements in American life."

Subjective writing expresses an author's feelings or opinions about a particular subject. Editorials or columns in newspapers and personal essays tend to rely on subjective judgments. Ruth Westheimer's "Women Know How to Fight" (p. 522) and Patricia McLaughlin's "Sis Boom Bah Humbug" (p. 566) are examples of subjective journalism. Writing frequently blends the subjective and objective together. See *Objective.*

Syllogism is a three-step deductive argument including a major premise, a minor premise, and a conclusion. For an illustration, see p. 508.

Thesis is a particular idea or assertion about a subject. Effective writing will always have an explicit or implicit statement of thesis; it is the central and controlling idea, the thread that holds the essay together. Frequently a thesis is stated in a thesis or *topic sentence.* See *Subject.*

Tone refers to a writer's or speaker's attitude toward a subject and audience. Tone reflects human emotions and so can be characterized or described in a wide variety of ways, including serious, sincere, concerned, humorous, sympathetic, ironic, indignant, sarcastic.

Topic sentence is a single sentence in a paragraph that contains a statement of *subject* or *thesis*. The topic sentence is to the paragraph what the thesis statement is to an essay—the thread that holds the whole together, a device to provide clarity and unity. Because paragraphs have various purposes, not every paragraph will have a topic sentence. When they do, topic sentences are frequently found at the beginnings or ends of paragraphs.

Transitions are links or connections made between sentences, paragraphs, or groups of paragraphs. By using transitions, a writer achieves *coherence* and *unity*. Transitional devices include the following:

1. Repeated words, phrases, or clauses.

2. Transitional sentences or paragraphs that act as bridges from one section or idea to the next.

3. Transition-making words and phrases such as those of
ADDITION—again, next, furthermore, last
TIME—soon, after, then, later, meanwhile
COMPARISON—but, still, nonetheless, on the other hand
EXAMPLE—for instance, for example
CONCLUSION—in conclusion, finally, as a result
CONCESSION—granted, of course

Understatement. See *Figures of speech*.

Unity is a oneness in which all of the individual parts of a piece of writing work together to form a cohesive and complete whole. It is best achieved by having a clearly stated *purpose* and *thesis* against which every sentence and paragraph can be tested for relevance.

Credits

Allport, Gordon, "The Nature of Prejudice." From *The Nature of Prejudice* by Gordon Allport. Copyright © 1979 by Addison-Wesley Publishing Company, Inc. Reprinted by permission of the publisher.

Angell, Roger, "A Baseball." From *Five Seasons* by Roger Angell. Copyright © 1972, 1973, 1974, 1975, 1976, 1977 by Roger Angell. Reprinted by permission of Simon & Schuster, Inc.

Angelou, Maya, "Sister Monroe." From *I Know Why the Caged Bird Sings* by Maya Angelou. Copyright © 1969 by Maya Angelou. Reprinted by permission of Random House, Inc.

Baker, Russell, "Computer Fallout." From *The New York Times*, October 18, 1987. Copyright © 1987 by The New York Times Company. Reprinted by permission of the publisher.

Berelson, Bernard R., "The Value of Children: A Taxonomical Essay." From *The Population Council Annual Report, 1972*. Reprinted by permission of the Population Council.

Bernstein, Theodore M., "Clichés." From *The Careful Writer: A Modern Guide to English Usage* by Theodore M. Bernstein. Copyright © 1965 by Theodore M. Bernstein. Reprinted by permission of Atheneum Publishers, an imprint of Macmillan Publishing Company.

Brownmiller, Susan, "Femininity." From *Femininity* by Susan Brownmiller. Copyright © 1984 by Susan Brownmiller. Reprinted by permission of Linden Press, a division of Simon & Schuster, Inc.

Brumberg, Joan Jacobs, "The Origins of Anorexia Nervosa." From *Fasting Girls: The Emergence of Anorexia Nervosa as a Modern Disease* by Joan Jacobs Brumberg. Copyright © 1988 by the President and Fellows of Harvard College. Reprinted by permission of the publisher, Harvard University Press.

Catton, Bruce, "Grant and Lee: A Study in Contrasts." From *The American Story*, edited by Earl Schenck Miers. Reprinted by permission of the U.S. Capitol Historical Society.

Cole, Diane, "Don't Just Stand There." From "A World of Difference," a special supplement to *The New York Times*, April 16, 1989. Copyright © 1989 by The New York Times Company. Reprinted by permission of the author.

Didion, Joan, "On Keeping a Notebook." From *Slouching Towards Bethlehem* by Joan Didion. Copyright © 1966, 1968 by Joan Didion. Reprinted by permission of Farrar, Straus and Giroux, Inc.

Dillard, Annie, "On Being Chased." From *An American Childhood* by Annie Dillard. Copyright © 1987 by Annie Dillard. Reprinted by permission of HarperCollins Publishers.

Edwards, Harry, "Educating Black Athletes." From *The Atlantic Monthly*, August 1983. Reprinted by permission of the author.

Villas, James, "E Pluribus Onion." From *Town and Country*, January 1985. Copyright © 1985 by James Villas. Reprinted by permission of the Robin Straus Agency, Inc.

Viorst, Judith, "How Books Helped Shape My Life." From *Redbook*, July 1980. Copyright © 1980 by Judith Viorst. Reprinted by permission of Lescher & Lescher, Ltd.

Ward, Andrew, "Yumbo." First published in *The Atlantic Monthly*, May 1977. Copyright © 1978 by Andrew Ward. Reprinted by permission of the author and the publisher.

Westheimer, Ruth, "Women Know How to Fight." From *The New York Times*, February 11, 1990. Copyright © 1990 by The New York Times Company. Reprinted by permission of the publisher.

White, E. B., "Once More to the Lake." From *Essays of E. B. White*. Copyright © 1941 by E. B. White. Reprinted by permission of HarperCollins Publishers.

White, William Allen, "Mary White." From *American Is West*, edited by John Flanagan. St. Paul: University of Minnesota Press, 1945.

Winn, Marie, "The End of Play." From *Children without Childhood* by Marie Winn. Copyright © 1981, 1983 by Marie Winn. Reprinted by permission of Pantheon Books, Inc., a division of Random House, Inc.

Winn, Marie, "Television Viewing as an Addiction." From *The Plug-In Drug* by Marie Winn. Copyright © 1977, 1985 by Marie Winn Miller. Reprinted by permission of Viking Penguin, a division of Penguin Books USA Inc.

Wolfe, Tom, "A Sunday Kind of Love." From *The Kandy-Kolored Tangerine-Flake Streamline Baby* by Tom Wolfe. Copyright © 1964, 1965 by Tom Wolfe. Reprinted by permission of Farrar, Straus and Giroux, Inc.

Woolf, Virginia, "The Death of the Moth." From *The Death of the Moth and Other Essays* by Virginia Woolf. Copyright © 1942 by Harcourt Brace Jovanovich, Inc.; renewed 1970 by Marjorie T. Parsons, Executrix. Reprinted by permission of Harcourt Brace Jovanovich, Inc., the Executors of the estate of Virginia Woolf, and the Hogarth Press.

Zinsser, William K., "The Transaction—Two Writing Processes." From *On Writing Well*, 4th ed. Copyright © 1976, 1980, 1985, 1988, 1990 by William K. Zinsser. Published by HarperCollins Publishers. Reprinted by permission of the author.